Welfare Policymaking in the States

American Governance and Public Policy Series
Barry Rabe, series editor

Selected books in the series

Budgeting Entitlements: The Politics of Food Stamps
Ronald F. King

Fenced Off: The Suburbanization of American Politics
Juliet F. Gainsborough

Improving Governance: A New Logic for Empirical Research
Laurence E. Lynn, Jr., Carolyn J. Heinrich, and Carolyn J. Hill

Preserving Public Lands for the Future: The Politics of Intergenerational Goods
William R. Lowry

The Politics of Unfunded Mandates: Whither Federalism?
Paul L. Posner

Lobbying Together: Interest Group Coalitions in Legislative Politics
Kevin W. Hula

Policy Entrepreneurs and School Choice
Michael Mintrom

The Politics of Ideas and the Spread of Enterprise Zones
Karen Mossberger

The Political Economy of Special-Purpose Government
Kathryn A. Foster

Welfare Policymaking in the States

The Devil in Devolution

Pamela Winston

GEORGETOWN UNIVERSITY PRESS / WASHINGTON, D.C.

Georgetown University Press, Washington, D.C.

Printed in the United States of America

10 9 8 7 6 5 4 3 2 1 2002

This volume is printed on acid-free offset book paper.

Library of Congress Cataloging-in-Publication Data

Winston, Pamela.
Welfare policymaking in the states : the devil in devolution / Pamela Winston.
p. cm — (American governance and public policy series)
Includes bibliographical references and index.
ISBN 0-87840-891-6 (alk. paper) — ISBN 0-87840-892-4 (pbk. : alk. paper)
1. Public welfare—United States. 2. Public welfare—Texas. 3. Public welfare—Maryland. 4. Public welfare—North Dakota. 5. United States—Politics and government. 6. Decentralization in government—United States. I. Title. II. American governance and public policy

HV95 .W574 2002
362.5'0973—dc21

2001040795

Contents

Appendices

Tables

Preface

It's become clear that devolution, at least of programs for low-income people, is here to stay for the foreseeable future. Welfare was the first and most basic safety-net program to be sent back to state control, although it may not be the last. It's less clear whether devolving the policymaking process will be good in the long run for low-income people—especially the millions of children who make up the majority of the poor in the United States.

This study was motivated by the desire to understand better what the process of developing welfare policies actually looks like in the states; what resources state-based actors have to draw on; how extensive the debate is; and, in particular, who really participates in it. Rhetoric about the states being "closer to the people" and more responsive to local needs was prevalent during the national welfare debate of the 1990s. Even before passage of the 1996 welfare law, states were gaining much greater policymaking control through federal waivers. My goal was to get beyond the rhetoric and to explore state policymaking under devolution in a more rigorous and systematic way, considering what the implications of this recent "revolution" are likely be for families that are most reliant on anti-poverty programs such as welfare.

This study could not have been completed without the support and assistance of a large number of people who contributed in a multitude of ways. First, several faculty members and scholars at Johns Hopkins provided invaluable guidance. Matthew Crenson and Benjamin Ginsberg were especially helpful, steering me in useful directions when I came into their offices in the early days of graduate school and said that I wanted to work on welfare reform but had no idea where it was going or how I wanted to approach it. They offered excellent ideas, constructive criticism, and consistent good humor and support. Andrew Cherlin and Robert Moffitt at the Welfare,

Children and Families study gave me a wonderful opportunity after finishing my Ph.D. to learn more about welfare reform and low-income families as a postdoctoral fellow at the study. Karen Bogen read every page and offered great advice, both substantive and editorial, as well as great friendship. Juliane Baron kept me up to date on the latest in Texas politics and provided essential feedback on draft chapters.

Several scholars in other organizations also helped me sift through ideas and approaches at critical stages. Kent Weaver at the Brookings Institution was particularly helpful, from my earliest information gathering to the final rewrites and revisions.

In addition, Barry Rabe, the editor of this series, and the anonymous reviewers who commented on the original manuscript provided detailed and valuable suggestions for rethinking, revising, and refining it. John Samples and Gail Grella at Georgetown University Press were enthusiastic, responsive, and generally very helpful.

The people I interviewed for my case studies in Washington and in the states were astonishingly generous, patient, and forthcoming. Many gave up as much as a day of their time to talk with me and guide me through the intricacies of welfare policy. I came away from my field visits to North Dakota, Texas, and Maryland impressed that people in state governments and in state and local organizations working with low-income families were as dedicated, smart, and kind as the people I met.

Several good friends and family members seemed to have no doubt I would complete this, even when I could not begin to imagine the end. Their faith reminded me that books are like marathons and that the only way to get to the finish line is through a zillion patient little steps. My parents first helped me understand that not everyone had what I did and that questions of equal opportunity really matter. Their belief in my abilities and their support and understanding have been critical.

Finally, I owe the fact that I completed this manuscript on deadline—and much, much more—to my husband, Leonard Bailey, and his unfailing love, support, and superb secretarial skills, which he offered when they were most needed.

1

Why Devolution Matters

On August 22, 1996, President Bill Clinton signed into law the Personal Responsibility and Work Opportunity Reconciliation Act of 1996 (PRWORA), which abolished Aid to Families with Dependent Children (AFDC). The Act ended the entitlement of poor families to assistance from the federal government, instituted a five-year time limit on federal cash benefits, devolved most details of welfare policymaking to the fifty states, and replaced AFDC and its federal matching funding structure with a fixed-sum block grant program called Temporary Assistance for Needy Families (TANF). It coupled new conservative national mandates with greater state flexibility in most other policy details. The nominal goal of these changes was to move single mothers with children who had been receiving AFDC out of "dependency" and into work outside the home. PRWORA paved the way for a radical change in political control over welfare policy.[1]

The 1996 welfare bill represented a critical moment in the development of American social policy. In signing it, Clinton essentially legitimated the Reagan "revolution" in social policy that had begun in the early 1980s—much as Dwight Eisenhower had effectively legitimated Roosevelt's liberal New Deal forty years earlier. AFDC had been created in 1935 as Title IV of the Social Security Act to provide federal matching funds to states for their programs for poor families; it established an open-ended entitlement to states and individuals that guaranteed to pay for aid to families who qualified for it. States set their own income eligibility requirements and payment levels, and they always varied widely. They also had moved significantly downward over the three decades leading up to passage of PRWORA. As long as states and their eligible poor had need, however, the national government provided money to match state expenditures, with some federal standards.

By the 1990s, the entitlement status of welfare was regarded increasingly as one of the causes of dependency, and political consensus coalesced around the belief that welfare mothers should work outside the home, leaving behind the income maintenance orientation of the past. State policymakers, along with many in Washington, revived the 10th Amendment and argued for greater state control over policy design and implementation.

The new law gave state policymakers much of the flexibility they sought, and they moved swiftly to alter the approach to welfare and work programs for recipients within their borders. They were aided by block grants that—because of declining caseloads—were far more generous than anticipated and greater than federal funding levels would have been under AFDC.

These changes in the law were predicted to alter radically the shape of American welfare policy, and by the end of the 1990s there already had been dramatic shifts in the way states approached welfare services and the number and nature of the people receiving benefits. Much has been made of the sharp decline in caseloads and the range of new state programs for low-income families. Many scholars and journalists in the past several years have provided insightful analyses of the national welfare debate.[2] The question of how welfare policy actually is made in the states and who is involved in making it has largely been ignored, however.

This book addresses the nature of state welfare politics under devolution and contrasts it with welfare politics on the national level. The reasons that welfare policy has taken the shape it has in Washington and in the states are many, and their complexity precludes a simple explanation. This study considers a range of political forces that have helped to shape welfare reform.[3] These forces include the states' political cultures and/or dominant ideologies, political party control and strength, the role of the media and public opinion, the strategic and policy goals of welfare reformers, the social diversity of state political actors, and the capacities of the states' political institutions. The book's emphasis, however, is on the influence of interest groups and other key actors in the legislative policymaking process on the national and state levels—in particular, the role of advocates for low-income families. This is an essential part of current welfare politics that has critical implications for the outcomes of the policymaking process and future well-being of low-income families, and it continues to receive short shrift as we begin to evaluate state policy decisions.

This study takes a neo-Madisonian approach, asking how the range and number of "factions" shift as the scope of the political "sphere" is altered by devolution. In particular, it focuses on the presence—and absence—of effective groups representing low-income families in the states, as well as the range of perspectives that have made their way into the policy debate in Washington and in three states that serve as case studies. The central question is the extent to which poor families—or groups that might represent their interests—have a voice in the welfare policymaking process under devolution.

At stake in this recent experiment in welfare reform are principles of equal opportunity, fairness, and self-determination. The outcomes of devolution also may have implications for our future political and social stability. Finally, though less urgently, this fundamental change can provide guidance about academically important ideas about the policymaking process.

Now that states have essential control over welfare policymaking, the results of their policy decisions will affect fundamentally the lives and opportunities of millions of poor children.[4] Often forgotten among the dominant images of nonworking welfare mothers was the fact that children made up two-thirds of the welfare caseload.[5] If the devolution experiment increases the number of families living in poverty over the long term; if it increases the intensity of child poverty; or even if it improves most low-income families' economic circumstances but sharply reduces adult guidance and supervision, it will place even greater limits on poor children's life chances. If children in some states are better off while those in others are worse off, it will be bad for children, and it will have made our social system markedly less fair.[6]

Of course, we have never lived up to the American ideals of fairness and equal opportunity for all our citizens, but these are beliefs most Americans hold dear.[7] If the PRWORA leaves no basic safety net for the children of parents who can't or won't work at a "livable" wage, it will have further compromised our national commitment to these values.

The 1996 welfare law raises additional questions about our commitment to political self-determination. Devolution of welfare policy also may be making it more difficult for poor families—or groups that represent them—to have a role in shaping the policies that most affect them if, in fact, it is harder for them to participate effectively in the states and localities than in the nation's capital. Americans commonly support the idea that parents should have a voice in education policy, old people should have influence on the shape of Medicare and Social Security, and business organizations should effectively express their views about regulation. These groups may not always get what they want, but it is regarded as entirely legitimate—in fact, necessary—that they have a role in the policymaking process in our pluralist system. If the effect of devolution, however, is to send welfare policymaking to political spheres where representatives of poor families are weakest, it will further diminish their political voice.

Certainly poor people are no longer regarded as a group with legitimate political grievances, as they were briefly during the New Deal and the Great Society. Most Americans do not appear to think a great deal about poor people, and when they do, it often is with pity or disapproval. Neither, however, are Americans in general likely to be entirely comfortable with the prospect that in a range of jurisdictions the perspectives of low-income families may have virtually no influence on the design of policies that are vital to their well-being.[8]

The welfare experiment also risks being politically unwise if it is not largely successful. If too large a proportion of our children become part of an "estranged poor," isolated and divested from the economic and political mainstream, the chances increase that they will have little interest in or ability to adhere to the rules of broader society. If these children become too great in number, they may pose a real risk to our future social and political stability.[9] The poverty rate for children in 1999 was about 17 percent—lower than in many years but nonetheless higher than in other industrialized nations—and the economic boom of the 1990s has lessened the immediate danger of sharp increases in poverty. With the federal five-year lifetime limit on cash assistance and some states' even shorter limits, however, it may be markedly more difficult for poor families to weather inevitable economic downturns.

Finally, the results of this venture matter to students of politics because they can provide insights into competing theories about the politics of policymaking. One school of thought has contended that smaller jurisdictions would be better suited to understand their inhabitants' needs—that is, that the "laboratories of democracy" of the states would experiment with welfare policy and develop the most effective means for aiding the poor families within their borders.[10] The "race-to-the-bottom" theory, on the other hand, suggests that states and localities would be less suited to make social policy than the national government exactly because they compete with each other and will face economic incentives to cut public assistance programs.[11]

A type of "institutionalism" has argued that changes in recipient behavior promised by welfare reform might not take place at all or might take place extremely slowly because of institutional resistance among governmental organizations, including welfare agencies. Finally, the neo-Madisonian perspective has contended that the national arena would allow for more effective participation by organizations that represent the interests and concerns of poor families and that, as E. E. Schattschneider has suggested, the shift to local control would inappropriately "restrict the scope of conflict."[12] The outcomes of the 1996 welfare reform bill can provide useful insights into these contending approaches.

WHY WELFARE REFORM AND DEVOLUTION?

The following chapter addresses the political motivations for welfare reform and devolution in more detail, but I highlight here several of the central thrusts of the PRWORA debate.

Welfare reform in 1996 was significantly motivated, I argue, by two principal and interrelated drives—one *reflecting* social and political change and the other intended to *serve* political change. The first was a response to larger shifts in social and political attitudes and circumstances. These shifts included growing skepticism about the role of government services, particularly social programs; the heightened expectation that all able-bodied Americans should be "self-sufficient"; and the widespread belief that women, particularly poor women, should work in the labor market. Growing welfare rolls—caused at least in part by the recession of the late 1980s and early 1990s—and rising out-of-wedlock birth rates contributed to the drive for some type of radical reform. Several national political developments also reflected and contributed to a markedly more conservative mood throughout the country, affecting the overall tone of the political discourse about welfare of both major political parties and the range of policy alternatives that received consideration. These developments included the newfound power of the most conservative elements of the Republican party, the ascendance of a Republican majority to both houses of Congress for the first time in forty-eight years, and the shift within the Democratic party away from New Deal liberalism and toward centrist New Democrat positions.

In addition, the "fiscalization" of national politics in the early and mid-1990s contributed to the strong presumption toward budget- and tax-cutting that supported changes such as cuts in programs for low-income people that were widely and incorrectly believed to be very costly. A lingering sense of economic anxiety also made Americans at all levels less tolerant of the non-working poor and contributed to the welfare policymaking environment of the mid-1990s. National mandates such as the end to the entitlement status of welfare, new work and behavioral requirements, and the five-year limit on federal aid reflected these new developments.

A second and equally critical thrust of welfare reform served strategic political ends for Republicans and Democrats alike.[13] Conservative welfare overhaul met the demands of key constituents of the new conservative Republican majority in Congress, and the Democratic president could fulfill his campaign pledge to "end welfare as we know it." It allowed members of Congress from both parties to satisfy public opinion and claim credit for solving "the welfare problem."

Welfare in the 1990s was widely regarded as a sinkhole that allowed poor—presumably minority—Americans and immigrants to avoid the pressures of work and responsibility that bore down on middle-class white taxpayers, who resented subsidizing this behavior.[14] Worse yet, AFDC seemed to give this dependency the imprimatur of the national government. In particular, Charles Murray's book *Losing Ground* popularized the idea that the structure of the federal system of assistance to poor families not only failed to help them but actually encouraged them to behave in aberrant and self-destructive ways.[15] A CBS/*New York Times* poll conducted in April 1995 found that 81 percent of white respondents believed that most recipients "are so dependent on welfare that they will never get off," despite evidence that about two-thirds of recipients used it for less than five years over their lifetimes (64 percent of black respondents held this view).[16] Time limits and devolution would allow Congress and the president to satisfy the demand that the government stop facilitating this dependency while avoiding the difficult work of actually formulating and passing a better alternative national welfare law.[17]

In addition, PRWORA's emphasis on devolution altered the distribution of power in welfare policymaking in essential ways. Sending policy decisions back to the states might reasonably be expected to constrain the range of constituencies that could play an effective role in determining the shape of welfare programs in the future. The national liberal advocacy groups, social service organizations, and public interest groups that had gained power in Washington since the 1960s would be largely replaced by a range of organizations in the fifty states, effectively "defunding the left" in the nation's capital. In addition, as of 1994 most of the nation's governors were Republicans, and state legislatures were moving in that direction. This shift could lead to state policy results that would be largely consistent with the national conservative agenda of smaller government and greater "personal responsibility" by low-income women that was reflected in PRWORA's mandates.

Some opponents of the effort to abolish AFDC suspected that its advocates pushed for a shift to state decision making exactly *because* the composition of the active constituencies in policymaking within the states would narrow and tend toward more conservative interests. They suspected that rather than making the politics of decision making more democratic, narrower boundaries would constrain representativeness, limiting the range of constituencies that could wield influence. They also expressed concern that shifting policy to the states and localities would reduce the visibility of welfare and make it more difficult to monitor the well-being of low-income families—in essence, "disappearing" the poor. Although several states, such as Wisconsin and Minnesota, historically had been relatively innovative and expansive in their programs for low-income families, others (such as Mississippi and Louisiana) had taken a much more restrictive approach. Some opponents of PRWORA foresaw a return to these highly uneven policies.

The idea of devolving welfare policy to the states took hold in Washington surprisingly quickly and with relatively little challenge. Proponents cited state welfare-to-work initiatives such as Wisconsin's "W2" program as evidence that shifting primary responsibility to the fifty states could only lead to improvements in the welfare system. Certainly, states had been exerting greater control over policy under the Clinton administration's liberal approach to welfare waivers. The jump from an expanded but still limited waiver policy to broad decentralization was dramatic, however.

As with most policy issues, the lines between the interests, ideologies, ideas, and conceptions of identity that were reflected in the welfare debate were blurred. Political scientist John W. Kingdon and others stress the point that the ways people make sense of the world, their ideas about it, often are practically and theoretically inseparable from the interests they hold and the goals they hope to achieve.[18] What met the demands of certain conservative interests for lower taxes and social spending also satisfied parallel ideological demands for more "freedom from government intrusion," and greater responsibility and adherence to the work ethic on the part of poor mothers receiving welfare. It also reinforced the identities of policymakers and middle-class Americans as virtuous taxpaying citizens—in contrast with welfare mothers, who personified for many Americans a range of deviant or pitiable characteristics, reflecting new ideas about the poor and resuscitating old ones.

Certainly some proponents of the 1996 welfare bill blamed the system and not the recipients, arguing that the structure of AFDC had trapped millions of worthwhile women and their children in dependency. Many proponents also held that the states knew best the causes of poverty within their borders and would be most responsive and compassionate in their policies toward poor people, even if that meant practicing a kind of "tough love" to cure them of their dependency. Regardless of whether proponents blamed recipients or the system, however, these ideas, the major social and economic changes, the political advantages of fundamental reform, and a feeling of helplessness about growing welfare rolls and out-of-wedlock birth rates helped set the stage for PRWORA.

THEORIES OF JURISDICTIONAL BOUNDARY

During the debate about devolution and welfare reform, few policymakers or other people discussed broader questions of how politics is practiced at different levels of government. Political theorists, however, have written about the effects of jurisdictional size since long before the devolution of welfare, asking how policymaking within a political sphere changes if we change its boundaries. Some of their ideas can provide a useful base for more detailed exploration of the effects of decentralized welfare policymaking. James Madison probably was the first and best-known American theorist to address this question, most explicitly in *Federalist #10*. A range of "neo-Madisonian" pluralists have followed—including Grant McConnell, Paul Peterson, and others—revising and updating Madison's theory, building on the idea that if you change the size of the jurisdiction within which policy is made, you change the distribution of power in policymaking.[19]

Madison basically argued that smaller jurisdictions would contain a narrower diversity of interests, thus increasing the danger that a powerful majority faction will oppress a minority. "Extend the sphere," he famously wrote, "and you take in a greater variety of parties and interests; you make it less probable that a majority of the whole will have a common motive to invade the rights of other citizens; or if such a common motive exists, it will be more difficult for all who feel it to discover their own strength, and to act in unison with each other."[20] In effect, he argues that a basic critical mass is necessary for something approaching a true pluralist political arena to exist.[21]

Although Madison's essential idea is an important stepping-off point, clearly in politics simple jurisdictional size alone is inadequate in determining policy outcomes—illustrating a key limitation to "pure" Madisonian theory. To explore fully the politics of welfare policymaking, we also must consider other factors that help determine the presence, diversity, and effectiveness of various groups. These factors include the states' political capacities (the professionalization of their legislatures, the relative strength of the executive, lobbying regulations, and other factors), socioeconomic level and diversity, party strength and control, political culture and ideology, and the diversity and relative strength of the states' political elites.

An evolution of Madisonian theory incorporates essential political characteristics of smaller jurisdictions and attends more explicitly to the presence—or lack thereof—of organizations that might represent politically weak groups, as well as questions of political capacity and the power of state and local elites, among other considerations.[22] It calls into question the long-standing American love of localism and decentralization, informality, private organizations, and fear of the coercive power of the national state. Although proponents of localism assume that decentralized decision making best fosters values of individualism, freedom, and efficiency, small organizations and jurisdictions are not necessarily more democratic than large ones.[23] In fact, this perspective argues, they may be *less* democratic and more prone to capture and domination by local or organizational elites that often have narrow economic interests. These elites' interests may masquerade as those of the community as a whole, stifling the power of more general, diffuse "collective goods" or the interests of marginal groups, such as poor people.[24] In addition, smaller political organizations often have constitutions and legal structures whose goals and practices may be incoherent or largely informal and whose enforcement may be casual and inconsistent.

This neo-Madisonian view also considers the blurring of lines between private and public that can arise from our preference for smallness, decentralization, and informality—a blurring that is clearly evident today in the tendency to use market organizations to provide previously public goods and services.[25] It asks the critical question of where, if anywhere, the legitimacy of private power lies: Private organizations often lack constitutions or other legal frames that can safeguard their members' rights. The compulsion exercised in smaller, decentralized, or private organizations can be far greater than that exercised on the national scale, this view argues—in part because they *are* more informal and lack the protections of explicit rules and due process.

Critics of this neo-Madisonian perspective argue that the states' political institutions have improved sufficiently in recent decades to warrant sending major new policy responsibilities to them. Most have undergone fundamental change. The U.S. Supreme Court's reapportionment decisions *Baker v. Carr* (1962) and *Reynolds v. Sims* (1964), as well as the federal Civil Rights Act (1964) and Voting Rights Act (1965), have been largely implemented, spurring important changes in state political and administrative capacity as well as patterns of representation. There has been an increase in party competition, greater professionalism in state legislatures and governors' offices, and proliferation of interest groups of many types (changes that are addressed in more detail subsequently). Despite these improvements, however, many of the political and administrative characteristics of the states remain highly uneven, suggesting that concerns about the political effects of decentralization may not be obsolete.

Another version of neo-Madisonian theory builds on the functional theory of public choice economist Charles Tiebout and others who argue that states or localities will put together varying packages of services and tax rates and that a mobile public will move among them to the jurisdiction that best suits their service and tax preferences.[26] State officials have incentives to compete with each other for economic development dollars, which bring things they want such as tax revenues, while discouraging costly poor people (who also are assumed to be mobile) from taking up residence.

Businesses, as rational actors, on the whole will prefer lower tax/lower social service jurisdictions, whereas poor people—who also are rational actors—will prefer jurisdictions that levy higher taxes (assuming they are not paying much of them) and provide more generous social services. Interstate competition to attract business and drive away poor people means that redistributive policy is not appropriate for devolution, according to this perspective. In fact, the lower the jurisdiction to which welfare is pushed, the more powerful the incentives to cut it. On this view, fear of becoming a "welfare magnet" and attracting expensive, nonproducing poor people will lead to a "race to the bottom" among states, which will cut their benefits to give poor people an incentive to move to the state next door.[27]

Although functional theory is useful in broad terms, it largely leaves out politics and does not sufficiently describe what has occurred to date in state welfare policymaking. States have developed widely varying approaches to welfare under devolution; they have not rushed wholesale to lower their benefit levels, and, according to my research and others', the behavior of their neighbors has been only one of many factors that policymakers consider in developing their new programs.[28] Equally important for some states has been the desire to be more innovative than the next state, which can occasionally, in fact, lead to more expansive policies.

State policymakers may feel greater pressure to embark on a race to the bottom in the future when money gets tight again, if the block grant or its maintenance-of-effort requirement are changed during reauthorization of the national welfare law in 2002, or as the national political spotlight shifts away from the states. In the years following passage of the 1996 law, however, they had more welfare funding than they knew what to do with, PRWORA prevented them from cutting spending dramatically, and there was still political credit to be gained through creative welfare reform, as well as declining caseloads.

METHODOLOGY AND STRUCTURE

This book does not offer only a single theory to explain why the federal bill took the shape it did, to understand why the states have done what they have in welfare policy, or to predict what they will do in the future. It builds on neo-Madisonian perspectives to investigate the changing patterns of welfare politics in the 1990s. I rely on empirical research over a limited but highly fertile period of welfare policymaking, asking how what we actually find in the policymaking process reconciles with the directions suggested by these theories and what this comparison may suggest about the future of welfare reform under devolution.

First I examine the context of the welfare policymaking process in Washington and each of three states, including the roles of electoral politics, the political parties, institutional capacity, the media and public opinion, and "policy feedbacks" from prior reform efforts.[29] Second, I explore the actors and organizations inside and, in particular, outside government that participated in the legislative process leading to welfare legislation. I focus on the formulation of the national welfare bill between January 1995 and August 1996. I look similarly at the actors who were most involved in shaping welfare reform in three states from 1995 to 1997 as they acted in anticipation of the federal bill as well as in response to it. I explore which groups appeared to be more effective in each arena. Finally, I consider the impact of these groups' activity on welfare policy outcomes. This is the most speculative part of my work, but it warrants exploration nonetheless. I have limited my analysis of welfare legislation to provisions related to cash assistance, including those replacing AFDC with programs under the TANF block grant. I do not emphasize provisions affecting the Food Stamps program or legal immigrants—these crucial programs suffered the heaviest budget cuts in the national bill, but they brought to the table a range of groups that had not previously been closely involved in AFDC policy.

In considering interest group participation in the national debate and in the state case studies, I have used hearing testimony at legislative public hearings—either delivered or submitted into the record—as a key measure of participation. My goal was to capture the universe of groups that attempted to influence policy. Although interest groups participate in policymaking in many ways, this measure is the most inclusive and objective available. I have found that it also is an effective proxy for other types of interest group activity, such as lobbying of individual legislators. I emphasize legislative politics, although groups also lobby governors' offices and bureaucratic agencies and use the court system to try to achieve their ends. As a rule, however, lobbyists have tended to concentrate on the legislative process, and we have some consistent records of this activity.[30]

In addition to witness lists—which, by definition, provide a limited view of groups and participants that were most active and effective in welfare policymaking—I have employed records of public hearings and conducted more than sixty semi-structured interviews with interest group staff members, legislators, legislative staff members, and other policymakers and key participants. These interviews lasted from a half-hour to more than three hours.[31] My goal was to understand better each state's political environment and to gauge interest group activity and influence more accurately, as well as to learn about any actors who participated entirely outside the hearings process. I also relied on official state publications and newspaper accounts.

In trying to assess relative interest group influence on policy outcomes, I assume that more liberal eligibility and participation criteria and fewer behavioral mandates, as well as increases in TANF benefits and/or more expansive employment and support programs, indicate greater political power on the part of poor people and their advocates. This premise is complicated by wide variations in how states have set up their TANF programs, which in some cases involve direct payments to private companies to provide jobs, employment support, or manage welfare programs. Under the new system, it also can be difficult to separate programs that benefit TANF recipients from those that benefit other low-income people. By and large, however, I assume that political power is reflected to a significant extent in the relative expansiveness of states' welfare and work programs, as well as the support services that accompany them. I also assume that more money usually leads to better results for poor families, though obviously this assumption is not always true.[32]

State Case Studies

I have selected a representative if limited set of states to examine in detail: Maryland, Texas, and North Dakota. Although three cases do not provide a large enough group on which to base overly broad conclusions, I selected these states to represent a range of state characteristics, allowing me to examine state welfare politics during the early years of devolution. The general criteria I used in selecting them included population size, regional diversity, poverty rate, median household income, ethnic mix, AFDC benefits in 1995 (as a proxy for historic approach to public assistance), and party control of the governor's office and legislature (see Appendix A).

In the mid-1990s, Texas had the second-largest population in the nation (about 19 million); is located in the Southwest; had a high poverty rate and low median household income, with high levels of income inequality; was ethnically mixed among whites (85 percent), blacks (12 percent), and a high proportion of Hispanics (28 percent);[33] offered the fourth-lowest cash benefits in the country; and had a Republican governor and a legislature that was Democratic in 1995 but became split between the parties in 1997. Maryland was mid-sized (nineteenth in population); eastern; below average in poverty and above average in median household income; largely biracial (26 percent black and 69 percent white); has urban, suburban, and rural areas; offered average cash benefits; and is dominated by Democrats in the legislature and the governor's office. North Dakota is in the Midwest; was forty-seventh in population (with about 640,000 inhabitants) and extremely rural; had a low poverty rate and low median income, with very low levels of income inequality; was about 94 percent white and 4.4 percent Native American; historically paid cash benefits above the national average; and had a legislature and governor's office that were controlled by Republicans.[34] An in-depth study of the welfare politics of these three states offers the opportunity to explore the direction that policy has started to take under devolution and enables us see if the concerns raised by neo-Madisonian theory appear to have credence in the case of welfare policy in the 1990s.

Structure of the Book

Part I examines national welfare politics. Chapter 2 provides the historical context for the most recent round of national welfare overhaul and analyzes national welfare politics between 1992 and 1996, with an emphasis on the role of political pressures from within government; chapter 3 explores the participation and influence of groups outside the federal government that were most active in congressional policymaking between the end of 1994 and mid-1996. In short, Part I provides an analysis of contemporary welfare politics when the "scope of conflict" was broadened. Part II examines welfare politics in the states. Chapters 4, 5, and 6 present the case studies of Maryland, Texas, and North Dakota, respectively. These studies provide a picture of welfare policymaking in the early days of state control and a narrower scope of conflict, allowing us to evaluate the merits of the neo-Madisonian argument, at least in these cases. Finally, chapter 7 draws lessons from this comparative research on national and state welfare politics and considers the long-run impact of devolution on the direction of welfare policy and the future well-being of poor families.

NOTES

1. The new law also limited the availability of food stamps—the nation's food voucher program for low-income people—and Supplemental Security Income for disabled people. It excluded legal immigrants from receiving many types of federal public assistance, although some of these cuts were reversed the following year.

2. Recent and useful analyses of welfare politics in the U.S. include R. Kent Weaver, *Ending Welfare As We Know It* (Washington, D.C.: Brookings Institution Press, 2000); Steven Teles, *Whose Welfare? AFDC and Elite Politics* (Lawrence: University Press of Kansas, 1996); Dan Balz and Ronald Brownstein, *Storming the Gates: Protest Politics and the Republican Revival* (Boston: Little, Brown and Co., 1996), especially chapter 6; and R. Kent Weaver, "Ending Welfare as We Know It," chapter 9 in *The Social Divide*, ed. Margaret Weir (Washington, D.C.: Brookings Institution Press, 1998). Michael B. Katz, *The Price of Citizenship: Redefining the American Welfare State* (New York: Metropolitan Books, 2001), puts recent changes in American policies for poor people in historical perspective, stressing in particular the growing dominance of private market models in determining who deserves assistance, and of what kind.

3. Welfare sometimes is regarded as meaning public assistance programs broadly, including food stamps and medical assistance. However, I use the term to refer specifically to the AFDC and TANF programs or to state programs developed to replace AFDC. Similarly, many people have expressed discomfort with referring to the 1996 bill as "reform" because that term implies improvement. Although I share some of their concerns, for simplicity's sake I do describe welfare overhaul efforts as reform.

4. A wide range of books and articles have been written about the determinants of child development. Recent popular work includes Daniel Goleman, *Emotional Intelligence* (New York: Bantam Books, 1995), and psychologist Penelope Leach's *Children First: What Society Must Do—and Is Not Doing—for Children Today* (New York: Vintage Books, 1995). Earlier work on the importance of parental influence in child development includes John Bowlby, *Attachment and Loss*, Vols. 1 and 2 (London: Hogarth Press and Institute of Psychoanalysis, 1969, 1973), and D. W. Winnicott, "The Theory of the Parent-Infant Relationship," in *Essential Papers on Object Relations*, ed. Peter Buckley (New York: New York University Press, 1986). For a more economics-oriented account, see Robert Haveman and Barbara Wolfe, "The Determinants of Children's Attainments: A Review of Method and Findings," *Journal of Economic Literature* 33, no. 4 (December 1995): 1829–78.

5. Weaver, *Ending Welfare As We Know It*, chapter 3, provides a useful discussion of policymaking "traps" in welfare politics, especially the "dual clientele" trap: Policymakers want to aid "deserving" children, yet at the same time they want to avoid aiding their "undeserving" parents.

6. As noted above, states have always set benefit levels, but the federal government sharply limited their ability to shape the system in other ways and established basic standards and procedures that kept states from excluding would-be recipients. Many supporters of devolution believed that poor children were at more risk under AFDC than under the new system.

7. Of course, Americans also hold competing values, such as self-reliance and independence. Jennifer Hochschild explores Americans' attitudes toward fairness and equal opportunity and the potential political costs of the disconnect between our aspirations and reality in *What's Fair?: American Beliefs about Distributive Justice* (Cambridge, Mass.: Harvard University Press, 1981) and *Race, Class, and the Soul of the Nation: Facing Up to the American Dream* (Princeton, N.J.: Princeton University Press, 1995).

8. No other group—except prisoners, children, and perhaps the mentally ill—is as broadly excluded from the formation of policies that most affect its members. During the most conflictual period of the PRWORA debate, the philosophy of "maximum feasible participation" of the 1960s seemed to have given way to something more accurately described as a "beggars can't be choosers" approach, informed by the widespread belief that welfare mothers were essentially defective or childlike. As I argue in more detail later in this book, however, surveys indicate support for the working poor, and as a growing number of welfare mothers move to low-wage work, one would expect less acceptance of their being objects of policymaking but not participants in it.

9. Hochschild, *What's Fair?*, chapter 1, uses the phrase "estranged poor" as an alternative to the problematic "underclass." She explores this point and cites theorists since Aristotle on the political dangers of allowing too great a divide between privileged people and poor people.

10. Justice Louis Brandeis, in his opinion in *New State Ice Company v. Ernest A. Liebmann*, 285 U.S. 262-311, U.S. SCt. Reports 76 L.Ed (1931) 771, compared the states to laboratories that can "try novel social and economic experiments without risk to the rest of the country." David Osborne revived the concept in his popular book *Laboratories of Democracy* (Boston: Harvard Business School Press, 1988). The welfare debates of the mid-1990s were striking in the degree to which policymakers at all levels assumed the scientific framework. Many of these policymakers assumed a high level of understanding of human behavior; they also assumed that designing the right welfare production function would result in appropriate behavior by recipients. One state legislator, commenting on the advantages of devolution, invoked the experimentation model with seemingly little recognition that the objects of it were primarily children: "That is the great thing about the state, we can try things that would be very difficult for the feds to do. We can have a little more risk. Even if we fail, it will be instructive to the rest of the country"; quoted in Judith Havemann and Barbara Vobejda, "After Getting Responsibility for Welfare, States May Pass It Down," *Washington Post*, January 28, 1997, A1.

11. See Paul E. Peterson and Mark C. Rom, *Welfare Magnets: A New Case for a National Standard* (Washington, D.C.: Brookings Institution Press, 1990); Paul E. Peterson, *The Price of Federalism* (Washington, D.C.: Brookings Institution Press, 1996).

12. E. E. Schattschneider, *The Semisovereign People* (Hinsdale, Ill.: Dryden Press, 1975), 10. See also Grant McConnell, *Private Power and American Democracy* (New York: Alfred A. Knopf, 1966), which provides a subtle and persuasive examination of the long-standing affection for decentralization in American political thought.

13. See Weaver, *Ending Welfare As We Know It*, especially chapters 10 through 12; and Balz and Brownstein, *Storming the Gates*, chapter 6.

14. See Martin Gilens, *Why Americans Hate Welfare: Race, Media, and the Politics of Antipoverty Policy* (Chicago: University of Chicago Press, 2000), for an insightful discussion of at least some of the reasons for the "racialization" of the welfare debate and the negative stereotypes of poor Americans, especially poor black Americans.

15. Charles Murray, *Losing Ground: American Social Policy, 1950–1980, Tenth Anniversary Edition* (New York: Basic Books, 1994).

16. "People, Opinions and Polls: Affirmative Action, Welfare, and the Individual," *The Public Perspective*, June/July 1995, 41.

17. See Weaver, *Ending Welfare As We Know It*, chapter 3, on the complexity of policymakers' motivations, including those of credit-claiming and blame avoidance; see also Teles, *Whose Welfare?*, 160–63, on the political appeal of block grants and allowing the states to grapple with the substance of welfare policymaking.

18. John W. Kingdon, "Ideas, Politics, and Public Policies," paper delivered at 1988 American Political Science Association annual meeting, Washington, D.C., September 1988. Political theorist William Connolly (personal communication) also notes the importance of competing conceptions of the "who" in Harold Lasswell's classic definition of politics in *Politics: Who Gets What, When, How* (New York: Meridian Books, 1958).

19. Some pluralists assume greater ease of access to representation in the policymaking process than is realistic, but many of their ideas are persuasive. David M. Truman's *The Governmental Process* (New York: Alfred A. Knopf, 1964) often is regarded as an example of this overly optimistic pluralist viewpoint.

20. Jacob E. Cooke, ed., *The Federalist* (Middletown, Conn.: Wesleyan University Press, 1961), 64. In opposition to Madison's association of largeness with freedom were the Anti-Federalists' association of smallness with virtue. See, among others, Herbert J. Storing, *What the Anti-Federalists Were For* (Chicago: University of Chicago Press, 1981).

21. Robert A. Dahl, in *A Preface to Democratic Theory* (Chicago: University of Chicago Press, 1956), 17, points out that Madison was something of a Hobbesian, asserting that "[i]f unrestrained by external checks, any given individual or group of individuals will tyrannize over others." Citing the work of political sociologists such as B. R. Berelson and Paul Lazarsfeld, Dahl notes that research on political behavior has found that socialized self-control is, in fact, quite possible. I would soften the assumptions of Madison's "realpolitik" to suggest that although most political actors may not actively and consciously oppress others, those with power, not too surprisingly, usually want to keep it. Motivated by this concern, they will tend to design and operate the systems they influence to ensure that they do, though much of this behavior they do not identify as self-interested.

22. Grant McConnell, *Private Power and American Democracy* (New York: Alfred A. Knopf, 1966), provides one of the best explications of this theory.

23. As Deborah Stone pointed out 30 years after McConnell, the assumptions underlying these values are potentially in conflict with many of the other values to which Americans aspire, such as equal opportunity and a classless society, and sometimes even conflict with each other. See *The Policy Paradox: The Art of Political Decision Making* (New York: W. W. Norton & Co., 1997).

24. Anyone who has read Arthur J. Vidich and Joseph Bensman's *Small Town in Mass Society: Class, Power and Religion in a Rural Community* (Princeton, N.J.: Princeton University Press, 1968) or lived in a small town may recognize McConnell's

account of informal social and political exclusion and see in it a significant problem, even while acknowledging its appeal to values of community.

25. These state and local projects include initiatives to send decision making about who receives welfare or health care benefits to private, for-profit corporations. Politicians talk enthusiastically about privatization of social services, although they focus little attention on the ways these services fail to meet criteria for efficient operation of competitive markets. The fact that the managers of publicly held private corporations are legally responsible for maximizing their shareholders' profits can lead to potentially harmful incentives when they manage services for vulnerable people who have limited information about their alternatives or few if any options for exiting the relationship. Recent controversies involving private, for-profit companies operating prisons, welfare systems, institutions that provide foster care for children, and Medicaid managed care underscore some of the risks in mixing the profit motive of corporate managers with the vulnerability of relatively powerless clientele who are not really "customers" in the usual business sense of the word.

26. Charles Tiebout, "A Pure Theory of Local Expenditures," *Journal of Political Economy* 64 (October 1956): 416–24. Paul Peterson is most closely associated with the modern version of this theory.

27. Although Peterson argues that higher benefits do spur recipients to migrate, other scholars have not found significant evidence of migration incentives among the poor. For example, see Phillip B. Levine and David J. Zimmerman, "An Empirical Analysis of the Welfare Magnet Debate Using the NLSY," University of Wisconsin-Madison Institute for Research on Poverty Discussion Papers, DP #1098-96, July 1996. The critical political consideration, however, is whether state decision makers *believe* that more generous benefits will draw poor people, whatever the empirical evidence—and it seems that generally they do.

28. See Carol W. Weissert, ed., *Learning from Leaders: Welfare Reform Politics and Policy in Five Midwestern States* (Albany, N.Y.: Rockefeller Institute Press, 2000), for an account of welfare policymaking in a selection of states.

29. See Margaret Weir, Ann Shola Orloff, and Theda Skocpol, "Introduction: Understanding American Social Politics," in *The Politics of Social Policy in the United States* (Princeton, N.J.: Princeton University Press, 1988), for a discussion of the role of policy feedbacks in American social policy.

30. See Kay Lehman Schlozman and John T. Tierney, *Organized Interests and American Democracy* (New York: Harper and Row, 1986) for tactics and strategies of interest group influence. See also Jeffrey M. Berry, *The Interest Group Society* (Boston: Little, Brown and Co., 1984), among others.

31. Some were off the record; as a rule, therefore, most interviewees are not identified by name.

32. Underlying my analysis is the assumption that the best remedy for poverty among families is either money (in the form of cash payments or vouchers) or help gaining employment at wages that are above the poverty level, along with support such as education, training, reliable and safe child care, job-hunting assistance, creation of

jobs, or transportation assistance. Current political and cultural biases clearly support the latter over the former, but questions remain about which is best for poor children and their mothers in the long run. Political scientist Cathy M. Johnson, in "Who Speaks for the Children? Representation in the Policy Process," a paper prepared for the annual meeting of the American Political Science Association, New York, September 1994, notes the shift in the underlying approach to welfare and family policy from one that is based on attachment theory (assuming that children—especially young children—need to be with their mothers) to role model theory (assuming that children are best off when their parents provide socially appropriate role models). Obvious problems with a work focus include less parental supervision and guidance for children who usually are being raised by only one parent; greater strain on poor women who are managing a household alone; scarcity of entry-level jobs that offer benefits or pay that are sufficient to raise a poor family out of poverty; jobs that are located far from recipients' homes; insufficient funding for and availability of good child care; and, in some states, provisions that force the mothers of very young children (as young as three months old, in at least six states) to work shortly after childbirth. Problems with continuing an income-support approach include its obvious political unpopularity as women across class lines increasingly work; a welfare system that was geared more to check distribution and eligibility verification than assisting women who want to work find and keep jobs; and some evidence of work disincentive effects.

33. Hispanics also could be included in the black or white categories.

34. Data are from *Statistical Abstract of the United States, 1996* (Washington, D.C.: U.S. Bureau of the Census, 1996) and from www.census.gov/population/estimates/state/srh/srh95.txt; U.S. House of Representatives Committee on Ways and Means, *1996 Green Book* (Washington, D.C.: Government Printing Office, 1997); Kathryn Larin and Elizabeth C. McNichol, *Pulling Apart: A State-by-State Analysis of Income Trends* (Washington, D.C.: Center on Budget and Policy Priorities, 1997).

Part I

National Welfare Politics

Setting the National Stage

In 1996, the enduring desire to reform welfare and poor people met the ongoing renegotiation of the balance of political power between the national government and the states. This latest "New Federalism" represented the most recent round in a long political and philosophical struggle over which level of government should make what kind of policies and over how to address the persistent issue of poor families among us. It was striking, however, for turning back sharply the decades-long trend toward greater centralization in Washington of policymaking for low-income families. Devolution in 1996 sent responsibility for most aspects of welfare policymaking back to the states, some of which have devolved it further to their localities.

For the nation's first 150 years, localities and then the states gradually joined private charities in providing assistance to poor people. With few exceptions, the federal government remained uninvolved. As a rule, state and local provision was modest and extremely inconsistent. During the Great Depression, these jurisdictions were overwhelmed by the scope of destitution and were unable to meet the growing demand for help. The federal government first took over broad aspects of American social policy with the 1935 Social Security Act; its role continued to grow over the following four decades.

Beginning in the 1960s, liberal organizations and interests worked hard to centralize policymaking in Washington, where they began to develop a greater presence and had a greater chance of influencing outcomes than they had in the fifty states. This movement toward policy centralization began to slow in the 1970s and especially the 1980s, with retrenchment in the national commitment to low-income people initiated by the Reagan administration, helping to set the stage for the radical shifts of the mid-1990s.

Chapter 2 reviews the history of American welfare policy and highlights the impact that federalism has had on social policy in the United States into the 1990s. It looks at the early Clinton administration's approach to welfare policy and examines the larger political influences and the pressures from within government that led to passage of the Personal Responsibility and Work Opportunity Reconciliation Act of 1996. Chapter 3 considers the role of organizations and actors outside the federal government—in particular, advocacy groups and others who tried to influence the final bill. It asks which groups and actors were most in evidence, most active, and most effective during the period of intense national debate between 1995 and 1996. Finally, chapter 3 explores some of the approaches these organizations used to try to affect policy outcomes, despite the radical changes in the political environment of welfare policymaking in Washington in the mid-1990s.

2

Reaching the Devolution Revolution: The History of Welfare in the United States

Welfare in the United States has been notoriously difficult to reform. It has been marked by incremental changes, with very occasional bursts of large-scale change such as that in the New Deal and the 1996 PRWORA. Americans have long been deeply ambivalent about poor people, reflecting an enduring tension between compassion and resentment; reformers in the United States have been fairly consistent—with a few important exceptions—in regarding the causes of poverty as individual in nature, rather than economic, social, or political. Americans also have long been worried that systems of relief themselves cause "poor" behavior. In the 1980s and 1990s, the sense of a dependency crisis caused by welfare programs contributed in critical ways to passage of PRWORA.

Americans have been debating the relative powers of the state and national governments for almost as long as they have debated how to deal with the needs of poor people. Although the relationship between the states and the central government over the first 150 years of the republic could be characterized as a system of "dual sovereignty," since the New Deal it has come to be more aptly described by Morton Grodzins' "marble cake" or "cooperative" federalism.[1] In the past three decades, policymakers have made several attempts to "sort out" government functions or to devolve federal responsibilities back to the states. Until 1995, the major recent efforts were the "New Federalisms" of Republican presidents Richard Nixon and Ronald Reagan.

This chapter reviews the history of American programs for poor people. It focuses on the period when states and localities determined their own welfare policies, as well as the era of increasing national standards for welfare and social policy. It briefly considers the development of American federalism and the role our federalist system has played in U.S. social policies. Finally, it explores the political dynamics around the centerpiece of the most recent New Federalism—the welfare reform act of 1996—emphasizing the institutions and actors within the federal government. The following chapter will look in detail at the role played by outside actors, including advocacy organizations and other groups representing low-income families.

RELIEF PROGRAMS BEFORE 1935: LOCAL AND STATE AUTONOMY

Between the early Colonial period and the nineteenth century, American attitudes toward the alleviation of poverty largely reflected British approaches, including the Poor Law of 1834. The Poor Law stressed the deterrent effect of meager aid and reinforced the ethic that people who were receiving welfare, whatever the reason, should always be worse off than those who worked.[2] The limited public aid that was available was almost entirely local, and local poor laws reflected the belief that individuals' spiritual, moral, mental, or physical weakness lay at the root of their distress; there was little emphasis on larger social or economic causes. At its most extreme, in the mid-1800s, a strand of social Darwinism regarded poverty as a sign of unfitness; advocates of this view argued that assistance was not only useless but dangerous because it allowed poor people to survive, multiply, and weaken the species.[3] By and large, an uneasy tension existed between the recognition that some people truly were unfortunate and a harsh skepticism that led some towns to drive the destitute from their borders and take children from their parents simply because they were poor.

During the 1800s, states became more involved in providing aid, but largely in the form of institutions—poorhouses and workhouses—and on a small scale.[4] Until 1865, the federal government took no responsibility for relief, leaving it entirely in the hands of local and state officials or private and religious charities. During the Civil War, however, Congress established "the nation's first federal welfare agency": the Bureau of Refugees, Freedmen, and Abandoned Lands, located within the U.S. War Department. The Bureau's main purpose was to aid slaves in transition to freedom during the war and immediately thereafter; although the Bureau demonstrated that the federal government had the capacity to alleviate poverty where states and localities could not or would not, it had negligible long-term influence on private and public social welfare policies.[5] In 1862 Congress also passed the first Civil War pension system for veterans and many of their dependents, and the program expanded markedly until 1910. Sociologist Theda Skocpol called it "America's first large-scale nationally funded old-age and disability system."[6] Congress discontinued the program in 1910, under charges of Republican patronage and corruption.[7] Some theorists argue that this failed experience with federal administration further slowed the expansion of national social programs in the United States.[8]

Unlike many European governments, the United States held back from founding a national social welfare system, for reasons that included its traditions of private support, concern about patronage in government programs, the existence of modest local and state programs, and the nation's decentralized federalist system.[9] The rapid industrialization, urbanization, and immigration of the nineteenth and early twentieth centuries, however, pushed some reformers and politicians to consider economic and social causes of poverty, in addition to the traditional personal explanations. During the early 1900s, support for public aid increased and state welfare institutions multiplied, becoming more competent and more professional.[10] Between 1917 and 1929, twenty-five states established public welfare agencies. Reformers and politicians began to feel that the "indoor" system of institutions such as poorhouses too often was inhumane, ineffective, and expensive. Institutions remained the predominant form of public aid, especially on the state level, but reformers were turning toward a system of "outdoor" aid, or assistance that supported poor people to remain, at least to some extent, within the community.[11]

In the first three decades of the twentieth century—during the Progressive era and beyond—many initiatives targeted toward women and children took hold. The active movement of voluntary women's groups, largely composed of educated upper middle class women, successfully pushed for state and federal programs benefiting mothers and children, even before women themselves gained the vote in 1921.[12] Many states started putting in place a system of modest mothers' or widows' pensions, providing aid to a limited group of "worthy" women and their children or occasionally to other caretakers. This system reflected a growing consensus among experts that children were better off staying with their mothers than going to institutions or foster homes.[13] Illinois was the first state to implement a mothers' pension system, in 1911. Within two years, twenty state legislatures had enacted them; by 1926, all but eight states had some sort of pension in place.[14] The speed with which mothers' pensions were adopted suggested new support for a degree of government assistance for poor families.

Through pensions, "deserving" mothers would be able to stay home with their children full time. Tying moral behavior to public aid was common to programs for men and women.[15] Although these programs were available in the majority of states by the late 1920s, they helped a very limited number of needy people. Instead, pensions only supplemented the earnings poor mothers already made in low-wage jobs, and overall spending was very low. Of the 3.8 million female-headed households living in the United States in 1931, only about 2.5 percent received aid.[16]

Although the federal government spent no money on general relief in 1929, other public aid was beginning to increase.[17] Reliable statistics are scarce, but one study of 16 cities found that "public outdoor aid" rose from $1 million dollars in 1911 to $7.4 million in 1928. Another study suggested that spending on welfare and social insurance (not including health and education) at all levels of government increased from about $114 million in 1913 to $500 million in 1929. Other estimates suggest that 4–10 percent of the population received some kind of public or private aid in that period.[18]

Undergirding the long-standing state and local autonomy over social programs was the American system of federalism. From the nation's founding to the 1950s, it was marked by strong deference to state authority—often for reasons motivated by the nation's system of racial apartheid, as well as concerns about central government oppression.[19] During the Constitutional Convention, delegates from the southern states had made clear that they would not join the union if the Constitution and the national government in any way interfered with their ability to import and own slaves, and northern delegates acceded in the interests of union and their own economic concerns.[20] Critically, the Constitution's "three-fifths compromise" gave southern states disproportionate power in Congress for most of the following century. Concerns related to slavery and race have lain beneath many of the most contentious debates about federalism as it has been practiced in the United States. After the Civil War—in which these issues were addressed in bloody confrontation—during the New Deal and into the 1950s, the linked traditions of American apartheid and "states' rights" continued to contribute to a national hands-off approach toward the states in social policy and other areas, in part to preserve the South's largely race-based system of low-wage labor. Even during the debate about PRWORA, the last major federalism initiative of the twentieth century, issues of race—though in less explicit forms—would continue to influence decisions about federalism and devolution.

THE NEW DEAL ERA

Until the election of Franklin D. Roosevelt in 1932, the U.S. Supreme Court generally interpreted the "commerce clause" and the "necessary and proper clause" narrowly and the Tenth Amendment broadly in disputes between the national government and the states, and the scale of the federal role remained small.[21] With the onset of the Great Depression, however, FDR received broad public support for using the power of the national government for economic relief, initiating the first of the two "big bangs" in American social policy—the New Deal—with the Social Security Act of 1935.[22] Aid to Dependent Children (ADC) was only one element of a three-pronged approach that emphasized temporary emergency and work relief, social and unemployment insurance, and federal matching assistance funneled through the states for unemployable people, particularly elderly widows and children. Roosevelt sold these initiatives politically as aid that the recipient had "earned" or as temporary relief, based on the assumption that the recipient would soon be self-sufficient again.

The programs' effect was significant, and by and large New Deal programs were within the capacity of the federal and state bureaucracies to carry out effectively.[23] By design, however, their structures and eligibility requirements limited the types and number of people who would receive help because this structure ensured the support of white southern Democrats. Old Age Insurance coverage excluded agricultural and domestic workers, thereby leaving out about 90 percent of black Americans who worked. The Social Security Act left unemployment insurance to state and local jurisdiction, and the states, in turn, left out many of the neediest, including agricultural workers, migrants, women, and African Americans.[24] States' mothers' pensions were the model for ADC, which provided federal matching grants to states for needy children; like those programs, ADC initially restricted most benefits to the children of white widows who were deemed worthy. Southern congressmen benefiting from the one-party Democratic South held key Congressional committee leadership positions and supported ADC legislation only on the condition that the right to set benefit levels and establish criteria for eligibility would remain under state control; federally set payment levels could have threatened the South's supply of largely black low-wage labor. This arrangement helped to reinforce regional and racial divisions in ADC receipt and benefit levels throughout the country.[25]

With the exception of ADC, which initially was small and uncontroversial, New Deal programs were not targeted at addressing the needs of the long-term poor or the causes of their poverty. The sheer scale of poverty during the Great Depression challenged, for a time, the concept that poor people themselves were to blame for their situations. The economic collapse was regarded largely as a temporary condition, however, not a reflection of fundamental structural inequities that had to be remedied. As Hugh Heclo writes, "For America's poor, the New Deal Domestic agenda was an exercise in social stabilization and not social engineering."[26] In 1939, Congress passed amendments to ADC that further bifurcated "deserving" and "undeserving" recipients, allowing the widows and children of workers who had been covered by Old Age Insurance to receive benefits from that program rather than ADC. Welfare became the last resort for women who were divorced, abandoned, or never married or the widows of men who were not covered by Social Security, many of whom were black.[27] In 1950, the federal government added a caretaker portion to the family grant and changed the program's title to Aid to Families with Dependent Children.[28]

During the 1940s and 1950s, states continued to set benefits and eligibility criteria, with wide variation, though the federal government attempted to impose some additional guidelines and make grants more liberal. The number of mothers and children covered by the program grew from 701,000 in 1945 to 3 million in 1960, and average monthly benefits increased by about 77 percent in real terms between 1940 and 1962, though they still differed markedly by state.[29] About one-fifth to one-sixth of poor families in America in the 1950s received either categorical aid, including AFDC, or state or locally administered general assistance. State benefit standards for those who received aid were modest; the national average in 1960 was $2,150 per year—below the poverty level of $3,000 and the Bureau of Labor Statistics' standard of "minimum comfort" of $5,464.[30]

Reminiscent of the variable administration of mothers' pensions, state AFDC restrictions included seasonal employment policies that cut mothers off during the cotton-picking season and "man in the house" rules that cut off recipients if they were found to be living with a man. These "absent father" regulations would later be blamed for breaking up poor families. Other state laws included lengthy residency requirements, slow or complicated application procedures, and denial of aid to families in which the father was believed to be living nearby or able to help support the children. "Suitable home" regulations enabled states to deny aid to families if the mothers were thought to be living improper lives. Louisiana put a "family cap" in place in 1960, cutting off aid to more than 23,000 children because their mothers had given birth to an out-of-wedlock child. About half of the families were reinstated after federal intervention.[31]

With the New Deal, the issue of federalism increasingly was addressed within the political rather than the judicial arena. After Roosevelt's threat to "pack" the Court paved the way for a more expansive interpretation of the appropriate role of the national government, the constitutional wall that had built up between federal and state authority and action significantly eroded.[32] The Court largely upheld the constitutionality of federal involvement in historically state functions in a variety of cases after 1937 (until the 1990s). The most important of these cases included *Brown v. Board of Education of Topeka* in 1954[33] and the reapportionment cases, *Baker v. Carr* in 1962[34] and *Reynolds v. Sims* in 1964.[35] The latter effectively ended rural domination in many state legislatures, bringing in more diverse, reform-minded representatives and attracting more competent and representative legislators and staffs, particularly in southern states.[36] The dramatic instances of federal political power forcing change in southern states, particularly in the area of racial desegregation, reminded a broad segment of Americans that states' rights had long-standing racial implications and contributed to passage and enforcement of the Civil Rights Act of 1964 and the Voting Rights Act of 1965.[37]

THE GREAT SOCIETY, PART I

Congress made changes to AFDC in the early 1960s, including legislation to allow states to provide benefits to families with unemployed fathers in residence—the AFDC-UP, or "unemployed parent," program—though initially few states did.[38] The 1962 Public Welfare Amendments increased federal funding for certain social services.[39] An innocuous Section 1115 of the 1962 amendments allowed the Secretary of the then-Department of Health, Education, and Welfare (HEW) to grant states waivers from many requirements of AFDC for the purpose of "any experimental, pilot, or demonstration project which, in the judgment of the Secretary, is likely to assist in promoting the objectives" of AFDC, with strict evaluation.[40]

Democratic President John Kennedy "rediscovered" poverty; in his decision to do something about it, he broke essentially with the political and policy approaches of the New Deal. Kennedy's successor, Lyndon B. Johnson, launched the Great Society—the second "big bang" of American social policy—and declared the War on Poverty in 1964, but Kennedy had laid much of the groundwork with his focus on the white rural poverty of Appalachia and the poverty of elderly people.

As a whole, the Kennedy-Johnson anti-poverty efforts differed from the New Deal in several crucial ways. They were not directed simply at short-term economic relief; instead, they aimed, in rhetoric at least, to end the causes of poverty. They reflected social scientists' beliefs that by controlling inputs they could change outputs—in this case, mass behavior. They focused on services such as training and education, as well as on community action, not on income maintenance or grant adequacy or on issues related to the larger relationship between poverty and the economy, such as underemployment.[41] They were started largely by social scientists—professional "technocrats" within government—not by the direct political demands of poor people themselves.[42] However, they were designed, at least in part and at the outset, to activate poor people politically and to incorporate them and their demands into the policymaking process. This experiment would be short-lived.

An essential element of the Economic Opportunity Act of 1964—the charter legislation for the War on Poverty—was the Community Action Programs (CAP), which provided federal money to state, local, and nongovernmental organizations for decentralized programs to meet the needs of low-income people. The language of the legislation included the now-famous requirement that community action programs involve "maximum feasible participation" by poor people in their development and administration. The design of the CAP was the work of a small group of liberal white policymakers within the White House's Office of Economic Opportunity, who drew up their plan rapidly and in relative political isolation.[43]

Several scholars argue persuasively (although along somewhat different lines) that the CAP was a response to the Civil Rights movement and was designed to remedy the "political poverty" of black Americans, rather than simply to improve program coordination and alleviate the economic poverty of poor people generally.[44] The CAP's specific provisions were not designed to satisfy the demands of particular civil rights organizations; these groups were not involved in its formulation. Instead, as the Civil Rights movement gained strength and the attention of a broad segment of white Americans, as well as liberal policymakers in the White House, anti-poverty efforts during the Johnson administration also became associated with sympathetic black Americans protesting racial injustice. Initially this "racialization" of anti-poverty efforts contributed to support for the CAP, which was regarded by its creators as a means for empowering black Americans politically and helping them learn the skills they would need to participate more effectively in the political process to demand services and improve their circumstances. According to Paul E. Peterson and J. David Greenstone's study of community action programs in five cities, "whenever community action took a participatory direction, it can be traced to a well-organized, militant black community that had developed during earlier civil rights efforts."[45]

This unprecedented emphasis on increasing the political participation of poor people in policymaking did not last, however, as community action programs were brought under the control of government agencies. The political empowerment strategy soon took shape beyond the control of White House policymakers and the political establishment in many cities.[46] Elements of the Civil Rights movement transformed into the more militant Black Power movement, unnerving many white people. Civil unrest and riots spread in many American cities, inflamed by the murder of Martin Luther King, Jr., and impatience with the rate of social and political change. Growing black political demands—in part from groups that had effectively gained political power through the community action programs—angered Democratic mayors such as Richard J. Daley of Chicago.[47] These mayors and others brought pressure to bear on the White House to contain this version of mass-based participation.

There were other reasons, of course, for the political failure of the War on Poverty. Welfare rolls began climbing, partially as a result of a concerted campaign by CAP organizers to enroll eligible families. The technocrats who developed War on Poverty programs oversold their potential, in part because of their faith in expert-designed government programs and in part to gain the popular and legislative support required for passage—setting the stage for their ultimate failure.[48] Johnson's decision to escalate the Vietnam War cost him essential support from the left and distracted him from his domestic "war."[49] The War on Poverty also was inadequately funded and badly coordinated.[50] The greatest vulnerability, however, probably arose from the fact that its programs were explicitly oriented to poor Americans—largely perceived as black—with no pretense to universalism and that they were initiated at a time of fleeting economic prosperity coupled with growing social insecurity. The War on Poverty required prolonged support from political constituents who were not its beneficiaries.[51]

By the late 1960s, War on Poverty programs faced a loss of support, white backlash, and the decline of their presidential sponsor, and they were largely abandoned. As Johnson's political fortunes faded, racially implicated law-and-order fears replaced racially implicated anti-poverty efforts for many white people, withering support for these programs.[52] Many white politicians, policymakers, and voters felt that they had listened to the "voice of the [black] poor"; ultimately, they didn't like what they heard.[53]

Finally, also as part of the Great Society programs, Congress established the Food Stamps program in 1964, under the jurisdiction of the Department of Agriculture, and the Medicaid program for low-income people in 1965 as part of the politically popular Medicare health program for the elderly.[54] In 1967, Congress passed another set of changes to AFDC, including requirements that most recipients register for training and work programs and that states provide child care for participants under a newly established Work Incentive Program (WIN) program. Revisions to AFDC also allowed participants to keep more of their earnings (the first $30 plus one-third of the remainder), in an effort to preserve the work incentive for welfare mothers.[55] The practical effect of WIN was minimal because it was costly for states to set up effective jobs programs and provide child care.

THE GREAT SOCIETY, PART II: NIXON'S FAMILY ASSISTANCE PLAN

Although the Johnson presidency often is depicted as the pinnacle of national authority over the states, especially in social programs, the Nixon presidency oversaw continued expansion of the federal role. Enhancing the "voice of the poor," however, was no longer on the political agenda, and President Nixon effectively ended the community action programs.

The last serious proposal to significantly expand welfare came from Republican Nixon. The number and percentage of Americans receiving cash assistance had risen dramatically from the early 1960s to the early 1970s, particularly between 1968 and 1972. One factor was a growing number of federal court decisions that limited the ability of states to set restrictive rules, and pushed them to apply criteria for AFDC eligibility more consistently. Several major U.S. Supreme Court decisions defined and protected due process and property rights of welfare recipients, contributing to wider availability of benefits.[56] Another factor was the efforts of the poor people's movement, which had worked to expand the rolls. At the same time, the value of welfare grew, in part because of increases in the food stamp program and the introduction of Medicaid.[57]

These changes in the welfare system took place against a backdrop of major cultural and social change. The women's movement and a tightening economy started to encourage women to work outside the home. Higher divorce and out-of-wedlock birth rates and concerns about the economy also were beginning to cast doubt on the idea that the nuclear family was the norm and realistically could be supported by the male breadwinner's salary alone.

Increasingly, black and divorced or never-married women had joined the welfare rolls, which were increasing at an annual rate of 18–20 percent at the end of the 1960s.[58] Nixon was elected in 1968 in an atmosphere of anxiety about the economy and a strong fear of social disintegration that centered on anti-war protests, the black power movement, and high inflation rates.[59]

Despite campaigning as a law-and-order Republican, with implicit racial appeals to white voters, Nixon indicated his interest in making welfare reform a priority early on. He decried widely unequal benefit levels among states and called for national standards for aid "that preserves the dignity of the individual and integrity of the family" for those who could not help themselves and "opportunity and incentive" for those who could.[60] However, Nixon's vision—a national guaranteed income for poor parents—focused on the white working poor as much as the minority urban poor. It also was proposed in response to governors, especially northern Republican governors, who perceived that growing welfare numbers and their costs were reaching epidemic proportions.[61] The enormous disparity between state benefit levels—which varied by nearly a factor of 10—contributed to the sense of crisis. In Mississippi, for example, 55 percent of residents lived below the poverty level, but only 14 percent received assistance.[62] Northern governors from high-benefit states expressed particular concern about the magnet effect of this gap; many argued that uniform standards would slow the migration of poor blacks from the southern states onto the welfare rolls of northern urban centers. National standards began to seem inevitable.[63]

Nixon's plan was conservative in origin—University of Chicago economist Milton Friedman had first proposed something like it in 1964—but seemed liberal in effect.[64] Despite the fact that Nixon was an unlikely president to initiate a plan as fundamentally radical as a guaranteed minimum income, he invested heavily in its success, at least initially. Like many others, he blamed the welfare system itself for the breakup of families, nonwork, and increasing rolls. The design of his Family Assistance Plan (FAP) was advertised as aiding the deserving working poor, reinforcing the work ethic, and encouraging responsible behavior. It offered the added virtue of punishing two groups toward whom the president felt particular antipathy: the federal social services bureaucracy and social workers. The FAP would weaken these two key Democratic strongholds by dismantling the human services apparatus that had built up under the Kennedy and Johnson administrations.[65]

The FAP did not particularly reward Nixon's traditional allies, however, and many people regarded it as inconsistent with his rhetoric and political positions, causing "ideological confusion."[66] Nixon's Southern strategy to woo southern whites to the Republican party had not won him black allegiance. Now he was in the unlikely position of proposing a program that would most benefit poor southern blacks and northern Republican governors. Blacks from low-benefit states would benefit disproportionately because they had been largely shut out of the Social Security and unemployment insurance systems and excluded from many state-run AFDC programs.[67] HEW estimated that the FAP would increase the number of welfare recipients in the South by 250–400 percent. Fifty-two percent of people covered by the FAP would be southern, and two-thirds of southern blacks would receive some payment.[68]

Nixon introduced the FAP as part of his "New Federalism" proposal, along with the General Revenue Sharing program and a plan to transfer training programs to the state and local levels. He regarded these three programs—to be followed later by block grant proposals—as part of a pattern of "sorting out" federal, state, and local responsibilities.[69] The FAP provided an opportunity for the national government to lead the states because no state had a guaranteed minimum income, and the fear of welfare magnetism made this approach unlikely. This strategy could work only at the national level.[70] Nixon was, in his way, an activist president who saw positive large-scale uses for federal power. As Richard Nathan, one of Nixon's aides, noted, "We accepted the paradigm of the Great Society."[71] Moreover, with approval ratings of 68 percent in 1969, Nixon initially had the political capital necessary for such a radical proposal.[72]

The initial FAP proposal would have replaced AFDC with a modest guaranteed minimum income provided by the federal government and accompanied by food stamps, Medicaid, mandatory job training, and child care.[73] The proposal was projected to add $4 billion to welfare expenses and more than double the rolls, drawing mostly from the working poor.[74] The income floor would surpass the AFDC benefit levels of 16 states; states with benefits above the floor would be required to maintain prior payment levels by means of cash supplements, although this maintenance-of-effort provision was later dropped.[75]

With Democrats controlling both houses of Congress, Nixon needed Democratic backing for any successful legislation.[76] Support for the plan was inconsistent, however. Initially, northern governors who wanted relief from rising rolls supported it. Liberal politicians and the advocacy groups that were beginning to spring up in Washington were hard-pressed—at least initially—to oppose creation of a national "right" to a minimum benefit for all poor families. Yet they were leery of the fact that Nixon had proposed a program that Johnson would not; as the debate continued they sought higher cash benefits, and their reservations grew. Religious organizations originally supported nationalized welfare for the poor, but their unity soon fractured as well. Protestant groups, in particular, responded to growing black dissatisfaction with the FAP.[77] Labor unions were divided. The AFL-CIO and United Auto Workers initially opposed it, concerned that it would use federal funds to subsidize private employers, but were won over by public jobs programs and wage commitments. The American Federation of State, County, and Municipal Employees (AFSCME), which represented state and local social workers, among others, opposed the bill because—as Nixon had intended—it would cut members' jobs.[78] Business interests also were at odds. The National Association of Manufacturers passively supported the bill; the Chamber of Commerce, representing more labor-reliant businesses, adamantly opposed it.[79]

The National Welfare Rights Organization (NWRO)—the largest of the welfare rights groups—was active in the FAP battle, opposing the training and work requirements and the modesty of the benefit levels. By this time, the extent to which the organization represented a broad membership was unclear, but with its provocative tactics the NWRO received ample attention.[80] Those it did represent were largely northern welfare recipients, and the NWRO sought to protect and if possible increase these members' welfare "rights"—or at least their benefit levels. The FAP, however, threatened to lower northern urban benefit levels at the same time it increased work requirements. The NWRO's members faced the possibility that they would have to start working in exchange for less money than they made by staying at home with their children. They opposed this prospect in the strongest terms, arguing for a higher annual benefit (the average in New York) and no work requirements.[81]

Ultimately, the NWRO pushed to "zap FAP" as liberal support transformed into opposition. Northern black elected officials followed their constituents' lead—at least the short-term interests of this group and others who shared their views—and in time opposed the FAP. All but one of the black representatives in the House had voted for the plan in 1969, but by 1971 all but one opposed it.[82]

Northern urban blacks on AFDC would have lost with the FAP, but large numbers of poor southern blacks would have won. Poor black southerners were not organized, however, and their interests were largely lost in the debate. Political participation in the South was fairly new—only a real possibility after the Voting Rights Act of 1965—and southern blacks still lacked representation in Congress and in the states.[83] The only black state representative in Mississippi, Robert Clark, testified in 1971 in favor of federal administration of the FAP, stating that under state control, Mississippi officials denied benefits to anyone "able to walk or crawl."[84]

On the other hand, the southern white politicians in Congress who controlled key committee chairmanships sought to preserve state autonomy. The average southern farm laborer made a median income of $1,034 in 1969, according to the U.S. Department of Agriculture. The FAP and food stamps together would have tripled that income, unaccompanied by hard labor. Despite the decline in the agricultural labor needs of the region since the 1950s, the guaranteed income posed a threat to the region's general system of low-wage labor. As Rep. Phil M. Landrum, Democrat of Georgia and one of three Ways and Means committee members to vote against the FAP, warned, "There's not going to be anybody to roll those wheelbarrows and press those shirts."[85] So as northern black opposition rose on the left, southern white opposition rose on the right.

The administration attempted to pass the FAP repeatedly but unsuccessfully from 1969 to 1972. Amendments to the Social Security Act approved in 1972, however, created the Supplemental Security Income (SSI) program for blind, disabled, and elderly needy people, creating a new program that further "creamed off" the sympathetic needy and left AFDC even more politically vulnerable.[86]

Nixon belonged in essential ways to the New Deal/Great Society period, and his New Federalism reflected this fact. He believed in legitimate uses for an activist national government, but he wanted to make its power (and his own) more efficient and effective. Political scientist Timothy Conlan calls Nixon's approach a rationalizing thrust to sorting out. Ronald Reagan's New Federalism, however, reflected and helped strengthen a national skepticism about central government action, and his administration marked the beginning of the age of devolution in welfare policy, with real cuts in federal social programs. It was under the Reagan administration's auspices that the federal government began a slow U-turn on national standards for income maintenance and began more energetically requiring work for welfare mothers.

INCOME MAINTENANCE GIVES WAY TO WORK: FROM THE FAMILY ASSISTANCE PLAN TO THE FAMILY SUPPORT ACT

Democratic President Jimmy Carter's Program for Better Jobs and Income proposal would have replaced AFDC, SSI, and food stamps with cash payments to about 32 million poor people and as many as 1.4 million public service jobs, but it did not go far.[87] The era of the guaranteed minimum income was ending, and the age of "fiscalized" welfare politics—with an emphasis on work, decentralization, and greater restrictions on assistance—was being ushered in.

The Reagan administration's 1981 Omnibus Budget Reconciliation Act (OBRA) reduced taxes and expenditures and made cost-cutting changes to AFDC that also had the effect of cutting benefits and the rolls.[88] OBRA signaled the end of serious discussion about adequacy of benefits. OBRA and Reagan's New Federalism also signaled a loosening of federal control as the administration granted increasing numbers of Section 1115 waivers to let states vary from the requirements of federal statute—a trend Presidents Bush and Clinton would continue. Some of these experiments were of long duration and had the effect of cutting benefits.[89] In addition, a 1982 "swap" proposal would have exchanged federal responsibility for fully funding Medicaid for state assumption of AFDC and the food stamps program, though it was never introduced in Congress.[90] These proposals marked the first serious effort in almost 50 years to turn welfare policymaking back to the states.

In contrast to the 1960s, the major problem with AFDC in the mid-1980s was neither escalating costs nor growing caseloads. Between 1975 and 1985, benefit expenditures at all levels of government had declined in real terms by

13 percent. The average monthly number of recipients had decreased somewhat, from 11.1 million to 10.8 million, despite a growing general population, and the size of welfare families became smaller.[91]

Nonetheless, experts, politicians, and the public increasingly expressed concern about welfare dependency and what was regarded as a growing "culture of poverty" that kept poor people poor. Far from considering poor people—of any race—a group with legitmate political or economic claims, policymakers and others increasingly considered them to be members of a burgeoning and dysfunctional or even dangerous "underclass." Charles Murray's 1984 book *Losing Ground* provided one of the most influential expositions of the growing belief that welfare was a leading *cause* of poverty, rather than a solution to it; he emphasized escalating rates of out-of-wedlock births as the source of a wide range of social ills, including the increase in crime. Even liberal experts and policymakers focused on welfare dependency and the urban underclass—largely understood to be black—which implicitly threatened other Americans.[92] These attitudes about the culture of welfare certainly were not new in the United States, though they had been crowded out for a time by competing conceptions of poor Americans during the 1960s and 1970s. The statistics behind dependency also told a more ambiguous story, however: The percentage of AFDC recipients who stayed on welfare for more than five years actually decreased somewhat in the years between 1979 and 1990.[93]

Growing support for women working in the labor market contributed to concern about welfare dependency: With more middle-class women in the workforce, welfare mothers also were expected to get jobs. Arguments about the value of child-rearing and other work traditionally done by women received scant attention in the welfare debate.[94] Daniel Patrick Moynihan—a central player in the FAP debate and later in the passage of the Family Support Act—had noted this inconsistency in 1973, but he expressed optimism that it would change:

> If American society recognized home making and child rearing as productive work to be included in the national economic accounts (as is the case in at least one other nation) the receipt of welfare might not imply dependency. But we don't. It may be hoped the women's movement of the present time will change this. But as of the time I write, it had not.[95]

By 1986, Moynihan was as worried about dependency as most of his peers. There was widespread agreement that women with children who received public assistance should work outside the home—implicitly assuming that it was better for children to be cared for by someone other than their mothers, at least in the case of welfare families. The consensus that a working welfare mother was a better mother first took hold in the late 1980s.

The welfare problem also was defined as a problem of parental irresponsibility, particularly on the part of fathers. Statistics from the Department of Health and Human Services (HHS) indicated that 52 percent of all women with children under twenty-one did not receive child support legally due to them.[96] After work, child support enforcement was the second major thrust of the next round of reform.

The Family Support Act of 1988 (FSA) was the last major welfare legislation before the 1996 PRWORA, and it attempted significant if incremental change. To be successful, the FSA would have to address basic problems inherent in jobs-oriented welfare initiatives. These problems included the availability of suitable jobs, the need for affordable child care, the loss of Medicaid when many low-paying jobs didn't provide health coverage, and logistical problems such as transportation to work. It also would have to contend with the fact that a recipient could work full-time at the minimum wage or above and still earn an income that was significantly less than the poverty level. Presaging the 1996 bill, the FSA also aimed to accomplish a range of other—sometimes inconsistent—goals, the most ambitious and amorphous of which was to "change the culture of the welfare system."[97] There was solid bipartisan assent on the broad strokes of the proposal, if often sharp disagreement about its details—in particular, work requirements, child care funding, and expansion of the two-parent families program.

The nation's governors and, later, Congress—not the Reagan administration—played the central role in getting welfare back on the national agenda. Two governors in particular—Michael N. Castle, Republican of Delaware, and Bill Clinton, Democrat of Arkansas—took the lead.[98] Their approach preserved state autonomy; this emphasis was congenial to the White House. Congress, the governors, and the White House did not agree, however, on the extent of control that should be left to the states or on whether work should be mandatory. The White House unsuccessfully proposed a plan to allow states freedom to experiment broadly with welfare, but without more federal money. The governors, not surprisingly, wanted flexibility, minimal federal mandates, and generous federal funding. After repeated failed attempts at welfare reform, however, members of Congress and the governors did not want to let this window of opportunity close.[99]

Clinton was called "the chief southern statehouse advocate" of the FSA, and he helped reduce the reservations of conservative southern Democrats who had contributed to the defeat of prior reform efforts.[100] Ultimately, this state-level base of political support provided welfare reform legislation with a powerful set of advocates, much as it would again in the mid-1990s. The other actors that had been vocal in the FAP debate were not as actively involved in the debate about the FSA. Some groups shared the general political consensus about work, and others regarded the FSA as an incremental proposal that did not stir the fears that the FAP had.

Many actors had been weakened since the 1970s, however, and conflict was muted. As Douglas Imig and others have noted, from the CAP and War on Poverty programs until the 1981 OBRA, the federal government was the main source of funding for many anti-poverty organizations and advocates. At the same time that the Reagan administration cut funding for these groups, foundations—their other major benefactors—were shifting their support from organizations engaged in political advocacy to those providing direct services. This period also saw the birth of a host of new think tanks, foundations, and other organizations whose orientation was more consistent with the Reagan administration's conservative priorities.[101]

Organized labor also had weakened, although AFSCME again expressed concern that work requirements would replace unionized government employees with welfare recipients, and that an influx of new low-wage workers would further weaken labor power. The NWRO had disbanded by the mid-1970s, and despite the survival of a smattering of state and local welfare rights organizations, the welfare poor were politically disorganized and weak. The organizations that now existed, such as the Children's Defense Fund and the Center on Budget and Policy Priorities, were largely the Washington-based research or "public interest" advocacy groups that had grown up since the 1960s, not the mass-based organizations envisaged by the CAP and the poor people's movement.[102]

After a two-year effort in Congress, and with only tepid support from the Reagan administration, the bipartisan FSA became law in October 1988. It was in effect until 1996. The FSA established the Job Opportunity and Basic Skills (JOBS) program to provide a federal match for nationally mandated state employment programs. Modest but gradually increasing work participation rates reached 20 percent by 1995. The FSA instituted automatic withholding of child support payments from noncustodial parents' paychecks and set mandated standards for states to establish paternity. States also were required to guarantee transitional child care and Medicaid for twelve months to parents who became ineligible for AFDC because of their income, and the FSA provided matching funding to states for child care. Finally, the FSA required the 26 states without AFDC-UP programs to institute them by October 1991.[103]

The results of the FSA fell far short of expectations; it succumbed to "money" and "overselling" traps.[104] The total amount of funding provided by the Act was modest—only $3 billion over five years for education, training, and jobs—particularly given its ambitious goals and the fact that administering work programs is markedly more complex than simply providing cash grants. The recession of the early 1990s compounded this problem. AFDC caseloads increased 30 percent between 1988 and 1994, at least in part because of the economy, and Medicaid costs soared, putting additional strain on state budgets.[105] The FSA required that states put up about 40 percent of the funds necessary for JOBS and other programs, but many simply didn't do this, drawing down only half of the federal money available for JOBS in 1991. Spending in 1991 for AFDC-UP in states that were mandated to set it up was only one-third the level predicted.[106] States had difficulty establishing new JOBS programs or revising their old employment systems to meet the new federal requirements. They also struggled to provide child care. By 1992, only 16 percent of nonexempt recipients participated in the JOBS program. This level of participation was a modest success, but it was far from changing the culture of welfare.[107]

Although the FSA did not meet the administration's goal of devolving policymaking to the states, other facets of Reagan's decentralization efforts were more successful. The administration's approach involved, to a great extent, getting government at all levels out of certain functions. It ended Nixon's General Revenue Sharing and proposed block grants, which were to be political "halfway houses" between federal categorical grants and complete termination of certain national programs. This strategy was very different from Nixon's sorting out approach.[108] As Reagan declared in his first inaugural address, "Government is not the solution to our problem. Government is the problem."[109] The Reagan administration was even willing to challenge state and local governments when they were regarded as too activist.[110] As with Reagan's ideological heirs in the mid-1990s, the guiding principle for Reagan's federalism was to push policies to the governmental level that was most likely to generate politically congenial outcomes—or abolish them altogether.

Ironically, some of the Reagan-era cuts in federal funding to states and localities actually may have encouraged states to take over certain functions and improved their ability to do so, rather than forcing these functions to wither away. After three decades of federal court decisions, legislation, and programs that compelled, cajoled, and enabled states to improve their political systems and capacities, some chose to take new action on their own when they faced federal cuts.[111] Richard Nathan calls this development "the paradox of devolution" under Reagan; it prepared some states to begin to develop innovative approaches to welfare reform, even before the 1996 bill.[112]

PERSONAL RESPONSIBILITY AND WORK OPPORTUNITY RECONCILIATION ACT OF 1996

Most Americans in the early 1990s, politicians included, seemed to have forgotten that Congress had passed the FSA. Those that were aware quickly judged it a failure because of the sharp rise in caseloads and the continuing increase in the out-of-wedlock birth rate: By 1993, almost 50 percent of welfare parents had never been married—about twice the rate for nonrecipients.[113] Some people also felt that the work requirements were too low and failed to satisfy the growing demand for work (see Table 2-1 for data on long-term AFDC use, costs, and related indicators).

These trends contributed to a general sense among middle-class voters and politicians in the early 1990s that the "welfare problem" was only getting worse. AFDC had become broadly unpopular, even among many liberals and recipients themselves. Rising costs added to the mounting pressure for reform as the federal deficit came to frame the domestic policy debate, and incremental change was politically inadequate to the demands of the early 1990s.[114] In 1992, presidential candidate Clinton effectively endorsed the view that nothing could be worse than the sixty-year-old AFDC system by adding to his campaign promises the pledge to "end welfare as we know it." Many accounts of the politics of PRWORA have been written, so I do not cover this well-trodden ground in great detail.[115] Several points deserve emphasis, however, particularly in preparation for an analysis of the relative influence of the governmental and nongovernmental actors that shaped the final welfare reform law in Washington.

HOW THE BILLS BECAME P.L. 104-193

103rd Congress (1993–1995)

Despite candidate Clinton's pledge to overhaul the welfare system, the social policy agenda of the 103rd Congress was dominated by the president's health care initiative. Clinton's election in 1992 with a plurality of 43 percent brought a Democrat into the White House for the first time in twelve years and briefly gave the Democratic party unified government. That unity fragmented quickly, however, and many aspects of the president's social policy proposals faced opposition from both sides of the aisle. After a bruising battle marked by intense opposition from a wide range of health care industry and business groups, the Democratic Senate majority leader pulled the plug on the president's crippled social policy initiative in October 1994, leaving a major political stain on Clinton's already shaky presidency. In many ways, the health plan represented the last gasp of national government activism in social policy, at least for the 1990s.[116]

Clinton sent no legislative proposal for welfare reform to Congress during 1993. HHS did, however, begin liberally granting Section 1115 waivers to states to experiment with new approaches to AFDC. Some states embarked on ambitious and innovative approaches, while others used their waivers to begin to limit eligibility. Time limits on benefits were not yet on most states' agendas, however. The value of states' monthly AFDC benefits had dropped in real terms by 28 percent, from an average of $523 per family in 1980 to $379 in 1994 (see Table 2-1).

The administration also established a welfare reform task force in 1993, which articulated the goal of shifting welfare from what many members

Table 2-1
Summary Data for Welfare and Related Indicators, Selected Years

Measure	1936	1940	1950	1960	1970	1980	1990	1994	1996
Benefit expenditures (millions of 1996 $)[a]	260	1,373	3,419	5,407	16,803	22,445	22,414	24,082	20,411
Administrative costs (millions of 1996 $)[b]	4.5	106	263	577	3,627	2,877	3,217	3,487	3,266
Average monthly welfare rolls (thousands), recipients[c]	546	1,222	2,233	3,073	7,429	10,497	11,460	14,226	12,649
Average monthly welfare rolls (thousands), children	404	895	1,661	2,370	5,494	7,220	7,755	9,590	8,673
Average recipient family size[d]	3.4	3.3	3.4	3.8	3.9	2.9	2.8	2.8	2.8
Average monthly benefit (1996 $)	322	312	440	559	734	523	470	397	374
AFDC enrollment as percentage of total U.S. population	0.4	0.9	1.5	1.7	3.7	4.6	4.6	5.5	4.8
General U.S. poverty rate (%)	N/A	N/A	N/A	22.2	12.6	13.0	13.5	14.5	13.7
Child poverty rate (%)	N/A	N/A	N/A	26.9	15.1	18.3	20.6	21.8	20.5

Sources: 1998 Green Book, Table 7-2 (original data from Congressional Research Service); poverty data from *1998 Green Book*, Table H-4 (original data from U.S. Census Bureau). Constant dollars calculated by using Consumer Price Index for all Urban Consumers (CPI-U).

[a]Benefit expenditures for 1936–1960 are from U.S. Department of Health and Education (HEW), Expenditures for Public Assistance payments and for Administrative Costs, by Program and Source of funds, Fiscal Years 1936–1970 NCSS Report F-5; 1936 data are for five months only. Later data are from Table 7-3 prepared by U.S. Department of Health and Human Services (HHS) but exclude foster care payments made in 1980. CPI-U was used to adjust current dollars for inflation.

[b]For years before 1980, administrative costs include some expenditures for service.

[c]Enrollment data for 1936–1960 are December numbers for 1970 Social Security Annual Statistical Supplement (Table 136). For later years, data are fiscal year monthly averages from Table 7-5 prepared by HHS but exclude foster care recipients in 1980.

[d]Calculated by dividing total recipients by number of families. This figure understates actual family size for 1936–1950 because the mother or other caregiver was not included as a recipient until after FY 1950.

regarded as a permanent way of life to temporary assistance that would be available only in the event of emergency. Like others before, the task force's plan emphasized moving welfare mothers into work in the labor market. It also included significant government assistance with child care, job training, transportation, and other related expenses, even though this approach clearly would cost more in the short run than simply issuing welfare checks. Clinton had proposed during the campaign to limit welfare recipients to two years of cash assistance, after which they would be required to work in private or public jobs. This approach was received cautiously by many liberal politicians and advocacy and research organizations, who were skeptical about the availability of low-skilled jobs paying a living wage and opposed limiting the entitlement to assistance. They were joined by groups representing state and city policymakers, such as the National Governors' Association (NGA), the National Conference of State Legislatures (NCSL), and the National League of Cities—all then dominated by Democrats—who feared federal mandates they were not equipped to meet.[117]

The broad framework was set early for the dramatic changes in welfare to come, with Democratic and early conservative plans shifting the debate rightward. House Republicans introduced a radical bill in early November 1993 to limit recipients to a maximum of two years of cash assistance throughout their lifetimes. It also would have required states to stop providing supplemental benefits to women who had additional children while on AFDC (the "family cap"); cut off women who didn't identify their children's fathers; end federal benefits for parents under the age of eighteen; block grant food programs, including food stamps and child nutrition; and limit a range of anti-poverty programs, including the earned income tax credit (EITC).[118] With Democrats in control of Congress there was little likelihood the bill would pass; nonetheless, it provided a reference point for Clinton and his welfare advisors. In light of liberal opposition to their stringent work requirements, they anticipated that they would need Republican support for passage of their own plan. Conservative Republicans introduced another exceptionally tough bill in 1994 that would deny all AFDC and food stamp benefits to women under the age of twenty-one who had children out of wedlock—and would deny benefits to their children as well.[119]

The administration's welfare proposal, the Work and Responsibility Act, was finally introduced in Congress in the summer of 1994, partly in response to Democratic pressure to offer a bill before the 1994 mid-term elections. No subcommittee acted on the legislation before November, however. Clinton's proposal certainly was more restrictive than AFDC, but markedly less so than the Republican proposals or the final 1996 welfare law.[120] Despite its new requirements, the president's plan preserved the individual entitlement to assistance and kept primary responsibility with the federal government, without block grants to the states. The work support provisions were projected to cost $9.3 billion in new funds over five years, so the plan was to be phased in, initially covering only recipients born after 1971.[121] Policymakers from all sides criticized the plan, but welfare received little concerted attention until after the 1994 mid-term election and the Republican takeover of Congress.

104th Congress (1995–1997)

The concerns and resentments of politicians and other Americans about welfare were fairly clear going into the 1994 mid-term election. The common—if not very accurate—perception that the government had waged an expensive war on poverty and lost held firm.[122] The entitlement status of welfare was regarded as sapping poor people of their ability to help themselves and giving poor women economic incentives to produce more children—or at least lessening the disincentives.[123] The budget deficit still was driving many political decisions, and welfare was perceived (incorrectly) as very costly. Clinton's "end welfare" promise, followed by the failure of health care reform and his administration's inaction on welfare, contributed to intense political pressure on the weakened president to sign a major overhaul bill before the 1996 election.

In November 1994, Republicans achieved a net gain of fifty-two seats in the House, giving them a majority of 230 seats. Thirty-five Democratic incumbents lost re-election; not a single Republican incumbent was defeated. In the Senate, Republicans gained eight seats. It was the first time in more than four decades that the Republicans controlled both houses of Congress, and their gains in the South were especially strong. At the same time they gained control of Congress, Republicans took control of thirty-one of the nation's fifty governorships as well, including those of most of the nation's largest states, and they controlled a plurality of state legislatures.[124] Democrats were stunned by the magnitude of their defeat, and even the Republican party seemed surprised by the sweep of its victory. The president was particularly shaken, and he quickly backed away from the relative activism of his first two years in office.[125]

The new Republican majority in the House wasted no time in pushing the welfare reform proposal contained in the Contract with America, the ten-point platform developed in the fall of 1994 that outlined sweeping policy changes. The Contract itself did not mention block grants, however. Welfare overhaul rated as a top priority for the Republican "revolutionaries," in part because it was the only provision that directly addressed the demands of social conservative and "family values" groups, such as the Christian Coalition and Family Research Council, that made up an essential and vocal part of their constituency.[126]

The Republican plan was introduced in early January 1995 as HR 4. It built on the two major Republican welfare proposals from the 103rd Congress and the Contract with America: ending the entitlement and consolidating AFDC and other poverty programs into state block grants, accompanied by lifetime limits on cash assistance of five years and a state option of cutting off recipients after two years. It also included work requirements and behavioral mandates. Unlike the Clinton proposal, HR 4 would affect all recipients almost immediately. It also aimed to get recipients into jobs without spending any additional money. In fact, it proposed to cut from the budget $64 billion over seven years.[127] HR 4 would cap the costs of welfare and other programs for poor people, though the bulk of the estimated savings came from cuts in benefits for legal immigrants and other programs not directly tied to AFDC. It granted states broad authority and in many ways represented the rediscovery of Grant McConnell's "cult of localism," reapportioning political power downward, accompanied by praise for the virtues of smaller jurisdictions.

The momentum of the Republicans' electoral victory and their goal of passing the Contract with America within the first 100 days of the 104th Congress propelled HR 4 through the House. The Ways and Means Committee began holding public hearings immediately, but much of the real bargaining took place behind closed doors—in particular, between key Republican members of Congress and an "inner circle" of Republican governors, primarily John Engler of Michigan and Tommy Thompson of Wisconsin. Engler and Thompson were radically transforming their own states' welfare systems and were believed to harbor national political ambitions. The Republican Governors' Association (RGA) also played a central role, with the bipartisan—and previously Democratic-dominated—NGA stymied by internal dissension and disagreement about funding formulas for apportioning block grant money to the states.[128] The speed of House action, coupled with the informal negotiations among influential Republicans, initially left the still-stunned Democrats (especially the liberal wing in Congress and many people in the advocacy community) essentially out of the debate.

The Republican governors and their partisan allies in Congress struck a deal in a marriage of interest and ideology. The governors wanted the states, especially their offices, to assume a higher profile in policymaking. They were willing to accept what was then expected to be less federal money for public assistance in exchange for greater autonomy; many objected to conservative behavioral mandates as federal micromanagement from the right. Some expressed concern about how they would cope with a regional or national recession under a block-grant system, but they were under real pressure from congressional Republicans to do everything possible to support the party's rise to power.

Many Democratic governors—though much less involved in the negotiations—also supported the movement toward devolution because most governors across party lines were eager to be free from federal mandates and seemed to believe that they could do a better job with welfare than the federal government. Moreover, with term limits in the majority of states, the governors could claim credit for solving the welfare problem but would be out of office if the economy turned downward and finding jobs for ex-recipients became more difficult.

House Republicans also supported states' rights for ideological reasons, taking on the identity of latter-day Anti-Federalists. In addition, some saw in devolution the opportunity to cut spending on social programs that benefited low-income people, who generally were not their constituents. Like Nixon in the 1970s, they also recognized that social service providers and advocates were disproportionately liberal, making welfare reform an opportunity to take on the liberal public interest and anti-poverty groups that had grown up in Washington since the 1960s. Simultaneously, efforts such as the Istook Amendment—which would have restricted the political activities of nonprofit organizations that received federal funds—though ultimately unsuccessful, added to the uncertainty of the environment in which these groups were operating. This dynamic was reinforced by the downward force on federal spending from the 1990 Budget Enforcement Act. Republican negotiators discussed making changes to hundreds of federal antipoverty programs, amounting to about $125 billion in annual federal spending.[129]

David Ellwood provides a typology of the key proponents of welfare reform that captures the range of motivations and goals. He groups them as "work-oriented reformers," who were willing to spend more on welfare to provide the jobs and support necessary to help recipients work and were not wedded to giving states the bulk of policymaking responsibility; "social policy critics," who regarded welfare as the root of the worst social problems and ideally would pull the government out of its provision almost entirely; "devolvers," significantly the governors, who argued that the states should hold decision-making power and would do better with it than the federal government if only they could receive block grants with minimal strings attached; and "budget cutters," who wanted to reduce the size of the budget, no matter what the means, and for whom AFDC, food stamps, SSI, and legal immigrants were the least protected targets.[130] Although this typology excludes symbolic and less tangible motivations for welfare reform, this framing of perspectives reconciles some of the competing interests and ideas involved in the debate of the 1990s.

In his January 1995 State of the Union speech, Clinton highlighted welfare reform and warned that he would not support any program that punished Americans simply for being poor, young, or even unmarried. Yet he did not state that he would veto HR 4, nor did he identify specific provisions to which he objected. This speech sent the first of many signals that Clinton might be open to a welfare bill that was notably more conservative than his own.

HR 4: The Congressional Debate

House Republicans took quick action on welfare reform, moving HR 4 through committee with remarkable speed. By early March 1995, Ways and Means had approved a plan to create a block grant to replace AFDC, end the individual entitlement to cash aid, and institute work requirements and a range of other new mandates.[131] The Economic and Educational Opportunities Committee (formerly Education and Labor) stirred up a political hornets' nest by proposing to block grant nutrition programs, abolishing the national school lunch and breakfast programs and the Supplemental Feeding Program for Women, Infants, and Children (WIC) and turning their functions over to the states. The bill also would have consolidated federal child care programs, abolished federal safety and health regulations, and frozen federal spending for five years. Committee Democrats, the administration, advocates, and the media charged Republicans with cutting popular, effective programs for children to fund tax cuts for wealthy Americans.[132] The Agriculture Committee, in turn, approved legislation aimed at curtailing the food stamp program.[133]

House Democrats offered two alternatives to HR 4, neither of which received serious consideration given the strength of the Republican majority.[134] The full House passed HR 4 in March, largely along party lines. It was projected to cut $66 billion over five years. Clinton assailed it as "weak on work and tough on children," stating that he would veto any final legislation that closely resembled HR 4.[135] Support in Congress also was tenuous: Only nine Democrats voted for it, and five Republicans voted against it. The politics of abortion further complicated the bill's passage.[136] Ultimately, however, House moderates' belief that the Senate would save them from themselves allowed them to approve the bill; one member noted, "I don't have to condition my support on perfection in the House vehicle. We all know the Senate will look at it closely."[137]

Many of the tensions that had simmered during the accelerated House debate came to the surface in the historically more cautious Senate. The Democratic minority had a greater range of tactics in the Senate, and the slower time frame also allowed opposition to mobilize. Moderate Republicans in the Senate also were beginning to put the brakes on their counterparts in the House, with influential members opposing the elimination of benefits for unwed teen mothers and their children and expressing reservations about cuts in benefits for legal immigrants. Presidential politics also came to the fore as 1996 approached, with likely Republican candidates—including Senate Majority Leader Robert Dole and Texas Senator Phil Gramm—jockeying for credit for tough reform.

The Senate Finance Committee took a more restrained approach to welfare and the use of block grants. In May 1995, the committee approved a welfare reform bill that followed the general thrust of HR 4 but created fewer block grants, left out some of the behavioral mandates, and eased the restrictions on legal immigrants.[138] The Committee on Labor and Human Resources provided a rare example of bipartisan agreement when it unanimously approved child care funding, maintaining federal health and safety standards.[139] The Agriculture Committee cut back spending on the food stamps program and gave states greater control. Dissension, particularly within the Republican party, delayed the full Senate's consideration of welfare overhaul over the summer, however. Continued disagreement over how to divide the money among the states and the lack of provisions aimed at out-of-wedlock-birth prevention were the thorniest issues.[140]

The Senate finally approved its version of HR 4 in September. It too ended the entitlement and created a welfare block grant, but it added $3 billion for child care and a "maintenance-of-effort" provision that required states to maintain at least 80 percent of their current welfare spending levels. Thirty-five of the Senate's 46 Democrats voted for it, in part because they sensed presidential irresolution, leaving them vulnerable to charges of being excessively liberal if they voted no.[141] The White House praised the Senate's efforts, and Clinton suggested that the legislation was sufficiently moderate to allow him to keep his campaign promise and sign a bill if it looked like this one, despite the fact that the Senate version was still markedly more conservative than Clinton's own proposal. This position further constrained the president's alternatives later on.[142]

The conference committee addressed welfare provisions on two tracks—with the separate bill (HR 4) and as part of the House and Senate budget reconciliation packages. Democrats wanted strictly a stand-alone bill, but including welfare reform in the reconciliation process clearly advantaged the Republican majority, allowing them to count the estimated savings toward their seven-year deficit reduction goal and limiting debate, among other benefits.[143]

Action on the budget bill came to a head first. Unlike HR 4, the reconciliation package also included a plan to overhaul Medicaid to the tune of $163 billion in savings over seven years.[144] Many Republicans believed that embedding reform in the budget legislation would force the president's hand, making it impossible for him to veto it.[145] Clinton did veto the bill, however, insisting that Republicans were trying to drive through major policy changes without deliberation.

The stand-alone HR 4 remained alive, but key committee chairs disagreed over block-granting school lunch and other child nutrition programs. Finally, in mid-December the GOP leadership brokered a compromise to allow a limited block grant. Clinton announced he would veto the conference HR 4 shortly before the House voted on December 21, saying it was too far from the Senate version and providing political cover for Democrats who wanted to vote no. The House approved the conference report and the full Senate adopted it the next day, along close-to-party lines. Although the president vetoed HR 4 in January 1996, the White House continued to suggest that if Congress sent the Senate version to the president, he might, in fact, sign it because it was within proximity of what he wanted.

Personal Responsibility and Work Opportunity Reconciliation Act of 1996

The history of welfare reform is littered with political failures, offering comparisons with the health care effort and hope to opponents of this version of welfare reform that it too might be doomed.[146] The impending 1996 elections raised the stakes, however, and helped to revive it. Haunted by the apparent relationship between the health care debacle and the Republicans' sweep of the 1994 mid-term elections, the president and many other Democrats—as well as congressional Republicans—clearly saw benefits to be reaped by passing reform. Poll data also indicated that Americans wanted some kind of welfare reform that stressed work for poor mothers, even if they were generally ill-informed about the details of the plan.[147] Governors and other state officials began to suspect that the strong economy and the downturn in caseloads might translate into more, not less, money than under AFDC.

The basic political and policy fault lines did not change significantly in 1996. The liberal wing of the Democratic party had recovered from the shock of the 1994 elections, however, and the voice of opposition grew louder. Some members of the Republican majority also were thought to have become more open to the perspectives of long-time participants in welfare policy, even those whose ideological orientation they disagreed with. The president, however, took the advice of key political advisors, following a policy of "triangulation" to position himself between the Republican majority and his more liberal Democratic colleagues in Congress. This strategy required him to move further to the right and, in turn, pushed the debate still further rightward as Republicans sought to maintain their leadership as tough on welfare.

In Congress, the impasse in federal budget negotiations dominated national politics from mid-November 1995 into 1996, adding to the pressure on the House and Senate to pass major legislation before the 1996 election. The perception that members of Congress were out of touch with the average voter had contributed to the expulsion of congressional Democrats in 1994, and it now appeared that policy overreaching might fell Republicans, as well.[148] Once again, congressional Republicans made welfare part of the budget reconciliation agreement that set the broad parameters for spending and revenue, this time for the fiscal year beginning October 1, 1996.

The NGA also helped to resuscitate welfare reform with an arduously brokered bipartisan but controversial proposal in early February 1996, which also proposed to block grant Medicaid. This proposal quickly became one of the most contentious issues, and Clinton again threatened a veto, calling Medicaid block grants a "poison pill."[149] Presidential candidate Dole intensified his attacks on Clinton, challenging him to resume negotiations over welfare reform, a balanced budget, and tax cuts. The administration insisted that it was, in fact, encouraging welfare reform in the form of state waivers: During

1995 and 1996, HHS had been granting Section 1115 waivers at an unprecedented rate. By early May 1996, thirty-seven states were instituting waiver programs and these programs, in fact, varied widely.

HR 3734: The Congressional Debate

The House Republican leadership's 1996 proposal was similar in most major respects to HR 4, although it also included Medicaid block grants.[150] The Ways and Means Committee approved its bill in mid-June. The Economic and Educational Opportunities Committee approved its welfare-related provisions the same day, including work participation rates of 50 percent by the year 2002—markedly higher than the 20 percent of HR 4. This time, the committee left the federal school lunch program alone.[151] The Agriculture Committee approved provisions to revise and cut the food stamps program.

The Senate worked on its version of the House bill during the last half of June. The Finance Committee voted along strict party lines to overhaul AFDC and Medicaid, and Chairman Roth articulated a common perspective when he stated, "It's time to end the incentives for staying in poverty." The Senate Agriculture Committee, like its House counterpart, voted to require work of adult food stamp recipients and cut individual benefits. The new Senate Majority Leader, Trent Lott of Mississippi, and House Speaker Newt Gingrich confirmed their intention in late June to send Clinton a welfare bill that also overhauled Medicaid. Ultimately, however, the GOP leadership dropped the Medicaid block grant and agreed to a welfare-only bill, succumbing to pressure from moderates and members up for reelection who did not want to lose the opportunity to claim credit for fixing "the welfare mess."[152]

In July, the House passed HR 3734 by a vote of 256 to 170, estimating that it would cut $61 billion over six years, most of it from food stamps, SSI, and immigrant social services.[153] The full Senate passed its version of HR 3734 by a vote of 74 to 24. Twenty-three Democrats voted against the bill, and 23 voted in favor. One Republican—Lauch Faircloth of North Carolina—opposed it because it was not tough enough. Senate Minority Leader Tom Daschle voted against the Republican bill, as did other influential Democrats, including John Glenn, Christopher Dodd, Daniel Patrick Moynihan, Ted Kennedy, and Paul Wellstone. A mix of liberals, centrists, and southern Democrats voted for it, including John Kerry of Massachusetts (who was in a close reelection battle against popular governor Republican William Weld) as well as John Breaux, Russell Feingold, Tom Harkin, and Joseph Lieberman. Many Democrats were eager to pass reform as the November election drew near. Wellstone was the only Senate Democrat seeking reelection who voted against the bill.[154]

Clinton again suggested that he might sign a variation of the Senate bill and moved for amendments to soften the House version, including a requirement that states continue to provide Medicaid to poor people who would have been eligible for it under AFDC.[155] These proposals alleviated some concerns of Republican moderates and Democratic centrists.[156] Republican leaders pushed to clear the bill before members left for the August recess and campaigning in their districts, and House-Senate conferees signed their agreement on July 30, 1996. The final bill moderated some of the most stringent House provisions but retained many restrictions, including broad cuts in benefits for legal immigrants.[157] Despite assertions that HR 3734 was largely similar to the legislation Clinton had twice vetoed, the administration positioned itself to finally sign welfare overhaul. "You have to say that it's moved considerably further towards the goal of the kind of welfare reform that the president has advocated," the president's spokesman said. "We are closer to that goal now than we ever have been."[158]

Clinton announced that he would sign HR 3734 right before the House's final vote on July 31, 1996, and the Senate's vote the next day—making it clear to congressional Democrats that if they opposed the bill, they would do so without political cover from the White House. Clinton's announcement also provided justification for members who were tempted to vote yes. In announcing that he would sign the bill, Clinton stated, "I will sign this bill, first and foremost, because the current system is broken; second, because Congress has made many of the changes I sought; and third, because even though serious problems remain in the nonwelfare-reform provisions of the bill, this is the best chance we will have for a long, long time to complete the work of ending welfare as we know it, by moving people from welfare to work, demanding responsibility, and doing better by children."[159]

The House approved HR 3734 by a vote of 328 to 101 just hours after Clinton's statement, with half of the Democrats voting for it. All but two Republicans endorsed the bill; these dissenters represented heavily Hispanic districts in Florida that would be sharply affected by the legal immigrant cuts.[160] The Senate voted on the bill the next day, with a final tally of 78 in favor and 21 opposed. Twenty-five Democrats voted for the bill and 21 against. All 53 Republicans sided with their party leadership and supported the legislation.[161]

Speaker Gingrich reiterated the position that ending AFDC was for the sake of poor children: "I think it's particularly important for children who are currently trapped in poverty. I believe this bill will dramatically help young Americans to have a chance to rise and to do better." Florida Republican Clay Shaw, chair of the Human Resources Subcommittee of the House Ways and Means Committee and a key architect of the bill, went even further: "This is an incredible day in the history of this country . . . July 31st has got to go down as Independence Day for those who have been trapped in a system that has . . . corrupted their souls and stolen their futures."[162]

Liberal Democrats were equally passionate in their disappointment. Charles Rangel, the New York Democrat who represented Harlem, branded the bill a "cruel monstrosity . . . the most radical and mean-spirited attack against the poor that I have witnessed during my service in government."[163] Other Democrats had jumped on the Clinton bandwagon, however—either out of fear of being marked as too liberal or because they truly believed that it was better than the status quo or trying yet again for a more amenable bill. One Democratic Congressman, Gary L. Ackerman of Queens, New York, spoke with striking candor about the political benefits of welfare reform, calling it "a bad bill but a good strategy. . . . Sometimes in order to make progress and move ahead," he said, "you have to stand up and do the wrong thing. If we take back the House, we can fix this bill and take out some of the Draconian parts."[164]

Enactment of P.L. 104-93

The Clinton administration had been deeply divided on whether the president should sign the bill. Pragmatic political advisors, including Vice President Gore and influential policy advisors such as Bruce Reed, gained over more liberal aides such as Chief of Staff Leon Panetta and HHS Secretary Donna Shalala, who opposed it.[165] Ultimately, however, ex-governor Clinton was said to be genuinely enthusiastic about devolution and welfare reform and appears to have signed the bill quite willingly. The president signed the Personal Responsibility and Work Opportunity Reconciliation Act (Public Law 104-93) into law on August 22, 1996.

PRWORA included a range of radical changes in U.S. welfare policy, including the following:

- Abolition of AFDC, with its federal-state match funding structure and the individual entitlement to assistance
- Creation of fixed-sum TANF block grants that gave states a total of about $16.5 billion annually and broad policy discretion and would have to be reauthorized by Congress in 2002
- A two-year time limit on cash aid without work and a five-year lifetime limit on all federal cash aid with exemption for up to 20 percent of the caseload
- Work requirements reaching 50 percent for single parents and 90 percent for two-parent families by 2002, with penalties on states that fail to meet participation levels
- A state option to impose the family cap or to refuse benefits to mothers under the age of 18
- $3 billion in additional funding for the child care block grant, although the guarantee of child care for working parents under JOBS was eliminated

- A maintenance-of-effort provision requiring states to continue spending 75–80 percent of their own current welfare funding[166]
- New requirements that states set up systems for establishing paternity, tracking absent parents, and enforcing child support orders
- The option for states to shift up to 30 percent of their TANF grants to the social services or child care block grants, accompanied by a 15 percent cut in the social services grant
- New restrictions on the availability of SSI disability payments
- Time limits and work requirements for many food stamp recipients who are not parents
- Abolition of cash assistance, SSI, Medicaid, and food stamp assistance to most legal immigrants, including those currently in the country and those arriving in the future.

Indian tribes were allowed to submit plans to administer their own TANF programs, independent of the states. The bill also allowed states with federal waivers—forty-three of them by mid-summer—to continue operating under those waivers, shifting to the requirements of the new legislation only after their waiver terms expired. Although this provision did not allow states to avoid overhaul wholesale, it slowed the speed with which they would be required to adopt the new federal requirements. The final bill was projected to cut $54 billion over six years—largely from the food stamp, SSI, and immigrant reductions.[167]

Radical though the legislation was, it did not include cuts to the EITC or overhaul and block granting of food stamps, child nutrition, child welfare, and foster care programs. Nor did it include block granting and overhaul of Medicaid. All of these proposals had been included in early versions of reform.

Implementation began three months later, on October 1, 1996, with the end of AFDC. States had until July 1, 1997, to decide whether to continue with their waivers or to convert to TANF and to file plans for their new programs with HHS. Individual recipients' clock on the five-year limit to federal aid started the date states submitted their plans. Because the TANF block grant levels were based on peak caseloads, however, states had an incentive to opt into the program as soon as possible to reap the TANF windfall that was resulting from the difference between those numbers and caseloads that had been declining for a couple of years.[168] The states were in control, and they had little time to waste.

Federal welfare reform was not entirely over, however. As part of the 1997 federal budget agreement—and in response to sharp criticism—Congress and the president agreed to reinstate about $11 billion to cover legal immigrants who were already in the United States at the time the new bill was signed. In addition, the budget included $3 billion in funding for "Welfare to Work" (WtW) grants, which states could use for jobs programs for poor people, including welfare recipients. Within several years, policymakers, advocates, researchers, and others began to look toward the required reauthorization of PRWORA in 2002.

CONCLUSION

Welfare policy in the United States can be broken down into three periods that broadly mirror trends in American federalism. The first period could be called the Age of State and Local Autonomy, dating from before the founding until the New Deal. State and local programs varied widely; many states and localities had no welfare programs or provided very limited aid. The second period could be called the Era of Encroaching Nationalism; it stretched roughly from 1935, with the Social Security Act, to the Great Society of the 1960s and early 1970s. The 1935 Act still left states enormous discretion to set their own policies, and the states' eligibility standards generally reflected the approaches they took during the period of state autonomy. Over time, however, federal institutions encouraged states to make their welfare benefits and standards more liberal, with some success. Briefly, through the community action programs of the 1960s, policymakers even focused on incorporating the perspectives of poor people directly into the political process. Richard Nixon's Family Assistance Plan to provide a uniform, national, guaranteed income to poor families fit generally into the Great Society model, although by then concern for the voice of urban poor people had given way to fears of violence and crime.

The third period—which we are in now—could be called the Era of Rediscovered Federalism. Ronald Reagan's victory in 1980 marked its real beginning. However, Democratic president Bill Clinton's election in 1992, followed by the 1994 election of a conservative Republican Congress, dramatically accelerated the trend toward decentralization. After six decades of "extending the sphere" in welfare politics, policymakers in the 1990s once again began rediscovering the appeal of localism, at least in this policy arena. The U.S. Supreme Court has reinforced this political shift with its findings in a range of cases from the past decade.[169]

A complex mix of factors led to passage of PRWORA in 1996. As John Kingdon notes in *Agendas, Alternatives, and Public Policies*, the joining of problem, policy, and political "streams" can open windows of opportunity that enable unusually radical policy changes, and this clearly was the case with welfare reform.[170] Finding a way to aid poor people without encouraging "dependency" has long been considered problematic. The structure of AFDC had been identified as a problem for several decades, especially as cultural attitudes shifted toward the expectation that most women—even those with children—would work in the labor market. Rising out-of-wedlock birth rates, crime, and the increase in single-parent households also were linked to the structure of the welfare system and fed into a sense of social decay made possible by government largesse. The economic downturn in the late 1980s contributed to a historic rise in caseloads, creating another "problem" for welfare reform to solve. Media portrayals of a growing underclass, however misrepresentative, also fueled the perception of a major dependency problem, and welfare recipients were regarded as dysfunctional rather than politically underrepresented.

The Family Support Act of 1988 produced policy feedbacks when many actors concluded that little had changed and, in fact, much had gotten worse. This conclusion spurred policy entrepreneurs across the political spectrum and inside and outside of government to push for change. Especially influential were members of the newly powerful conservative think tanks and "traditional values" organizations, such as the Heritage Foundation and the Family Research Council. The 1992 presidential election softened the ground for major reform with Clinton's campaign pledge to end welfare, and the failure of his health care initiative in 1994 raised the political stakes for successful completion of this policy initiative. The mid-term election of 1994 undoubtedly was the most influential development within the political stream, however, as the Republican party took over both houses of Congress and a majority of the statehouses. By the 1994 election, a national mood of intensified cynicism about the usefulness of the central government and the ability of social science to solve social problems had taken hold.[171] Although the general public was largely unaware of the details of competing welfare proposals, Americans expressed strong enthusiasm for the *idea* of welfare reform, with all its symbolic potency, providing further justification for political action. Political rhetoric reflected and contributed to a common belief that welfare recipients were bad mothers, predominantly black, who lived deviant lives. Few people in the policymaking process suggested that recipients' views were inadequately represented in the formulation of welfare reform.

Despite broad support for reform, welfare was an extraordinarily partisan issue in Washington during the mid-1990s, marked by a high degree of mistrust. The Republicans' Contract With America—of which welfare overhaul was a crucial provision—provided a unifying theme that enabled party members on all levels to move swiftly, as well as a benchmark of the success of the Republican "revolution." Moreover, as political scientist Kent Weaver points out, members of Congress in both parties, as well as the president, faced strong "micro-incentives" to claim credit for welfare reform or at least avoid blame for blocking it. The results of the 1994 mid-term election seemed to haunt the Democratic party over the succeeding two years, particularly the president, and exacerbated anxiety about the impending 1996 election. Clinton had campaigned in 1992 as a New Democrat, and his post-1994 strategy of triangulation indicated that he was willing to disaffect traditional Democratic constituencies to outmaneuver Republicans by coopting their issues. His approach to welfare reform was in keeping with this strategy. By sending consistently mixed signals about how far he was willing to take welfare reform, however, Clinton essentially weakened his bargaining position and gave his administration little room to maneuver for specific provisions of the bill as the 1996 elections approached. As one commentator observed, "In these negotiations, and in talks over the congressional bills, Mr. Clinton . . . drew lines in the sand against some Republican proposals, then erased them."[172]

The ballooning budget deficit of the 1980s and 1990s and changes in the law and practices of the budgeting process—in particular, the 1990 Budget Enforcement Act and the use of large budget reconciliation bills—also put general downward pressure on spending and gave the majority in Congress additional tactics to enforce their program. This was especially the case for spending on politically weak constituencies. Welfare was widely, if inaccurately, regarded as an expensive entitlement, and cutting its costs was considered an essential component of a balanced budget.

Finally, devolution also was ideologically consistent with the conservative agenda of smaller, decentralized government and the preference for localism. It helped pare back the generally liberal federal bureaucracy; the wide range of public interest and anti-poverty organizations that focused on the concerns of disadvantaged groups could no longer count on the "extended sphere" of Washington to exert influence. Because the Republican party had swept the 1994 governors' races, the new welfare policies formulated in smaller political arenas could be expected to significantly parallel the conservative policy developments on the national level. The governors, too, could claim credit for facilitating welfare reform, and most would be out of office when the vibrant economy slowed and the difficulties of moving large numbers of unskilled workers permanently into jobs showed themselves—thus deferring potential political blame. To be sure, many governors were genuinely enthusiastic about designing innovative reform plans that were distinctive to their states and passionately disliked the HHS waiver process. However, expectations that devolved welfare policymaking would be responsive to a narrower range of voices and less influenced by the kinds of energetic advocacy groups that were so prevalent in Washington also helped spur national Republicans' enthusiasm for devolution.

Of course, the federal welfare bill was not shaped only by political actors within the national government. A wide range and large number of "outside" organizations and individuals participated actively in the policymaking process in Washington, as Madison might have predicted. Many—across the political spectrum—had an essential effect on the final outcomes of the welfare debate. The following chapter looks in greater detail at these outside actors and their critical involvement in formulating the 1996 welfare law.

NOTES

1. Morton Grodzins, *The American System: A New View of Government in the United States*, edited by Daniel J. Elazar (Chicago: Rand McNally, 1966).

2. James T. Patterson, *America's Struggle Against Poverty, 1900–1994* (Cambridge, Mass.: Harvard University Press, 1994), 20–21.

3. Walter I. Trattner, *From Poor Law to Welfare State: The History of Social Welfare in America*, 5th ed. (New York: Free Press, 1994), 90–91.

4. Trattner, *From Poor Law to Welfare State*, 59–63.

5. Ibid., 84–86; George Brown Tindall and David E. Shi, *America: A Narrative History*, 3d ed. (New York: W. W. Norton & Co., 1984), 697–98.

6. Theda Skocpol, *Protecting Soldiers and Mothers*. (Cambridge, Mass.: The Belknap Press of Harvard University Press, 1992), 1.

7. Joel F. Handler, *The Poverty of Welfare Reform* (New Haven, Conn.: Yale University Press, 1995), 21.

8. See Skocpol, *Protecting Soldiers and Mothers*, among others.

9. Skocpol, *Protecting Soldiers and Mothers*, 4; also see 11–30 for a succinct summary of the most prevalent theories explaining the United States' late and partial entry into social welfare provision, and Margaret Weir, Ann Shola Orloff, and Theda Skocpol, "Introduction: Understanding American Social Politics," in *The Politics of Social Policy in the United States* (Princeton, N.J.: Princeton University Press, 1988).

10. Trattner, *From Poor Law to Welfare State*, chapter 11.

11. Patterson, *America's Struggle Against Poverty*, 29, notes that as late as the 1920s, most state (as opposed to local) aid still went to indoor relief; a 1923 survey reported 2,046 almshouses holding 85,899 inmates nationwide.

12. Skocpol, *Protecting Soldiers and Mothers*, ix. This apparent anomaly is one of the focuses of her book.

13. Ibid., 425.

14. Patterson, *America's Struggle Against Poverty*, 27. Almost all of the eight states were southern: Kentucky, Mississippi, North Carolina, New Mexico, Alabama, Georgia, and South Carolina. The latter two did not implement programs until after the Social Security Act of 1935. See Skocpol, *Protecting Soldiers and Mothers*, 457.

15. Skocpol, *Protecting Soldiers and Mothers*, 471.

16. Patterson, *America's Struggle Against Poverty*, 29.

17. Ibid., 29.

18. Ibid., 27–29.

19. The reality, however, was that even from the beginning of the republic, the nation's structure could never have been described as an entirely neat "layer cake"; from early on, the national government played a role in certain "local" functions of national importance, such as education. Morton Grodzins and Daniel Elazar, "Centralization and Decentralization in the American Federal System," in *A Nation of States: Essays on the American Federal System*, 2d ed., ed. Robert A. Goldwin (Chicago: Rand McNally College Publishing Company, 1974), 3. For general discussions of American federalism, see David B. Walker, *The Rebirth of Federalism* (New York: Chatham

House, 2000); Alice M. Rivlin, *Reviving the American Dream: The Economy, the States and the Federal Government* (Washington, D.C.: Brookings Institution, 1992), 83; Gerald Gunther, *Constitutional Law*, 12th ed. (Westbury, N.Y.: Foundation Press, 1991), 66–67; Richard P. Nathan, "Federalism—The Great 'Composition,'" in *The New American Political System*, 2d ed., ed. Anthony King (Washington, D.C.: American Enterprise Institute, 1990).

20. David B. Robertson and Dennis R. Judd, *The Development of American Public Policy: The Structure of Policy Restraint* (Glenview, Ill.: Scott Foresman, 1989), 170–72.

21. See Gunther, *Constitutional Law*, chapters 2 and 3.

22. Weir, Orloff, and Skocpol, "Understanding American Social Politics," 16. See also Frances Fox Piven and Richard A. Cloward, *Regulating the Poor: The Functions of Public Welfare* (New York: Vintage Books, 1971), especially chapters 2 and 3, for a discussion of the pressures caused by mass unrest that helped spur the New Deal.

23. Hugh Heclo, "The Political Foundations of Antipoverty Policy," in *Fighting Poverty: What Works and What Doesn't*, ed. Sheldon H. Danziger and Daniel H. Weinberg (Cambridge, Mass.: Harvard University Press, 1986), 314–16; Skocpol, *Protecting Soldiers and Mothers*.

24. Handler, *The Poverty of Welfare Reform*, 27.

25. Jill Quadagno, *The Color of Welfare: How Racism Undermined the War on Poverty* (New York: Oxford University Press, 1994), 119.

26. Heclo, "The Political Foundations of Antipoverty Policy," 317. See also Piven and Cloward, *Regulating the Poor*, for their argument that New Deal programs were used—largely successfully—to circumvent large-scale social and economic protest.

27. Quadagno, *The Color of Welfare*, 119.

28. Patterson, *America's Struggle Against Poverty*, 67; Trattner, *From Poor Law to Welfare State*, 313.

29. Patterson, *America's Struggle Against Poverty*, 86.

30. Ibid., 86–87.

31. Ibid., 87–88.

32. In 1937, Roosevelt initiated "reform" measures to enlarge the size of the Supreme Court, thereby allowing him to place his own appointees in the new seats and tilt the balance toward support for his policy agenda. While Congress was debating the proposal, the Court backed off its opposition to the president's programs and began to hand down decisions that sustained federal regulatory laws. A key justice also retired, marking a shift in the Court's approach toward federal involvement in state affairs.

33. 347 U.S. 483 (1954).

34. 369 U.S. 186 (1962).

35. 377 U.S. 533 (1964).

36. Gunther, *Constitutional Law*, 1658–59; Rivlin, *Reviving the American Dream*, 105.

37. Gunther, *Constitutional Law*, 145. Attempts to pass federal legislation to end the de facto segregation of the North, particularly residential segregation, were less successful.

38. Quadagno, *The Color of Welfare*, 120.

39. Patterson, *America's Struggle Against Poverty*, 131–32.

40. Lucy A. Williams, "The Abuse of Section 1115 Waivers: Welfare Reform in Search of a Standard," *Yale Law and Policy Review* 12 (1994): 10.

41. Margaret Weir, *Politics and Jobs: The Boundaries of Employment Policy in the United States* (Princeton, N.J.: Princeton University Press, 1992), 69–71.

42. Samuel H. Beer, "In Search of a New Public Philosophy," in *The New American Political System*, ed. Anthony King (Washington, D.C.: American Enterprise Institute, 1978), 16.

43. See John C. Donovan, *The Politics of Poverty* (New York: Western Publishing Company, 1967), especially chapter 3, for one account of the development of the CAP. See also Daniel Patrick Moynihan, *Maximum Feasible Misunderstanding* (New York: Free Press, 1969), for another, more critical account of the CAP.

44. Frances Fox Piven and Richard A. Cloward, *Poor People's Movements: Why They Succeed, How They Fail* (New York: Vintage Books, 1979), 179. See also Paul E. Peterson and J. David Greenstone, "Racial Change and Citizen Participation: The Mobilization of Low-Income Communities through Community Action," in *A Decade of Federal Anti-Poverty Programs*, ed. Robert H. Haveman (New York: Academic Press, 1977). Peterson and Greenstone presented their study in greater detail in *Race and Authority in Urban Politics: Community Participation and the War on Poverty* (Chicago: University of Chicago Press, 1973, 1976).

45. Peterson and Greenstone, "Racial Change and Citizen Participation," 266–67.

46. See Peterson and Greenstone, *Race and Authority in Urban Politics*, for an account of community action in five major cities.

47. Tensions related the Great Migration of rural black families into the major cities of the North after the mechanization of southern agriculture contributed to the response of mayors to community action programs in their cities.

48. Beer, "In Search of a New Public Policy," 15–18; Heclo, "The Political Foundations of Antipoverty Policy," 333.

49. Heclo, "The Political Foundations of Antipoverty Policy," 322; Stephen Skowroneck, *The Politics Presidents Make: Leadership from John Adams to George Bush* (Cambridge, Mass.: Belknap Press of Harvard University Press, 1993); Weir, Orloff and Skocpol, "Understanding American Social Politics," 25; Skocpol, *Protecting Soldiers and Mothers*, 59.

50. Beer, "In Search of a New Public Philosophy," 33; Skocpol, "The Limits of the New Deal System and the Roots of Contemporary Welfare Dilemmas" in *The Politics of Social Policy in the United States*, 305–306.

51. Weir, Orloff, and Skocpol, "Understanding American Social Politics," 18–19, 23; Skocpol, *Protecting Soldiers and Mothers*, 307.

52. Heclo, "The Political Foundations of Antipoverty Policy," 323. See also John Reider, "The Rise of the Silent Majority," and Thomas Byrne Edsall, "The Changing Shape of Power: A Realignment in Public Policy," both in *The Rise and Fall of the New Deal Order*, ed. Steve Fraser and Gary Gerstle (Princeton, N.J.: Princeton University Press, 1989).

53. Organizers of poor people in the United States faced an inevitable dilemma: If poor people or black Americans participated along socially and politically acceptable consensual lines, within the pluralist tradition, they were effectively drowned out (or coopted, in the view of Piven and Cloward) and made less "dangerous." If they used militant tactics and effectively challenged the established political regime, however, they would be deemed too threatening and support for their mobilization would be withdrawn.

54. Patterson, *America's Struggle Against Poverty*, 164–69.

55. Ibid., 12.

56. In particular, *Shapiro v. Thompson* in 1969 limited waiting periods and residency requirements, and *Goldberg v. Kelly* in 1970 held that due process required states to grant welfare recipients hearings before cutting off their aid. See R. Shep Melnick, *Between the Lines: Interpreting Welfare Rights* (Washington, D.C.: Brookings Institution Press,1994).

57. These benefits increased more later on, however, *after* the period of greatest expansion in welfare caseloads. R. Kent Weaver and William T. Dickens, *Looking Before We Leap: Social Science and Welfare Reform* (Washington, D.C.: Brookings Institution Press, 1995), 42.

58. Vincent J. Burke and Vee Burke, *Nixon's Good Deed* (New York: Columbia University Press, 1974), 9; Moynihan, *Maximum Feasible Misunderstanding*, 34–35. Economist William Dickens of the Brookings Institution notes, however, that during the 1960s, family breakdown on the whole did not cause the caseload increase; instead, more female-headed families were using AFDC benefits for which they qualified. Weaver and Dickens, *Looking Before We Leap*, 42.

59. *1969 Congressional Quarterly Almanac* (Washington, D.C.: Congressional Quarterly, 1970), 107.

60. Daniel Patrick Moynihan, *The Politics of a Guaranteed Income* (New York: Random House, 1973), 67.

61. Burke and Burke, *Nixon's Good Deed*, 41.

62. *1969 Congressional Quarterly Almanac*, 833; Quadagno, *The Color of Welfare*, 128.

63. *1969 Congressional Quarterly Almanac*, 833; Burke and Burke, *Nixon's Good Deed*, 44, 74.

64. Milton Friedman, *Capitalism and Freedom* (Chicago: University of Chicago Press, 1962, 1982), 190–95.

65. Burke and Burke, *Nixon's Good Deed*, 67; Timothy J. Conlan, *New Federalism: Intergovernmental Reform from Nixon to Reagan* (Washington, D.C.: Brookings Institution, 1988), 79; Desmond S. King, "Citizenship as Obligation in the United States: Title II of the Family Support Act of 1988," in *The Frontiers of Citizenship*, ed. Ursula Vogel and Michael Moran (New York: Macmillan, 1991), 23; Conlan, 32.

66. Lawrence M. Mead, *The New Politics of Poverty* (New York: BasicBooks, 1992), 188.

67. Conlan, *New Federalism*, 171; Jill Quadagno, "Race, Class, and Gender in the U.S. Welfare State: Nixon's Failed Family Assistance Plan," *American Sociological Review* 55 (February 1990): 15; see also Moynihan, *The Politics of a Guaranteed Income*.

68. Quadagno, *The Color of Welfare*, 129–30.

69. *1969 Congressional Quarterly Almanac*, 77-A, 78-A; Conlan, *New Federalism*, 29–30.

70. Moynihan, *The Politics of a Guaranteed Income*, 205.

71. Nicholas Lemann, *The Promised Land: The Great Black Migration and How It Changed America* (New York: Vintage Books, 1992), 207.

72. Conlan, *New Federalism*, 77, 196.

73. *1969 Congressional Quarterly Almanac*, 833, 836; Moynihan, *The Politics of a Guaranteed Income*, 139.

74. *1969 Congressional Quarterly Almanac*, 833, 836; Moynihan, *The Politics of a Guaranteed Income*, 139; Conlan, *New Federalism*, 77–81.

75. Moynihan, *The Politics of a Guaranteed Income*, 163.

76. *1969 Congressional Quarterly Almanac*, 109.

77. Moynihan, *The Politics of a Guaranteed Income*, 179, 295–98.

78. Ibid., 185; Burke and Burke, *Nixon's Good Deed*, 140, 143–46.

79. Quadagno, "Race, Class and Gender"; 1971 *Congressional Quarterly Almanac*, 521.

80. Piven and Cloward, *Poor People's Movements*, chapter 5, suggests that by this time the NWRO was no longer a mass-based organization and instead represented a fairly narrow group of recipients who composed its leadership. Shortly after the FAP battle, it disbanded.

81. Burke and Burke, *Nixon's Good Deed*, 174; Quadagno, *The Color of Welfare*, 133.

82. Moynihan, *The Politics of a Guaranteed Income*, 339–40.

83. Lester M. Salamon, "The Stakes in the Rural South," *The New Republic* (1971), cited in Quadagno, "Race, Class and Gender," 24.

84. Burke and Burke, *Nixon's Good Deed*, 144.

85. Quadagno, "Race, Class and Gender," 24; Burke and Burke, *Nixon's Good Deed*, 147.

86. Moynihan, *The Politics of a Guaranteed Income*, 472–73; Burke and Burke, *Nixon's Good Deed*, xvii–xxii.

87. *1988 Congressional Quarterly Almanac*, 349.

88. U.S. House of Representatives Committee on Ways and Means, *1994–95 Green Book*, (Washington, D.C.: Brassey's, 1994), 439.

89. Williams, "The Abuse of Section 1115 Waivers," 16–18.

90. King, "Citizenship as Obligation in the United States," 11–13; Rivlin, *Reviving the American Dream*, 101, 123–24.

91. *1994–95 Green Book*, 325.

92. Only a small percentage of poor people would have been considered "underclass" by any reasonable definition of the concept. See Christopher Jencks, "The Underclass," in *Rethinking Social Policy: Race, Poverty and the Underclass* (Cambridge, Mass.: Harvard University Press, 1992). For a more critical analysis, see Adolph I. Reed, Jr., "The Underclass Myth," *The Progressive* 55 (1991): 18–20.

93. Peterson, *The Price of Federalism*, 114.

94. For a useful discussion of these issues, see Wendy Sarvasy, "Reagan and Low-Income Mothers: A Feminist Recasting of the Debate," in *Remaking the Welfare State*, ed. Michael K. Brown (Philadelphia: Temple University Press, 1988), 253–76.

95. Moynihan, *The Politics of a Guaranteed Income*, note 17.

96. *1988 Congressional Quarterly Almanac*, 350.

97. Mary Jo Bane and David T. Ellwood, *Welfare Realities* (Cambridge, Mass.: Harvard University Press, 1994), 23. See also Michael B. Katz, *The Undeserving Poor* (New York: Pantheon Books, 1989), 229–32, on the goals of the Family Support Act.

98. *1988 Congressional Almanac*, 350.

99. Ibid., 349–50.

100. Ibid., 556.

101. Douglas Imig, *Poverty and Power* (Lincoln: University of Nebraska Press, 1996), 37–39; see Demetrios Caraley, "Washington Abandons the Cities," *Political Science Quarterly* 107 (spring 1992): 1–30, on the effect of Reagan-era cuts on the cities and urban interests.

102. See Mead, *The New Politics of Poverty*, 200, on labor and the Left generally.

103. Program information from *1994–95 Green Book*, 431–32; *1988 Congressional Quarterly Almanac*, 353–64.

104. See R. Kent Weaver, "The Politics of Welfare Reform," in Weaver and Dickens, *Looking Before We Leap*, 92–100, for an early version of his analysis of the common political "traps" in welfare reform generally.

105. Federal and state spending on AFDC benefits increased 9 percent in real terms during this period; *1996 Green Book*, 386.

106. Bane and Ellwood, *Welfare Realities*, 24; *1994–95 Green Book*, 435.

107. Bane and Ellwood, *Welfare Realities*, 24–25.

108. Conlan, *New Federalism*, 2–4.

109. Ibid., 1.

110. Ibid., 224.

111. Ibid., 229.

112. Nathan, "Federalism," 233–34.

113. Images of unmarried teen welfare mothers informed much of the rhetoric, although teen mothers made up only about 7 percent of the caseload; *1996 Green Book*, 516.

114. Benefit and other expenditures were only slightly higher in real terms in 1994 than in 1975, although more than 3 million additional recipients were on the rolls.

115. As I note in chapter 1, R. Kent Weaver, *Ending Welfare As We Know It* (Washington, D.C.: Brookings Institution Press, 2000) is particularly useful, as are Steven M. Teles, *Whose Welfare? AFDC and Elite Politics* (Lawrence: University Press of Kansas, 1996) and Dan Balz and Ronald Brownstein, *Storming the Gates: Protest Politics and the Republican Revival* (Waltham, Mass.: Little, Brown and Co., 1996).

116. See *1993 Congressional Quarterly Almanac*, 335–39, 373–75, and Balz and Brownstein, *Storming the Gates*, 252–53, on the early welfare and health care plans. On health care, see Theda Skocpol, *Boomerang: Clinton's Health Security Effort and the Turn against Government in U.S. Politics* (New York: W. W. Norton and Co., 1996).

117. *1993 Congressional Quarterly Almanac*, 373–75.

118. Ibid.

119. *1994 Congressional Quarterly Almanac*, 364. See also Balz and Brownstein, *Storming the Gates*, 275–83, on Republicans' move rightward.

120. Condensed from *1994 Congressional Quarterly Almanac*, 364–65. See also Rochelle L. Stanfield, "Growth Curve," *National Journal*, 23 July 1994, 1728–32, for policymakers' reactions to the president's plan.

121. R. Kent Weaver, "Ending Welfare as We Know It," in *The Social Divide: Political Parties and the Future of Activist Government*, ed. Margaret Weir (Washington, D.C.: Brookings Institution Press, 1998), 382–83.

122. See John E. Schwarz, *America's Hidden Success: A Reassessment of Public Policy from Kennedy to Reagan* (revised), (New York: W. W. Norton and Co., 1988), and Wendall Primus et al., *The Safety Net Delivers* (Washington, D.C.: Center on Budget and Policy Priorities, 1996), for an opposing evaluation of the cost and success of the "war on poverty."

123. A 1995 Kaiser Foundation/Harvard University survey on public attitudes about welfare suggests that most Americans considered welfare an overwhelmingly minority program populated by people who really could work. Yet in many ways their specific ideas about what should be done were more consistent with the original Clinton plan than those advocated by the Republican Congress. Kaiser/Harvard Program on the Public and Health/Social Policy, *Survey on Welfare Reform* (Menlo Park, Calif.: Henry J. Kaiser Family Foundation, 1995).

124. Timothy Conlan, *From New Federalism to Devolution: Twenty-Five Years of Intergovernmental Reform* (Washington, D.C.: Brookings Institution Press, 1998), 232, 278; Balz and Brownstein, *Storming the Gates*, 55.

125. A particularly good analysis can be found in Balz and Brownstein, *Storming the Gates*, chapter 6.

126. Ibid., 281.

127. This and the following are from *1995 Congressional Quarterly Almanac*, 7-35 to 7-52, unless otherwise noted.

128. Ibid., 7-35 to 7-36; as well as interviews with participants.

129. *1995 Congressional Quarterly Almanac*, 7-36.

130. David Ellwood, "Welfare Reform As I Knew It: When Bad Things Happen to Good Policies," *The American Prospect* (May–June 1996); also lecture at Johns Hopkins University on February 6, 1997.

131. The vote basically was along party lines, though one Democrat (who switched to the Republican party after the bill passed) voted with the Republicans.

132. *1995 Congressional Quarterly Almanac*, 7-41; also interviews with congressional staff.

133. As in Ways and Means, one Democrat crossed party lines to vote with the Republicans.

134. Weaver, *Ending Welfare As We Know It*, 386–69; also Balz and Brownstein, *Storming the Gates*, chapter 6; interviews.

135. *1995 Congressional Quarterly Almanac*, 7-35.

136. In several instances, the bill's social engineering goals conflicted with each other. Here the question essentially became how best to use national legislation to keep unmarried women from having children while also keeping them from having abortions. Some conservative Republican abortion opponents, including Rep. Henry J. Hyde (R-IL) and groups such as the National Right-to-Life Committee, opposed provisions such as the family cap and cutting off teenage mothers, fearing they would encourage more young women to have abortions. Other socially conservative groups, such as the Christian Coalition and Heritage Foundation, supported the new mandates. *1995 Congressional Quarterly Almanac*, 7–43. See also Eliza Newlin Carney, "Legitimate Questions," *National Journal*, 18 March 1995, 684.

137. Rep. James C. Greenwood (R-PA) quoted in *1995 Congressional Quarterly Almanac*, 7-43.

138. *1995 Congressional Quarterly Almanac*, 7-44.

139. Ibid., 7-46; interviews.

140. Ibid., 7-47; interviews.

141. Ibid.; Weaver, "Ending Welfare as We Know It"; interviews.

142. *1995 Congressional Quarterly Almanac*, 7-50.

143. It also precluded a filibuster and forced an up or down vote on the entire budget bill, not just on welfare and related provisions. Reconciliation effectively neutralized the weapons that the minority, particularly in the Senate, could use to block legislation it opposed and weakened potential veto points. The Byrd Rule—a Senate provision that discouraged inclusion of extraneous policy provisions within budget bills—meant that some of the "pure" policy clauses of the welfare bill would be knocked out, but the main financing provisions, including block grants, would be preserved. Republican leaders also regarded inclusion of welfare overhaul in the budget bill as a backup, in case HR 4 failed. See Weaver, "Ending Welfare as We Know It," 376–78. See also Allen Schick, *The Federal Budget: Politics, Policy, Process* (Washington, D.C.: Brookings Institution Press, 1995), especially 82–88 on reconciliation and the Byrd Rule.

144. *1996 Congressional Quarterly Almanac*, 6-4.

145. Jeffrey L. Katz, "School Lunch Fight Bogs Down Overhaul Agreement," *Congressional Quarterly*, 2 December 1995, 3662; Katz, "Clinton Vows to Overhaul Measure," *Congressional Quarterly*, 23 December 1995, 3889.

146. Judith Havemann, "Overreaching Once More for Reform: Welfare Bill Echoes Health Care Effort," *Washington Post*, 15 January 1996, A1. Economist Henry Aaron and other scholars also have written about why welfare has been so hard to reform.

147. The polls by the Kaiser/Harvard Program on the Public and Health/Social Policy suggest that Americans' views were significantly more moderate than the "hard" time limits and many other provisions of the Congressional plan; in many ways, the public's views more closely resembled a plan like Clinton's 1993 proposal.

148. See John Ferejohn, "A Tale of Two Congresses: Social Policy in the Clinton Years," in *The Social Divide: Political Parties and the Future of Activist Government*, ed. Margaret Weir (Washington, D.C.: Brookings Institution Press, 1998), 49–82.

149. *1996 Congressional Quarterly Almanac*, 6-3.

150. Ibid., 6-6 and 6-7.

151. According to participants in the debate, there was something of a "bidding war" between Democrats and Republicans to be seen as serious about work that drove participation requirements well above those the Republicans had proposed in their most stringent bill in 1993. *1996 Congressional Quarterly Almanac*, 6-8; interviews.

152. *Congressional Quarterly Almanac 1996*, 6-11. There was a certain irony in both branches' eagerness to sign legislation to devolve welfare: It essentially fixed the problem by pushing it down to the much less visible arena of the fifty states, where policymakers still had to figure out how to reform it. Stephen Teles, David Ellwood, and others have made this point. Teles, in particular, criticizes members of Congress for being unwilling to make tough policy decisions that would be necessary to reform but still maintain the national commitment to welfare.

153. *1996 Congressional Quarterly Almanac*, 6-11 to 6-12.

154. Barbara Vobejda and Helen Dewar, "Bill to Overhaul Welfare Clears Senate, 74 to 24: Clinton Calls for Further Revisions," *Washington Post*, 24 July 1996, A1; Robert Pear, "Senate Approves Sweeping Change in Welfare Policy: Big Role to States," *New York Times*, 23 July 1996, A1. Wellstone won reelection in November 1996.

155. Governors bemoaned this provision as an administrative nightmare because it required that they maintain two eligibility systems—one for their new TANF system to determine who gets welfare and a second under their old AFDC eligibility criteria to determine who is eligible for Medicaid. In the years after welfare reform went into effect, Medicaid rolls dropped sharply.

156. Vobejda and Dewar, "Bill to Overhaul Welfare Clears Senate"; Pear, "Senate Approves Sweeping Change in Welfare Policy"; *1996 Congressional Quarterly Almanac*, 6-22.

157. One conference provision actually was harsher than either the Senate or House version: States were prohibited from penalizing a mother on welfare who doesn't work because she cannot find day care for a child under the age of six. The Senate and House versions had covered women with children under the age of eleven.

158. Barbara Vobejda, "Welfare Bill Opponents Turn Up Pressure," *Washington Post*, 27 July 1996, A4.

159. Robert Pear, "Clinton to Sign Welfare Bill That Ends U.S. Aid Guarantee and Gives States Broad Power: After Hearing President, More in Party Back Measure in House," *New York Times*, 1 August 1996, A1.

160. Pear, "Clinton to Sign Welfare Bill"; "House's 328-101 Roll Call Vote," *Washington Post*, 1 August 1996, A8.

161. Robert Pear, "Senate Passes Welfare Measure, Sending It for Clinton's Signature," *New York Times*, 2 August 1996, A1. See also Robert Pear, "The

Democrats: Many Subtleties Shaped Members' Welfare Votes," *New York Times*, 4 August 1996, 22.

162. Quotes from "The Republicans' View: Remarks by Gingrich and Other G.O.P. Supporters," *New York Times*, 1 August 1996, A25.

163. Jerry Gray, "The Liberals: Amid Praise, a Peppering of Criticism and Dismay," *New York Times*, 1 August 1996, A24.

164. Pear, "Many Subtleties Shaped Members' Welfare Votes," 22. The Democrats did not take back the House, but some of the legal immigrant cuts were restored in 1997 budget amendments.

165. Pear, "Clinton to Sign Welfare Bill"; Pear, "The Democrats."

166. If states meet their work participation requirements, they must maintain 75 percent of previous spending. If they do not, they must maintain 80 percent.

167. Robert Pear, "Agreement Struck on Most Elements for Welfare Bill," *New York Times*, 30 July 1996, A1; Barbara Vobejda and Helen Dewar, "Conferees Finish Work on Welfare Bill: Clinton Indicates Desire to Sign Measure, but Offers No Endorsement," *Washington Post*, 31 July 1996, A1. For details of the bill, see U.S. Department of Health and Human Services, "Personal Responsibility and Work Opportunity Reconciliation Act of 1996 (HR 3734), Summary of Provisions," Office of the Assistant Secretary for Planning and Evaluation, 18 March 1997, and David Super et al., *The New Welfare Law* (Washington, D.C.: Center on Budget and Policy Priorities, 1996).

168. States could choose as their base year fiscal year FY 1994, 1995, or an average from FY 1992 to 1994, whichever was highest.

169. These cases include *New York v. United States*, 505 U.S. 144 (1992); *United States v. Lopez*, 514 U.S. 549 (1995); *Printz v. United States*, 521 U.S. 898 (1997); *Alden v. Maine*, 527 U.S. 706 (1999); and *United States v. Morrison*, 529 U.S. 598 (2000). The 2000 session included decisions upholding the supremacy of federal law in certain cases related to foreign policy, but the general movement in domestic policy has been toward greater deference to state authority.

170. John W. Kingdon, *Agendas, Alternatives and Public Policies* (New York: HarperCollins, 1984, 1995).

171. The moral mandates embedded in the welfare law suggest, however, that for some policymakers this skepticism about "social engineering" pertained mainly to liberal programs that cost money and benefited traditionally Democratic constituencies.

172. Peter T. Kilborn and Sam Howe Verhovek, "Clinton's Welfare Shift Reflects New Democrat," *New York Times*, 2 August 1996, A18. This comment was echoed by numerous interviewees.

3

The Role of "Factions" in the National Welfare Debate

In keeping with neo-Madisonian theory, a broad range of actors outside the national government participated in the national welfare debate during the 104th Congress—though some, such as Republican governors Thompson of Wisconsin and Engler of Michigan and the conservative Heritage Foundation, were more active than others. Nonetheless, there also was a large and energetic—if not always welcome—community of groups in Washington representing low-income people. This chapter looks in detail at the involvement of organized interests and other outside actors and considers the range and mix of groups that participated in the debate about national welfare reform, particularly those that had arisen in the previous three decades to advocate for low-income families. As other scholars have noted, interest groups did not alone establish the broad parameters of the welfare debate during the 1990s, nor did they alone determine its narrow provisions. Kent Weaver notes, "The influence that interest groups exercise in welfare reform or any other policy sectors depends on complex attributes of the groups, of politicians, and of the issue itself."[1] Nonetheless, they did have critical influence over the essential policy details in the final reform legislation.

I define "interest group" broadly as any organization or actor that took an active role in commenting on or trying to influence the shape of welfare reform during congressional public hearings or by other means, even though many of these groups are not technically lobbyists.[2] I use a typology of groups that reflects the various actors that were, in fact, involved in the politics of welfare policy during the 104th Congress—one that reflects reality as I found it. As I note in chapter 1, for the purposes of this study I initially define interest participation as the presentation and/or submission of hearing testimony before committees with primary jurisdiction for the AFDC-replacement portions of the bill. I do not consider groups that tried specifically to influence provisions concerning SSI, food stamps, and benefits for immigrants; these provisions were addressed in hearings largely separately from AFDC. This criterion limits the analysis somewhat because these programs and others are closely linked with cash assistance. Examining them, however, would have brought in a range of groups that historically have not been especially active in AFDC politics.

I use hearing testimony as a stepping-off point because it provides the broadest and most objective measure of a group's intention to influence the policymaking process, regardless of whether it ultimately is successful in doing so. Hearing participation clearly is a limited measure of the desire to affect policy, however, and an even more limited indicator of an organization's success in doing so. Although participants in the welfare debate said that hearing testimony could affect the eventual shape of the law, they stressed the role of other strategies as well.

Interest groups in Washington use a range of tactics; they rely on direct contact, personal relationships, and other approaches, as well as participation in congressional hearings. These other approaches are harder to measure systematically, however, so I use information about them that I gleaned from my interviews and other sources to supplement an analysis of participation in public hearings. As I note in chapter 1, I also include in this analysis actors that only submitted written testimony and may not have been invited to testify orally. In Washington, the opportunity to provide oral testimony itself often is political, subject to negotiation between the committee majority and minority. By considering written testimony as well, I capture the universe of actors and organizations that desired to shape welfare policy outcomes. I also found that hearing participation was a generally effective proxy for other types of activity (with a few exceptions that I discuss below).

Through interviews with key policymakers and interest group representatives, which lasted between a half-hour and more than three hours, I explored the additional strategies these groups used. These strategies included cultivating direct relationships with legislators and their staffs; mobilizing grassroots or mass activity; "going public" through appeals to the media; reverse and cross-lobbying; and other, less documentable approaches.[3] I also learned about groups that acted entirely behind the scenes and would not appear to be active if their activity were gauged only by hearing participation. I incorporate the results of these interviews, supplemented by press accounts and other sources, into my analysis of pressure group activity. I also try to identify characteristics of groups that were particularly effective in influencing policy decisions.

Through this examination of the organizations that tried to influence welfare policy on the national level during the 104th Congress, I ask which types of groups appeared most frequently on the national level, which were most active, and which were most influential. In particular, I focus on the existence and activity of organizations that reasonably can be defined as representing the interests of low-income families.[4] I explore the relative presence, activity, and influence of these types of groups in state welfare reform in chapters 4 through 6.

THE ROLE OF PRESSURE GROUPS IN POLICYMAKING

American pluralists from James Madison to David Truman and Robert Dahl have suggested a model of national political activity that resembles a vibrant marketplace of interests, each representing a different segment of society as they haggle with each other and with lawmakers to reach some more or less "fair" set of policy outcomes.[5] Other scholars of organized pressure groups note, however, that interests and concerns are by no means represented equally in Washington or state capitals and that different constituents' effectiveness in attaining their goals vary widely. In particular, a strong class bias skews the concerns that receive an effective hearing in the political arena. As E. E. Schattschneider so memorably put it, "The flaw in the pluralist heaven is that the heavenly chorus sings with a strong upper-class accent."[6]

Particularly in welfare policymaking, it bears repeating that low-income people and children have less political power than other American citizens. They tend to vote at lower rates (obviously, children can't vote), and neither group is likely to have the time, money, independence, or other resources required to organize into political action groups or to give money to pressure groups, political parties, or candidates. Money and votes are the major currencies of politics, so it is not surprising that low-income people and children have tended to be underrepresented in the policy process.

There have been exceptions, however, such as the briefly influential "poor people's organizations" coming out of the War on Poverty and the Community Action Program (CAP) discussed in chapter 2. Although the CAP did not result in a permanent political voice for the poor, neither was it a complete failure, programmatically or politically. Ultimately—as Peterson, Greenstone, and others have argued—it addressed, at least for the time, "the regime-threatening potential of race conflict in America" by helping to bring middle class black Americans into the political order. Although the result was not full political equality, the CAP did help to increase black political power, if not the political power of poor Americans broadly.[7]

Another effect of the CAP was the development of the poor people's organizations in the mid-1960s. These organizations arose in part as a result of a strategy of CAP-funded organizers to sign up eligible low-income families for welfare and other benefits for which they qualified and to organize them politically into mass-based organizations. The NWRO was founded in 1967, and a range of local and state groups arose as well. The lives of most of these groups were relatively short, and it was not clear—particularly in the case of the NWRO—how much they represented their membership and how much they represented their leadership. For a time in the late 1960s and early 1970s, however, they played some role in shaping anti-poverty policy.[8]

The story of these groups illustrates the difficulties of organizing low-income people into stable, politically effective, mass-based organizations, either for their own material gains or for more abstract goals related to greater equality of opportunity.[9] Poor people as a rule have fewer resources, less time, and less education about and socialization toward political participation, and they may not regard their problems as rooted in political causes because they tend to share mainstream values about individual responsibility. Kay Lehman Schlozman and John T. Tierney describe these difficulties in the case of one state welfare rights organization:

> Consider the organizational maintenance problems confronted by the organizers of the Massachusetts Welfare Rights Organization. Committed to organizing welfare recipients, a constituency with little experience in and few resources for political participation, these activists adopted a strategy that allowed them to generate support for collective goods—increased welfare rights and benefits from the government—by supplying members with selective ones. Having no resources to provide selective benefits on their own, the organizers generated support for their group by helping members obtain government benefits for which they were already eligible. This was a sound strategy for attracting members but was of little use in inducing welfare recipients to support the organization in a sustained fashion. Once members had acquired whatever government benefits were available (the selective benefits), they tended not to participate in the organization's efforts to exact collective benefits from the government. The costs of group participation on behalf of policy goals—baby-sitters, bus fares, and so on—were simply prohibitive to the poor, who could not afford to expend their scarce resources for the potential achievement of less immediate collective goals. All this helps us understand why not only the interests of diffuse publics but also the interests of the poor are underrepresented in politics. For those with few resources the costs of organizational membership are rarely low enough to justify efforts to seek collective benefits.[10]

Although poor people's organizations were not very successful politically, the new federal emphasis on social programs and the centralization of domestic policymaking did encourage formation in Washington between the 1960s and the 1980s of public interest groups representing low-income people.[11]

Most of the advocacy groups involved in the 1990s welfare debate simply did not exist during the Great Society. In fact, the failures of organizing poor people directly may have helped to encourage the development of the more centralized, professional, and "elite" advocacy and research groups representing the concerns of low-income people in the policymaking process by working within its pluralist structure. The existence of these new organizations reflected and reinforced the centralization of policymaking for poverty programs as advocates realized that they could reach greater numbers and wield greater influence in Washington than in each of the states.[12] Political scientist Douglas Imig describes their growth, citing twenty-four new advocacy and research organizations focusing on domestic anti-poverty issues that were formed in Washington between 1965 and the end of the 1980s.[13]

The tactics that interest groups across the spectrum use to shape policy vary widely. These tactics include testifying at hearings; direct contact with administrators, legislators, and staff; monitoring and disseminating information about legislative and governmental activity; and cultivating relationships with the media. They also conduct and present research to the public and government; maintain constituency contact; mobilize grassroots support; and conduct letter, telephone, and e-mail campaigns, including orchestrated "astroturf" campaigns that are designed to look like true grassroots activity. They make financial contributions to parties and candidates, instigate litigation, organize civil disobedience and protests, and form coalitions with other groups. These interest organizations—along with their issue-related counterparts in congressional committees and the executive branch—form "policy domains," "subsystems," or "issue networks" that focus on substantive policy areas.[14]

One survey of pressure groups indicates that the most common tactics are hearing testimony, direct contact with government officials, presentation of research results, and communicating with membership and constituents about activities. Research and anecdotal evidence suggest that direct contact with policymakers—informal and formal relationships developed over time—are most effective.[15] Most of these techniques for exerting influence require money, and even those that are not capital-intensive clearly benefit from sufficient numbers of skilled staff. Business groups and other well-heeled organizations usually will be in the best position to exploit these methods.

Although Washington is not the pluralist heaven of Truman, however, neither is it a game in which the outcome is at all times rigged in favor of a simple "power elite." Though these private interest groups certainly are dominant, they are not always a monolithic force. The number and range of lobbyists in Washington have soared in past decades, and in this atmosphere of "hyperpluralism," even business groups often are at odds with each other on specifics of legislation. The number of groups representing low-income citizens also has increased since the 1960s, as have other public interest organizations.[16] Although this growth is not sufficiently countervailing to balance the power of wealthy private groups, these interests are not completely ignored, especially on the national level.

Increasingly, since the failure of efforts to organize widespread membership-based poverty groups during the Great Society era, poor people are represented in Washington by the aforementioned professionalized advocacy organizations, often funded through liberal national foundations. It has been some time since a group with wide membership of low-income people themselves has been influential. By and large, the actors in Washington who represent their concerns do not directly receive the benefits. Secondary advocacy groups such as organized labor also often represent the concerns of low-income families, while representing other interests as well.[17] When the interests of their other clients and these families conflict, however, poor people may lose out. So although it would be simplistic to state that political power is held only by a narrow few—scholars such as Schlozman and Tierney, Walker, and Heinz have found significant dispersal among pressure groups—interest politics nonetheless is characterized by "tremendous inequalities in representation and influence."[18]

Some students of interest group politics have suggested that strong parties are a better vehicle for translating the sheer numbers of low-income citizens into political influence because when these citizens are mobilized they have the power to vote, even if they have little money. Political parties in the United States are considerably weaker than in most developed democracies, however, and the old decentralized mass-based party system has evolved into an advertising-focused national system with party strategies that increasingly have shifted from labor-intensive electoral mobilization to expensive "high-tech" campaigns that further reward wealthy people.[19]

Mancur Olson, Schattschneider, and others have discussed the difficulties of organizing people into groups that advocate for collective, nondivisible goods rather than selective and divisible concrete benefits. Collective, or public, goods are characterized by the fact that they cannot be divided among those who successfully advocate for them: By definition, those who benefit from them cannot be limited. The "free rider" effect, these theorists argue, discourages people from giving money and otherwise supporting organizations that lobby for public goods such as clean air and water or the care of mentally ill people living on the street—goods that also benefit those who do not help to support them. This difficulty makes these groups harder to form and maintain.[20] Similarly, it is difficult to persuade citizens to give money to support and maintain organizations that lobby for benefits for people other than themselves. This is the challenge that many advocates for poor people and for children face, contributing to the small staffs and tight budgets with which many of them operate.

Even with these limitations, however, groups that advocate at the national level for programs for low-income people and their children, encouraged by the social movements of recent decades, have arisen and have been maintained. In Washington these groups have a national pool from which to draw support for the people and issues they represent, which helps significantly in fundraising. Often they are successful in shaping policy outcomes, either by limiting or blocking provisions they oppose or by gaining provisions they support. They can try broadly to set the agenda, and they can focus on the details of legislative language, where many of the biggest decisions are made. The following sections explore groups and actors that played a role in trying to shape the 1996 welfare bill, first looking briefly at participation in congressional hearings and then examining in more depth the participation of interest groups across the spectrum.

ORGANIZATIONS ACTIVE IN WELFARE HEARINGS IN 1995 AND 1996

During the 104th Congress, between the beginning of January 1995 and August 1996 when the president signed the new welfare law, the House and Senate held twenty-five hearings on welfare-related topics. These hearings ranged between a half-day to six days in length. The topics included replacement of AFDC with block grants, work opportunities for recipients, teen parents, child care, and child support (see Appendix B for a list of committees, hearings, and dates). I examined witness lists from these hearings, which were held by the five committees with primary jurisdiction over welfare policy during the 104th Congress: the Senate Finance Committee and Senate Labor and Human Resources Committee and the Ways and Means, Education and Economic Opportunities, and Agriculture committees in the House. I also examined a welfare-related hearing addressing information technology held by the Senate Committee on Governmental Affairs.

I have categorized groups into nine types, reflecting the nature of the organizations that were actually involved in welfare policy, rather than attempting to develop a theoretically comprehensive schematic of all possible types of groups. Others—including Kay Lehman Schlozman and John Tierney, as well as Jack Walker—have done this in an effort to theorize broad interest group activity and influence more rigorously. My goal is simpler, and the typology reflects what I found in looking at welfare hearings and at other kinds of participation. Interviews and press accounts helped to identify the actors who participated through other means; I discuss them below. My research indicates, however, that the vast majority of major actors in welfare reform overall also participated actively in public hearings.

The nine broad categories (described further in Table 3-1) are advocates, including child advocacy groups, nonprofit and charitable organizations, and unions; intergovernmental organizations and officials; nonpartisan research organizations and academic experts; think tanks; "traditional values" groups; for-profit service providers and business organizations; professional associations; individuals with no obvious organizational affiliations; and

Table 3-1
Interest Group Categories

Advocates—child advocacy organizations, nonprofit and charitable service providers, unions: Largely between the center and the left politically, with the goal of advocating for more expansive programs for low-income families, though some groups were not easily labeled ideologically. Most advocacy groups also conducted research or provided direct services, including the Center on Budget and Policy Priorities (CBPP), the Center for Law and Social Policy (CLASP), the Children's Defense Fund (CDF), the Coalition on Human Needs, the National Welfare Rights and Reform Union, and the National Women's Law Center. Providers' primary activity was direct service provision, although some also conducted advocacy and research. Includes local programs such as Kansas Food Bank Warehouse and Focus: Hope, as well as national groups such as Catholic Charities USA and the Child Welfare League of America. Category also includes public-sector unions, such as AFSCME, as well as other unions such as the AFL-CIO and the United Auto Workers (UAW).

Intergovernmental organizations and officials: Includes intergovernmental organizations such as the National Governors' Association (NGA) and the National Conference of State Legislatures (NCSL), as well as individual governmental officials from all levels (excluding members of Congress and the administration). Includes state, county, local, and tribal leaders. Elected officials such as governors, state legislators, and mayors, as well as appointed officials such as heads of state social services departments and county health centers participated.

Research organizations and academic experts: Nonpartisan organizations or individual academics affiliated with universities or private or government research organizations. Includes academics such as David Ellwood of Harvard University and Lawrence Mead, then of Princeton University (now of New York University), as well as organizations such as the Manpower Demonstration Research Corporation (MDRC) and the U.S. Government Accounting Office (GAO—a governmental but largely independent, nonpartisan research agency of Congress).

Think tanks: These participants tended to have a more ideological orientation (across the political spectrum) than research organizations did, though there was potential overlap. Although groups such as the Heritage Foundation played major roles in welfare reform, many have 501(c)(3) tax status, which technically prohibits them from lobbying. Participating think tanks included the American Enterprise Institute (AEI), Heritage, the Brookings Institution, Cato, and the Progressive Policy Institute (PPI).

"Traditional values" groups: A range of socially conservative organizations advocating policies to shore up "family" or "traditional" values, such as the nuclear family structure. Includes the Christian Coalition, Concerned Women for America, the Family Research Council, the Traditional Values Coalition, and the National Fatherhood Initiative (less conservative than the others). Some of these groups, such as the Children's Rights Council, sound like liberal advocacy groups but because of their conservative policy positions on welfare reform are categorized here.

For-profit service providers and business groups: For-profit welfare-to-work management companies such as America Works and EDS Government Services Group, child-support collection firms, and smaller for-profit child care providers. Categorized separately from nonprofits because as for-profit

Table 3-1

Interest Group Categories *(continued)*

enterprises their incentive structures must be fundamentally different. Some coalitions of child care providers had a mixed for-profit/nonprofit membership but are assigned to this category if the majority appeared to be for-profit. Also includes peak business groups such the U.S. Chamber of Commerce and trade associations such as the National Grocers Association and the Apricot Producers of California.

Professional associations: Membership organizations of professionals. Includes the National Bar Association, the National Association of Social Workers (NASW), the American Society for Payroll Management, the National Child Support Enforcement Association, the American Academy of Matrimonial Lawyers, and the American Academy of Pediatrics.

Individuals (with no obvious organizational affiliation): A significant number of individuals from around the country testified in hearings or submitted comments for the record. Although many certainly did so at the request of or with the encouragement of organizations or policymakers, it was not feasible to identify their patrons or to differentiate them from people who submitted testimony strictly on their own.

Miscellaneous: Several groups did not fit logically into any other category, such as the Citizens' Jury on Welfare Reform and the Christian Science Committee on Publication.

Note: Appendix C provides a detailed listing of the organizations in each category.

miscellaneous groups. (Appendix C provides a detailed listing of organizations in each category.)

Organizations did not always fit neatly into categories. Many are hybrids by definition: Advocates also may conduct research and perform education functions, and many service providers also do advocacy and research. Coalitions of daycare providers may include nonprofit, religious, and for-profit centers. There is an inevitable degree of subjectivity in many of these assignments, but I attempted to categorize organizations according to their predominant activity or orientation. Some groups are temporary coalitions. I treated them like other, more permanent organizations and did not remove their member groups from my count, on the premise that a coalition is a substantively different entity than its member groups.[21] Some groups have names that make them sound like liberal advocates when in fact they are conservative. Lobbyists working on contentious or ideological issues, in particular, may disguise the identity of their primary patrons.[22]

Many organizations—whether they have mainly private, material interests or an ideological emphasis—frame their arguments as public interest claims. As political scientist Cathy M. Johnson notes in her paper on the representation of children in the policy process, "We are all pro-child."[23]

During the welfare debate, we also were all pro–poor people. The organizations that were involved in national welfare overhaul represented a wide range of ideologies and interests and posed some challenge in evaluating competing claims to represent the good of poor people. The "tough love" approach of the right often was in sharp conflict with the benefits emphasis of the left. The categories used here assume that more rather than less government spending on programs for low-income families—particularly spending for child care, work support, and cash assistance—benefits them, and organizations taking these positions are defined as advocacy groups.[24]

HEARINGS PARTICIPATION

Overall, 310 different organizations or actors outside Congress or the administration testified or submitted written statements into the record in the twenty-five welfare-related hearings leading up to passage of PRWORA. These groups testified a total of 410 times, orally or in writing; several groups and actors testified multiple times (see Table 3-2). The most constant nongovernmental presence at welfare hearings was Robert Rector, welfare analyst for the Heritage Foundation, who participated in about one-third of the hearings. Officials from the U.S. General Accounting Office (GAO), the nonpartisan Congressional research agency, and representatives from Manpower Demonstration Research Corporation (MDRC), the nonprofit research organization that evaluated several early welfare pilots, also testified frequently. Other especially active participants included Catholic Charities USA, the Child Welfare League of America (CWL), academic Lawrence Mead, the Center on Budget and Policy Priorities (CBPP), the National Organization for Women (NOW) Legal Defense and Education Fund, the Center for Law and Social Policy (CLASP), and the Children's Defense Fund (CDF). The American Civil Liberties Union (ACLU), AFSCME, officials from the California and Michigan social services departments, Governor Engler of Michigan, Governor Thompson of Wisconsin, and the head of the Riverside County (Calif.) Department of Public Social Services (the site of early welfare "experiments") also testified several times (see Table 3-3).

As Table 3-2 illustrates, the greatest proportion of actors participating in welfare-related hearings were advocacy groups, nonprofit and charitable providers, and labor unions.[25] Intergovernmental organizations and officials were the second most prevalent and active category; considering the focus on devolution of poverty policy, the intensity of involvement in numbers and frequency by these interests seems understandable. Surprisingly, individuals ranked third, though again it was difficult to differentiate between those who came at the behest of organizations and those who were simply interested citizens submitting testimony. Research experts were the next most active group, followed by for-profit service contractors and business and trade associations.

Table 3-2
Activity of Interest Groups in Congressional Welfare-Related Hearings, by Category, 104th Congress

Category	No. of Organizations/Actors	No. of Times Testifying
Advocates: child advocacy, nonprofit and charitable providers, unions	112	148
Intergovernmental	64	83
Individuals	38	39
Researchers	30	48
For-profit companies, business groups	19	20
"Traditional values" groups	14	19
Professional associations	14	17
Think tanks	12	29
Miscellaneous	7	7
TOTAL	**310**	**410**

Sources: Witness and testimony submission lists from welfare-related congressional hearings between January 1995 and August 1996. See Appendices B and C for complete lists of hearings and organizations that testified or submitted written statements.

The latter were in evidence but were not particularly active in the hearings process.

Traditional values groups and professional associations participated in roughly equal numbers. A dozen think tanks across the ideological spectrum testified. They constituted only a small fraction of the number of total participants, but they were especially active (particularly Rector of the Heritage Foundation).

Overall, advocates, service providers, and organized labor, combined with researchers, represented 142 of 310 groups—slightly less than half of those involved in welfare hearings—and provided about half of the total testimony. Although few "poor people's organizations" were in evidence, this group of participants could be defined as generally supportive of more generous policies toward low-income people (obviously, not all researchers held this view,

Table 3-3
Congressional Frequent Testifiers

Organization/Actor	No. of Times Testifying
Robert Rector, Heritage Foundation	8
U.S. General Accounting Office (GAO)	8
Manpower Demonstration Research Corporation (MDRC)	7
Catholic Charities USA	5
Child Welfare League of America	5
Lawrence Mead	4
Center on Budget and Policy Priorities (CBPP)	4
Center for Law and Social Policy (CLASP)	4
NOW Legal Defense and Education Fund	4
Children's Defense Fund (CDF)	3
American Civil Liberties Union (ACLU)	3
American Federation of State, County and Municipal Employees (AFSCME)	3
California Department of Health and Human Services	3
Michigan Department of Social Services	3
Gov. John Engler of Michigan	3
Gov. Tommy Thompson of Wisconsin	3
Riverside County (Calif.) Department of Social Services	3

Sources: Witness and testimony submission lists from welfare-related congressional hearings between January 1995 and August 1996. See Appendices B and C for complete lists of hearings and organizations that testified or submitted written testimony.

Note: These acts of testimony include oral testimony before congressional committees and written statements submitted for the record by actors who were not invited to testify orally.

but most tended to). More than one-third of those who testified were social welfare advocates, nonprofits, and charities. Much as the neo-Madisonians might have predicted, a relatively broad range of actors participated in welfare politics in Washington, with a significant proportion representing the interests of low-income people.

INTEREST GROUP INFLUENCE IN THE LARGER CONTEXT OF WELFARE POLICYMAKING

In addition to public hearings, much of the activity on the welfare bill was conducted in more informal ways, often behind closed doors. Through interviews and press accounts, I have tried to gauge which actors had meaningful access to national policymakers and which were able to affect the shape of the final welfare bill. As one key participant noted, the best way to influence policy is through established and trusting relationships with primary legislative staff and key committee members, and the quality of these relationships is only rarely reflected in official records. I turn now to the larger picture of welfare policymaking, exploring which outside actors also were particularly active through means other than hearing participation and which were considered especially effective in influencing the legislation during the 104th Congress.

Legislative committee staff members who were closely involved in formulating the welfare bill cited Robert Rector as one of the participants who was most often at their door, and the majority of other participants I interviewed mentioned Rector as one of the small handful of the most influential players outside the hearing room (in addition to inside). Committee staffers and others also said that state policymakers, particularly the "inner council" of Republican governors and their senior staff, were closely consulted and eagerly involved in the formulation of the bill at all stages. Among the advocacy groups, two in particular—the CBPP and CLASP—were cited repeatedly as heavily involved and relatively influential in shaping legislation. Catholic Charities USA and the United States Catholic Conference (USCC) also had some access and influence over time, working with staff and members. Among researchers, the MDRC was said to have been trusted, and to the extent that congressional policymakers considered research results at all, they attended to the organization's work. Several participants also mentioned Lawrence Mead, now of New York University and an active scholar of social policy.

All of these actors also appeared among the frequent testifiers at welfare-related hearings. However, some actors who did not appear in hearings were said to be involved behind the scenes, and others had far more influence, or less influence, than might be apparent from their level of hearing activity.

Advocacy Organizations, Nonprofit Providers, and Organized Labor

During much of 1995, commentators noted the relative silence of progressive interest groups, civil rights organizations, and other advocates. Many groups—including women's groups, immigrant groups, and those in the child welfare community—seemed surprisingly inactive in the early days of welfare reform. Senator Moynihan publicly criticized advocates for their passivity, and one high-level Republican committee staff member called their initial performance "dismal" and "inept."[26]

The results of the 1994 election and the speed and momentum of the new Republican majority's action on welfare stunned many liberal groups, according to participants. Whereas Republicans in the House worked on the issue intensively in anticipation of their 1994 victory and hit the ground running, many Democratic constituents apparently could not conceive of a conservative win and after that win occurred were slow to respond and mobilize. Advocates for low-income people took a much more aggressive and vocal stance by the second round of reform in 1996, and civil rights groups began to stir, but even then some could not believe that the president really would sign HR 3734. This wishful thinking appeared to inhibit their ability to act forcefully.[27]

Criticism seems a bit unfair coming from conservative policymakers, however, because they were among the essential players who no longer were attending to the viewpoints of many liberal organizations while they were proposing sweeping changes to national social programs. The welfare policy domain in Washington had changed with astonishing speed, and the old domain was fundamentally fractured. Advocates themselves noted the sheer breadth of the programs that the new Republican majority had put up for radical overhaul: Medicaid, food stamps, the EITC, child nutrition, housing, child welfare, SSI, immigrant programs, and legal services, in addition to cash assistance and work programs. This left them scrambling to mount any kind of coherent defense. "Vision" now belonged to the Republican party and the ascendant conservative interest groups setting the political agenda.[28] Organizations representing poor families pressed hard to stave off attempts to overhaul almost every major program for low-income people. Conservative Republicans in the House also fought to limit political activity by nonprofit organizations receiving federal grants with the Istook Amendment. Opponents of this effort labeled it an attempt to further "defund the left," which already had experienced sharp cuts in government funding during the Reagan administration.[29] Although the amendment ultimately was unsuccessful in 1995 and 1996, it posed yet another threat for advocates and providers to fight off.[30]

Child Advocacy Organizations

Self-professed liberals in positions of power were increasingly hard to find, either in the national government or in states and localities, as Americans as a whole joined in the shift rightward. Advocates' objections to the Republican proposals often were dismissed by the Right as "defending the status quo." Not all advocates were ineffectual, however, even under a newly conservative Republican Congress. Two left-of-center research and advocacy groups, the CBPP and CLASP, were identified as particularly active and effective in the welfare debate. They worked together closely and with other liberal groups as part of the Coalition on Human Needs, and even conservative Hill staff praised them. Staffers noted the quality of these organizations' analysis and their ability to negotiate cooperatively and effectively with the newly powerful conservative policymakers, whose ideology they obviously did not share.

Participants cited both organizations—in particular, the larger CBPP—for their energetic and "reasonable" involvement and the high quality of the reports they produced. The CBPP's staff members were described as "playing fair" and "completely trustworthy," and they were said to discuss the effects of policy proposals largely on their merits without resorting to heated rhetoric. The group also seemed to select its battles carefully, despite being faced with the broad array of programs up for revision; it determined that wholesale opposition was futile in the political environment of the mid-1990s. Instead, it concentrated on a limited number of top priorities, most of which were successful. These priorities included preservation of the entitlement to food stamps, preventing the block granting of Medicaid and cuts in immigrant programs, and requiring state maintenance-of-effort provisions. The organization focused in particular on protecting the EITC for low-income families from early proposals to make sharp cuts, according to the staff director of Ways and Means's human resources subcommittee and CBPP staff. That federal program was spared. The subcommittee staff director, a Republican, noted only half-jokingly that "if I could change any person in Washington, I would make Bob Greenstein [the CBPP's director] a conservative."

Other liberal advocacy and research groups also were intensely concerned about the welfare bill but took a more "purist" approach that kept them largely out of the inner sanctum, and even out of the anteroom. Republican committee staffers described the CDF, in particular, as having cut itself out of debate. Marian Wright Edelman, one-time Clinton friend and political ally, had founded and now directed the CDF, and she adamantly opposed welfare reform in strong language from the early days of HR 4. In a widely publicized "open letter to the president" that was published in the *Washington Post* and *New York Times* in November 1995, Edelman called the Senate and House bills "morally and practically indefensible" and dismissed the argument that welfare reform would help children by cutting the federal deficit as "the domestic equivalent of bombing Vietnamese villages in order to save them."[31]

Although the CDF's language reflected the views of many of the bills' opponents, the organization's approach alienated some of the participants on the Hill with the greatest influence. Many congressional Republicans working on welfare would have little to do with the group, despite the fact that it was no more liberal than the CBPP. Several participants did suggest that CDF staff influenced child support enforcement provisions, however (long an area of expertise for the organization). Participants in more research-oriented groups also pointed out that the nature of the organization—which relies at least somewhat on grassroots membership—required that it be able to mobilize its political base. Passionate language often is an effective way to do so. They also argued that

Republican criticism of the CDF was a bit unfair, given that conservatives had never been particularly eager to consult with the organization.

One participant in welfare reform, in fact, expressed the wish that the CDF had been more political and used its June 1996 "Stand for Children" as a rally to oppose the de-entitlement of cash assistance rather than maintaining an apolitical stance, as it did. It seemed that after harsh criticism of the group's earlier style of opposing welfare reform, it bent over backward to make the children's rally one that would appeal to potential sponsors and participants across the political spectrum.

Civil rights organizations were described as "in disarray" on the issue and were largely absent from the policymaking table, according to my interviews and analysis of hearing participation, despite their periodic appearance in the media opposing the Republican bills.

Nonprofit Service Providers and Charities

By and large, the community of nonprofit service providers and charities was in the same boat as most advocacy groups. Several were very active, including Catholic Charities USA and the CWL. Participants cited Catholic Charities and the USCC, in particular, as having access to key players and some influence on the final legislative product. Catholic Charities' chief lobbyist noted that although the organization was largely shut out of the debate in its beginning months, she had already established relationships with Republican policymakers; they had sometimes shared goals in other areas such as school prayer and government aid to religious schools. These relationships helped the group gain a hearing with conservative lawmakers by mid-1995, privately and in public hearings. The political clout of the Catholic Church also helped it to gain access with key political decisionmakers. Officials from the USCC and Catholic Charities met with Clinton, bringing along two bishops, to petition him to maintain the individual entitlement to cash assistance. The president was said to have side-stepped the issue, however, instead discussing only what they already agreed on.

The CWL was described as being in complete opposition to the bill, much like the CDF, and similarly was largely ignored by Republican staff. A coalition of Christian and Jewish groups called for a veto in late 1995, branding the bill "unholy legislation."[32] A group of liberal Protestant evangelicals (not all evangelicals were part of the Religious Right) staged a public protest in the Capitol rotunda in December 1995, which resulted in mass arrests but was largely ignored by policymakers.[33] Some religious service-providing organizations indicated support for Senator John Ashcroft's (R-MO) "charitable choice" amendment, which loosened constraints on federally funded religious service organizations, though opponents warned that it lowered the wall between church and state.

Nonprofit and charitable providers helped to moderate the direction of welfare legislation when their concerns were picked up by the media and threatened to generate a backlash of public opinion. The strong public response to the proposal to block grant the national school lunch and other child nutrition programs, for example, contributed to the House's decision to abandon the idea. Many nonprofit providers—religious and secular—were regarded by conservative policymakers, however, as beneficiaries of a "bankrupt federal welfare state" and lacked legitimacy among many of them.

Unions

Organized labor joined with other groups to publicly oppose the bill in its various incarnations, and AFSCME submitted testimony several times. It also was active in the Coalition on Human Needs. The union's top priorities were protecting low-wage unionized workers from displacement by recipients meeting the bill's work requirements and preserving the entitlement to assistance—in part to ensure that eligibility determination would be done by public employees, as required by federal law under AFDC. Not surprisingly, unions had little access to or influence with Republican staffers. Democratic members and staff listened to the concerns of labor, but that access was of limited use given the Republican majority and unity. In general, the private-sector unions considered welfare reform a public-sector issue, and unions at all levels were working full-time on issues of more immediate concern to their key constituents. Labor would be more effective in fighting off new legislation to encourage privatization of welfare services after PRWORA passed and in extending federal labor standards to workfare participants.[34]

Several committee and interest group staffers noted that the lack of established relationships between congressional Republicans and advocacy groups and organized labor had several effects. First, because Democrats had held power on the Hill for years, these groups had built relationships with the Democrats—who played a larger role in setting legislative priorities and drafting bills—rather than with their Republican counterparts. Obviously, most advocates had less access to the Republicans who now were making social policy. Second, because Republicans historically had tended to focus on issues other than social policy, even the pressure groups that had well-developed relationships with Republican congressional staffs tended not to be organizations that were concerned with welfare. One outgrowth of this fracturing of the welfare issue network linking advocates and legislative social policymakers was that those who now were in power had few obligations or political debts to these groups. This situation gave policymakers "incredible freedom," according to one staffer, enabling the truly radical change represented by the welfare bill, which was so different from the incremental approach typical of the legislative process.

It also was more difficult for these groups to fight off proposals to end the entitlement and block grant welfare when most of the nation's governors—Republican and Democratic—supported them so enthusiastically. As a staff member of one liberal group noted, "An important aspect of our strategy was to have some governors on our side, hopefully from both parties. We knew it would not be easy, but it was more than that. It didn't happen." Another participant commented that "the stars were aligned" for block grants.

This assessment is not intended to suggest, however, that advocates, nonprofit providers, and labor had no influence on the legislation. The final bill looked markedly different from the early proposals in part because of the efforts of many of these organizations, as well as some intergovernmental actors and others. As one advocacy group official commented, they were negotiating over a package of proposals, and to preserve or make gains in one area, they had to be willing to make concessions in other areas. Although loss of the entitlement to cash assistance was major and occurred early in the debate, they were able to help fend off the numerous other proposals such as block granting of Medicaid, food stamps, and child nutrition and welfare programs, as well as cuts to the EITC. They also influenced decisions to increase funding for child care, set state maintenance-of-effort requirements, and soften moral mandates such as the family cap.

States and Other Intergovernmental Actors[35]

Governors

One of the early questions in the politics of welfare reform was why state officials—governors in particular—and other intergovernmental actors were so enthusiastic about devolution and welfare reform. Whatever the short-run gains, the welfare bill threatened to saddle their states with mushrooming social costs in the long run. The administration's expanded waivers already were allowing most states to "experiment" widely with welfare under AFDC, even though the waiver process was widely regarded as unwieldy and time-consuming. Certainly, devolution represented a legitimate philosophy that would be expected to appeal in particular to governors, but initially it looked like block grants would mean less money, and it wasn't clear at that point how much caseloads would drop.

With the majority of the nation's governors now Republican and state legislatures moving swiftly in that direction, these officials clearly shared many of the ideological motivations of their partisan colleagues at the national level, as well as many of the same constituents. They also would be expected to show loyalty to the party, especially at the beginning of its new reign in Congress. Despite differences between moderates and conservatives, the party remained consistently "on message."

The structure of block grants also provided a short-term financial motivation to sign on to devolution because states could cut their welfare spending, even with the limits imposed by the 75–80 percent maintenance-of-effort requirements, which were expected to mitigate the temptation to "race to the bottom." This incentive intensified once the welfare rolls began to drop and the economy to improve. By 1995, welfare rolls had started to dip in most states, yet the block grants were based on peak caseload levels—sweetening the deal for states with welfare "windfalls." Although some participants in reform stress that the caseload declines were not yet readily apparent and wouldn't be until after Clinton signed the 1996 bill, others suggest that many state officials individually suspected that their states would fare well financially under block grants. The provision allowing states to transfer 30 percent of TANF funds to their federal social services or child care block grants also could free up previously earmarked state general revenue funds.

Many of the risks of devolution were longer term and would not come up for some time—until the five-year time limits hit large numbers of the hardest-to-employ recipients or a regional or national recession struck and reduced tax revenues at the same time the need for welfare grew. Some state officials seemed extraordinarily optimistic, expressing the belief that the problems of welfare recipients across the board could be solved in five years—or might simply disappear in the face of firm limits on aid. The payoffs, on the other hand, were immediate, bringing the chance to jump on the reform bandwagon and design innovative programs, the potential of financial windfalls, and the opportunity to claim political credit. Governors with national ambitions were particularly active in welfare reform. For most state politicians, the immediate benefits, political and financial, outweighed potential future costs.[36]

The nation's Republican governors were immensely influential in shaping the bill and were the most influential force outside Congress, according to key committee staffers and other participants. The NGA was beset with partisan dissent, however, and was largely absent from the negotiating table on many major provisions until early 1996. This absence contrasted with the essential unifying role the NGA had played in the FSA in 1988, when Democratic governor Clinton and Republican Castle of Delaware were the central representatives for the governors on welfare.

Although Democratic governors obviously did not respond to the Republican call for party unity, the former generally agreed with their now-majority Republican colleagues that the states should have more control over the delivery of welfare, had similar dislike for the waiver process, and in some cases itched to compete with other states in welfare innovation. Governors across party lines shared the belief that Washington too often imposed untenable constraints on the states, and this belief combined with the long-standing view that state officials knew better how to handle policy within their borders than did out-of-touch and often arrogant bureaucrats in the nation's capital. HHS waivers were insufficient to meet their demands. A spokesperson for Wisconsin governor Thompson, reflecting the prevalent tone, said, "No longer would we have to go to Washington and kiss somebody's ring," and noted that about two-thirds of Wisconsin's waiver requests to the federal government in recent years had been rejected.[37]

Democratic and Republican governors disagreed, however, on many of the details of the early welfare bills—especially the end to the national entitlement. Initially Democrats blocked the NGA from taking a stand supporting the block grant approach (the organization required a supermajority to take an official policy position), expressing particular concern over how the states would manage to fund welfare during a recession. Some Republican committee staff members also said that at the beginning of the session they didn't fully trust NGA staff members, many of whom had worked on social policy when Democrats were dominant. Although these NGA staffers were informed on the issues, Republican staffers on the Hill suspected them of excessive liberalism. Only with time were they brought back into the policymaking circle, though never the inner ring.

The Republican leadership and House committee members and staff largely avoided working with Democratic governors—individually or through the Democratic Governors' Association (DGA)—and instead negotiated closely with individual Republicans, especially Thompson, Engler, and the RGA. Thompson and Engler were described as "the most important players" and "fearless" in the political debate. Both led early and high-profile efforts at major welfare overhaul in their states and were believed to hold national political ambitions, and both enjoyed strong relationships with Chairman Clay Shaw of the Ways and Means subcommittee on human resources and his staff. To a lesser extent, Hill committee staffers also consulted with governors Weld of Massachusetts, Allen of Virginia, and Wilson of California.

The degree of involvement by this inside group of governors was called "unprecedented" in legislative social policymaking, with staff sending actual draft language to Thompson and Engler for review and feedback. One key staffer said "there were people [in their offices] I was on the phone with ten times a week." A small cadre composed of the Republican leadership, Republican governors, and committee leadership and staff framed the bill very quickly—largely between the RGA's strategy meeting in Williamsburg, Virginia, shortly after the November 1994 election, and early 1995 when Shaw introduced HR 4, the first welfare bill of the 104th Congress. Thereafter, this structure defined and constrained the agenda. Advocacy organizations played a role in essential details, but the Republican governors helped set the broad framework of the debate.[38]

Some governors outside the inner circle who were concerned about expenses the states would have to absorb criticized the 1995 legislation for a lack of adequate funding, the family cap, and restrictions on aid to teen mothers and especially legal immigrants. In fact, however, the governors helped resuscitate welfare reform in early 1996 after two presidential vetoes. By then, caseloads had been dropping for almost a year, and governors seemed to be realizing more widely that block grants could bring immediate windfalls rather than greater costs. This realization fostered agreement among them.

After Clinton announced that he would sign the welfare bill, Republican governors responded enthusiastically, though some criticized it for falling short on greater state flexibility. They warned about conservative micromanagement from Washington in the moral mandates, high work participation rates, requirements that states maintain dual eligibility systems for Medicaid and TANF (so that recipients who were still eligible for the health program but no longer eligible for cash assistance would not get cut off), and child support enforcement provisions. Governor Wilson said he was disappointed with the bill for failing to revise Medicaid or child protection provisions, but he labeled it an improvement nonetheless. Engler had threatened in the eleventh hour to denounce the bill right before it went to conference in July 1996, objecting to the dual TANF/Medicaid eligibility systems, but was dissuaded when the leadership added $500 million to cover increased state administrative costs for the provision. Governor George Voinovich of Ohio supported even greater devolution of control to the states but was enthusiastic that the bill "reformed" welfare and cut the budget deficit.[39] Ultimately, even the DGA supported the president's decision to sign the bill, despite its similarities to earlier Republican plans that had been developed almost solely in consultation with the RGA and individual governors.

State Welfare Directors

The American Public Welfare Association (APWA)—the association of the state welfare directors—also worked to shape the bill.[40] Typically, the NGA would draw the broad strokes of policy proposals, and the APWA, whose members work for the governors, would flesh out the details. The APWA initially was somewhat limited by a long-standing reputation for liberalism, according to some participants on the Hill. After 1994, however, the organization began moving rightward, becoming more cooperative with Republican goals, though it still was not among the most influential advisors. This shift was significantly related to Republican gains among the governors, who appoint state social service directors, as well as the intense involvement of Gerald H. Miller, Michigan's social services director. Miller served as APWA president and as Engler's point person on the national bill. Ways and Means staffers spoke with him almost daily on some provisions of the bill. He also gained publicity shortly after its passage by leaving the public sector to take a job as director of Lockheed-Martin's new welfare reform services division.

Nonetheless, according to the APWA's lead lobbyist on the issue, neither the APWA nor the NGA had seriously considered ending the entitlement status of welfare or block grants until Clinton got the ball rolling with his Work and Responsibility Act and its "two years and you work" pledge. Clinton's shift in orientation, she suggested, set the stage for the more radical Republican proposals to end the entitlement.

Certainly Miller and Jason Turner, Wisconsin's social services director (who later became New York City's human services commissioner), played central roles in shaping the plan. Staffers cited both as influential, though often behind the scenes. Miller appeared in hearings several times, for Michigan and for the APWA, but Turner never testified. Eloise Anderson of California also was cited as an important proponent of reform. Other state welfare directors were less sanguine about the pending changes, however: Shortly after the president signed PRWORA into law, some state officials began to express anxiety about their abilities to implement it.[41]

Among other contributions to negotiations over the welfare law, APWA staffers were widely credited with influencing members of Congress to drop the proposal to block grant child protection programs, which would have capped federal spending for the growing problem of child abuse and neglect.

State Legislatures

Before the 1994 election, Democrats maintained control of a plurality of state legislatures: 25 were Democratically controlled, 16 were split, and 8 were dominated by Republicans. After the election, however, Republican dominance reached the state legislatures as well: Only 18 were Democrat-controlled, 12 were split, and 19 were controlled by Republicans.[42] The National Conference of State Legislatures (NCSL) was divided in part because of the inevitable fragmentation of the institutions it represented, seven of which met only for several months every other year. Rapid changes in party representation among state legislatures also split members.

During the decades of Democratic congressional dominance, NCSL staff members were said to have concentrated on relationships with Democratic, not Republican Hill staffs. Although they were considered highly competent and were included in discussion, initially they remained outside the central group of policymakers, despite the increasingly important role state legislatures would play under devolution. By the summer of 1996, however, the NCSL was dominated by Republicans, and the organization sent a letter to President Clinton, encouraging him to sign HR 3734.

A top priority for the NCSL was the "Brown Amendment," which became Section 901 of the new welfare law and required state legislative appropriation of all TANF funds.[43] This provision ensured that the state legislatures, not just the governors, would be involved in formulating state welfare reform. In a note that would be amplified months later, however, the NCSL warned that the provisions cutting off legal noncitizens left states with a large financial burden if they chose to fund this support.[44] The legislatures also were concerned about child support enforcement provisions, which imposed more, not fewer, federal controls on the states. The NCSL's lobbyist noted that the organization also might have supported a reform bill that maintained the individual entitlement.

GOP party unity did not hold all the way down the political chain, however, and some Republican local officials opposed the bill. New York City

Mayor Rudolph W. Giuliani, in particular, lobbied hard against it, saying that it could sharply increase the city's costs. About one-seventh of New York's population received some type of public assistance in 1996, and many were immigrants. Guliani's stand put him markedly to the left of the nation's Democratic president and many Democratic legislators, although he soon became an enthusiast of efforts to get recipients off welfare and into jobs.[45] The nation's largest cities were disproportionately Democratic as the nation's population and political base moved increasingly to the Republican-leaning suburbs. Certainly the new Republican congressional majority did not count among its key constituents the residents of the nation's largest cities, many of whom are members of minority groups. The two Washington-based organizations that represented urban areas, the United States Conference of Mayors and the National League of Cities, both opposed the welfare bills. Neither group had much influence among Hill staff drafting the bill (one described the mayors as "out of it"), however, nor did they testify more than a couple times at hearings. One staffer suggested that lobbyists for the cities assumed they'd be ignored and made little effort, but other participants argued that Republican members and staffers in fact shut them out of the Hill debate.

Other intergovernmental groups and actors—including those representing the counties, tribes, and schools—also criticized specifics of the bill and argued that they needed to be consulted more about its financial and program ramifications.[46] The National Association of Counties (NACo) and the Council of State Governments (CSG) had little presence in the debate and little influence, however. Republican House staffers mentioned NACo as notably absent from the political debate, despite the fact that many states would further devolve responsibility for welfare policy-setting and administration to the counties. NACo was less Democratically dominated than the cities' organizations and might have been able to affect the debate; instead, however, the group largely followed the NGA, reportedly in part because of organizational in-fighting.

Some individual local welfare officials played a role in helping to shape the welfare bill, however, and committee staff members were in frequent contact with those whose perspectives and experiences were useful to the goals of the Republican-controlled welfare agenda. The director of Riverside County, California, social services appeared in hearings several times, and was consulted by staff. Riverside was the site of an early pilot project that used the "work first" model now finding favor.

Experts and Research Organizations

A small number of research organizations and experts were somewhat influential in the welfare debate. By and large, however, in the mid-1990s the results of research had little impact on the broad agenda or legislative detail unless it supported policymakers' established positions. Several people noted that whereas the FSA clearly was informed by research, such research was largely irrelevant to PRWORA. One key staffer, however, cited the MDRC as a "completely honest" organization with reliable data that helped shape the bill. Its representatives testified frequently at welfare hearings. The Urban Institute, which participated in hearings a couple of times, was regarded by some conservatives as overly liberal in orientation. Other participants suggested that it had influence with the White House instead.

Otherwise, few individual researchers or experts were considered particularly active or effective. Charles Murray, author of *Losing Ground*, did not get involved in lawmaking and had little direct impact on the specifics of the welfare legislation. Several participants, however, credited his book with helping to shift the direction of the welfare debate toward the right since the mid-1980s, reflecting and reinforcing widely held ideas about the disincentive effects of the structure of AFDC.

One researcher/advocate suggested that research really couldn't offer much to the discussion of the radical changes Congress was debating in 1995 and 1996. Research could be useful in informing incremental reform, such as the FSA, because existing work analyzed the results of similar, if smaller-scale, efforts. However, no one had really studied the effects of hard time limits, de-entitlement of cash assistance, or block granting because nothing like them had been attempted in recent history.

Think Tanks

Among think tanks, the Heritage Foundation was the most effective and certainly the most active, in hearings and behind the scenes.[47] Robert Rector was in constant contact with policymakers and staffers, consistent with the frequency with which he participated in hearings. Rector was described by one central player as "the single most important outside person" in shaping the bill, "very smart," and a "true conservative [who] never deviates." Others also said that much of his effectiveness lay in his consistency, his energy, his apparent willingness to be unpopular, and his character as a "true believer."[48]

Part of Rector's power also came from the fact that he was one of only a handful of truly conservative "intellectuals" who focused on welfare issues. He knew how to harness data to make his case with intuitive appeal and the strong appearance of validity. Where Democrats could call on a large number of social policy scholars, Republicans' strengths typically had been in economic and other areas. Once they turned toward social policy, Rector moved in quickly to fill the vacuum, providing conservative policymakers with data and interpretations they needed to support their policy goals. This also meant that when there was a need to balance testimony by liberal or centrist experts, Rector was eager and available to provide a more conservative perspective.

Rector worked closely with the family values groups, which often lined up behind him. They, in turn, were able to activate strong grassroots support, which most of the advocacy groups lacked. This alliance gave the family values groups the ability to make their displeasure felt in congressional offices through phone calls and letters if Rector's demands were ignored, including his demands to testify. He was reported to have the ability to make policymakers "miserable" if they did not at least give him a voice on issues he cared about. As the interest group literature notes, the most active groups often are the most extreme, and Rector was said to speak forcefully for traditional values groups that attended to the issue of welfare.

Rector was willing to play hardball. "He carries a threat," said one participant; "he's one of those few people who's willing to say bad things about people publicly." Rector also had strong relationships with the House Republican leadership, especially Majority Leader Richard Armey, and was close to Governor Thompson's welfare chief, who could echo Rector's concerns through the governor. This coherence and "interconnection of outside forces" helped Rector shape the welfare bill. Provisions within the bill to promote abstinence education were said to be "95 percent his," as was a bonus for states that reduce out-of-wedlock birth rates. He also was very influential on the work requirements. Rector's sometimes-harsh approach alienated several influential policymakers, especially moderates. Nonetheless, few actors matched his intensity or effectiveness.[49]

The lobbyist for one Catholic organization commented that Rector and others in the traditional values community who were most concerned with illegitimacy "thought that welfare caused sex; if there was no welfare, then no sex. . . . We're a 2,000-year-old organization," she noted somewhat facetiously, "and we've been trying to stop sex for a long time, and it hasn't worked." Rector, however—like Charles Murray—regarded out-of-wedlock births as the source of most social problems and welfare as the cause of out-of-wedlock births.

Scholars associated with the American Enterprise Institute (AEI) testified at several hearings, and AEI generally was considered more moderate and less ideological than Heritage. Several participants cited AEI's experts, particularly Douglas Besharov, as somewhat influential, as were people associated with the Cato Institute. The Progressive Policy Institute (PPI)—the think tank of the centrist Democratic Leadership Council (DLC)—influenced the decision to give states "performance bonuses" and the idea of "second chance" group homes for teen mothers, although it was not especially active in hearings. The PPI provided policy proposals to support the DLC's advocacy of welfare reform. The DLC supported Clinton's endorsement of HR 3734, praising him for returning to his New Democrat roots. Bruce Reed, one of the major White House reform architects, had been the domestic policy director of the DLC.[50]

Conservative "Traditional Values" Groups

A core group of traditional values organizations were said to be one of Rector's biggest resources, giving his ideas a grassroots base. Among Rector's "foot soldiers" on welfare were the Christian Coalition, the Family Research Council, Concerned Women of America, and the Eagle Forum, among others. Not surprisingly, they advocated a tough approach toward welfare, including stringent work requirements and lower benefits. One conservative staffer called these groups helpful in providing public support for Republican proposals. Several fathers' rights groups joined them, largely in favor of policies to shore up the traditional family structure.

The traditional values groups differed sharply from most Jewish and Catholic organizations, as well as liberal evangelicals, who themselves provided services for low-income families and typically advocated more generous programs for poor people, even if they sometimes took a tough anti-abortion stance. Christian Right groups generally advocated more restrictive benefits for poor families, with strong moral mandates—particularly anti-illegitimacy measures such as the family cap (even at the risk of increasing abortion rates). The usually conservative National Right-to-Life Committee was praised by one participant for being "very gutsy" in standing up to the Family Research Council and others to oppose the cap for fear it would increase abortions.

For-Profit Contractors and Business and Trade Associations

For-profit service providers were said to have little explicit part in trying to influence the bill. Some, such as America Works and Electronic Data Systems (EDS), had representatives who testified at congressional hearings. According to Republican Hill staffers, however, they played little direct role behind the scenes. Other interviewees, however, suggested that they had more influence behind closed doors than conservative policymakers were willing to admit. One representative of a large charitable organization noted that a lobbyist for Lockheed-Martin whom she knew personally was at all the welfare hearings, "presumably for a reason," though he did not testify. She noted the change in the numbers and types of people attending to the welfare debate, however, suggesting a growing presence by businesses seeing new opportunities: "I've been doing this for 20 years, going to mark-up [sessions]. I knew everyone there. There was never any danger of not getting in. Suddenly, there were all these people in nice suits that I'd never seen before, and a line out the door."

Business-oriented interest groups generally followed the bill and supported the final version. The United States Chamber of Commerce submitted testimony and publicly praised the president and the bill's support for "America's work ethic."[51] The National Federation of Independent Businesses (NFIB) and other business groups expressed concern that the legislation's stringent child-support enforcement provisions, including employer withholding requirements, might burden businesses. For-profit child support collection firms and day care providers also testified. On the whole, however, business groups played little significant direct role in shaping the legislation, despite its emphasis on moving welfare recipients into private-sector jobs. They were broadly supportive of its direction, which they found congenial for partisan and ideological reasons, and they attempted to stay abreast of negotiations about it, but otherwise they invested their resources elsewhere. One staffer involved in the welfare-to-work provisions commented that business and trade organizations would save their political "chits" for issues that really mattered to them. With welfare going in a conservative direction, they didn't need to get very involved.

Other Actors

Individual citizens—some presumably sent to testify by organizations that were not identified—provided about 10 percent of hearing testimony, but they had little effect on policy, according to congressional staffers and other participants. Professional associations that represent practitioners, including nonprofit practitioners, also were weak. The National Association of Social Workers (NASW) offered testimony but was cited by no one as particularly active in other ways, nor as effective.

Finally, members of the media obviously would not appear in hearings witness lists, nor would they petition committee staffers, except for information. By most definitions, they are not themselves a pressure group. They had an indirect role in the welfare debate nonetheless. They widely reported on Democratic charges that Republican lawmakers were proposing to cut essential programs for children to fund a tax cut for the wealthy (see chapter 2). Not surprisingly, conservative policymakers regarded the press as having a liberal slant, echoing advocates' charges of mean-spiritedness; they cited the enormous publicity given to the proposal to block grant the school lunch program as especially unfair. The media typically gave time to proponents of welfare reform as well, however. Moreover, early stories about dysfunctional, welfare-reliant families—such as the 1994 *Washington Post* series on the extended family of Rosa Lee Cunningham—in fact gave life to the conservative argument about welfare's degenerative effects.[52]

Major news outlets did provide an important tool for advocacy groups and others now outside the inner circle, however, allowing them to "go public" to appeal to public opinion—which, in turn, could put pressure on the lawmakers they themselves had difficulty reaching. The major papers, at least, kept the progress of welfare reform highly visible and allowed a large number of people to follow the details of the debate. Many major newspapers, in particular the *New York Times* and the *Washington Post*, reported on welfare reform closely and consistently. Several strongly opposed the final bill.[53]

CONCLUSION

Certainly no policy area is determined by interest groups alone, especially an area as fraught with symbolism as welfare reform. The 1994 congressional elections had a dramatic effect on the shape of welfare reform and the composition of the Washington welfare policy domain. National welfare policy during the 104th Congress took a radical new direction, reversing a decades-long trend toward centralization, with the more highly politicized House acting as the catalyst. It moved with unusual momentum, particularly in light of the congressional tradition of incremental politics. One participant who had worked in Congress and within the administration suggested that the 1994 elections had provided a unique window of opportunity for change of this magnitude—that it would not have been possible even during the somewhat more moderate 105th Congress. Whether the 104th Congress provided a one-time policy window or not, the confluence of forces—Kingdon's "streams"—certainly was essential. In the face of these changes, the effect of the national interest groups that were active on the broad agenda was constrained unless they further justified the radical shift already under way, as did the Republican governors and the socially conservative organizations. Ideology, ideas, and partisan interests significantly set the overall parameters and drove the bill.

The essential details of the final bill were fundamentally affected, however, by the work of a broad range of "factions" in the nation's capital. Furthermore, the debate in Washington saw the continued presence, activity, and influence of a sizeable community of organizations that reasonably could be said to represent low-income families.

A large number of different organizations—310 of them—participated in the welfare debate in 1995 and 1996, as defined by hearing testimony. They ranged widely across the political spectrum, from the CDF on the left to the Christian Coalition and the Heritage Foundation on the right. Although few direct representatives of low-income families were in evidence, about half of the participants—advocates, nonprofit providers, organized labor and researchers—generally were in favor of more- rather than less-expansive programs for poor people. In the previous thirty years, these organizations (of which there were more than 100) had become fairly effective representatives in Washington of the interests of low-income people. Along with the Democratically controlled Congress and the federal social services bureaucracy, these organizations had formed a fairly stable welfare policy issue network over the previous few decades. Its members typically preferred more rather than less federal spending on social programs and federal oversight of state administration.

The elections in November 1994 disrupted these policymaking relationships but, I argue, did not destroy them. Advocacy groups and others attempted to participate in the newly defined welfare debate, and some were successful with certain key priorities. Initially, they were stunned by the speed of the change and the sheer breadth of the programs under attack. Many were simply excluded. They also were in the difficult position of appearing to defend "the status quo"—a public assistance system that was widely regarded as deeply flawed, even by welfare recipients themselves.

The broad outlines of the new approach to welfare already had been framed by the small and highly focused "inner council" composed of the Republican leadership, especially in the House; Republican committee chairs; staffers; conservative think tanks and pressure groups; and the newly powerful Republican governors and their welfare directors. This group was beholden to virtually none of the actors who had been part of the old welfare network. One Republican legislative staffer described the process leading up to the new welfare law:

> This bill was different. Usually you gather pieces from various groups and put together a bill from their input. Here, the bill came first and then groups would react, and you would see how much of the bill you could keep and what you had to give on to still keep your vote together. This was the usefulness of the governors and the welfare directors—they provided a rationale, a justification for what we'd done.

Conservative researchers also provided a justification in the new welfare era. The difference between the liberal and conservative framings of welfare policy was dramatic, and those now in power had little motivation to allow groups who represented the "bankrupt federal welfare state" to help set the agenda. One well-known conservative intellectual summed up the hostility to "the status quo," declaring "liberalism is not only wrong, but cruel."[54]

The furious pace of change left advocates reeling—first simply trying to grasp its magnitude and second trying to protect in some way the multitude of social programs that suddenly were up for fundamental overhaul. They also had to try to establish relationships with a whole new cast of policymakers who held very different perspectives from their own. Even when they recovered from the shock of the Republican victory, some underestimated the seriousness of the threat, unable to believe that a Democratic president actually would sign legislation to end this fundamental part of the Social Security

Act. Many advocates also felt they received little support from politicians or from a public that wanted reform but was largely disinterested in policy details and indifferent and/or hostile to the welfare poor. Initiatives such as the Istook Amendment further distracted them.

Initially, the new Republican majority had little motivation to listen to left-leaning advocates. Republican policymakers didn't have to deal with the myriad demands made by the liberal interest groups that so often slowed the pace of congressional policymaking under the Democrats, sometimes to a standstill. This freedom also exposed them to risks, however. Republican members of Congress, especially conservatives, typically had not been involved in social policy, and they and their staffs possessed less expertise on welfare issues than did their Democratic counterparts. Without their own expertise or that provided by interest groups they trusted, the new majority was in danger of making policy mistakes. Several conservative and moderate participants acknowledged the dangers of moving rapidly into a new and complex policy area without substantial analysis.

Over time, several advocates gained access to the welfare negotiating table. The most successful seemed to be those who relatively quickly accepted the fact that radical change had become inevitable, even if they never supported it. They concentrated on a handful of top priorities, rather than opposing the changes wholesale. Those who had reputations for conducting high-quality analysis, such as the CBPP and CLASP, were reported to be most effective. Among other things, they helped to fill the expertise vacuum the new majority faced (on the other end of the spectrum, the Heritage Foundation and the Family Research Council also were said to provide analytical assistance to the most conservative members). These liberal groups dealt with their political opponents with civility and had something useful to offer them, essentially earning themselves a place at the table.[55] Some large direct-service groups such as Catholic Charities USA also were said to exert influence.

These organizations could not shake the framework that had been established—de-entitlement, block grants, and devolution of welfare apparently were nonnegotiable—but they played an essential role in damage control, limiting cutbacks, and making certain conservative provisions optional rather than mandatory for the states. The bill that passed undoubtedly was far different than it would have been in their absence. With the exception of work participation requirements—which were increased in part by the "bidding war" between congressional Democrats and Republicans—and some food stamp cuts, it was notably less radical than the original House proposals and included more money for child care. Republican policymakers themselves cited an array of cuts and other constraints on programs for low-income people that didn't occur as a result of these groups' active lobbying.

In short, the welfare debate in the national political arena was marked by the participation of a wide variety of organizations and a large number of groups that reasonably could be said to represent poor families. Poor people themselves have long been largely absent from political participation, and this absence seems to be even more pronounced as methods of politics become more professionalized and expensive. In recent decades, however, the growing community of advocacy and related groups in Washington has provided low-income families with fairly vigorous representation in legislative politics. Although the speed of welfare policy overhaul after the 1994 election left many of these groups out of the decision-making process, at least initially, over time they regained some influence. Others were able to add their perspectives to the debate almost from the beginning of the 104th Congress. They measured their success largely in terms of their ability to limit losses rather than to make new gains for low-income families. These successes were significant, however. These organizations effectively opposed the block granting of the Medicaid, child welfare, child nutrition, housing, and food stamps programs; successfully fought cuts to the EITC; and pushed for maintenance-of-effort requirements for state funding. They also moderated some of the moral mandates. Without the presence and activity of advocates and other representatives of low-income families in Washington, the changes in the 1996 welfare bill undoubtedly would have been even greater.

NOTES

1. Weaver, *Ending Welfare As We Know It*, 218.

2. Others have addressed definitional issues more closely. See Kay Lehman Schlozman and John T. Tierney, *Organized Interests and American Democracy* (New York: Harper and Row, 1986); Jeffrey M. Berry, *The Interest Group Society* (Boston: Little, Brown and Co., 1984), 4–8; and Mark P. Petracca, "The Rediscovery of Interest Groups Politics," in *The Politics of Interests* (Boulder, Colo.:Westview Press, 1992), 5–7. Some actors were asked to testify at welfare hearings because of their expertise and tried to maintain an apolitical posture. Others, such as the Heritage Foundation, have 501(c)(3) tax status and are legally prohibited from lobbying.

3. See Schlozman and Tierney, *Organized Interests and American Democracy*, chapter 7, for an excellent exploration of the range and types of approaches interest groups use. Kevin W. Hula's *Lobbying Together: Interest Group Coalitions in Legislative Politics* (Washington, D.C.: Georgetown University Press, 1999) provides a full discussion of the growing use of coalitions. See also Allan J. Cigler and Burdett A. Loomis, *Interest Group Politics*, 5th ed. (Washington, D.C.: CQ Press, 1998); Berry, *The Interest Group Society*; and Petracca, "The Rediscovery of Interest Group Politics," among others.

4. Obviously, the issue of who represents the "true" interests of poor people is debatable and was one of the more contentious ideological issues of the national welfare debate. This study defines traditional advocacy groups, nonprofit and charitable

providers, researchers, and labor organizations as largely representing the concerns of poor families. There is some fuzziness in these categories, of course. Moreover, some conservatives challenged a "poverty industry" that was said to be acting more in its own interests than in the interests of poor people.

5. As I discuss in chapter 1, this excessive optimism probably is the greatest weakness in Madison's theory.

6. E. E. Schattschneider, *The Semi-Sovereign People* (Hinsdale, Ill.: Dryden Press, 1975), 34. See also Sidney Verba, Kay Lehman Schlozman, and Henry Brady, "The Big Tilt: Participatory Inequality in America," *The American Prospect*, May–June 1997; Jack L. Walker, "The Origins and Maintenance of Interest Groups in America," *American Political Science Review* 77 (June 1983), 390–405; Berry, *The Interest Group Society*; Schlozman and Tierney, *Organized Interests and American Democracy*.

7. Paul E. Peterson and J. David Greenstone, "Racial Change and Citizen Participation: The Mobilization of Low-Income Communities through Community Action," in *A Decade of Federal Anti-Poverty Programs*, ed. Robert H. Haveman (New York: Academic Press, 1977), 269–74.

8. See Piven and Cloward, *Poor People's Movements*, chapter 5, for an account of the NWRO and other welfare rights organizations.

9. See also Piven and Cloward, *Poor People's Movements*, and Jeffrey M. Berry, *Feeding Hungry People* (New Brunswick, N.J.: Rutgers University Press, 1984), on the difficulties of organization by low-income citizens.

10. Schlozman and Tierney, *Organized Interests and American Democracy*, 130–31.

11. Economist Robert Inman, among others, has explored the ways in which antipoverty policy is a "public good" and the broad negative "spillover effects" of poverty (Johns Hopkins Lecture, January 1997).

12. See Berry, *Feeding Hungry People*, and Piven and Cloward, *Poor People's Movements*, for aspects of this movement.

13. Douglas R. Imig, *Poverty and Power: The Political Representation of Poor Americans* (Lincoln: University of Nebraska Press, 1996), 41.

14. The concept of the "iron triangle" generally is considered a bit too simple. John P. Heinz et al., *The Hollow Core: Private Interests in National Policy Making* (Cambridge, Mass.: Harvard University Press, 1993), describe policy domains; Hugh Heclo, "Issue Networks and the Executive Establishments," in *The New American Political System*, ed. Anthony S. King (Washington, D.C.: American Enterprise Institute, 1978), suggests a web of issue-related actors, which he calls "issue networks."

15. Schlozman and Tierney, *Organized Interests and American Democracy*, 150; author's interviews with legislative and interest group staff.

16. See Walker, "The Origins and Maintenance of Interest Groups in America," 395, on patrons and the growth of citizen and nonprofit groups since the 1960s; Berry, *Feeding Hungry People*; and Andrew S. McFarland, "Interest Groups and the Policymaking Process: Sources and Countervailing Power in America," in *The Politics of Interests*, ed. Mark P. Petracca (Boulder, Colo.: Westview Press, 1992). See also Weaver, *Ending Welfare As We Know It*, chapter 8.

17. Schlozman and Tierney, *Organized Interests and American Democracy*, 399–401.

18. Ibid., 399.

19. See Margaret Weir, "Political Parties and Social Policymaking," in *The Social Divide* on changes in the parties and their tactics.

20. Mancur Olson, Jr., *The Logic of Collective Action* (Cambridge, Mass.: Harvard University Press, 1965); Schattschneider, *The Semi-Sovereign People*, chapter 2.

21. See Hula, *Lobbying Together*, for members' motivations in creating and maintaining coalitions and their increased activity in Washington politics.

22. See Schlozman and Tierney, *Organized Interests and American Democracy*, 31; also Jane Fritsch, "Sometimes, Lobbyists Strive to Keep Public in the Dark," *New York Times*, 19 March 1996, A1, for an example in the context of product litigation.

23. See Cathy M. Johnson, "Who Speaks for the Children: Representation in the Policy Process," paper presented at American Political Science Association annual meeting, Washington, D.C., September 1994.

24. Some conservatives argued that traditional values organizations and right-leaning think tanks such as the Heritage Foundation were advocating more effectively for the true interests of low-income families.

25. Within the broad category, child advocacy organizations were most prevalent and slightly more active (64 groups participated 85 times), followed by nonprofit service providers (43 participated 56 times). Five unions participated 7 times in welfare-related hearings.

26. Tamar Lewin, "Liberal Urging Has Given Way to Eerie Hush," *New York Times*, 24 November 1995, A1; interviews.

27. Ibid. Some also did not wholeheartedly oppose welfare reform, even though they had misgivings about the details of the legislation.

28. Ibid.

29. Ibid. See also Imig, *Poverty and Power*, on the effects of Reagan-era cuts on advocates and nonprofit providers.

30. John E. Yang, "Plan Limiting Nonprofits Is Labeled 'Extreme,'" *Washington Post*, 29 September 1995, A4.

31. Marian Wright Edelman, "Say No to This Welfare 'Reform,'" *Washington Post*, 3 November 1995, A23. Dana Milbank, "Children's Defense Fund and Its Lauded Leader Lose Clout as Social Policy Shifts to the States," *Wall Street Journal*, 28 May 1996, A28.

32. Peter Steinfels, "Christian and Jewish Groups Call for Veto of Welfare Bill," *New York Times*, 10 November 1995, A27.

33. Francis X. Clines, "Christians against Welfare Cuts Are Arrested in Capitol," *New York Times*, 8 December 1995, B15.

34. Interviews; Weaver, *Ending Welfare As We Know It*, 205.

35. For an early analysis of the role of the intergovernmental lobby, see Donald H. Haider, *When Governments Come to Washington* (New York: Free Press, 1974), and, more recently, Anne Marie Cammisa, *Governments as Interest Groups* (Westport, Conn.: Praeger Publishers, 1995).

36. See Weaver's discussion of politicians' choices and opportunities in welfare politics, including credit claiming and blame avoidance, in chapter 3 of *Ending Welfare As We Know It*; interviews.

37. He did not, however, note what the rejected waivers were for or why they had been rejected. Dirk Johnson, "Wisconsin: Big Cuts Already, and More Ahead," *New York Times*, 21 September 1995; B10.

38. Interviews; Balz and Brownstein, *Storming the Gates*, 284–87.

39. Dirk Johnson, "The Governors: Republicans Endorse Turning Welfare Over to the States," *New York Times*, 1 August 1996, A23.

40. The organization is now called the American Public Human Services Association (APHSA).

41. Peter T. Kilborn, "With Welfare Overhaul Now Law, States Grapple with the Consequences," *New York Times*, 23 August 1996, A22.

42. National Conference of State Legislatures, "Partisan Control of State Legislatures, 1938–2000," available at www.ncsl.org/programs/legman/elect/hstptyct.htm.

43. *1996 Green Book*, 1395; interviews with NCSL staff.

44. Johnson, "Republicans Endorse Turning Welfare Over to the States."

45. David Firestone, "New York Area Sees Huge Costs in Welfare Bill," *New York Times*, 1 August 1996, A1, and "For Giuliani, Move to Left: Welfare Goals Put Him Beyond Clinton's Stand," *New York Times*, 5 August 1996, B1.

46. Kilborn, "States Grapple with Consequences."

47. See Nicholas Lemann, "Citizen 501(c)(3)," *The Atlantic Monthly* (February 1997), on the growing tendency of Heritage and other foundations on the right and the left to engage in explicit political activity, despite the prohibitions of their tax status.

48. Interview; Hilary Stout, ""Behind the Scenes: GOP's Welfare Stance Owes a Lot to Prodding from Rector," *Wall Street Journal*, 23 January 1995, A1.

49. Balz and Brownstein, *Storming the Gates*; interviews.

50. Jerry Gray, "The Liberals: Amid Praise, a Peppering of Criticism and Dismay," *New York Times*, 1 August 1996, A24; interviews.

51. Gray, "The Liberals."

52. Weaver, *Ending Welfare As We Know It*, 135–36.

53. "A Sad Day for Poor Children," *New York Times*, 1 August 1996, A26; "Whose Welfare?" *Washington Post*, 31 July 1996, A26; "Welfare Bills Suffer from Politics," *Atlanta Constitution*, 28 July 1996, R4.

54. William Bennett, quoted in Balz and Brownstein, *Storming the Gates*, 271.

55. One highly respected researcher/advocate took issue with the idea that his organization had filled any "expertise vacuum," suggesting instead that with such radical reform there was less room for expertise and that the new majority basically had what it needed. The House Ways and Means human resources subcommittee staff director, however, credited him and others with providing reliable and useful analysis. Another influential advocacy participant gave credence to the idea that they filled an expertise breach and noted that they also sometimes assisted Democratic committee members who had lost staff when they went from the majority to the minority.

Part II

State Welfare Politics

Welfare Politics in the States: An Introduction

With the 1996 federal welfare bill transferring most welfare policy-making from Washington to the states, the question remained whether low-income people would have a significant voice in the policy-making processes of the fifty state capitals. The neo-Madisonians' work suggests that the range of actors involved in state politics would be markedly narrower than in Washington and that effective representatives of poor people and other disadvantaged groups would be harder to find in the states and localities. Part II examines whether these concerns appeared to be warranted in the devolution of welfare policy in the 1990s.

Many states already had started welfare reform through waivers before 1995. Others, seeing federal welfare reform in the offing, began to develop reform proposals in anticipation of action in Washington. Despite the notice that welfare policy was beginning to get, policymaking within the states generally received far less attention than that on the national level. Since the 1960s, scholarly and popular attention had shifted away from the states as policymaking and financing centralized in Washington. For a time, some students of federalism were even predicting that the states would become a political anachronism and eventually would wither away. This prediction, of course, has not been borne out.

Scholars who study federalism generally agree that much has changed in the states since the period before the Social Security Act of 1935 or the more recent era of "states' rights" in the 1950s, when the southern states used arguments about their sovereignty to defend their systems of racial inequality. The trend toward greater federal activism, particularly in civil rights enforcement, as well as the Supreme Court's reapportionment decisions in the early 1960s, have helped to compel or enable state political institutions to become more representative, professional, and competent. State legislatures now are more representative of urban areas, less dominated by rural residents and a small handful of powerful interests, and less prone to "the politics of friends and neighbors," to borrow V. O. Key's phrase. They also have become more racially representative.[1]

Where, exactly, did these changes leave the states in the 1990s, however, and how prepared were they to take over the design of programs for low-income families? Had the limitations that led to "federalization" of government functions in the first place disappeared? What are the characteristics of the states and their governmental institutions today? And what might be the implications for welfare policymaking?

STATE FISCAL CAPACITY

Remarkably absent from the national welfare debate and its praise of states as "laboratories of democracy" was the simple fact that some of these laboratories are much better equipped than others. Some states are poor and others are wealthy; despite recent improvements, this fact can limit the reform options of poorer states such as Mississippi, West Virginia, and Arkansas. States also are vulnerable to regional economic ups and downs that affect the number of people who need assistance and the amount of revenues the states can raise. The double-edged sword of balanced-budget requirements that are common in the states means that in tight economic times, when states may most need to borrow, they are unable to do so. We have lamented the federal government's tendency to run a deficit, but during recessions, when tax revenues are stagnant or dropping, this borrowing ability can make the difference between being able to fund programs for residents facing hard times and not being able to help them.

Two of the most important factors related to assigning greater fiscal and policy responsibility to the states are their individual capacities to raise revenue—or their wealth—and the political decisions they make about what to do with the capacities they have, or their will to draw public income from that wealth. The now-defunct Advisory Commission on Intergovernmental Relations (ACIR) developed an index for gauging these two factors and comparing states to each other, with a benchmark of 100 as the average for all states.[2] Obviously we can make judgments about the political influences behind the choice of types of taxes and their relative virtues in terms of equity and efficiency, but the ACIR steered clear of these questions.

The outcomes of the final survey, published in 1993, though somewhat dated, highlight the wide discrepancies in state capacity and financing decisions.[3] The top five states in capacity were Alaska (178), Hawaii (146), Wyoming (134), Connecticut (130), and Nevada (128). The bottom five were

Mississippi (68), West Virginia (77), Arkansas (78), Alabama (81), and Idaho (82). The top five jurisdictions in tax *effort* were the District of Columbia (157), New York (156), Alaska (119), Wisconsin (118), and Rhode Island (115). The bottom five were Nevada (73), Montana (78), Delaware (80), Alabama (81), and Wyoming (81). Each of the bottom five states in effort had chosen either not to have a general sales tax or not to have an individual income tax. Twelve states (including Nevada and Wyoming) had high capacity but low effort.[4]

Some of these states' economic circumstances have changed since the early 1990s, but these data illustrate the underlying fact that states have different fiscal capacities and different political interest in exploiting them. Despite formula adjustments that Congress made in apportioning the TANF block grants to compensate low-income states with high population growth, as well as the maintenance-of-effort requirements, over time these discrepancies are likely to be exacerbated again. The old federal matching system of AFDC had helped even them out by giving more federal money per dollar of welfare spending to poor states, but block grant amounts are fixed. In the long run, we may get wonderful models out of the laboratories of some innovative and wealthy states. At the same time, however, we may get meager results from those that lack the financial resources or the political willingness to raise state revenues for the purpose of aiding low-income families.

The theory of interjurisdictional economic competition suggests that states with the lowest fiscal capacity are likely to feel the greatest pressure to keep taxes and programs for low-income people to a minimum, as a way to attract business to the state. Certainly interstate competition was not the only thing motivating state policymakers, but it seemed to influence economic and social policymaking in important ways. In 1996, one news report noted that the state of Alabama spent at least $150,000 per job in tax abatements and infrastructure improvements to lure a Mercedes Benz plant into the state. The same year, Alabama provided a maximum of $164 per month, or $1,968 per year, to a family of three on welfare. It was not the only poor state with very low welfare benefits to use generous financial incentives to attract new industry.[5]

STATE POLITICAL CHARACTERISTICS AND INSTITUTIONS

Several decades ago, McConnell, Schattschneider, and Key, among others, raised concerns about a relative lack of political capacity and meager representation of economically and socially disadvantaged people within many states. This situation was most egregious in the case of black Americans in the South. The states have changed markedly and today have much-improved political capacities and practices of representation. However, notable differences remain in their political cultures, histories, institutions, and practices.

Political Culture and Ideology

Despite changes in information technology, transportation, and other developments that have made our nation seem smaller and more homogenous, the states' political cultures still appear to vary significantly. Daniel Elazar, in his classic work on federalism, *American Federalism: A View from the States*, identified three state political subcultures, which he defined as individualistic, moralistic, and traditional. These categories were not pure and simple, of course, and many states reflected more than one orientation, but they described general tendencies.[6]

The "individualist" states, Elazar proposed, stress the market and material motivations for politicians and bureaucrats to serve. These states stretch roughly from Massachusetts, Rhode Island, and New York in the east out to Illinois, Nebraska, Wyoming, and Nevada. In contrast, Elazar's "moralist" subculture emphasizes the commonwealth and regards furthering a general sense of the public interest as government's responsibility. In this subculture, politics are issue-oriented and of concern to all citizens. Bureaucracy is viewed favorably, and corruption is not tolerated. These tendencies predominate in northern New England, he suggests, as well as in much of the northern Midwest to the Pacific Northwest and down to California. Finally, in Elazar's "traditional" subculture, the main purpose of government is to maintain the existing social and economic hierarchy; political activity is the domain of the elite. Bureaucracy is regarded as interfering with prevalent informal political relationships and therefore is suspect. These attitudes tend to predominate in the South, stretching out to Texas, New Mexico, and Arizona. These generalities obviously can be overdrawn, and they are weakening as information and transportation technology increase interstate mobility.

Other scholars have questioned, refined, and updated Elazar's framework—including Rodney E. Hero, who argues that racial/ethnic diversity among the states has greater impact on their varying ideologies, politics, and policies, which Elazar's model largely misses.[7] The concept of regional political culture and Elazar's general categories still seem to hold a surprising degree of accuracy, however, in describing political perspectives and practices, individual attitudes, and policy outcomes in the states, including decisions about policies for low-income people.[8]

State Legislatures and the Parties

Among state political institutions, legislatures in particular were long considered political backwaters. With the increase in power that the federal welfare bill granted to the states, the extent to which this assessment remains true becomes a renewed concern. By the 1990s, most states had made marked improvements in their institutional capacities. The legislatures of many states, especially large ones, were highly professionalized and competent. California, New York, and Illinois, among others, had full-time, well-paid legislatures that met year round. Alan Rosenthal's *The Decline of Representative Democracy* depicts dedicated and hard-working elected officials struggling to govern but limited by growing public demands and mistrust of representative democracy.[9]

According to one 1999 assessment, however, the political characteristics of state legislatures were still uneven. Nine states had full-time legislatures with sizable salaries and staffs; sixteen still had "citizen" legislatures that were part-time, had small staffs, and were paid minimal amounts; and twenty-five were a hybrid. As of 1999, eighteen states also had legislative term limits. Some scholars argue that by spurring legislative turnover, such limits pass greater power to interest groups that have the staff and resources to develop lasting substantive expertise that short-term lawmakers lack and give greater influence to legislative staffs and the executive branch. Term limits also make it harder for legislators to learn about and address complex issues.[10] In addition, seven legislatures met only every other year in biennial sessions, contributing to legislators' difficulty in developing expertise.[11]

By the late 1990s, the political parties had grown more competitive in state legislatures, especially in the South. Between 1976 and 1996, Democratic legislative dominance faded, particularly in the South, though the share of Democratic seats in state legislatures nationwide remained over 50 percent. There was general agreement, however, that the parties as a whole had weakened considerably throughout the states, signaling the decline of the mass-based party structure and increasing interest group influence.[12]

The Executive Branch

The past thirty years also have seen an increase in the professionalism of the governors' offices and the states' executive branches more generally, though again there was wide variation. States differ with regard to the formal powers of the governor's office relative to the legislature (such as appointments and budgeting), how executive power is apportioned among the governor and other officials such as the lieutenant governor or attorney general—who could be independently elected and of the opposing party—and the use of gubernatorial term limits and the line-item veto. Governors' institutional powers varied markedly: Maryland, New Jersey, New York, and Ohio were at the high end of one index of institutional power, and North and South Carolina, Rhode Island, and Vermont were among the states at the low end.[13]

State bureaucracies had grown markedly in recent decades, suggesting improvements in the administrative capacity of many states to handle policy responsibilities. While federal employment remained fairly steady, state employment rose by 33 percent between 1985 and 1995.[14] State governments took on markedly different functions: Some ran extensive university systems, and others took over broad direct service responsibilities. In addition, the growth in federal spending in the 1960s and 1970s contributed to the increase in state employment because states took on responsibility for administering federally funded programs. Other states continued to offer fairly minimal public services, however, choosing instead to keep tax rates low.

Interest Groups

We can begin to get a better sense of the applicability of neo-Madisonian theory to state policymaking by examining the interest group environment within the states. As Alan Rosenthal and other students of the states have noted, interest groups do not single-handedly determine legislative outcomes.[15] Nonetheless, the federalist system, the separation of powers, and the particularly fragmented structures of many state governments prescribed by their constitutions have offered ample opportunity for interest groups to take action, and in the past several decades more of them have been doing so. State interest politics have grown markedly more complex; there are far more interest organizations and a greater variety of types than there used to be, and their activity is more intense.

Business-oriented groups still are the most plentiful and largest, and they control the most money. New types of organizations have been added to the mix, however, and—consistent with changes in other state political institutions—lobbying has become more professional and more sophisticated in its strategies and tactics. A 1998 evaluation of the types of interests and their presence and influence in the states found that general business organizations, teachers' organizations, utilities, lawyers, health care organizations, insurance companies, general local government actors, and manufacturers were among the most commonly involved and active interests. Anti-poverty organizations ranked last in influence, as part of a "miscellaneous social issues groups" category, and were classified as "less/not effective" in forty-three states. These findings alone raise concerns about the representation of low-income families in a system of devolved welfare policymaking.[16]

Simple interest group presence does not necessarily translate into effectiveness in influencing policy. As in Washington, the degree to which officials want or need a group's services and resources, as well as the amount of money it has, probably are most essential in determining its political influence in the states. Other important factors include the skills of an organization's leadership; its potential to enter into effective coalitions; the strength of its opposition; whether its goals are primarily defensive or promotional (the former typically are easier to achieve); its membership size, cohesion, and geographic distribution; and the general political culture and climate. The right blend of these factors can offset, at least in part, a lack of money or other concrete benefits. Moreover, participation in politics, at least in the public hearings process, typically is relatively easy in the states—at least, it is easier there than in Washington, where the opportunity to provide oral hearing testimony is more tightly controlled. Without money and services or resources that politicians care about, however, a group is unlikely to wield much power—driving home the difficulties for groups that represent the poor.

As with most things that relate to the states, however, the extent and type of interest group activity differ by state. The power of interest groups in state politics generally and the power of specific types of groups are determined by a range of factors, including the state's level of socioeconomic development, its political culture and ideology, the strength of the parties, the level of campaign spending and sources of contributions, and the professionalization of state government. Other important considerations include the extent and enforcement of lobbying and campaign finance laws (which generally, though not always, are weaker than federal controls), the state's constitutional and legal authority over policymaking, the degree of fragmentation of the policy process, and state policy and budgetary priorities. The South, where the political parties are still weakest, remains the region with the most powerful interest group systems, followed by the West and Midwest. The Northeast has the least powerful systems of interest groups, according to scholars Clive Thomas and Ronald Hrebenar.[17] Although the informal insider politics of which V. O. Key warned is markedly less prevalent than it used to be, it still exists to some extent in the South and the West. "Good old boy" lobbyists no longer abound, certainly, but neither have they entirely died out; instead, they have become more sophisticated. The South also has the most fragmented policy process, providing groups with more access points to reach into the policymaking process. (Texas provides a good example of this fragmentation.) Increasingly, state administrative agencies also have become targets for the lobbying groups that are proliferating in many state capitals, and where political power is divided among many actors, opportunities for interest groups to influence policy grow.

As the costs of "high-tech" campaigning grow at all levels of government, the ability of certain interest groups to provide campaign contributions appears to be playing a larger role in determining who gains access, though the extent to which access contributes to influence remains unclear.[18] Party reforms such as the direct primary have had unforeseen consequences—significantly weakening state and local party influence and, in turn, possibly weakening the power of social groups whose influence was felt more through their numbers and participation in parties and elections, rather than their ability to contribute money. Certainly some states have seen relative growth of organizations representing the poor, and some of them have had considerable access to policymakers, mirroring the growth of public interest groups in the nation's capital.

Even though the number of advocacy groups and others representing poor people has increased in the past couple of decades, however, their presence in the states and localities remains highly uneven, as my case studies suggest. Certain large urbanized states such as New York, California, New Jersey, and Maryland have relatively large numbers of organizations attempting to represent low-income families in the political process. Others, however—particularly rural states and many states in the South and West—have a relative dearth of such organizations or the kinds of resources necessary to support them. These organizations and people generally have a harder time competing with larger and better-funded interests for legislators' and governors' scarce attention.[19] In some states, numerous advocacy organizations participated in the welfare policy debate, and several were active on a regular basis. The extent of their influence was highly uneven, however, particularly when their positions were opposed to those of better-funded organizations. In many states, moreover, a very narrow range of such organizations participated in the debate, limiting the range of perspectives that received a hearing and the involvement of poor people.

Public Opinion and Media Coverage

Finally, public opinion data in the 1990s did not suggest great enthusiasm among Americans for their state governments, despite the widespread rhetoric about the states being closer to the people. Findings showed a shift in public support from the federal government to local government, however, with attitudes about the states holding fairly steady (and relatively negative). National surveys conducted over a twenty-year period for the bipartisan Advisory Commission on Intergovernmental Relations found that when people were asked, "From which level of government do you feel you get the most for your money?" in 1972, 39 percent of respondents said the federal government, 26 percent said local government, and 18 percent said the state. In 1993, 38 percent said local government, 23 percent said the federal government, and 20 percent said the state.[20] This study also suggests that the general public was largely uninterested in the details of state policymaking—at least, welfare policymaking.

Nor was there evidence that the media were following the policymaking process in the states closely. One study noted that over time, press coverage of state governments had markedly decreased in most states, despite rekindled political enthusiasm for devolving poverty policy and other issues.[21]

POLITICAL AND SOCIAL CHARACTERISTICS OF MARYLAND, TEXAS, AND NORTH DAKOTA

As discussed in chapter 1, this study examines a sample of states—Maryland, Texas, and North Dakota—that were selected to provide a range of characteristics, including regional diversity, population size, political culture or ideology, poverty rate, median household income, ethnic mix, 1995 AFDC benefits, and partisan control of the governor's office and legislature. I recognize that a study of three states can provide only a snapshot of devolved welfare politics. By choosing these case studies carefully, however, I hope to offer a useful picture of welfare policymaking to date under devolution.

These states' tax capacity and effort varied widely. In 1991, Maryland had the greatest capacity and effort: 106 and 103, respectively (100 was the national average). Texas had a capacity of 97 but an effort of only 87, and North Dakota had a capacity of 91 and a slightly higher effort of 92.[22] Their political cultures also differed significantly. According to Elazar, Maryland had an individualist culture (though I would argue it has become more moralist over time), Texas was traditionalist, and North Dakota a hybrid of moralist and individualist.

Their legislatures differed widely in terms of professionalism and staff capacity. At the time of this study, none had legislative term limits, though turnover still tended to be relatively high. Texas and North Dakota were among seven states with legislatures that met only every other year. This fact was striking, given that Texas was the second most populous state in the union. In North Dakota the legislative session was 80 days; in Texas it was 140 days. Maryland's General Assembly met every year for 90 days. In all three states, legislative committees met periodically during the interim session.

Maryland's legislature, though technically part-time, was considered fairly professional, and members received salaries of about $30,000 per year. North Dakota's was a true "citizen legislature," with no funding for personal staffs or offices and limited central staff assistance; members made about $12,000 per year. In Texas, professional staff support was greater, but members earned only about $8,000 per year—limiting the position to people with alternative sources of income and necessarily diverting their energies from their legislative responsibilities. Maryland generally was considered to be a strong-governor state, whereas Texas and North Dakota had governors with weaker institutional powers, largely by constitutional design (especially in Texas). In Texas and North Dakota, however, the short biennial legislative sessions meant that if the governor vetoed a bill toward the end of the session, it was difficult for the legislature to override it. This factor and the fact that the governor was in office year round could give him relatively greater de facto power, as could the unity of his voice.

I turn now to a detailed examination of the welfare policymaking process in these three states, considering how key political and social characteristics contributed to the politics of welfare reform and exploring the political dynamics and actors that helped shape these states' initial forays into welfare policymaking in the early days of devolution. The study focuses in particular—though not exclusively—on the participation of groups in the legislative debate and on the role of nongovernmental organizations (NGOs) and actors that represent low-income families. I begin with Maryland, the state most like Washington in this regard.

NOTES

1. For one assessment of the states' governing capacity after these and other changes, see David M. Hedge, *Governance and the Changing American States* (Boulder, Colo.: Westview Press, 1998). See also Rivlin, *Reviving the American Dream*, 105, and Clive Thomas and Ronald Hrebenar, "Interest Groups in the States," in *Politics in the American States*, 5th ed., ed. Virginia Gray, Herbert Jacobs, and Robert Albritton (Washington, D.C.: CQ Press, 1990).

2. The Commission was defunded during the 104th Congress. Advisory Commission on Intergovernmental Relations (ACIR), *RTS 1991: State Revenue Capacity and Effort* (Washington, D.C.: ACIR, 1993), iii.

3. The 1993 survey used data from 1988 to 1991, which was a period of recession that hit states unevenly.

4. ACIR, *RTS 1991*, 18–19.

5. "Newshour with Jim Lehrer," 14 October 1996, transcript from "Strictly Business," 10–12; *1998 Green Book*, 429.

6. For a more complete discussion, see Daniel Elazar, *American Federalism: A View from the States*, 2d ed. (New York: Thomas Y. Crowell Co., 1972); Virginia Gray, "The Socioeconomic and Political Context of the States," in *Politics in the American States*, 7th ed., ed. Virginia Gray, Russell L. Hanson, and Herbert Jacobs (Washington, D.C.: CQ Press, 1999).

7. Rodney E. Hero, *Faces of Inequality: Social Diversity in American Politics* (New York: Oxford University Press, 1998). Joel Lieske, "Regional Subcultures of the United States," *Journal of Politics* 55 (November 1993): 888–913, also attempted to update Elazar's typology; he developed a typology with ten regional subcultures that account for demographic changes since 1966, when Elazar developed his categories.

8. A range of political scientists still rely on Elazar's work—including welfare scholar Lawrence Mead, who is using his political culture categories to explain, at least in part, the varying policy approaches that states are taking to welfare reform under devolution. See Lawrence M. Mead, "Governmental Quality and Welfare Reform," paper presented at annual research conference of Association for Public Policy Analysis and Management, Seattle, November 2000.

9. Alan Rosenthal, *The Decline of Representative Democracy: Process, Participation and Power in State Legislatures* (Washington, D.C.: CQ Press, 1998).

10. See John M. Carey, Richard G. Niemi, and Lynda W. Powell, *Term Limits in the State Legislatures* (Ann Arbor: University of Michigan Press, 2000), for a discussion of the effect of term limits.

11. Keith E. Hamm and Gary F. Moncrief, "Legislative Politics in the States," in Gray, Hanson, and Jacob, *Politics in the American States*. Data also from National Conference on State Legislatures (NCSL).

12. NCSL statistics; see also Kim Quaile Hill, "Political Party Competition," chapter 3 of *Democracy in the Fifty States* (Lincoln: University of Nebraska Press, 1994).

13. Thad Beyle, "The Governors," in Gray, Hanson, and Jacob, *Politics in the American States*, 191–231.

14. Richard Elling, "Administering State Programs: Performance and Politics," in Gray, Hanson and Jacob, *Politics in the American States*, 271.

15. Alan Rosenthal, *The Third House* (Washington, D.C.: CQ Press, 1993), 207–09.

16. Clive S. Thomas and Ronald J. Hrebenar, "Interest Groups in the States," in Gray, Hanson, and Jacobs, *Politics in the American States*, 134–35.

17. Ibid., 135–37.

18. Ibid.; Rosenthal, *The Decline of Representative Democracy*.

19. A 1995 report found that among 177 state legislative leaders who were interviewed, few could name the child advocacy organizations in their states. Legislators also complained that many advocates did not adequately understand the legislative process. The report provided useful analysis of the effectiveness or lack thereof of advocacy groups working with state legislatures and suggestions for how these groups could be more influential. See *State Legislative Leaders: Keys to Effective Legislation for Children and Families* (Centerville, Mass.: State Legislative Leaders Foundation, 1995), 22.

20. Advisory Commission on Intergovernmental Relations, *Changing Public Attitudes on Governments and Taxes*, 1993, Report S-22 (Washington, D.C.: ACIR, 1994), 3–4.

21. Charles Layton and Mary Walton, "Missing the Story at the Statehouse," *American Journalism Review* (July–August 1998), 2. A follow-up article noted that press coverage of the state capitols had increased in sixteen states between 1998 and 1999; it had decreased in eleven states. Mary Walton, "The Jersey Giant," *American Journalism Review*, October 2000, 61.

22. ACIR, *RTS 1991*, 18–19.

4

Maryland: Welfare Policymaking in a Diverse Environment

The politics of welfare reform in Maryland in the 1990s saw the involvement of a wide range of governmental and outside actors—in particular, an active and energetic community of groups that were attempting to represent the low-income families. Geographically, Maryland is a fairly small state; it had a population of about 5 million people. Despite the state's relatively modest size, the advocacy community in Maryland resembled that in Washington more than those in the other two states I studied. Its communities were diverse—from the city of Baltimore, with high concentrations of minority low-income people as well as affluent urbanites and significant black political power, to the rural counties of the west and south and the wealthy (and usually liberal) Washington suburbs of Montgomery County. Maryland was one of the original 13 colonies; a sense of history permeates its capital, Annapolis, which is located about 25 miles east of Washington, D.C. The Democratic Party had long dominated the state, though Republicans had gained ground in recent years, especially in suburban and rural areas. Overall, the state's approach to welfare reform in the mid-1990s reflected a fairly liberal political climate.

In addition the community of advocates, input from several researchers played an important role throughout the welfare policymaking process, particularly compared to the situation in Texas and North Dakota. Initial policy outcomes reflected the influence of both of these groups. Most notably, state lawmakers resisted the temptation to use welfare reform and declining caseloads as a way to cut the budget. Instead, most of the savings recouped from the declining cost of cash benefits were plowed back into a "dedicated purpose account" that was legislatively earmarked for programs intended to support welfare recipients who were moving to work and working poor people more generally.

This is not to say that Maryland's proposals have always been expansive toward welfare recipients. In the early and mid-1990s, when the state's economic situation was still tight and caseloads were high, policymakers considered and implemented several proposals to cut cash benefits.[1] In 1995, Maryland abolished its general assistance program for single poor and disabled people, though the program was partially reinstated later.[2] By 1996, however, when it became clear that caseloads were declining and federal money would be more plentiful than anticipated, the state followed a relatively generous approach toward getting recipients off welfare and into jobs.

In addition to reflecting the relative influence of groups representing poor people, this approach indicated the importance of the state's political culture, Democratic Party domination, and the relative power of Baltimore and the liberal Prince George's and Montgomery County suburbs. It also suggested the attachment of key legislators in both parties to welfare reform, as well as the strong economy and wide availability of money for welfare programs.

The significant policymaking capacity of Maryland's political institutions also affected the outcomes of the welfare debate. Although lawmakers met full-time for only three months, they convened every year, and committees met regularly during the interim. Legislators were paid relatively well—the most of the three states I studied.[3] Several important legislators and their staff members had considerable expertise on social programs. The state welfare agency also possessed capable staff and research capacity and, along with key legislators, initiated a relatively open and inclusive policymaking process. Although, not surprisingly, fewer different interest groups and fewer types of groups participated in Annapolis than in Washington, Maryland nonetheless exhibited a stronger advocacy community than many other states.

This chapter looks briefly at the context of welfare policy in Maryland, leading up to 1996. It then examines in detail the political and environmental factors that helped shape the successful legislation, key players inside and outside the government, and policy outcomes. It first considers the 1996 legislative session, when the General Assembly took on a major welfare reform initiative in anticipation of the federal welfare bill, and then analyzes the state's comprehensive response to the new national law during the 1997 session. It then looks briefly at welfare policy adjustments since 1997. Throughout the chapter I emphasize the role that groups outside government played, as well as that of public officials. In particular, I focus on participation by organizations and actors that reasonably could be said to represent the interests of low-income families, asking how neo-Madisonian theory contributes to an understanding of Maryland welfare politics.

EARLY EFFORTS AT WELFARE REFORM

As in most states, welfare caseloads in Maryland rose dramatically during the late 1980s and into the early 1990s. In 1995, the caseload peaked at about 228,000 recipients.[4] By the early 1990s, state politicians—in particular, Democratic Governor William Donald Schaefer—began to see political advantages and policy motivations for jumping on the welfare reform bandwagon. Encouraged by Bill Clinton's campaign pledge to alter fundamentally the national welfare system, as well as well-publicized efforts by officials in other states, officials began to rethink Maryland's programs.

The Early 1990s

With Governor Schaefer in his second and last term (the state has gubernatorial term limits) and eager to make his mark as a welfare innovator, state social services officials announced in the early 1990s new requirements for welfare parents, backed by the threat of reductions in cash grants. No one could provide a politically adequate explanation for the state's growing welfare rolls, and Schaefer wanted to initiate radical change.[5] His administration moved quickly to design a "Primary Prevention Initiative" to submit for federal waiver approval. Schaefer used his considerable institutional powers, including an executive budget process, and his own personal powers of persuasion to push the plan through.[6]

The program originally was conceived (and supported by a range of advocates and others) as one that would provide financial incentives to recipients to get their children immunized, keep them in school, and take them for regular medical check-ups. What began as a "carrot" approach, however, turned in its final version into a "stick" program—employing financial penalties on recipients who neglected to do these things. The recession of the early 1990s and the requirement that waivers be cost-neutral to the federal government, as well as Schaefer's determination to do something relatively dramatic about welfare, contributed to this reversal.[7] The plan was approved by the legislature in early 1992, as was a proposal to tighten the state program for disabled single people and abolish emergency assistance altogether. The primary prevention program later ran aground on implementation difficulties and was scrapped.[8]

Whatever the policy failings of this effort, welfare reform was off and running. In January 1994, in his last State-of-the-State address, Governor Schaefer proposed a package of changes that were based on the interim report of the Governor's Commission on Welfare Policy, a broad-based group that had met for two years. According to one key participant, the governor saw his gubernatorial peers, particularly Engler of Michigan and Thompson of Wisconsin, reaping political rewards for their initiatives and was determined to embark on major welfare innovation as well. The plan called for a pilot program that would have covered about two-thirds of the welfare caseload.[9] It included work requirements; transitional child care and medical benefits for people moving to work; the mandate that teen mothers live with their parents or another adult; and, most controversially, a "New Jersey-style" family cap. The plan received mixed reviews from legislators, many of whom were disturbed by the cap—as were advocates. The public, however, indicated support for the idea of freezing benefits for women who had additional children, despite a lack of evidence that caps worked to discourage births.[10] Ultimately, the version that came out of the General Assembly in the final hours of the legislative session was stripped of the cap, and the governor vetoed the bill, arguing that the benefit freeze was necessary for the program to remain cost-neutral.[11] Welfare reform was dead for the 1994 General Assembly session.[12]

1995: Welfare Reform Pilot Proposals

Welfare reform arose once more at the beginning of the legislative session in January 1995. The 1994 national congressional and state elections had brought major change. Parris N. Glendening, another Democrat, won the governorship in a tight race against Republican Ellen Sauerbrey. The new governor had not made welfare a major campaign issue. On welfare reform, Glendening took a back seat to the legislature and his own Department of Human Resources (DHR).[13]

At the beginning of the 1995 session, key legislators—supported by new DHR Secretary Alvin C. Collins and his program deputy, Lynda G. Fox—resurrected the waiver pilot program. Most of the political appointees at the agency had turned over, although nonpolitical professional staff members remained. This continuity among mid-level agency staff and other participants in the welfare debate contributed to generally collegial relations among members of the state's welfare policy domain. Fox and Collins, in particular, were credited with improving relations among participants and bringing in local officials as well.[14]

An hour away, in Washington, the new Republican majority used the Contract with America and HR 4 to signal that it was making welfare policy a top priority for the 104th Congress. The Clinton administration's welfare plan had effectively died, but HHS expanded further its policy of granting state waivers. Although the economy was improving, money was still understood to be tight in Maryland and nationally; deficit politics influenced federal policy alternatives and limited state options. State officials and others believed that block grants would be accompanied by "the virtual certainty" of reduced funding, and they anticipated having to execute their reforms with less money than they received under the AFDC match system.[15] Maryland's 1995 caseloads were even slightly higher than 1994 levels.[16]

After the rancorous 1994 session, the General Assembly successfully passed a three-jurisdiction welfare reform pilot in 1995, and Governor Glendening signed the bill in May. The 1995 law also successfully brokered a compromise family cap that was to be implemented statewide. It awarded no new cash for additional children born while their mothers were on welfare but provided the value of that benefit (about $80 per month) to a third party who would be responsible for giving the family goods and services for the child. Administration of this "child-specific benefit" faced strong opposition from many people in the religious and nonprofit communities, which were expected to act as the third party, but the benefit passed in the General Assembly nonetheless.

The advocacy community offered mixed enthusiasm: Support for the pilot program was tempered by general opposition to the modified cap.[17] The fact that the pilot was time-limited, with evaluation, rather than a statewide leap into major reform reassured some advocates and others who worked with low-income families. After the bruising family cap battle of 1994, the compromise reached in 1995 generated less opposition from abortion foes or liberal advocates.

With the debate in Washington centering on block grants, reduced funding, "hard" lifetime limits to cash assistance, possible mandatory family caps, and stringent work requirements, it also was widely recognized that radical welfare reform was becoming politically inevitable. In comparison to some of the ideas being bandied about in Congress, the Maryland pilot plan was moderate. Advocates argued, however, that its "work first" approach failed to address the need for longer-term education and training to help recipients move out of poverty and complained that there was too little attention to job creation. They also lobbied unsuccessfully for a "fill-the-gap" approach to cash assistance that would moderate the loss of aid when recipients found a job.[18] The failure of the state to adopt this policy drew harsh criticism several years later. One study placed Maryland third from the bottom among the fifty states in a ranking of the income level at which working recipients got cut off from cash aid entirely. Only West Virginia and Texas removed their working recipients from the rolls at lower income levels.[19]

A child support initiative within the 1995 welfare bill generated particular controversy. It would privatize child support enforcement in Baltimore City and Queen Anne's County for a test period of four years. Child support collections in the city, in particular, were low, and many policymakers felt that almost anything was worth a try to bring them up.[20] Lockheed-Martin, with its growing social services division, lobbied legislators privately for the plan, although its representatives did not testify in public hearings. Other participants suggested that they gained little through public testimony because they had sufficient access privately. The legislation specified a competitive bidding process; Lockheed ultimately received the contract.[21] Organized labor—especially AFSCME—surprisingly was not adamantly opposed to the privatization effort, although the bill contained provisions to require the contractor to hire state employees who otherwise would have lost their jobs, as well as other protections for those already working under Lockheed.[22] In 1995, the legislature also passed a "Work, Not Welfare, Tax Incentive" bill that offered tax breaks to businesses hiring welfare recipients.

The broad welfare reform pilot would never be fully implemented; after the session, DHR and the legislature agreed to anticipate federal welfare reform by introducing a comprehensive statewide system of changes that rendered the pilot obsolete after it was passed in 1996. The child support privatization pilot and the tax credit were not repealed, however.[23]

1996: COMPREHENSIVE REFORM

By 1996, caseloads began to drop. During the summer of 1995, DHR deputy secretary Fox had pulled together a broad-based steering committee to help formulate the state's approach to welfare reform. The task force was composed of DHR officials and staff, legislators, local social service directors, advocates, community and religious leaders, and at least one influential researcher.[24] It included about forty people, who met for a two-day retreat during the summer followed by subcommittee meetings to hash out proposals for overhauling the state's system. The approach was far-reaching and, according to several participants, marked by a sense of inclusiveness and overriding concern for low-income families, even when there was heated disagreement about policy options. The breadth of participation further helped build and strengthen a network of relationships that eased the policymaking process over the next several years.

The belief that federal welfare reform would mean less money drove several of the proposals under consideration. Committee members discussed seriously the possibility of cutting grants across the board, as well as counting federal SSI disability payments as income for the purpose of grant calculation (thus lowering welfare grants for SSI recipients). Toward the end of the year, Governor Glendening warned of the need to cut $25–50 million from the $650 million DHR annual budget—the amount his office estimated the state would lose from its federal payment.[25] The state eliminated its Disability Assistance and Loan Program (DALP), which served single poor and disabled adults, in the summer of 1995, although it was partially replaced with a more limited program. There was evidence that shortly afterward, homelessness increased in Baltimore.[26]

In October 1995, DHR Secretary Collins announced that the state would cut benefits by 10–30 percent as of January 1996, anticipating passage of a federal bill, although he dropped the proposal several months later when the financial outlook brightened.[27] According to officials, the agency was betting that block grants and greater state flexibility would be coming out of Washington in 1996, and DHR was eager to move ahead with statewide reform. If a federal bill failed to pass, the state could still apply for waivers. Like Governor Schaefer earlier, state policymakers were drawn to the possibility of taking the lead as innovators in statewide reform.[28]

In January 1996, the state's maximum grant level for a family of three—$373—was lower than grant levels in 1990 because the legislature cut them during the state recession. Overall, the benefit had declined in real terms by 42 percent between 1970 and 1996.[29] The demographic breakdown of the caseload was about 26 percent white, 70 percent black, 1 percent Hispanic, and 1 percent Asian.[30] The overall state population was about 69 percent white, 26 percent black, 3 percent Hispanic, and 4 percent Asian.[31] In 1995, the city of Baltimore made up about 46 percent of the total caseload; it was followed by Prince George's and Baltimore counties.[32]

Maryland's welfare system was significantly decentralized in a somewhat awkward structure. The central agency was located in downtown Baltimore. In addition, there were twenty-four local departments of social services—one for each county and one for Baltimore City. These local offices provided direct services to clients; they handled eligibility determination, cash assistance, child care, and job placement and support services. They had the option of contracting out aspects of these services, though not eligibility determination. The directors were jointly appointed by the DHR secretary and by the county executive or county commission. In some counties, these offices also contended with a county advisory board on social services. Their budgets were entirely state funded, however, and until 1996 policy was set largely by the central state agency. Several counties were developing interesting new initiatives, however. For example, Anne Arundel County sold old agency cars to welfare recipients who needed them to get to jobs.[33] Until the implementation of reform, case management largely involved eligibility determination, including checking and verifying income, employment, and other information.

The Legislative Debate

The next and most radical wave of reform took place with the Welfare Innovation Act of 1996 (SB 778), replacing AFDC and its emphasis on income maintenance with a Family Investment Program that stressed "work first." Legislators introduced the bill early in 1996, and the governor signed it into law in May. In addition to the legislation that became law, nine other major welfare-related bills received consideration during the session. A bill titled "Work, Not Welfare, Tax Incentives" also became law, broadening the business tax incentive first passed in 1995. The Maryland House Appropriations Committee and Senate Finance Committee had primary jurisdiction over the comprehensive welfare bills.[34] The tax incentive bill was considered in the state's House Ways and Means and Senate Budget and Taxation committees.[35] The House Judiciary Committee and Senate Judicial Proceedings Committee considered child support legislation. These committees held nine hearings on major welfare-related proposals (see Appendix D for a list of bills, hearings, and witnesses).[36] Delegate Samuel I. Rosenberg (D-Baltimore) chaired the Appropriations Subcommittee on Health and Human Resources, and Senator Martin G. Madden (R-Howard and Prince George's Counties) headed up the state's Welfare Subcommittee of the Senate Finance Committee. Both were sponsors of the major bills in their chambers and played central roles throughout the debate. Both also had participated in the DHR welfare reform steering committee.[37]

The Appropriations Committee held one hearing in February on the House of Delegates' major bill, HB 1061.[38] This bill generated significant response, especially from the advocacy community, which came out for the hearing in force and largely in opposition to its two-year limit on cash assistance without work and five-year cumulative limit on cash, even though these elements were not yet mandated by federal law. The bill also proposed to count the money that families received for disabled children under SSI as income for the purpose of calculating grants and to funnel the savings into child care and other programs for low-income families.[39]

Senator Madden and twelve other state senators across party lines introduced SB 778 at the beginning of the 1996 session; in late March, after one committee hearing, the full Senate approved it unanimously. The debate on reform in the House was more heated, resulting in the adoption of floor amendments. One in particular, proposed by a Democratic delegate from Montgomery County, dropped the SSI income proposal. Finally, the full House voted out its version of SB 778, also unanimously, on April 2.[40] The Senate refused to concur with the House version, and two days later a conference committee, chaired by Madden and Rosenberg, met to work out a compromise, reaching agreement quickly. The conference version was adopted by the full legislature the evening of April 8, during the final hours of the session. In the Senate the vote was 47 to 0, and in the House it was 125 to 5. The governor signed SB 778 into law on May 14.[41]

The final deliberations on the bill were conducted with the General Assembly coming down to the wire on its ninety-day session. The most controversial issues included whether to have a lifetime limit on welfare receipt when federal law didn't yet require it, the SSI income proposal, what activities should count as work, and preserving the entitlement to assistance. The family cap was not revisited. There seemed to be a feeling among proponents and opponents of the cap alike that if it were revisited, the outcome might be even less to their liking than the compromise.[42]

The tone of the legislative debate in Maryland was more pragmatic, and less ideological or partisan, than that in Washington during the 104th Congress. Although the family cap had generated heat, it was basically settled by 1996. Everyone, from liberals to conservatives, seemed to agree with the emphasis on work and "self-sufficiency." Disagreement arose, however, over how fiscally conservative the new system should be, time limits, and the need to affirmatively protect children if their parents were cut off. Madden, in particular, was an issue entrepreneur: One person who was closely involved in reform called him "the godfather of welfare reform." Madden pushed provisions such as the increased role for charitable and religious organizations as third-party payees and the use of savings for demonstration projects such as group homes for recipients and school-based programs. Despite conflict over these and other specifics of the legislation, however, the tone of the debate was largely collegial, and the range of viewpoints was within narrower bounds than those debated in Washington.

Other Government Actors

The state DHR took a lead role in developing and advocating for welfare reform in 1996. In particular, participants cited Deputy Secretary Fox as active, open to a variety of viewpoints, and committed to low-income families. She was described as "a believer in research" who used it to guide the state's initiatives. One leading advocate called her a good example of how one person can affect the tone and approach of policymaking. Secretary Collins, though less closely involved day-to-day with reform, was described as an enthusiastic and supportive department head. Several long-time DHR staffers also were mentioned as extremely knowledgeable and influential. Department personnel, including Collins and Fox, testified at eight of the nine hearings. Although the orientation of reform was entirely consistent with the work-first paradigm, the department also sought information on recipient well-being, not only job placements and caseload declines, continuing a long-standing research relationship with the University of Maryland's School of Social Work.[43]

One agency goal was to "change the culture of welfare offices"—an idea that had come to permeate the welfare debate and was first broadly addressed in Mary Jo Bane and David Ellwood's 1994 book, *Welfare Realities*.[44] The department's new practice of referring to recipients as "customers" reportedly began at Collins's urging, as a way of signaling to workers that their clients deserved to be treated with respect and attentiveness.[45] Under Collins, the central agency also advocated greater local flexibility in policymaking. Fox was the central force behind the welfare reform steering committee, and this group's work contributed to the substance of the 1996 legislation and to the sense of relative inclusion that marked the policymaking process in Maryland. Fox also was said to be accessible to advocates and others outside of government. Although Governor Glendening took a greater role in 1996 than he had in 1995, his office was not particularly involved with reform and did not take the lead.[46]

Several intergovernmental groups participated in public hearings and worked to shape the bill, which contained proposals to increase decentralized authority (see Table 4-1). These groups included the Maryland Association of Social Service Directors, as well as individual county governments and local departments of social services, including the Baltimore City welfare agency. In the past, according to one active director, the attitude of the state DHR toward the locals had been "adversarial." Although this attitude began to change in the early 1990s, Collins in particular was credited with improving relations between the state and county agencies. After 1995, local departments were particularly involved—participating in the welfare reform steering committee, testifying at hearings, and attending other legislative and executive branch meetings.[47]

Several county executives' offices and county commissions also testified, but the Maryland Association of Counties was most in evidence on welfare reform, at least as indicated by hearing participation. Officials from the city of Baltimore participated infrequently in hearings and were relatively absent from debate, despite the fact that the city accounted for about half of the caseload.[48]

Nongovernmental Participants

Maryland's traditionally individualist political culture (according to Elazar's typology) historically has left ample room for business and other material interests to gain control of the policy agenda. The state's long-standing lack of party competition also provided room for interest groups seeking to fill a power vacuum. Weak parties generally have allowed for a greater role by interest groups in many of the states than in the federal government or in other Western industrialized nations.[49] However, a recent increase in party competition, the proliferation of state interest organizations of many stripes, and the relatively professional legislature and bureaucracy have helped to inhibit the ability of single groups to dominate the policy process. Maryland interest groups are said to have moderate strength and operate within a complex political environment, suggesting the broad range of groups that exist in the state.[50] In total, during the 1996 welfare debate, 41 different organizations of all types were active in the nine hearings in 1996, presenting testimony 75 times (see Table 4-1).

The Advocacy Community

In the past two decades, Maryland has seen a notable increase in the number of organizations representing the interests of low-income people, supported by newer "moralist" strains in the state. Welfare Advocates, one of the organizations that has been most active in lobbying on welfare reform, was founded in 1979 and, according to its vice president, was part of a small core

Table 4-1
Activity of Maryland Interest Groups in Welfare-Related Hearings, by Category, 1996 General Assembly Session

Category	No. of Organizations/Actors	No. of Times Testifying
Advocates: child advocacy, nonprofit and charitable providers, unions[a]	20	35
Intergovernmental	9	12
For-profit companies, business groups	6	18
Professional associations	3	5
Individuals	3	5
Researchers	0	0
Think tanks	0	0
"Traditional values" groups	0	0
Miscellaneous	0	0
TOTAL	**41**	**75**

Sources: Data from audiotapes, witness lists, and copies of testimony in the bill files of nine House and Senate public hearings, Department of Legislative Services Library. Author's calculations.

[a]As with national groups, the lines between advocacy and nonprofit service or charitable organizations often are blurry. Some advocacy groups also provided services, and some charitable groups also were committed to advocacy.

of such groups. In 1996, numerous different advocacy organizations (seventeen of them) participated actively in welfare-related legislative hearings, offering testimony twenty-nine times. They were joined by three nonprofit providers. More participated the following year. Advocates also had influence with many individual legislators, played an important role in the DHR welfare reform steering committee, and had access to agency officials. Madden, the Republican chair of the welfare reform subcommittee of the Senate Finance Committee, called them "the legislature's conscience."[51] His counterpart in the House, Delegate Rosenberg, had been the director of an advocacy group for the homeless before joining the General Assembly and was considered sympathetic to social concerns.[52]

This is not to say that organizations representing low-income people were a monolithic group or that their views went unchallenged. They had to share the policy stage with other influential and usually more conservative actors, including DHR and the intergovernmental groups, as well as a range of business organizations that were closely involved in the tax incentive bill.[53] They did gain several of their key priorities during the 1996 debate, however, and had considerable presence and influence.[54]

As in most states, advocacy groups and those providing services to poor people often overlapped; in most cases the strongest advocates were also religious, nonprofit, or charitable organizations that worked with low-income families. One leading participant noted the difficulty in getting support for straight advocacy activities because few funders are willing to support groups that eschew direct service. She also commented on the long-standing difficulty of forming organizations composed of recipients themselves, saying "We'd get a cadre of folks excited, but six weeks later, their lives would change." She noted, however, that several organizations were trying to organize low-income people through homeless organizations and Head Start centers.

By the mid-1990s, Welfare Advocates was composed of more than 400 state and local advocacy and service organizations, individuals, and state and local public agencies. According to interviews and hearing participation, the most influential actors in 1996 also included the Maryland Catholic Conference, Maryland Catholic Charities (whose director for social concerns also was the vice president of Welfare Advocates), Action for the Homeless and the Maryland Food Committee (later merged into the Maryland Center for Poverty Solutions), and the Homeless Persons Representation Project. These groups and others also formed overlapping coalitions to address specific issues. The Arc of Maryland (formerly the Association for Retarded Citizens) was cited as especially influential on issues related to disabilities, including the SSI income proposal. One central participant noted that there were "about ten people [who] have leadership roles in these organizations. If we wanted to call a meeting about changes in the welfare system, there are ten that I'd call into a room."

Other members of the religious community participated actively. The Maryland Interfaith Legislative Committee, an interdenominational organization representing state groups with a heavy presence of Baltimore City and suburban Washington organizations, testified frequently. The Presbytery of Baltimore and several Jewish organizations also were cited as especially involved. Maryland Catholic Charities and the Maryland Catholic Conference wielded special clout, however, because they represented the Archdioceses of Baltimore and Washington, as well as the Diocese of Wilmington. One participant noted the power of these groups' lobbying arsenal: "If they don't like what you do, they can send the Cardinal to talk to you. . . . They mattered very much in this equation. . . . When pressed, they have two Archbishops, plus the Cardinal."

The advocacy community was united in the spring of 1996 in its opposition to HB 1061, the first bill to have a hearing, which included the five-year hard time limits and SSI proposal and lacked an entitlement to assistance. They were more ambivalent about the Senate bill that passed, stressing the need for a continued safety net and lobbying hard to have the state's benefit levels indexed to changes in the cost of living rather than left to the discretion of DHR or the legislature to set each year. They also fought to include an affirmative entitlement to assistance for recipients who met eligibility criteria, to require the state to continue to spend 100 percent of its prior funding levels, and an appeals process for families who were sanctioned.

One of the major Washington advocacy/research organizations, CLASP, participated in Maryland hearings twice during 1996. Its representatives took no position on legislation, but they provided an overview of federal welfare reform efforts and information on what other states were doing with waivers. CLASP participated only when requested by state organizations, but its considerable expertise on welfare issues seemed to get the attention of legislators.[55]

Organized labor was absent from the 1996 welfare debate, according to hearing testimony and interviews. Labor was described as generally weak in the state; one leading participant noted, "AFSCME was very busy with the privatization of the entire child support enforcement system in Baltimore. That was a much bigger perceived threat for labor."

Other Actors

The tax incentive bills, not surprisingly, brought out a range of business interests lobbying to increase the number of tax exemptions when they hired welfare recipients, among other concerns. Active groups included the state Chamber of Commerce and the "Work Not Welfare Coalition," a group of businesses and organizations that included the Maryland Hotel and Motel Association, Lowe's Home Centers, and Pizza Hut of Maryland. The coalition was especially focused on tax credits.[56]

Several professional organizations—the American Academy of Pediatrics, the Maryland chapter of the NASW, and its lobbying arm, the Maryland Legislative Council of Social Workers—were active and sometimes effective. The pediatricians' group was cited as particularly influential on children's issues. One participant (and NASW member) criticized the social workers' group, however, for sometimes seeming more concerned with protecting their members' professional turf than the success of welfare reform and the needs of low-income families.

Two research organizations were cited as particularly influential on the shape of welfare reform, but their representatives never testified at public hearings. The University of Maryland's School of Social Work housed the "Welfare and Child Support Research and Training Group," directed by a long-time welfare researcher. Her work informed DHR, the advocacy community, and the state legislature, as well as others in the research community within the state and nationwide. The director also had served as head of Welfare Advocates in the past. The other organization, the Regional Economic Studies Institute, provided analysis of the region's employment situation, caseload projections, and other data related to the welfare-to-work push. Fox and other policymakers cited the institute's work and stressed their own desire to design policies that were based on research when it was available.[57] Maryland legislators also seemed to be more concerned than policymakers in many other states with basing their decisions on research.

No think tanks—either Washington- or Maryland-based—participated in the hearings process, and conservative groups such as the Heritage Foundation, which were so influential in Washington, basically ignored Maryland's welfare reform despite its proximity. In contrast to the influence of relatively liberal religious groups, the Christian Right also was largely invisible. The Maryland Right-to-Life Committee took a stand on the family cap in 1995, but that seemed to be its only welfare issue.[58]

Welfare Innovation Act of 1996

The final version of SB 778 made many essential changes preceding passage of PRWORA. Most fundamentally, it repealed the welfare reform pilot and replaced AFDC with a Family Investment Program, including a temporary cash assistance (TCA) component to provide "last resort" short-term cash benefits to families that meet income criteria.

The underlying assumptions of the legislation, as expressed in the preamble, were strikingly similar to the language of the national welfare debate, even though the tone of the legislative debate itself had been notably more moderate. The bill began as follows:

> Whereas, The State of Maryland recognizes that for too many families, welfare has become what it never was intended to be: a permanent way of life, and this system of continuous income maintenance . . . destroys all incentive for an individual to become self-sufficient. . . .The state's welfare system does not reward work or any effort to seek and secure a job. . .

It further noted that "the State's role is to promote family and community responsibility for nurturing children, not to take their place . . . " and that the General Assembly established welfare reform "with the intended goal of achieving a significant reduction in the number of citizens who are enrolled in the Aid to Families with Dependent Children (AFDC) program. . . . " The current system, it charged, "fosters dependence, low self-esteem, and irresponsible behavior." The new one must be "one that rewards work and fosters self-reliance, responsibility, and family stability."[59]

The provisions of the Welfare Innovation Act of 1996 included the following:[60]

- Hard time limits only on the condition they were required by the federal government
- A limit on cash assistance of two years if the client did not participate in work activities
- Maintenance of an affirmative entitlement to assistance
- A floor for grants combined with food stamps at 61 percent of the state's Minimum Living Level—the amount determined to provide a basic level of subsistence—indirectly indexing the grant to inflation[61]
- A mandate that program savings that were not set aside for demonstration projects be retained in a "dedicated purpose account" limited to welfare-related purposes such as child care, welfare-avoidance grants, and work support services
- The "quasi" family cap
- A requirement that minor parents live with their parents or other adult relative
- A "personal responsibility agreement" between recipients and the local department of social services
- A requirement that applicants apply for child support at the same time they apply for TCA and conduct a job search before receiving cash
- One-time "welfare avoidance" cash grants to recipients with emergency needs, instead of signing them up for regular benefits
- Wage subsidies funded by TANF money when firms hired recipients (known as "grant diversion")
- Increased program flexibility for local social services departments, accompanied by mini-block grants and greater service integration[62]
- Establishment of a permanent legislative oversight committee, the Joint Committee on Welfare Reform, composed of five senators and five delegates
- Ten percent of the savings from caseload declines earmarked for welfare demonstration projects, including cooperative living, intensive case management, and school-based initiatives.

Finally, in recognition of the long-term implications of welfare reform, the bill mandated a follow-up study of recipients who left the rolls, from the outset of implementation. This ongoing study was conducted by the welfare reform group at the University of Maryland.

1997: AFTER THE FEDERAL BILL

U.S. Senator Paul S. Sarbanes (D-MD) and U.S. Representative E. Elijah Cummings (D-Baltimore) voted against PRWORA in Congress, despite President Clinton's announcement in the summer of 1996 that he would sign it. Senator Barbara Mikulski and the rest of the Maryland delegation voted for the new law.[63] Maryland's waiver request also received federal approval in August, giving the state the option of either implementing the provisions of SB 778 for the waiver term of three years or amending state law still further to comply with the new federal bill as soon as possible.[64] In mid-September, DHR announced that it would drop the waiver and make the changes necessary to comply with federal law.[65] It had become clear that under the new block grant the state would, in fact, receive more money than under AFDC or its waiver—estimated at more than $10 million more for the first year, or almost $1 million per month. DHR officials cited this financial advantage in announcing its decision to abandon the waiver.[66]

In September, Governor Glendening also announced that the state would provide cash assistance, nutrition, early child care, and medical benefits to legal immigrants already in the country in August who would have been cut off by the 1996 federal bill. He also said that the state would provide medical coverage and cash assistance to children regardless of when they arrived in the country, using savings reaped from welfare reform and dropping caseloads.[67]

The new Joint Committee on Welfare Reform got to work after the 1996 session, met six times during the interim, and issued a detailed report in December 1996.[68] Republican Senator Madden and Democratic Delegate Rosenberg were co-chairs. The report's proposals included a drug-testing requirement for all applicants, with the mandate that the state provide treatment for everyone who needed it. Churches and other charitable organizations again were expected to act as third-party payees for recipients whose grants were cut for not complying with drug testing or treatment but whose children would still be eligible for payments.

Even before the 1997 session started, the drug-testing proposal met with vehement criticism from advocates, religious groups, and others as unduly harsh and an attempt to shift the burden of caring for poor people from the state to charitable organizations.[69] Others objected that the drug-testing provision and the new demand for treatment would be too expensive; the state's existing treatment capacity was widely acknowledged to be inadequate.[70] In mid-December 1996, fifty-five church leaders representing almost 250 Maryland congregations met with Glendening to ask that he postpone implementation of the new welfare system, indicating that the effort to push more responsibilities onto the charitable sectors would face strong opposition. The governor rejected the request, however.[71]

The Legislative Debate

The 1997 General Assembly session saw the introduction of a range of welfare reform proposals, but SB 499, the "Welfare Innovation Act of 1997," represented the most comprehensive response to the changes spurred by federal reform. SB 499 was cross-listed in the House as HB 653.[72] Senator Madden and eleven co-sponsors from both parties introduced SB 499 in January 1997. As introduced, it codified into law benefits for legal immigrants, expansion of the types of groups that could act as third-party payees and payment of an administrative fee to the third party, and a substance abuse screening requirement. In the face of the widespread opposition, the mandatory drug-testing requirement had been modified to a drug-screening provision. The screening would require that recipients go through several interviews, with multiple opportunities for them to identify themselves or to be identified by a social services or health care worker as having a substance abuse problem. If they did not participate in treatment (if it were available), they could have their grant cut.[73]

The committees with primary jurisdiction held ten welfare-related hearings, with some hearings considering multiple bills (see Appendix D for bills, hearings, and witness lists). The Finance Committee held its hearing on SB 499 on February 19, 1997, and on March 6 reported out the bill. The full Senate considered it on March 12. In the House of Delegates, the Appropriations Committee held its hearing on SB 499 on March 25 and reported it out with amendments on April 2. Again the Senate and House could not concur, and a conference committee was named, again co-chaired by Madden and Rosenberg. The conference version of SB 499 passed unanimously in the Senate and in the House by a vote of 123 to 10.[74]

The most contentious issue was still the substance abuse proposal. The central questions involved how screening and referrals would work and whether DHR, the local departments and their caseworkers, and the managed care organizations that would be responsible were adequately prepared for implementation. Because the bill cut benefits to parents who would not cooperate with treatment, the stakes were particularly high. One concern was that parents would not identify themselves as substance abusers for fear of having their children taken away. Another was that the current system did not have enough treatment slots and that it lacked sufficient different types of treatment.

Another major concern about the bill was that welfare recipients pushed into jobs would replace full-time paid workers, displacing people from low-wage jobs and possibly into welfare themselves.[75] There was widespread legislative support for protecting individual workers but less so for protecting job slots, especially because businesses opposed this strategy, arguing that tax credits would not be useful if they were limited to newly created jobs.

Judging from the tone of public hearings and the vote tallies, however, the legislative debate in 1997 again was fairly congenial and focused more on the details than the broad orientation of the proposals. Shortly after the session closed, however, in one of the more dramatic moments of welfare reform, one group of advocates staged a rally on the front lawn of Delegate Rosenberg's house. They criticized his drug-screening initiative and gave him "failing grades" for the previous session, despite the fact that he usually was one of their staunchest allies in the General Assembly.[76]

Other Government Actors

Once again, Secretary Collins, Lynda Fox, and others from DHR participated actively. In 1997, however, the legislature—in particular, the new Joint Committee on Welfare Reform—seemed to take more of a lead role in initiating new proposals. SB 499 and HB 653 were very similar to the proposals outlined in the committee's 1996 interim report.

Fox and others at DHR did express concern about the agency's ability to implement quickly some of the drug-screening and referral requirements, as well as the ability of managed care organizations to get reliable and timely information back to the department without greater phase-in time. The department's management information systems weren't yet sufficiently accurate to be the basis of decisions to cut recipients' benefits, and DHR requested a delay of one year in several facets of the reporting requirements.[77] The state Department of Labor, Licensing, and Regulation also testified in opposition to the proposal to protect job slots from being transferred to workfare openings.

A greater number of intergovernmental actors participated in 1997, testifying sixteen times (see Table 4-2). Higher education groups that participated were largely concerned with a proposed mentoring initiative for welfare families. A few individual county officials also testified. The city of Baltimore was more active in 1997; the director of the city's welfare department was particularly concerned about the need for more—and more effective—drug treatment options and the implications of the new proposal for Baltimore's welfare recipients, a substantial number of whom faced substance abuse problems.[78] The Maryland Association of Counties did not testify, however, nor did the county executives' offices or the social services directors' group.

Table 4-2
Activity of Maryland Interest Groups in Welfare-Related Hearings, by Category, 1997 General Assembly Session

Category	No. of Organizations/Actors	No. of Times Testifying
Advocates: child advocacy, nonprofit and charitable providers, unions[a]	37	88
For-profit companies, business groups	21	34
Intergovernmental	11	16
Professional associations	3	14
Individuals	3	11
Researchers	0	0
Think tanks	0	0
"Traditional values" groups	0	0
Miscellaneous	0	0
TOTAL	**75**	**163**

Sources: Data from audiotapes, witness lists, and copies of testimony in bill files of ten House and Senate public hearings, Department of Legislative Services Library. Author's calculations.

[a]As with national groups, the lines between advocacy and nonprofit service or charitable organizations often are blurry. Some advocacy groups also provided services, and some charitable groups also were committed to advocacy.

Nongovernmental Participants

An even greater number of outside groups participated in hearings in 1997 than the year before. All told, 75 organizations testified more than 160 times, and they were active in a range of other ways as well.

Advocacy Community

At the beginning of the 1997 session, members of the advocacy community spoke out about the need to preserve programs for low-income people, despite the political pressure on Governor Glendening to push through a personal income tax cut now that economic recovery was finally underway. A representative of the Maryland Alliance for the Poor—a new coalition of groups that included Welfare Advocates and the Maryland Food Committee—testified at a House Appropriations Committee hearing that food pantries and other emergency services actually had experienced marked increases in demand despite the general improvement in the economy.[79]

The advocacy community again was closely involved in hearings and through other means. They were led once more by Welfare Advocates, the Maryland Catholic Conference, the Maryland Food Committee, and Action for the Homeless. Several groups that were not particularly active in 1996 participated more frequently in 1997, including Advocates for Children and Youth and the Presbytery of Baltimore.

Baltimoreans United in Leadership Development (BUILD) and the Maryland Industrial Areas Foundation (MIAF)—which are related church- and labor-affiliated advocacy and direct action organizations—participated in legislative hearings for the first time in 1997. They typically lobbied the executive branch more than the legislature and had some success there. They also marked a leftward edge to the debate, helping to position other groups—which used more conventional political strategies—as relatively more centrist. BUILD was established in the late 1970s, following the Saul Alinsky model of community organizing. It was affiliated with AFSCME and the MIAF and had used protests and other direct action, as well as lobbying the executive branch, to try to effect political changes. It tended not to coordinate with the other more mainstream advocates on welfare policy. One advocate described the Glendening administration as "kind of terrified of them" and their tenacity, suggesting that at times this gave her a relative advantage in negotiating with the administration because in comparison she seemed very moderate.[80]

Maryland Catholic Charities again was particularly involved, but its director of social concerns also was the lead spokesperson for the Welfare Advocates coalition, so the level of participation is not clear from looking at incidents of testimony alone because she tended to testify under the auspices of the larger coalition. Some groups represented suburban Washington organizations. Another of the national Washington-based advocacy and research organizations, the CBPP, testified in support of a House bill that died in committee.[81]

Advocates' top priorities included trying to make the drug-screening program as useful to recipients as possible, in particular by increasing funding for treatment, which they estimated would require about $40 million in new money.[82] They favored assistance for legal immigrants; providing health care for children pushed off SSI by the national bill; and ensuring that the state try to track what happened to those families that left the rolls. They also sought to broaden the state's definition of work to allow more than the single year of education that counted under federal law. [83]

Although their overall goals were similar, these organizations sometimes stressed different issues and took different approaches. BUILD, AFSCME, and the MIAF focused on job creation and protection. BUILD in particular was instrumental in Baltimore's adoption in 1994 of a city "living wage" to bring low-wage workers out of poverty. The MIAF lobbied the governor's office hard and successfully for an executive order to address job displacement. More mainstream groups such as Welfare Advocates and the Maryland Catholic Conference emphasized opening jobs in the existing labor market to recipients and improving their skills so that they would be equipped to perform them. Advocates' views on the drug-screening program also were mixed. Whereas a representative of the Maryland Catholic Conference testified that the organization supported the aim of pushing substance-abusing parents to get treatment, others opposed it as punitive.[84]

Although these groups were not closely coordinated, the direct action of BUILD at times complemented the more conventional lobbying tactics of other advocates. Some participants felt, however, that BUILD's organizers at times focused on their own agenda at the expense of the priorities of the larger advocacy community.

Organized labor entered the legislative fray for the first time in 1997, largely trying to keep public jobs held by full-time workers from being filled by welfare recipients. In particular, they wanted tax credits for hiring welfare recipients to be available only when companies created new jobs for recipients. Two local Maryland councils of AFSCME testified multiple times, as did representatives of the national AFSCME office in Washington.[85]

Other Actors

The Work Not Welfare Coalition and several corporations doing business in the state participated once again, this time testifying on proposals to establish a "work not welfare enterprise zone" and tax credits for the creation of new jobs. Maryland Works, Inc. (a for-profit welfare services contractor) and a company that sold drug-screening systems also testified several times. Again, the large contractors such as Lockheed-Martin, Maximus, and EDS did not participate in hearings. Trade associations participated most frequently on the enterprise zone and tax proposals. The Maryland Hospitals Association and the Maryland Association of Health Maintenance Organizations, however, expressed particular concern about the drug-screening program, which would require health maintenance organizations (HMOs) to identify substance abuse during clients' initial health assessment. They feared that the screening would lead to new costs that were not included in their capitation agreements with the state and that the system as it stood could not yet coordinate effectively among agencies.

The Maryland Legislative Council of Social Workers was extremely active in testifying. Researchers at the University of Maryland School of Social Work's welfare project and the Regional Economic Studies Institute again were influential, although none participated in legislative hearings. As in 1996, no think tanks or "traditional values" groups testified. Several individuals participated, although they appeared to have little influence.

Final Welfare Innovation Act of 1997

In its final form, the Welfare Innovation Act of 1997 codified the governor's decision to maintain assistance for legal immigrants who were pushed off the rolls by the national bill in 1996. It also directed the state health department to apply for a federal waiver to continue providing medical assistance to disabled children who were removed from the SSI program. The bill established the drug-screening program. It also broadened the types of organizations that could serve as third-party payees, offered legal immunity and liability coverage for groups that provided the third-party service, and allowed for payment of an administrative fee to offset their costs.[86]

For recipients who found unsubsidized work, the income disregard (the amount of income recipients could keep that did not count as income for purposes of grant calculation) was increased from 20 percent to 26 percent of income. The legislation also instituted a mentor program between students at Maryland colleges and universities and welfare families—a sort of modern-day "friendly visitors" program.[87]

SB 499 extended the requirement that savings from the Family Investment and Purchase of Child Care programs for fiscal year (FY) 1997 and FY 1998 remain in the multiyear dedicated purpose account reserved for program-related expenses. Local departments of social services were permitted to keep savings from one fiscal year into the next. They also could apply to the state DHR for time-limited waivers from the program requirements of the Family Investment Program, allowing counties to experiment with their own innovations. Counties were granted greater flexibility from state procurement and other regulations for certain pilot projects. Finally, the new law set up a grievance procedure for cases in which worker displacement by welfare recipients was charged.[88]

1998 AND THE FUTURE

At the end of June 1997, Governor Glendening signed the anti-displacement executive order barring companies from replacing permanent employees with state-subsidized welfare recipients.[89] Implementation of the 1996 and 1997 bills moved apace. Between January 1995 and May 1997, the caseload had dropped 31 percent. By June 2000, it had dropped a total of 68 percent.[90] The economic recovery continued, and unemployment was low.

After the major welfare reform legislation of 1996 and 1997, the General Assembly continued to make incremental changes to the state's system and focused on related anti-poverty initiatives. The legislature passed yet another "welfare innovation" bill in 1998. It made permanent the dedicated purpose account (which originally had been set up for a period of only two years) and protected money in the account from reverting back to general revenues. It required DHR to establish a "job skills enhancement pilot program" in at least three counties, mandated that certain state contractors try to hire welfare recipients for entry-level jobs, and required DHR and other state agencies to "redesign the Family Investment Program service delivery system from the 'ground up.'" The bill also required DHR to study "finger imaging" as a way of reducing fraud in the welfare and food stamps programs.[91]

The General Assembly enacted several other related bills that were designed to aid low-income people during the 1998 session. These bills included extension of the employer tax credit, establishment of a Maryland Emergency Food program within DHR, expansion of the state's EITC to make it refundable (meaning that low-income people who owed no taxes nonetheless would receive checks from the state), and provision of Medicaid for families at or below 200 percent of the poverty level.[92] Advocates and the media declared the 1998 session a relative victory for low-income Marylanders, after seeing a 10 percent reduction in personal income taxes and generous funding for sports arenas pass during prior sessions.[93] However, they noted that although these programs certainly would help, even with the strong economy the numbers of people seeking emergency assistance were growing.[94]

The legislature continued to revise the details of the welfare system with annual "Welfare Innovation Acts." In 1999, the major elements were establishment of a new Family Investment Administration within DHR to administer cash assistance, food stamps, and medical assistance; a requirement that the state develop and implement a plan to hire welfare recipients into executive agency jobs; and a child support enforcement pilot project that had state-run and privatized jurisdictions competing with each other. It established "the Joseph Fund," which had been advocated by BUILD and set aside $10 million for anti-poverty programs. The legislature also raised the state's earned income disregard from 26 percent to 35 percent. In 2000, the legislature revised drug screening procedures to incorporate addiction specialists earlier and more closely and to make the process more effective. It expanded the "Work, Not Welfare" tax credit and elected to end the federal prohibition on cash aid to drug felons under certain circumstances. The emphasis was turning toward workforce development programs to help welfare parents and other low-income people get and keep jobs, especially jobs that would bring them above the poverty level.

The fifth interim report of the "Life After Welfare" research project at the University of Maryland School of Social Work was released in 2000. It found that about 50 percent of ex-recipients were working in the first six months after leaving cash assistance, and about 70 percent worked at some point after leaving, most in sales or the service industry.[95] About 12 percent of families had been sanctioned off welfare, and 17–35 percent "cycled back" to cash assistance in the first year after leaving. Few children became involved in the child welfare system after leaving. The report noted, however, that recipients who had left more recently were more likely to have been sanctioned off or had their cases closed for failing to provide eligibility information; they were less likely to have "earned income above limit" as a reason for leaving. The report stressed that welfare reform was becoming more complicated and that "a broad, deep and diverse array of post-exit services needs to be funded and available if, in the coming years, we are to continue to achieve the success of reform's first few years."[96]

Among these hard-to-serve individuals were long-term recipients, many of whom lived in very poor and isolated neighborhoods within Baltimore, as well as in rural areas with few jobs and services. The proportion of the caseload that lived in Baltimore grew by 12 percent in four years, to 59 percent in fiscal year 1999.[97] As has been noted elsewhere, the suburbs of Maryland had experienced significant job growth, but transportation networks to get recipients from inner-city neighborhoods out to suburban jobs often were fragmented.[98] In addition, recipients who remained after the "successes" left were more likely to suffer from multiple problems, such as low education levels, substance abuse, and mental illness.[99] Even if the drug-screening and treatment initiative succeeded in pushing or encouraging significant numbers of recipients into recovery, drug and alcohol addiction often were effectively treated only after repeated attempts.

Although these troubled recipients were subject to the two-year limit to cash receipt without work, which hit in January 1999, caseworker discretion to extend benefits for people in hardship and relatively broad interpretation of mandated work activities had softened the impact of these limits.[100] It was less clear how they would fare in 2002 when they faced the end to their five-year lifetime access to federally funded cash assistance. Under the requirements of the federal bill, the 20 percent exemption to the federal time limit would apply to the caseload as it existed at the time. If the caseload continued to shrink, in five years it could be made up almost entirely of the hardest-to-employ recipients and their children, only 20 percent of whom would be exempt (although the state could elect to support parents and children entirely with state funds).[101]

Another formidable implementation task that confronted DHR, local offices, and poor families arose from the new emphasis on initial case assessment, caseworker counseling, and local discretion. These approaches, though undoubtedly effective in many jurisdictions, increased the necessity to train welfare caseworkers for newly complex jobs that required them to exercise considerable judgment. In some jurisdictions, local officials and workers seemed to be rising effectively to the challenge; in others, such as Baltimore City, staff members' skills were said to be more limited. This raised serious concerns about their ability to perform these functions effectively without more training and time for adjustment (time that recipients, with their ticking clocks, didn't have).[102]

Social services officials also noted major problems with the state's management information system, which was unable to provide the breadth or depth of information required for case tracking under the new system.[103] Major implementation problems also arose over the drug-screening program; legislators responded during the 2000 session with changes to the system.[104] The availability of substance abuse treatment continued to be a problem.

Welfare rolls continued to decline while the economy remained strong, although the rate of decrease was expected to slow. Many ex-recipients were employed, and many of those who did not appear in state employment records were thought to have additional forms of income, including jobs that were "off the books." Transitional medical and child care benefits helped people in their first year off the rolls, and the EITC would help the working poor to some extent. The degree to which welfare reform in Maryland could help these families out of poverty was unclear, however.

Some participants in reform argued that this criterion was the wrong expectation of the reform initiatives—that the changes were too small and the program was too limited to justify expecting it to "solve the poverty problem." One researcher noted that if this were the yardstick, reform was destined to fail. Advocates and others emphasized the need to resist declaring welfare reform a success on the basis of caseload decreases, however. The large numbers of now working poor held jobs that usually did not offer health care or other benefits, and they had difficulty finding affordable child care during their often-irregular work hours. Affordable housing was increasingly scarce, and the state cut off cash aid to working families relatively quickly.[105] If welfare reform were to be judged a success, they argued, the state and the nation had to grapple with the question of whether these families' lives in fact had been made better, rather than simply celebrating that they were no longer on the public dole.

Finally, several related issues would help to shape the future of Maryland welfare reform. Although the state's voters reelected Democrat Glendening and maintained the Democratic majority in the General Assembly in 1998 and 2000, future electoral contests in the state and on the national level clearly would affect the direction of social policy. The partisan alignment of the governor's office and the General Assembly, as well as the fate of the individual legislators who were most committed to welfare policy, had major implications for the future of reform. The long-term economic health of the region and state also would affect how generous state policy decisions would be in coming years, as would the attention span and commitment of state politicians, social services officials, advocates, and the public. The long-term challenges of helping recipients would grow tougher as a greater proportion faced significant barriers and often-unsympathetic problems.

CONCLUSION

The pattern of interest group involvement in Maryland welfare reform provided some challenges to neo-Madisonian theory. Although the number and types of actors participating in the debate certainly were more modest than in Washington (there were basically no very conservative organizations), the state still saw the presence of a strong community of groups representing low-income families. In many ways these groups reflected their counterparts in the nation's capital one hour away. They did not always get what they wanted, but they had real influence on policy outcomes.

In total, 95 different groups attempted to influence policy by participating in legislative hearings, with intense activity by several organizations during consideration of the major welfare bills in Maryland in 1996 and 1997. This figure compares with a portfolio of 310 organizations and actors who participated in the national hearings process (see Table 4-3). All told, 46 organizations that could be said to represent low-income families (advocates, nonprofit and charitable providers, and unions, as well as researchers) were active in the debate, as indicated by hearings participation, compared with 142 such organizations in Washington, including advocates and researchers (see also Table 4-4).

On the whole, the policy outcomes of the state's welfare reform process have been fairly liberal, and according to my respondents, advocacy groups played a key role in framing the agenda and shaping the details of legislation. In particular, they were instrumental in decisions to preserve the entitlement, set a floor for benefit levels, establish the dedicated purpose account, and conduct long-term research on families who have left the rolls. The state also took a relatively soft approach to the family cap (though having one at all generally was not considered liberal) and provided benefits to legal immigrants out of state funds. Not all aspects of the bills could be considered generous—the drug-screening provisions and full-family sanction were opposed by many advocates, as were the low income levels (earnings eligibility limits) at which cash aid was cut off—and some people objected to using public welfare funds to subsidize private-sector jobs. Although the state was criticized for not using more money from its bulging coffers for welfare and working poor people, on the whole Maryland invested more rather than less in helping recipients move off welfare. The considerable size and activity of the advocacy community contributed to the relatively liberal shape of Maryland welfare reform.

Applying David Ellwood's typology of welfare reform proponents (see chapter 2)—work-oriented reformers, social policy critics, budget cutters and devolvers—to the Maryland policymaking process suggests the relative primacy of actors who focused on assisting recipients to make the transition to work, even at greater cost to the state. Conservative social policy critics were almost entirely absent from the debate, and as one participant noted, in Maryland "welfare reform was not sold as a budget cutter," at least during

Table 4-3
Maryland- and Washington-Based Organizations Involved in Welfare-Related Hearings, by Category

Category	Maryland: No. of Organizations/Actors	Washington: No. of Organizations/ Actors
Advocates: child advocacy, nonprofit and charitable providers, unions[a]	46	112
For-profit companies, business groups	23	19
Intergovernmental	18	64
Individuals	5	38
Professional associations	3	14
Researchers	0	30
Think tanks	0	12
"Traditional values" groups	0	14
Miscellaneous	0	7
TOTAL	**95**	**310**

Sources: Data from audiotapes, witness lists, and copies of testimony in bill files of nineteen House and Senate public hearings, Department of Legislative Services Library. Author's calculations.

[a]As with national groups, the lines between advocacy and nonprofit service or charitable organizations often are blurry. Some advocacy groups also provided services, and some charitable groups also were committed to advocacy.

the beginning years of devolution, despite the opportunities provided by the block grant structure.[106]

It is worth noting that the active interest groups in Maryland included several Washington-based organizations, such as CLASP, the CBPP, and the national office of AFSCME, the public sector employees' union. These groups somewhat altered the portfolio of organizations participating in the welfare debate, and the state's proximity to Washington organizations was said to have provided valuable resources to advocates and others, with something of a political spillover effect.

Even without the Washington groups, however, the number of organizations that were active in welfare reform in Maryland was considerable, as was their level of activity. The question remains why. As discussed earlier, a refined reading of neo-Madisonian theory should include a range of political factors such as political culture/ideology and social diversity, party, the

Table 4-4
Maryland Frequent Testifiers

Organization/Actor	No. of Times Testifying
Maryland Legislative Council of Social Workers/NASW	11
Maryland Catholic Conference	9
Welfare Advocates	8
Maryland Food Committee	8
Action for the Homeless	8
Maryland Chamber of Commerce	8
Maryland Interfaith Legislative Committee	7
Presbytery of Baltimore	7
Advocates for Children and Youth	7
Maryland Association of Nonprofits	6
Work Not Welfare Coalition	6

Note: These acts of testimony include oral testimony before legislative committees and written testimony or positions registered with no oral testimony given.

professionalism and capacity of the state's institutions and welfare bureaucracy, the commitments and motivations of individual policy entrepreneurs inside and outside government, and the relative heterogeneity of politically powerful groups within the state. These elements contributed to the extent and power of the advocacy community and exerted their own influence on welfare reform in Maryland.

The proximity of Washington not only added several national organizations to the debate; its spillover effects also increasingly helped to shape the political culture of the state as a whole. Washington suburbs in Montgomery, Prince George's, and other counties have grown rapidly, many of their inhabitants are federal employees, and they tend to be fairly liberal. Although Elazar considered Maryland "individualist," and in the past its politicians behaved so (for a time, corruption appeared to be endemic), I argue that in recent years it has grown more "moralist" with the influence of these residents as well as those in the city of Baltimore. Certainly they have contributed to the state's greater social diversity and a relatively liberal political environment.

The Democratic Party controlled both branches of government and had for some time, and the Republicans who were most involved in welfare reform were moderate, which also contributed to a more liberal tone. The two chairs of the central House and Senate committees—Madden (representing Prince George's County) and Rosenberg (representing Baltimore)—were widely considered to be committed to the issue and knowledgeable about it. In addition, the newly created Joint Welfare Committee met regularly, including during the interim periods between legislative sessions. The relatively professional legislature had competent professional staff assistance on welfare issues, and the lack of term limits helped ensure a continuity of expertise. Certain key members, committee leaders, and staffers, then, exhibited significant welfare policymaking capacity.

The political power of Baltimore City also was considerable, even though city government officials were not especially active during the period of greatest change in welfare policy. Many black political leaders from Baltimore were well-established and respected, which helped to reduce the potential racial divide in welfare politics. Several participants mentioned the influence of the city's General Assembly delegation. In addition to Rosenberg, Senator Barbara Hoffman (chair of the Senate Budget and Taxation Committee), Senator Thomas Bromwell (chair of the Senate Finance Committee), and Delegate Howard Rawlings (chair of the House Appropriations Committee) were cited as particularly attentive to the needs of their jurisdiction. The advocacy and social services groups also tended to be centered in Baltimore, even if their reach was statewide. BUILD focused largely on Baltimore's low-income families, and the city's black churches were unusually active.

State welfare agency officials also were widely considered to be dedicated to and well-informed about welfare policy. Although those at the top levels of DHR were relatively new appointees, they were highly regarded, and several influential mid-level personnel had been there for some time. The capacity of the state's welfare bureaucracy was considerable as well. There was a cohesion in the state's welfare policy domain—including advocates, the legislature, and the executive branch—that eased the policy process while still incorporating a fairly wide range of viewpoints. Moreover, expertise and research were valued in the debate.

Yet there still is reason to be concerned about the long-term prospects for devolved welfare reform, even in a state with as vibrant an advocacy community and liberal political environment as Maryland's. Reform during the mid-1990s occurred under almost ideal circumstances, with a strong economy drawing recipients into jobs and block grants ultimately paying more than anticipated as caseloads declined. The state remained vulnerable to economic downturns, however. As recently as the early 1990s, lawmakers lowered basic grant levels and cut the state's Disability Assistance and Loan Program general assistance program, and welfare advocates were in fact considered quite weak.[107] With the TANF block grant system and its constant level of federal funding no matter what the demand, every additional dollar the state would spend must come entirely from its own coffers, making increased welfare spending during recessions difficult.

Although many policymakers clearly were concerned about the well-being of low-income families, lawmakers often bow to the demands of the business interests that provide tax revenue and jobs before those of poor people who frequently do not vote. This analysis suggests that the concern about interstate competition still may have merit in the long term, if not immediately. As recently as early 1996, when it looked like block grants would reduce state funding, the governor proposed cuts in welfare grants at the same time he discussed future sports arena deals with the owners of the area's National Football League teams. Given the frequently expressed concern about Virginia's competitive advantages in attracting business, during an economic downturn development priorities may be expected to take precedence over programs for poor families once again. How effective the state's energetic community of advocates will be in counterbalancing these forces remains to be seen.

NOTES

1. For one account of reform in the early 1990s, see Donald F. Norris and James X. Bembry, "Primordial Policy Soup, Bureaucratic Politics, and Welfare Policy Making in Maryland," in *The Politics of Welfare Reform*, ed. Donald F. Norris and Lyke Thompson (Thousand Oaks, Calif.: Sage Publications, 1995).

2. Norris and Bembry, "Primordial Policy Soup"; interviews; Gady A. Epstein, "Needy Unlikely to See Aid Rise," *Baltimore Sun*, 5 March 2000.

3. Salaries were about $30,000 per year, and turnover had been somewhat in excess of 30 percent in recent elections. Data from Maryland Department of Legislative Services.

4. Written testimony of Lynda G. Fox, Deputy Secretary for Programs and Local Operations, Maryland Department of Human Resources, "Briefing to the Joint Committee on Welfare Reform: Cash Assistance Caseload Trends," 6 October 1998, 5.

5. Norris and Bembry, "Primordial Policy Soup"; interviews.

6. Ronald C. Lippincott and Larry W. Thomas, "Maryland: The Struggle for Power in the Midst of Changes, Complexity, and Institutional Constraints," in *Interest Group Politics in the Northeastern States*, ed. Ronald J. Hrebenar and Clive S. Thomas (University Park: Pennsylvania State University Press, 1993).

7. Norris and Bembry, "Primordial Policy Soup"; interviews.

8. Ibid.

9. Editorial, *Baltimore Sun*, 14 January 1994, 18A.

10. Poll results reported in Laura Lippman and Marina Sarris, "Schaefer Welfare Reform Proposes 'Family Cap,'" *Baltimore Sun*, 27 January 1994, 1B.

11. Robert Timberg, "Welfare Reform Bills Clash," *Baltimore Sun*, 29 March 1994, 1A; John W. Frece and Marina Sarris, "Schaefer Agenda Is Gutted," *Baltimore Sun*, 12 April 1994, 1A; Deborah A. Liederman, "County's Lawmakers Back Welfare Reform," *Baltimore Sun*, Howard County Edition, 6 March 1994; interviews.

12. Several Commission members wrote a minority opinion dissenting with the family cap recommendation. Maryland Governor's Commission on Welfare Policy, "For the Good of the Whole . . . : Making Welfare Work," final report of Governor's Commission on Welfare Policy, June 1994; interviews.

13. Norris and Bembry, "Primordial Policy Soup"; Frank Langfitt, "Glendening Supports Welfare Reform Proposal," *Baltimore Sun*, 21 March 1995, 2B; interviews.

14. Interviews. Fox would take over Collins's job when the latter joined the federal HHS several years later.

15. Editorial, *Baltimore Sun*, 3 February 1995, 10A.

16. Caseloads in January 1995 were about 228,000 recipients—an increase from about 221,000 the year before. Caseloads in most other states peaked in 1993 or 1994, suggesting that their economies rebounded more rapidly than did Maryland's. Fox, written testimony, "Briefing to the Joint Committee on Welfare Reform," 6 October 1998, 3–5.

17. Written testimony from bill file for SB 754.

18. Terry M. Neal, "Family Cap Debate Holds Up Md. Welfare Legislation," *Washington Post*, 10 April 1995, B1; also written hearing testimony on SB 754 by Welfare Advocates and Lutheran Office on Public Policy, among other groups.

19. Report by Maryland Budget and Tax Policy Institute, cited in Donna St. George, "Aid Cuts Make It Hard for Some Going from Welfare to Work," *Washington Post*, 25 February 1999, B5.

20. Interviews.

21. Marina Sarris, "Welfare, Ethics Law Among Tall Hurdles," *Baltimore Sun*, 10 April 1995, 1A; hearings witness lists; interviews.

22. Written testimony from AFSCME, Council 92, on SB 754, from bill files available from Legislative Services Reference Library.

23. Lockheed had met only the minimum collection levels required by the contract by the end of 1997, and the work would go to another for-profit contractor in 1999. The tax credit also was said to have been only modestly effective. Robert E. Pierre, "Tax Incentive Little Used in Maryland," *Washington Post*, 3 December 1997, A18.

24. Michael Abramowitz, "Federal Cuts Put Squeeze on Welfare; Maryland Pilot Program at Risk, Task Force Says, *Washington Post*, 7 October 1995, B1. Also, interviews with participants in task force meetings.

25. Abramowitz, "Federal Cuts Put Squeeze on Welfare."

26. Laura Lippman, "Needy, Allies See Welfare Reform as Rising Storm," *Baltimore Sun*, 2 October 1995, 1A.

27. John W. Frece, "Md. Welfare Payments to Be Pared," *Baltimore Sun*, 12 October 1995, 1B.

28. Interviews.

29. Abramowitz, "Federal Cuts Put Squeeze on Welfare"; *1996 Green Book*, 446.

30. *1998 Green Book*, 452.

31. 1995 Census estimates, available at www.census.gov/population/estimates/states/srh/srh95.txt.

32. Fox testimony, 6.

33. Editorial, *Baltimore Sun*, 17 January 1996, 12A.

34. Power within the Maryland legislature tends to be centralized within the leadership and committee structure. Lippincott and Thomas, "Maryland: The Struggle for Power," 136.

35. This and the following information, unless otherwise noted, are from the General Assembly website, "Bills by Subject: Welfare—1996 Regular Session," available at mlis.state.md.us (accessed September 1998). Also from individual bill files available from Legislative Services Reference Library.

36. Ibid.

37. Interviews.

38. General Assembly website, "Bill Information—1996 Regular Session—HB 1061."

39. Testimony and witness lists from Legislative Services Department bill file for HB 1061.

40. From General Assembly website, "Bill Information—1996 Regular Session—SB 778"; interviews.

41. Ibid.

42. Interviews.

43. Interviews.

44. Bane and Ellwood, *Welfare Realities*, chapter 1; interviews.

45. The implication that the status of "customer" carries with it a claim to greater respect than that of "citizen" seems to indicate the diminution in the standing of public institutions and identities in comparison with the private market.That is another book, however.

46. Interviews.

47. Testimony from bill files; audiotapes; interviews.

48. Witness lists, testimony from bill files; audiotapes of Senate Finance Committee hearings on SB 778; interviews.

49. Thomas and Hrebenar, "Interest Groups in the States," 131.

50. Lippincott and Thomas, "Maryland: The Struggle for Power," 139–43, 164; interviews.

51. Interviews.

52. Maryland Department of Legislative Services, *General Assembly of Maryland: List of Committees and Roster, 1998 Session*, February 1998, 92.

53. Interviews.

54. One list of gains made by advocates in 1994–1997 is contained in "Welfare Reform: 15 Positive Policies, 15 Welfare Reform Issues Addressed by Advocates in Maryland," Maryland Catholic Charities Division of Community Services; available at www.catholiccharities.md.org/welfare.htm.

55. Audiotape of public hearings on SB 778.

56. Testimony from bill files.

57. Interviews.

58. Interviews.

59. Maryland General Assembly, *Maryland Session Laws of 1996*, Ch. 351, Preamble, 2373.

60. Information on final bill from *Maryland Session Laws of 1996*, Ch. 351 (Senate Bill 778), 2370–2426; "SB 778 Welfare Innovation Act of 1996" description contained in bill file, Department of Legislative Services; Maryland Catholic Charities, Division of Community Services.

61. The Minimum Living Level (MLL) was set by a governor's commission focusing on welfare reform in 1980 after research into the cost of living in the state; by law, it was adjusted for inflation each year thereafter. The 61 percent figure was established because it was the percentage of the 1996 MLL that was equal to the state's food stamp and cash assistance grant that year. The state's cash grant had lost almost half its real value in the prior twenty-six years, and advocates and others regarded legislation that permanently linked welfare and food stamps to the MLL as guarding against future erosion. The proposal created little controversy or resistance.

62. Jon Jeter, "Social Services in Md. Get Rare Opportunity," *Washington Post*, 9 January 1996, B1; interviews.

63. C. Fraser Smith, "Sarbanes' 'New Deal' Stance," *Baltimore Sun*, 6 August 1996, 2B.

64. John Jeter, "Maryland Gets Leeway on Welfare Reform," *Washington Post*, 17 August 1996, B4.

65. Sean Scully, "Maryland Decides to Go with Federal Law," *Washington Times*, 18 September 1996, C6.

66. Bart Jansen, "State Gets More Welfare Funds, More Questions," *The Capital* (Annapolis), 18 September 1996, D1; Scully, "Maryland Decides to Go with Federal Law."

67. Michael Dresser, "Md. to Pay Benefits to Immigrants," *Baltimore Sun*, 17 September 1996, 1A; Joint Committee's 1996 report, 15; Jansen, "State Gets More Welfare Funds."

68. Maryland General Assembly, *Joint Committee on Welfare Reform: Report of the 1996 Interim* (Annapolis: Department of Fiscal Services, 1996).

69. Kathy Lally and Jonathan Bor, "Drug Testing for Welfare Faces Hurdles," *Baltimore Sun*, 8 December 1996, 1A.

70. Jon Jeter, "Drug Testing Plan Could Balloon Maryland Welfare Costs," *Washington Post*, 5 December 1996, E1.

71. Jon Jeter, "Glendening Rejects Church Groups' Main Demands," *Washington Post*, 13 December 1996, G2.

72. Maryland General Assembly, "Legislative History, Bill Information—1997 Regular Session—SB 499"; available at mlis.state.md.us/1997rs/subjects/welfare.htm.

73. Presentation by Madden, audiotape of hearing on SB 499, 19 February 1997. Also "Legislative History, Bill Information—1997 Regular Session—SB 499," at General Assembly website.

74. "Legislative History, Bill Information—1997 Regular Session—SB 499," at General Assembly website. The House held a major hearing on HB 653, along with

related legislation, on February 18th, but much of that bill ultimately was folded into SB 499.

75. Senate Finance Committee hearings on SB 499, from audiotapes.

76. John Rivera, "Anti-Poverty Coalition Gives Poor Grades to Assembly Performance: Baltimore Delegates Singled Out by Groups," *Baltimore Sun*, 15 April 1997.

77. Fox testimony at Senate Finance Committee hearing on SB 499, from audiotapes.

78. Yvonne Gilchrest testimony at Senate Finance Committee hearing on SB 499, from audiotapes.

79. Ivan Penn, "Legislators Warned Poverty Is Increasing," *Baltimore Sun*, 11 January 1997.

80. Interviews; Center for Community Change, "Church and Neighborhood: BUILD-ing Beyond Congregations," organizing newsletter, no. 12, January 1999, available at www.communitychange.org/organizing/build12.htm. See also Robert H. Wilson, Pat Wong, and Heywood T. Sanders, "The Policy of Community in Public Policy," in *Public Policy and Community: Activism and Governance in Texas*, ed. Robert H. Wilson (Austin: University of Texas Press, 1997).

81. In contrast, CLASP—the other Washington-based participant—took no position on the legislation the prior year.

82. Welfare Advocates 1997 testimony on SB 499, from bill file.

83. Maryland Catholic Charities, Division of Community Services; interviews; advocacy group testimony from SB 499 and HB 653 bill files.

84. Appleby testimony on SB 499 from bill files; John Rivera, "Anti-Poverty Coalition Gives Poor Grades to Assembly Performance," *Baltimore Sun*, 15 April 1997; interviews.

85. AFSCME representatives' testimony at Senate Finance Committee hearing on SB 499, from audiotapes.

86. Nonetheless, several participants called the third-party payment structure "an administrative nightmare." Maryland General Assembly, Senate Bill 499, Enrolled Bill; "Summary of SB 499, The Welfare Innovation Act of 1997," from SB 499 bill file, Department of Legislative Services Library, undated document; interviews.

87. SB 499, 6; Sen. Martin Madden, co-sponsor of bill, audiotape of Finance Committee hearing on SB 499.

88. SB 499, 27–31.

89. Governor's Press Office, "Maryland at the National Forefront in Welfare Reform Efforts and Initiatives," 30 June 1997; also "Comments by Governor Parris N. Glendening, Executive Order Signing: Displacement and Family Investment Program, Monday, June 30, 1997," available at www.gov.md.state.us.

90. U.S. Department of Health and Human Services, Administration for Children and Families, "Changes in TANF Caseloads," 14 December 2000, available at www.acf.gov/news/stats/caseload.htm.

91. Maryland General Assembly, Department of Legislative Services, Senate Bill 686, Enrolled Bill; Maryland Department of Human Resources, "Report on

Legislation Enacted During the 1998 Session," available at www.dhr.state.md.us/dhr/profile.htm.

92. Maryland became one of only eight states to offer a refundable EITC (a non-refundable credit means that people who owe taxes get no financial benefit from the credit because they have no tax debt against which to claim it). Robert E. Pierre, "Maryland Session a Success for Poor: Reversing Trend, Spending Increased," *Washington Post*, 13 April 1998, B1.

93. C. Fraser Smith, "Assembly Cuts Taxes 10 Percent," *Baltimore Sun*, 4 April 1997; C. Fraser Smith and Thomas W. Waldron, "Stadium Aid Could be Key for Govenor," *Baltimore Sun*, 25 February 1996.

94. Pierre, "Maryland Session a Success for Poor."

95. Welfare and Child Support Research and Training Group, *Life After Welfare: Fifth Report*, executive summary, School of Social Work, University of Maryland, October 2000. The authors note that the study used, among other sources, state employment data that include all employers covered by state unemployment insurance law—about 93 percent of employers. People who worked for the other 7 percent of employers and those who worked "off the books" would not be included.

96. Ibid., iv–vii.

97. Maryland Department of Human Resources, Secretary of Planning, "DHR Fact Pack," 27, available at www.dhr.state.md.us/pi/index.htm.

98. Senator Madden proposed during the 2000 session a program to assist 1,500 welfare families, about half of whom would be from Baltimore, in moving to job-rich areas in the suburbs. This plan met with strong opposition, echoing white suburbanites' virulent opposition to an earlier program to move residents of Baltimore's public housing to neighborhoods outside the city. Gady A. Epstein, "Plan to Help Move Poor Is Scrapped," *Baltimore Sun*, 2 February 2000.

99. Interviews.

100. Gerard Shields, "Welfare Cuts Loom for 9,000: State, Baltimore Seek to Cushion Impact of Jan. 1 Deadline," *Baltimore Sun*, 28 August 1998; interviews.

101. In 2001, the legislature established a fully state-funded program to aid families who hit the five-year time limit, but it was still too early to know how the program would be implemented or how expansive it would be. See SB 541, Welfare Innovation Act of 2001, available at mlis.state.md.us/2001rs/billfile/sb0541.htm.

102. Interviews.

103. Fox testimony before Joint Committee on Welfare Reform, 6 October 1998; interviews.

104. Avram Goldstein, "State Rehab Program for Welfare Recipients Goes Unused," *Washington Post*, 5 September 1998, B4; House Bill 1160, Enrolled Bill, 2000 Regular Session, Maryland General Assembly, available at mlis.state.md.us/2000rs/billfile/hb1160.htm; interviews.

105. St. George, "Aid Cuts Make It Hard." A family of three no longer received cash aid when its income reached $520 per month.

106. Devolvers on the national level advocated shifting from federal to state control. Although some states devolved control further to the local level, this was a less clearly articulated theoretical position during this period.

107. Norris and Bembry, "Primordial Policy Soup," 177.

5

Texas: Reforming Welfare in a Low-Benefit State

Texas, the second-most populous state in the nation, joined the union in 1845 after a bloody war with Mexico and ten years of independence as the Republic of Texas. This sense of independence still permeates its political culture, as does a rhetoric of individualism and general skepticism about government. Both have contributed to a fragmented system of limited government and a history of modest social programs, including very low welfare grants. Texas's identity as a "low benefit state" has been strong.

With more than 19 million people, the state certainly would qualify as a large jurisdiction, and the Madisonian expectation that a greater variety of "factions" would participate in policymaking in fact holds true, at least in the case of welfare policy. During the mid-1990s, basically the same types of organizations participated in Texas as in Washington. The welfare debate in the legislature was more restricted in terms of the sheer number of actors participating, however, with far fewer groups than in Washington and fewer even than in Maryland. A modest proportion of these actors were advocates for low-income families—although some of these were very active—and an even more modest number had significant influence in a debate whose parameters were narrow. The state fit Elazar's traditionalistic political culture, with a fairly limited group of people exercising political power (voter turnout has been quite low) and a distinct emphasis on the market and business interests.[1] Despite increased party competition in recent years, with Republicans gaining influence, the ideological divide between Democrats and Republicans was narrow, and many of the former still fit the old conservative southern Democrat mold.[2] Although Texas's political institutions have grown more professional and representative in recent years, they are highly fragmented, and the professionalism of the legislature, in particular, was limited by its biennial sessions and by members' low pay. With a salary of less than $8,000 per year, legislators had to have other sources of income, which drew away from the time they could spend on government business. The policymaking process around welfare reform in the mid-1990s was largely collegial; most of the actors agreed on the basic framework for approaching it. The limited parameters of the debate contributed to a generally conservative approach to low-income families.

This chapter considers welfare reform in Texas during the 1995 and 1997 biennial sessions. It briefly explores the political context of welfare policymaking and policy for low-income families as it had developed in the state. Then it examines the political processes that led to the 1995 passage of HB 1863, the state's major welfare reform bill—which created Achieving Change for Texans (ACT), the Texas waiver program. It also explores the political influences on legislation in 1997, the state's appropriations decisions after the federal government passed PRWORA, and the push toward privatization between 1996 and 1997. As in the analyses of welfare policymaking in Washington, D.C., and Maryland, this chapter looks at pressures within government and the part that nongovernmental actors played in shaping the state's approach to welfare overhaul. Finally, it briefly considers efforts to revisit reform during the 1999 session, the future of policy for low-income families in the state, and the lessons of Texas welfare policy in the mid-1990s for the application of neo-Madisonian theory.

CONTEXT OF WELFARE POLICYMAKING IN TEXAS

As in other southern states, the Civil War and Reconstruction have cast a long shadow over Texas politics. Texas joined the Confederacy in 1861 and after the Civil War ended was occupied by Republican Reconstruction forces until the 1870s, when the Democratic Party regained power. It was a slave state prior to the Civil War, it passed Black Codes and Jim Crow laws in the 1870s and the early 1900s, and it practiced legal segregation and restrictions on black political participation until federal intervention in the 1950s and 1960s.[3] Like many southern states in recent years, Texas has been shifting from long domination by conservative Democrats to growing Republican Party strength. Members of both parties within the government, with some exceptions, tended to be essentially conservative, and in the mid-1990s the partisan divide on welfare was narrow. Although a few issues were contentious, the overall direction of welfare policy had broad bipartisan support.

Despite the presence of high-profile wealthy residents such as Ross Perot and Sid R. Bass, Texas is a poor state. The poverty rate (19.1 percent in 1994) was well above the national average, placing the state forty-seventh in the nation. The child poverty rate remained steady at 26 percent between 1990 and 1997. The median household income was $30,755 in 1994, compared with a national figure of $32,264. Income inequality was fairly high: One study ranked it twelfth highest in the nation. The state had no income tax; instead, it relied on property and general sales taxes, which tend to be regressive, as well as severance taxes.[4]

In the mid-1990s, the ethnic composition of the state was diverse: 85 percent white, 12 percent black, 28 percent Hispanic, 2.5 percent Asian, and 0.5 percent Native American.[5] About 11 percent of the population were noncitizen immigrants in 1996—behind only California and New York. Texas was growing fast, at almost twice the rate of the nation. It also was increasingly urban: About 84 percent of residents now lived in cities, although 196 of the state's 254 counties were still rural. The state's rural legacy and sheer physical size (second only to Alaska) contributed to a political culture that emphasized individualism and self-sufficiency.[6]

TEXAS WELFARE POLICY

In the mid-1990s, Texas provided financial assistance only to low-income families with children and had no statewide general assistance program. Welfare benefits were low: In 1995, a family of three received a maximum of $188 per month in cash benefits. This amount was the fourth lowest level in the country, leading only Mississippi ($120), Alabama ($164), and Tennessee ($185). The national median was $389.[7] The average size of a family on welfare in Texas was three—one female parent and two children—and the average cash grant was $160. Only 40 percent of families with children who were living under the poverty level received assistance, and since 1970 the grant had lost 69 percent of its real value.[8] Nonetheless, an increase was not on the agenda in either 1995 or 1997 (though the legislature would increase it by $13 in 1999).

As several participants noted, the state didn't really have a "welfare problem" as much as it had a serious "working poor problem" because almost no one could support a family on what welfare paid, even with the average $313 monthly food stamp allocation. People on welfare, therefore, also had to work, though if they made more than about $400 per month they were ineligible for any cash assistance.[9] Texas's poor residents particularly tended to be "cyclers," using cash assistance intermittently for short periods of time when they were hit by job loss, family upheaval, or illness, rather than the "long-term dependent" whose image drove much of reform nationally.

Texas's identity as a low-benefit state permeated the political dynamics of welfare reform in 1995 and 1997. Aspects of the debate reflected the intense rhetoric and political pressures of the national debate. On the whole, however, Texas avoided many of the more extreme proposals pushed by ideological conservatives in Washington. Many Texas conservatives identified welfare as a budget issue, but no one could reasonably argue that it was, by itself, a big-ticket item. Nor did the meager benefits lend much credence to the widespread moral arguments that cash aid, or grant increases for additional children, were likely to draw poor Texans into dependency and encourage immoral behavior. (Nonetheless, a few legislators clung to this view.)

About 3.2 percent of the Texas population (600,128 people) received cash assistance in state fiscal year 1997. This figure represented a decrease of 24 percent from a peak caseload of 786,313 in 1994; the numbers kept dropping through 1998, though they began to rise somewhat in 1999.[10] The largest caseloads were in the Houston and Dallas areas, as well as the rural Rio Grande Valley, which had the greatest share of two-parent AFDC/TANF families and high unemployment rates. The lowest caseloads were in the rural northwest region of the state and the eastern region near the Louisiana and Arkansas borders. Despite the size of their caseloads, Houston and Dallas also experienced the greatest declines, aided by their strong economic growth; caseloads there dropped by more than 40 percent between 1994 and 1997. About 22 percent of families on welfare in Texas in September 1997 were white, 44 percent Hispanic, and 33 percent black, with Native Americans and Asians each making up less than 1 percent.[11]

Like most other governmental functions in the state, the structure of the social services bureaucracy was highly fragmented, with diffuse lines of authority. The Health and Human Services Commission (HHSC) was established in 1991 to improve coordination of the state's social services agencies. Its chair was a gubernatorial appointee, and its members (also appointed by the governor) had staggered terms. The chair during part of 1995 and all of the 1997 session was Michael D. McKinney, who was appointed by Governor George W. Bush. The HHSC had broad oversight and coordination responsibilities and could veto Human Services department decisions, but it was widely considered ineffectual as structured.[12] It would play a major role in the 1996 privatization controversy, however.

During the 1995 session, Burton Raiford was the commissioner of the Texas Department of Human Services (DHS). He resigned, and Terry Trimble served as interim commissioner during 1997. The fragmentation and staggered terms of HHSC members meant that changes in the governor's office tended to trickle down to DHS staff only with time as a greater proportion of HHSC members became appointees of the incumbent governor. During the initial welfare debate, DHS personnel and operations were buffered somewhat from the political shifts after Democratic Governor Ann Richards lost to Republican Bush. One participant described agency personnel as "very client-oriented." By late 1997, when DHS commissioner Eric M. Bost was hired, the department was more affected by the decisions of Bush appointees.[13]

1995: THE POLITICS OF MAJOR OVERHAUL

The Texas House of Representatives is a cumbersome body of 150 members and 50 committees whose chairs and membership turn over fairly frequently.

Despite this fragmentation and lack of continuity, the House took on welfare reform in 1993, led by the newly appointed chairman of the House Human Services Committee, Rep. Harvey Hilderbran (R-Kerrville). Hilderbran was said to be eager to learn more about welfare policy, though he was new to the subject. Despite the fact that he was a conservative Republican in the Democratically controlled House, he chaired a House Human Services interim committee requested by the House speaker in 1994 to study the issue.[14] He also headed up a welfare study group of the Texas Conservative Coalition, a bipartisan organization of conservative legislators. Gubernatorial candidate Bush called for welfare reform in his 1994 campaign, attacking the Richards administration for increases in the welfare rolls and—like so many other politicians—taking advantage of welfare reform's symbolic value. The legislature did not initiate major action until 1995, however.[15]

Although Texas had not been a leader in social policy, in the 1990s state politicians were feeling and reflecting the same swings in national mood and political incentives that led to Bill Clinton's "end-welfare-as-we-know-it" pledge and Republican Congressional interest in the issue. As more states undertook waiver projects, politicians talked to each other, competed with each other to be innovative, and increasingly identified welfare policy as an area that offered rich opportunities for credit-claiming. Like other Americans, few Texans knew much about the details of the existing program or reform plans, nor did they get closely involved in the debate, despite widely reported public support for "reform." Several participants noted the general public indifference during the Texas welfare debate.

In the winter and spring of 1995, during the 74th session, the legislature passed the state's major welfare reform plan, HB 1863, and directed DHS to apply for federal waivers to implement the new program, called Achieving Change for Texans. The federal Department of Health and Human Services granted the waivers in March 1996. As in Maryland, one impetus for the new system, according to participants, was the belief that national welfare reform—or at least greater state flexibility—was becoming inevitable. State officials said they wanted to anticipate this development and design a system tailored to the distinctive characteristics of Texas and its poor residents.

The Legislative Debate

HB 1863 was rooted in a range of sources, including the House Committee on Human Services' 1994 interim report,[16] the report of the Texas Conservative Coalition,[17] and the state comptroller's Texas Performance Review report for 1995, titled "A Partnership for Independence: Public Assistance Reform Options."[18] The comptroller, who was independently elected, certified the state's balanced budget and wielded considerable influence. His biennial report analyzing government services also earned him real clout. This particular report had been requested by the late Bob Bullock, and officials borrowed liberally from it. Bullock, a Democrat, at the time was lieutenant governor; he also was independently elected and was widely considered the most powerful official in the state.

The first two reports were the source for the House committee's first comprehensive welfare bill, which Hilderbran introduced with bipartisan sponsors in January 1995. The thirty-one-member Senate, in turn, embraced the comptroller's report as the base for its more moderate early welfare reform bill, introduced a month later. As at the national level, the Senate was considered more centrist than the House. Governor Bush also flagged welfare reform as a key issue in his 1995 State of the State address, calling for two-year time limits and a family cap.[19]

The House interim report had the disadvantage of presenting no actual plan for overhaul. The House committee's composition was bipartisan, and although members agreed on the major issues, they could not reach consensus on what to do about them. The comptroller's report, on the other hand, made a specific set of recommendations, and his office certified that these proposals would cut costs.[20] The report of the Texas Conservative Coalition offered concrete recommendations as well and helped establish the range of alternatives.[21]

It is essential to remember that the backdrop to welfare reform in Texas, as in the other states, was the ascendancy of conservative Republicans in Washington during early 1995. Some Texas legislators saw themselves as engaged in a guessing game with the federal government and suggested that if they developed their own plan they could avoid having to implement more radical changes being advocated in Washington (and by Governor Bush), such as a cumulative two-year time limit and family caps.[22] It is unclear, however, if this attitude was used to justify or to repel radical change in state policy.

Consistent throughout the political debate in Austin was the desire to avoid spending money, although concerns about moral decay—presumably caused by welfare—also were raised. The debate also included genuine philosophical disagreement about the best way to help low-income families join the mainstream: through programs and supports, or by pushing them into self-sufficiency through a "tough love" approach. Many participants saw no inconsistency between cutting costs and making fundamental changes in welfare to bring recipients out of "dependency." In fact, for some policymakers cutting costs was the major goal. Comptroller John Sharp stated that the goal of reform was to "change the checkbook and the rulebook of the system." His "Partnership" report identified five other broad goals, some at odds with the others: encouraging personal responsibility and family preservation; preventing at-risk Texans from depending on cash assistance; stopping returns to welfare; enabling Texans with disabilities to leave public aid; and streamlining the system and reducing fraud. Legislators also cited cutting caseloads, preserving a safety net for children, and strengthening child support enforcement.[23]

The House Committee on Human Services held two public hearings during February 1995. In its original form, the House bill included a proposal to provide a single flat grant of $184 per month awarded to a family regardless of its size. It introduced the idea of tiered time limits that depended on recipients' experience and education: Those with the most experience and education would receive only three months of cash assistance; those with less would be eligible for somewhat more time on cash assistance. It required a "personal responsibility agreement," including mandated child immunizations and cooperation with the state's efforts to identify the fathers of children born out of wedlock. It also introduced the idea of "finger imaging" recipients to reduce fraud.

In the Senate, Health and Human Services Committee chair Judith Zaffirini (D-Laredo) filed her bill, SB 22, about a month later, with seven coauthors drawn from both parties. The committee held two public hearings. Most other welfare-related bills were folded into SB 22 or dropped. The Senate bill was more moderate than its House counterpart, with no family cap and time limits tested on a pilot basis. The human services committees of the two chambers clearly were in competition over welfare reform. The House took the lead and moved more quickly toward radical and statewide change; members of the Senate committee suggested that their work represented a more thoughtful and responsible approach.[24]

Between March and April, the House Committee on Human Services held two more public hearings and considered more than fifty amendments. One of the most unexpected amendments allowed alimony payments in the case of divorce, for the first time in the state's history. It would be limited to marriages that lasted ten years or more and provided very modest amounts. Attempts to introduce alimony to the state had been unsuccessful for years, but when it was finally pitched as a way to shift the financial burden of assisting a recently divorced woman from the welfare system to her ex-spouse, the concept gained real support for the first time.[25]

Another major amendment took many legislators, advocates, and policymakers by surprise and caused controversy for several years to come. It was more than 100 pages long and would consolidate and make major changes to the state's workforce programs. The proposal would send money to the localities in the form of block grants and fundamentally restructure the division of responsibility for welfare, work, and child care programs between DHS and a new Texas Workforce Commission (TWC). The TWC would be controlled by a three-person board appointed by the governor, and its programs would be managed by as many as twenty-eight local "workforce development boards" controlled by local business, government, and labor leaders. The emphasis was on radical decentralization. DHS would retain responsibility for welfare eligibility determination, but the new workforce commission and local boards would take over the JOBS/CHOICES training program, child care, Job Training Partnership Act (JTPA) (later the Workforce Investment Act [WIA]), and food stamp employment training programs, as well as twenty-four other work and training programs.[26]

The amendment was introduced in the Senate at the end of April 1995 and was scarcely debated in the House or the Senate during the session's final days, despite the massive changes it entailed. Its sponsor, Sen. Rodney Ellis (D-Houston area), was said to have incorporated it into the new welfare bill to force better coordination of the state's very fragmented workforce programs. It had liberal and conservative proponents: The former saw it as a way to get more out of the state's employment programs and destigmatize welfare-to-work efforts, and the latter saw it as a means to increase private-sector control. The TWC amendment was approved with the clock ticking down on the 74th session during the final rush to pass the welfare bill.[27]

Some details of the House and Senate bills approved earlier still differed significantly, requiring that they go to conference committee. The conference negotiated a compromise during May; the House approved the bill on May 27th, and the Senate passed it the next day. Governor Bush signed HB 1863—the comprehensive welfare bill—in June 1995, and it went into effect on September 1, 1995.[28]

All told, the House committee with primary jurisdiction held four public hearings on its major welfare reform bills, and the equivalent Senate committee held three public hearings on its major welfare reform legislation. To be fair, many advocates and others participated in formulating the comptroller and House interim committee reports that provided the base for HB 1863. Moreover, as several participants noted, in Texas as elsewhere, many details of legislation are hashed out through private discussions and negotiations even before it gets to committee. Nonetheless, the massive statewide overhaul moved through the legislature and into law very quickly.

The central provisions of the ACT plan were as follows:[29]

- *Tiered time limits*. Recipients with a high school diploma or its equivalent, or eighteen months of work experience, received 12 months of cash assistance; those with three years of high school or at least six months' work experience received assistance for 24 months; and those with less than three years of high school and less than six months of work received up to 36 months of assistance. The caretakers' grants—but not the children's—were time-limited.

- *Welfare "freeze-out."* Once their time limits ran out, parents or caretakers were "frozen" out of the program for five years, after which they could reapply.

- *Personal responsibility agreements (PRAs)*. Recipients were required to sign "personal responsibility agreements" that addressed drug and alcohol use, the right to quit jobs, child immunization and health care, and paternity establishment. The PRAs did not require reciprocal state responsibilities, such as providing substance abuse treatment for addicted parents.

- *Transitional benefits.* Under AFDC, all recipients had been guaranteed 12 months of transitional child care and Medicaid when they left the rolls for work. Under TANF/ACT, Texas lawmakers continued 12 months of Medicaid coverage for most recipients but limited child care for some recipients.
- *Work requirements.* The "clock" on time limits began once a recipient had been called into the JOBS office for a work referral (later this would be known as the CHOICES work program). Thus, the clock did not start on recipients until they were assisted in finding work. The 10 percent of recipients who lived in counties without JOBS programs were exempt from time limits. The definition of work was broader initially than in the national bill; Texas counted vocational and higher education.
- *Exemptions for parents with young children.* Parents with children under the age of five (shifting to kids under age four in 1997 and eventually reaching children under age one—the federal standard—by mid-2001) were exempt from work requirements and time limits. With a cash grant of $188, it was cheaper for the state to pay parents to stay home than to provide child care.
- *Child support enforcement.* New provisions included revocation of state recreational, professional, and business licenses, but these revocations were limited to noncustodial parents of children on welfare. Enthusiasm for tougher child support enforcement crossed ideological lines. The bill included job placement assistance for noncustodial parents.
- *Higher asset limits.* ACT raised asset limits from $1,500 to about $4,600 and disregarded the income of dependent children in benefit calculation.
- *Consolidation of workforce development programs.* The bill consolidated twenty-eight work and training programs and established the TWC. ACT's goal was better program coordination and integration and removal of the stigma from welfare-to-work programs.

ACT also increased the availability of aid to two-parent families, implemented the new alimony law, and undertook the "finger-imaging" pilot project to reduce fraud.[30] It included a test of "fill-the-gap" budgeting, which would allow recipients moving to work to keep some of their benefits as they earned income, phasing them off welfare more gradually. Conferees dropped proposals for family caps and requirements that teen parents live with their parents. Some conservative lawmakers believed the cap would discourage mothers from having more children, despite the fact that the additional per-child grant was little more than $30 per month. They faced strong opposition, however, from liberal and moderate social welfare advocates, as well as from the Catholic Church and antiabortion forces. Zaffirini, the chair of the Senate Human Services Committee who also represented the heavily Hispanic and Catholic Rio Grande Valley, made clear that under no circumstances would she approve a welfare bill with a family cap, and it was removed in conference.[31]

Not surprisingly, the proposal for such short time limits, even with the freeze-out, was controversial. Advocates for low-income families and others expressed concern about the skills assessment and assignment to tiers because the shortest time limit was now only one year. The PRA, the work requirements, and the breadth of exemptions and harshness of sanctions also spurred debate. The legislature's language applying sanctions and time limits only to the caretaker's portion of the grant, not to the children's, was said to be the result of confusion on the part of some members; it was unclear whether they all understood the difference between "cases" and "caretakers" and realized that the sanctions would be so limited. These issues, particularly exemptions, pitted conservatives' desire for a tough bill with strong behavioral and work mandates against their determination not to spend any more money on welfare recipients (provisions such as drug testing are costly). The legislature decided to cut funding for the JOBS employment program at the same time it passed tough new work requirements. This decision received particular criticism.[32]

HB 1863 also included a "competitive government provision" that created a task force to examine the possibility of privatizing automation and determination of eligibility for welfare. Privatization would soon dominate Texas welfare reform and have national repercussions.[33]

Other Government Actors

Governor Bush played a supporting role in 1995; he was enthusiastic about the need for major overhaul but did not personally lead the way. His staff was closely involved, however, negotiating with the legislature. Bush supported family caps and was eager to cut caseloads, but he did not issue any ultimatums or otherwise "play hardball." Bush was more assertively and sometimes effectively involved after 1995 in attaining the waiver package from the federal HHS, pushing the state's privatization initiatives, and trying to move future revisions to the state's welfare system in a more conservative direction.[34]

Comptroller's office staff members, in addition to providing the base for the Senate's original legislation, testified frequently and participated in more direct ways. An experienced staff member who had worked on the comptroller's welfare report was assigned to the Senate Health and Human Services Committee during the 74th session to work full-time on reform. Although this cross-branch staffing arrangement was controversial, it was not challenged legally.

DHS representatives, particularly then-commissioner Raiford, also testified frequently at hearings, though they were precluded by state law from taking a position on legislation. In addition, Chairman Hilderbran relied on DHS staff to educate him on welfare issues from his first term, during the 73rd session. Agency staff also worked with key actors within the advocacy community. A handful of regular representatives appeared as resource witnesses from DHS, the state Department of Health, the comptroller's office, the Attorney General's child support enforcement division, and the University of Texas.

Members of the delegation from Texas to the U.S. Congress—in particular Republican Senator Phil Gramm and conservative Democratic Representative Charles Stenholm—were vocal about the welfare bill in Washington but largely ignored Texas's overhaul efforts. In fact, several participants in Texas reform, including one conservative within the executive branch, expressed resentment about Gramm's position on the federal bill, charging him with putting his own national political ambitions before the interests of the state. Gramm's enthusiasm for tough work requirements and short time limits, in particular, was cited as especially bad for Texas, given its regions of high unemployment.[35]

The model of the private market and recipients as rational profit-maximizing actors was widely accepted throughout the government and by many outside actors. "If you build the incentives properly, you get what you want," stated one welfare advisor to the governor, and this perspective was echoed by other state policymakers. This language was prevalent in "traditionalist" Texas.

Nongovernmental Participants

The institutional weakness of the state's system of government placed significant power with numerous but relatively weak public officials. This fragmentation gave Texas interest groups important power. Their money, permanence, and expertise provided them with resources that the part-time state legislators often lacked. The decentralized structure of the executive branch also provided multiple access points to lobbyists. Interest groups wield unusual influence in Texas for other reasons as well. One study of the state's interest groups in the 1990s noted that the "lack of party competition and cohesion, the state's weak party structure, and its traditionalistic and individualistic political culture" have given them "a very influential role."[36]

This study found that by far the greatest proportion of the state's registered interest groups—65 percent—were business organizations. The second biggest category, 16 percent, were "non-economic" groups that focused on issues such as education, taxation, morality and ideology, public participation, environmental conservation, and ethnicity or nationality. The study authors noted the relative weakness statewide of black civil rights groups, although they wielded significant influence in local politics, such as in Houston. The research for this study also suggested similar statewide weakness of groups representing Mexican-Americans, although as a rule they were said to be more integrated into the economy and political system than black Texans. As several people I interviewed pointed out, Texas was Mexico before it was Texas, and the border has been fairly fluid. Mexican-Americans' views also are diverse, ranging from conservative to liberal.[37]

Scholars have noted that interest groups tend to be strongest in states with low levels of urbanization, per capita income, industrialization, and political knowledge, as well as weak parties, electorally and within the legislature. State legislatures with short sessions, high turnover, low salaries, limited research capacity, low visibility, and limited professionalism will provide environments in which interest groups can flourish. Even with the political changes of the past thirty years, these conditions still obtain in Texas.[38]

Despite the relative power of interest groups as a whole, however, the community of interests involved in welfare reform in 1995 was constrained. The details of the 1995 welfare bill drew little attention from the general public or from organized interests of any kind, beyond the usual rhetorical support. In contrast to the crowded hearing rooms in Maryland, one participant from the Texas comptroller's office noted, "When they were debating the issue on the House floor, the lobby wasn't very full. Usually, it's packed with lobbyists on phones, full with high-paid lobbyists. [But] few groups here are dealing with poverty issues."

I turn again to hearings testimony as an objective indicator of participation in the legislative welfare policymaking process (although I recognize the importance of other approaches—including, in particular, personal contact). A total of twenty-eight outside organizations or individuals participated in the six public hearings held on welfare reform bills by the House Committee on Human Services and the Senate Committee on Health and Human Services during the 74th session. As in Washington and Maryland, this total includes actors who testified orally and those that only submitted testimony or registered their position without testifying. In addition to interviews, data sources included audiotapes of hearings, written minutes and other records from the House and Senate legislative support offices, the legislative library, and the legislature's website.[39] The hearings process often involved one long hearing at which the committee considered multiple bills—often a large number—

under its jurisdiction. Witnesses usually did not have to make separate appearances on each separate bill in separate hearings. (See Appendix E for a list of bills, hearings, and witnesses.)

The community of advocates for poor people that participated in legislative hearings in 1995 was small. Eight organizations participated, only three of which explicitly represented welfare recipients and other low-income people. The others were women's organizations and representatives of disabled citizens, who testified on the supported employment clauses of the welfare bill (see Table 5-1). In addition, three nonprofit providers participated. No unions participated.[40]

A range of interested individuals testified, from current and ex-welfare mothers who objected to the stereotype of recipients as irresponsible and blameworthy to opponents of welfare as a "moral problem" and evidence of a recipient's "choice to not be responsible."[41] A small number of local government agencies participated, as did one for-profit provider and a University of Texas researcher. The researcher acted as a key source of relatively objective expertise, buffered from more intense political pressures in the executive agencies. The Texas chapter of the NASW participated, as did several "fathers' rights" groups, which advocated that children should go to their fathers rather than stay with a mother on welfare. Although the fathers' groups are idiosyncratic and difficult to label ideologically, I categorize them as traditional values organizations because their major goal was to make divorce more difficult and to give a father with money priority over a mother without it in custody decisions. Representatives of think tanks, independent research organizations, and civil rights and Hispanic organizations were notably absent. No Washington-based groups participated directly.

Several of these twenty-eight actors were surprisingly active, however. The low-income advocacy community, though modest, was energetic—in particular the Austin-based Center on Public Policy Priorities (or CPPP, also known, somewhat facetiously, as "the Center on too many Ps"). A representative of the Houston Welfare Rights Organization (it was unclear if the organization staff exceeded one person) and representatives of an organization of teen parents also were particularly involved in hearings. Of the eleven advocacy groups, including those for disabled persons, representatives participated twenty-five times. The other active interests were the social workers' association and the fathers' rights groups, whose three representatives testified multiple times under various organizational names.

Texas Advocacy Community

Despite the fact that Texas advocacy organizations generally were small and ill-funded, several were active and sophisticated in their lobbying. The CPPP was cited repeatedly as unusually effective in helping to shape HB 1863. The CPPP also organized a coalition of advocacy groups, nonprofit providers,

Table 5-1
Activity of Texas Interest Groups in Welfare-Related Hearings, by Category, 74th Session (1995)

Category	No. of Organizations/Actors	No. of Times Testifying
Advocates: child advocacy, nonprofit and charitable providers, unions[a]	11	25
Individuals	7	9
Intergovernmental	3	3
"Traditional values" groups	3	6
Researchers	1[b]	1
For-profit companies and business groups	1	1
Professional associations	1	4
Think tanks	0	0
Miscellaneous	1	2
TOTAL	**28**	**51**

Sources: Information from audiotapes and minutes of six House and Senate public hearings. Author's calculations.

Note: See Appendix E for a list of hearings and witnesses. Each hearing could cover a wide array of bills, not only those related to welfare reform.

[a]As with national groups, the lines between advocacy and nonprofit service or charitable organizations often are blurry. Some advocacy groups also provided services, and some charitable groups also were committed to advocacy.

[b]This University of Texas researcher technically is a government employee and therefore "inside" government; much like the GAO, however, the University of Texas provided generally well-regarded and objective research.

and government participants to monitor and try to influence the direction of welfare reform. Some advocates did not themselves lobby, relying instead on the CPPP's associate director and other staff as their most effective spokespersons.[42]

The Texas Industrial Areas Foundation (TIAF)—the state's counterpart to the MIAF and BUILD in Maryland—was not directly involved in legislative hearings on welfare reform in 1995 and 1997, although it was a member of the advocates' coalition. The TIAF has been an effective representative for the state's low-income families, but it tended to focus on job training and child care after initial development of the ACT program.[43]

Although the CPPP was relatively successful, it was not typical of Texas advocates in that it had money and staff resources that most others lacked. Founded in the 1980s, the CPPP was funded by a group of Benedictine nuns through the Benedictine Resource Center. During the 1990s, it received significant assistance from the Washington-based CBPP, as well as CLASP, and received Ford Foundation funding as a part of a CBPP project. It also received funding as part of the Annie E. Casey Foundation's "Kids Count" project. Certainly, its staff was talented, assertive, and resourceful, but it seemed to have been spared some of the survival scramble that so often confronts advocacy groups for the poor, in part because of continued assistance from Washington-based groups and its original funding from the Benedictine Center.

In addition to testimony, the CPPP used numerous other strategies to shape welfare policy. These strategies were similar to those used by the most successful Washington groups. Its staff produced high-quality analyses quickly and in easily accessible form, such as fact sheets; provided draft legislative language to lawmakers; and cultivated relationships with individual legislators and the media. The CPPP's main welfare lobbyist stressed the importance of developing good relationships with lawmakers because the Texas welfare policymaking domain was so small. The CPPP's policy expertise was cited repeatedly as one of its most effective tools, especially given the lack of legislative staff resources on this issue, at least at the beginning of reform. Like the major Washington groups, the CPPP accepted the general direction of welfare reform as a given but then acted to shape critical details, particularly in areas in which the legislature lacked information.[44]

The CPPP, at least, was relatively influential in shaping the 1995 bill, first as part of the working group that participated in developing the comptroller's "Partnership for Independence" and second with the legislature, especially Hilderbran. Like the CBPP and CLASP on the national level, the Texas group helped to fill an expertise gap, especially for the House Committee on Human Services (the Senate seemed to rely more on the comptroller's office).

Nonetheless, the advocacy community had an uphill fight in 1995. The range of alternatives was relatively narrow, and the agenda in Texas and the nation had moved rightward to the point that provisions such as time limits, PRAs, and sanctions had become givens. The state did not always adopt the most conservative options—Texas welfare policy was a mixed bag—but neither were most liberal proposals politically viable in 1995. Advocates for poor Texans had no political action committee (PACs), and their constituents obviously wielded little financial or political power. The state mood in many ways mirrored the national mood that helped drive the conservative approach in Washington.

Other Organizations and Actors

Independent researchers or think tanks, either on the national level or based in Texas, participated very little. Staff members from the Heritage Foundation spoke with the governor's policy staff privately, although their views were considered largely irrelevant to the concerns of Texas policymakers. One policy advisor said, "If we did what they wanted, it'd put me in a ditch. I can't put factions together and get political results." Phyllis Schlafly's Eagle Forum also had some contact with the governor's office, but it was more concerned with education. Other national conservative groups made no appearance in hearings but were said to have tried to influence individual legislators and governor's staff. The American Legislative Exchange Council (ALEC), the conservative organization of state legislators across the nation, worked with individual members and the Texas Conservative Coalition.[45]

For-profit contractors also had little presence in the hearings process; their appearances were limited to a single company that provided finger-imaging services. Again, the sense was that they gained little through public participation. Many participants stressed, however, that they played a major role behind the scenes, particularly when privatization took off after the 74th session. The governor's policy advisor for health and human services called them "big-time players" in welfare reform, noting, "I was relying on that. Lockheed-Martin was the first vendor to do the entrepreneurial approach with the federal government, and I knew they'd be willing to do something similar with us. I was pleased because they could be allies."

The overall orientation of welfare reform was overwhelmingly industry-driven—consistent with the state's pro-business culture, which focused on meeting the labor needs of Texas businesses by making welfare mothers into workers that they would want to hire. One area in which business gained influence was the new TWC, with its structure of local boards and career centers. The new law required that these centers be operated by nonprofit or for-profit contractors, and the TWC's mission stated explicitly that its first goal was to meet the needs of Texas employers and, secondarily, those of Texas workers.[46]

1997: WELFARE REFORM AS BUDGET POLITICS

Welfare reform during the 75th session was dominated by budget politics. The state received its federal waiver in March 1996 and started to implement the ACT program. Several provisions, such as time limits, were phased in, finally going into effect statewide in January 1997. Restructuring between the new TWC and DHS proved to be extraordinarily difficult, exacerbated by the state's efforts to privatize eligibility determination and other services. In several regions, formation of the decentralized TWC workforce boards aggravated local political tensions as power over major funding streams changed hands.[47]

When President Clinton signed PRWORA, Texas had to decide whether to comply with its new requirements immediately or maintain the state's waiver until 2002. It also had to determine how to spend $973 million that it would now receive each year in TANF block grant money from the federal government. This amount exceeded what the state needed to continue its existing programs at projected service levels by almost $400 million because of declining welfare rolls. Caseloads were expected to decline by 33 percent between FY 1994—the base year for calculating the block grant amount—and FY 1999. This difference would become a surplus "windfall" for the state. These questions occupied the 75th Session, which met from January to May 1997.[48]

After the federal bill passed, the state opted to operate under its waiver for another six years. Legislators introduced a slew of bills to make programmatic changes, liberal and conservative, although money was the big issue during the session. Much of the debate centered on how the state would use its TANF funds at a time when caseloads were shrinking but recipients also faced tough new time limits and work participation requirements. The rhetoric of the 1995 session—that welfare reform was a compassionate initiative designed to help poor mothers gain self-sufficiency—was put to the test in 1997. Now the state had a large federal windfall that could be used for long-underfunded jobs, child care, and transportation programs. It also could be diverted, however, from programs for low-income families to replace state revenues in other programs or even to lower taxes.

Governmental Participants

The legislature considered dozens of bills to make alterations in the welfare system, but most of these bills did not pass. Those that did included proposals to establish a cashless welfare system, using electronic benefits transfer (EBT), and to restrict recipients from using TANF funds for goods such as cigarettes or alcohol; to provide assistance to recipients who were victims of domestic violence; to establish the "Texans Work" program, using JOBS funds for job training; and to require that TWC jobs centers help recipients apply for the federal EITC. These and related bills were considered in fourteen public hearings. The Senate went from Democratic to Republican in 1996, but Zaffirini continued as chair of the Senate Health and Human Services Committee. Her committee and Hilderbran's once again heard the majority of witnesses. (See Appendix E for a list of bills, hearings, and witnesses.)

The comptroller's office was less involved in 1997 than in the previous session, but the governor was more active. Bush proposed a plan to cut property tax revenues by $1 billion, and this tax cut overshadowed budget negotiations because it put pressure on all areas of the budget and increased the temptation to siphon off TANF money. A $65 million shortfall in the Department of Protective and Regulatory Services—one of the agencies that could be funded with TANF money—and doubts about the competency of the new TWC also affected the 1997 budget debates. The state had long underfunded the Texas JOBS program, which the TWC took over, and even without stringent new work requirements and the confusion of reorganization it was ill-equipped to meet service demands.[49] With the intensified federal work requirements, the agency had to ratchet up the range and effectiveness of its programs. It was trying to do so, however, in an environment of institutional chaos and widespread political mistrust.[50]

In addition to various proposals to amend the ACT system, then, the main issue was how much of Texas's federal windfall would be appropriated for welfare-to-work, child care, income support, and related services and how much would be used for other purposes. The real source of budget power and much oversight responsibility in Texas was the Legislative Budget Board (LBB), which played a pivotal role. Its members included the lieutenant governor, the House speaker, the chairs of the House Appropriations and Ways and Means Committees and the Senate Finance and State Affairs Committees, and four legislative members appointed by the lieutenant governor and speaker. They served all year, not only during the session, and with a strong professional staff, the LBB exercised important power.[51]

Because of the timing of the budget process, the LBB initially issued a preliminary budget in 1996 that was based on welfare cost projections under AFDC, with declining caseload numbers and without the TANF block grant. When the biennial budget negotiations began a year later, the LBB still had not publicly revised its base plan. This preliminary budget gave advocates and others a benchmark by which they could gauge how much the state would have spent on welfare in the absence of the new block grant and identified the amount of extra money—$393 million—Texas would receive under TANF.[52]

There undoubtedly was some confusion within the LBB about how TANF funds could be administered under the new system; HHS had not yet issued final federal regulations. Ultimately, however, this inaction led to charges that the agency was being secretive and was unwilling to let the comptroller, the governor, advocates, and others know how it was planning to allocate the money.[53] Thus, the budget process began in January 1997 with almost $400 million in additional funds and no plan to spend them. Although DHS, TWC, and other agencies wanted the new funds, none had proposed a specific plan. The CPPP offered a detailed outline for spending the TANF surplus to the Senate Finance and House Appropriations and Workforce Development Oversight committees. This group subsequently was included in Appropriation's TANF work group. Inclusion of the major advocacy organization for low-income families, according to some participants, allowed key legislators to claim credit for a more open and representative process.[54]

The LBB identified areas of the state budget previously funded by general revenues or the federal Title XX social services block grant that now could qualify (at least arguably) for TANF funding.[55] Ultimately, an estimated 39 percent, or $152 million, of the state's TANF surplus replaced state general revenues. In numerous instances, such as family planning services, the state simply swapped one funding stream for another without increasing services. When legislators replaced federal social service block grant dollars or state general revenues with TANF money, the freed-up state funds could be allocated to other purposes, such as the governor's property tax cut. Only $126.3 million, or 32 percent of the surplus, actually went to expanded welfare-to-work services, and $30 million of this was unavailable for current spending because it was earmarked in a fund for the TWC on the condition that the agency met performance targets.[56]

Child care services, along with JOBS and other employment programs, had been transferred from DHS and other agencies to the TWC after the 1995 session. DHS had earned high praise for its statewide child care management system (it was not clear how this system would fare under the TWC's radically decentralized structure), but state funding for child care had always been insufficient. Of the $26.6 million in TANF funds allocated for child care, only $2.6 million was for new services; $24 million replaced other federal block grants. There was considerable evidence that this level of funding was not enough to meet the demands for child care under a system of mandated work.

The state's modest allocations of its "found money" to child care and welfare-to-work programs, as well as the diversion of almost 40 percent of the TANF surplus into the general revenue pool, raised questions about the widespread rhetoric of helping poor families achieve independence.[57] One gubernatorial aide commented, "My goal is that we not spend Texas general revenue money on welfare. People either work or should be on [federal SSI] disability." The budget outcomes of 1997 certainly seemed to move the state in this direction: The broad goal of cutting state spending on low-income families prevailed in the legislative and executive branches. Even with hundreds of millions of "extra" dollars, no one in legislative hearings that year seriously discussed raising the state's benefit levels, and the attempt to provide food assistance to legal immigrants failed.[58]

Nongovernmental Participants

The number and variety of outside actors participating in the 1997 programmatic debate expanded from the 74th session, despite the fact that the programmatic bills considered during the 75th session were less radical. Whereas twenty-eight different groups or individuals testified or registered their opinions on the comprehensive 1995 overhaul, thirty-seven participated on the twenty-one less-significant bills considered in 1997. Their level of activity also increased markedly (see Table 5-2).

In 1997, 23 advocacy groups, including social service providers and organized labor, participated in the hearings process; in 1995, only 11 had. These

Table 5-2
Activity of Texas Interest Groups in Welfare-Related Hearings, by Category, 75th Session (1997)

Category	No. of Organizations/Actors	No. of Times Testifying
Advocates: child advocacy, nonprofit and charitable providers, unions[a]	23	71
Individuals	5	22
Miscellaneous	3	7
For-profit companies, business groups	2	3
Professional associations	2	4
Researchers	1[b]	1
"Traditional values" groups	1	2
Intergovernmental	0	0
Think tanks	0	0
TOTAL	**37**	**110**

Sources: Information from audiotapes and minutes of fourteen House and Senate public hearings. Author's calculations.

Note: See Appendix E for a list of hearings and witnesses. Each hearing could cover a wide array of bills, not only those related to welfare reform.

[a]As with national groups, the lines between advocacy and nonprofit service or charitable organizations often are blurry. Some advocacy groups also provided services, and some charitable groups also were committed to advocacy.

[b]This University of Texas researcher technically is a government employee and therefore "inside" government; much like the GAO, however, the University of Texas provided generally well-regarded and objective research.

23 groups testified a total of 71 times, compared with 25 times in the previous session. Whereas organized labor was entirely absent in 1995, it suddenly appeared and was quite active in 1997. Several different unions participated and offered their views multiple times. The individuals who testified in 1997 were active, although they were not cited as influential. Two associations—the NASW and the Children's Hospital Association—participated in 1997 (only the former had in 1995), and a couple of business groups testified in 1997, compared with none the session before. The same researcher from the University of Texas acted as a resource witness, but otherwise no think tanks or independent researchers took part in the debate. Some groups were less

active, and others were still absent. One fathers' rights group was the only traditional values organization that appeared. No intergovernmental actors or for-profit contractors testified.

Advocacy groups provided more than half of all testimony in 1997. Almost half of this testimony was by just two people: Patrick Bresette of the CPPP and Bruce Bower of the Houston Welfare Rights Organization and Texas Legal Services. Bresette alone accounted for about 20 percent of all testimony on these bills in 1997. Bower also seemed to be well respected by legislators, but he was less involved, in part because of the small size and limited resources of his organization. Surprisingly, organizations representing black and Hispanic Texans were almost entirely absent from hearings. The Mexican-American Legal Defense Fund (MALDEF) testified once, but it was the only such group to do so. Interviews confirmed that these groups were largely inactive. Other groups involved in the debate included those for disabled people (as in 1995), the Texas Consumers Union, and the ACLU. As on the national level and in Maryland, organized labor was activated by fears that welfare recipients would be hired to replace unionized workers and that private contractors would take jobs from union members. The Texas AFL-CIO testified five times, and the state employees' union and AFSCME participated with similar frequency. There is little evidence that they were especially effective in the political environment of Texas, however: The bill to prevent job displacement—one of their major priorities—was vetoed by Governor Bush.

The conservative ideological think tanks and traditional values groups, such as the Heritage Foundation and the Family Research Council, again were absent from the hearings process. Business groups—specifically, the Texas Retailers Association and Small Business United—testified, primarily on policies such as the use of the Lone Star Card for EBT for recipients and funding for jobs programs rather than on welfare more broadly.

Otherwise, the groups and individuals that participated in the hearings process were fairly similar to those who participated in 1995. The lack of intergovernmental actors was noteworthy given the TWC's push toward decentralization, although the cash-assistance part of the system remained state- rather than county-administered. These changes were complex, however, and many people appeared to be unaware of how they would be affected.

Advocates and others seemed to be easier to mobilize in 1997. There had been a general consensus on the need for welfare reform in 1995 and an understanding that in some ways the Texas plan was less radical than alternatives being considered in Washington. Advocates in 1995 seemed to be reluctant to push for more liberal and probably politically unfeasible proposals, given the state's conservative environment. This factor, along with general indifference to the issue, had contained opposition. In 1997, however, with many smaller changes under consideration, advocates and others came out in larger numbers. The availability of real money to spend on new programs in that session undoubtedly activated participants. The fact that welfare had simply been on the agenda for a longer time, as well as the passage of the high-profile PRWORA in Washington, undoubtedly also contributed to an increase in the awareness and activity of nongovernmental groups.

PRIVATIZATION

Privatization became an extremely contentious issue after the 74th session and into the 75th session, despite the fact that it received little attention in public hearings and none of the major private contractors testified. They did, however, get a warm reception in the governor's office. Language within the 1995 welfare bill required the HHSC to streamline health and welfare eligibility services, cut administrative costs, and examine ways to reduce fraud and error rates. A provision also required the HHSC and the state's Council on Competitiveness in Government to study privatization and, if it were determined to be effective, recommend services that could be provided better through competitive bidding and contracting with private firms. This innocuous language quickly led to a highly controversial effort to privatize statewide the process of deciding who was eligible for cash assistance, food stamps, and Medicaid. It also severely strained relations between the new TWC and DHS at exactly the time they most needed to cooperate on implementation of the new welfare and work systems.[59]

Governor Bush had cited privatization of welfare as a key goal during his 1994 campaign and continued to identify it as a top priority. In August 1995, shortly after the major reform bill passed, the HHSC (chaired by Bush appointee McKinney) and the Council on Competitive Government began to go well past the language of the law to design a comprehensive privatization plan called Texas Integrated Enrollment Services (TIES).[60] The services being considered for privatization cost about $520 million each year and delivered about $8 billion in benefits. Many lawmakers were taken aback by how quickly the HHSC pursued "wholesale privatization" and were skeptical that the reform legislation granted the commission the authority to make such sweeping changes. Bush's zeal for privatization and lobbying by Lockheed and other for-profit contractors were widely suspected to be behind the push.

Blurring public and private boundaries, the HHSC plan would allow either private companies or public-private partnerships to bid competitively to run the state's eligibility-determination system. The seven-year contract was estimated to be worth as much as $2.8 billion. DHS announced its intention to bid with private-sector partners EDS and Unisys. The entire DHS eligibility staff—about 13,000 people—faced the prospect of losing their jobs, providing strong motivation for the agency to take the lead. The TWC later announced that it too would bid on the contract, along with Lockheed Martin's Information Management Systems division and IBM (Anderson

Consulting joined as a third, entirely private, potential bidder). Some people raised questions about the legality of these public-private arrangements.[61]

The fact that the welfare and workforce agencies were now competitors for a massive state contract had two major ramifications. First, the HHSC had to treat them as potential bidders and therefore could not draw on them for help in designing the TIES system, leaving the commission short on expertise. Second, the sense of competition kept agency personnel from talking openly with each other and impeded their ability to implement the restructuring required by Texas law and the new federal legislation. This competition set implementation back by at least two years and fostered significant ill will between the agencies that took several years to fade.[62] One legislative staffer called it "a disaster."

The HHSC moved swiftly but faced growing opposition. The expected groups—advocates, nonprofits, and unions (especially the public-sector unions)—protested within the state and nationally.[63] Several state lawmakers also grew increasingly uncomfortable with the direction of privatization. Their concerns included the obvious worry about the incentives built into for-profit companies—that their managers would tend to favor their responsibility to maximize shareholders' profits over the well-being of welfare clients who could not take their "business" elsewhere. There also was concern that several of these companies (Lockheed in particular) had questionable records, including charges of bribing public officials and major program failures and cost overruns.[64]

The Texas State Employees Union also alleged improper lobbying by Lockheed because of its hiring of state officials, including a top Bush aide. He had worked on privatization under the governor but quit to set up a lobbying shop with clients that included Lockheed. This allegation led to a criminal investigation by the Travis County district attorney. Another fear was the emphasis on cost savings, with HHSC officials claiming that privatization could reap potential savings of 25–40 percent but providing little evidence that recipients' well-being would be protected. It also was unclear what obligation, if any, a privately held company had to provide data about its finances and administration, raising concerns about public accountability. Finally, this approach was not being tested first, as it was in other states exploring privatization (such as Wisconsin), but was to go into effect statewide immediately.[65] The extreme secrecy in which the project was cloaked aggravated these concerns. One legislator was quoted as wondering if the project hadn't been "wired for Lockheed Martin" from the start. Only after the Clinton administration rejected the draft proposal in 1997 did the HHSC publicly release it.[66]

In May 1997, HHS in Washington notified McKinney that the plan would not comply with federal law; whereas the 1996 welfare law clearly allowed private employees to determine eligibility for TANF, existing food stamp and Medicaid law still required that eligibility for these programs be determined by public employees. So although TANF could be privatized, the two other programs could not, frustrating a central goal of service integration.[67] McKinney and the governor expressed outrage about this "intrusion" of the federal government, as did the Texas delegation to Congress. The delegation's members responded with a "Welfare Flexibility Act of 1997" in the U.S. House and Senate, expressly authorizing the use of private employees to determine eligibility for Medicaid, food stamps, and WIC programs. Ultimately, however, this effort failed. Senator Kay Bailey Hutchison also attempted to add an amendment to the 1997 federal budget agreement to accomplish the same goal, but it was rejected as nongermane.[68]

The state finally abandoned the original TIES proposal and moved toward a more modest "son-of-TIES" plan that emphasized service integration and automation but not eligibility determination or replacing public employees with private employees. Lockheed and other contractors, however, continued to bid for and win contracts with the TWC's local workforce development boards to run their career centers.[69] EDS won the new TIES contract to improve automation and streamline state services in August 1997. This approach was expected to result in service delivery improvements for welfare clients and a move toward "one-stop shopping." During the 75th session, the state legislature passed a bill to limit the governor's and the HHSC's control over privatization, insert legislative oversight, and encourage a more incremental approach.[70]

The Texas privatization story is useful for several reasons. First, privatization appears to be a growing trend among the states, raising questions of public accountability and the nature of the types of services that appropriately belong in the private market and those that are better left to organizations that are not subject to market pressures. Of the three states I examine in this book, Texas was the only one that pursued statewide privatization of welfare eligibility services, but many other states have been exploring it. Second, privatization was a major political episode in Texas's welfare debate, yet it appeared almost nowhere in the records of legislative hearings during the session preceding it. Although the large contractors such as Lockheed Martin and EDS lobbied the governor's office, they never appeared in the public hearings I examined. There was little public debate on the state's original TIES proposal. Finally, as noted earlier, the privatization debate provided a rich illustration of the neo-Madisonian concern about the tendency of smaller, more informal jurisdictions to blur the lines between public and private.

One could argue that there is an encouraging moral to the Texas tale: that large corporations and a small cadre of political insiders tried to circumvent "the public will"—as represented by the state legislature—and were foiled. Opponents certainly mounted strong resistance to the secretive and fast-track privatization effort. It is not at all clear, however, what would have happened if the federal government had not rejected the plan. Although state lawmakers objected to the process and the plan, and it wreaked havoc on implementation of the welfare bill they had passed the prior session, there was no guarantee that they could have stopped it, absent federal intervention.

AFTER REFORM

Initially Texas policymakers were concerned about their ability to meet the federal work requirements while still living under the ACT waivers, given the state's system of exemptions, benefit "freeze-outs," and parent-only sanctions. The federal government's decision to grant all states the "caseload reduction credit" that adjusted required participation rates downward, however, saved Texas and many other states from losing part of their TANF grants.[71]

While the TWC and the local workforce boards and career development centers were finally getting up and running after the privatization controversy, there still was sharp criticism of their implementation and operations. In 1999, a state audit charged that the TWC had inadequately monitored how contracts were awarded by the local workforce development boards, jeopardizing millions of dollars in federal employment program funds that were contingent on state oversight and accountability. Among other problems, the audit cited thirteen incidents of inappropriately awarded local service contracts awarded by the TWC under TANF and stated that the process "did not ensure that it [the state] paid a fair price for services or that the bidders were financially sound."[72] Coordination between the TWC and DHS improved but continued to have problems.

The underlying structures and philosophies of the two agencies were very different: DHS was state administered, with uniform standards and no major plans for devolution, whereas the TWC's heavy emphasis on decentralization and privatization allowed each region to run its child care and job training programs differently. Reconciling these differences while providing "seamless" services to recipients was not easy. One advocate called the structure "a complete nightmare." In several sparsely populated rural areas, the local political and business elites that took control of funding for job training under "second-order devolution" were an extremely small group. In very rural areas, one state official commented, "You could get them all at a barbecue together." Echoing neo-Madisonian concerns about localism and informality, he observed, "You can tell them they must have new reporting and fiscal relationships, but these have been and continue to be largely based on relationships. It's personal. It's hard to change."

In Texas as in the rest of the nation, welfare reform was measured by reduced caseloads and widely hailed as a success. Welfare rolls dropped by

59 percent between 1994 and January 1999.[73] As elsewhere, however, this rush to credit-claiming generally underplayed the role of the strong and unusually sustained economic growth, which eventually would slow or reverse. Less noticed was a 5 percent increase in welfare caseloads in the state during 1999, which suggested the complexity of helping people leave welfare permanently for work that could support their families, especially in a state that often was reluctant to spend money on programs for low-income people. In 1998, DHS released a report that found that about 55 percent of Texans who had left welfare were working, with an average wage above the minimum. This work rate was similar to that in other national and state studies. The findings were preliminary, however, and were based on a response of 51 percent—low for reliable surveys.[74]

Incremental reform continued during the 76th legislative session in 1999. Governor Bush had campaigned for reelection (and had begun campaigning for the presidency) in 1998 on a platform that included more welfare changes.[75] His "carrot and stick" approach included the following:

- Eliminating benefits for the entire family (full-family sanctions) if a parent refused to work or wouldn't cooperate with child support enforcement
- Cutting a parent off welfare for life the first time she/he intentionally misrepresented income
- Removing convicted drug felons from assistance for life, though continuing it for their children
- Providing an additional $100 million for child care
- Allowing recipients to receive aid for several additional months after finding a job as they made the transition to work.[76]

Bush reiterated these priorities in his 1999 State of the State address and pushed for the legislature to pass his package in the form of an omnibus welfare reform bill. Later that year, he also announced $500,000 in grants to Christian organizations to help people stay off welfare, calling these organizations the "armies of compassion" and referring to this approach as "the next bold step in welfare reform."[77]

In 1999, however, the House Human Services Committee had a new and more liberal chair. House Speaker Laney ousted Republican Harvey Hilderbran at the beginning of the session and replaced him with liberal-leaning Elliot Naishtat, Democrat from Austin and an ex-VISTA volunteer.[78] This change underlined the importance of committee leadership, particularly when it was receptive to the perspectives of the state's low-income families and advocacy community. The final 1999 legislation provided most of the governor's proposed carrots but none of the sticks. It included $100 million more for child care; four months of transitional cash assistance for people just leaving the rolls for work; $35 million over three years in state matching funds for the federal Welfare to Work (WtW) program; and a modest grant increase to $201 per month for a family of three, as well as a yearly "back to school" grant of $60 per child.[79] Naishtat described the negotiations with the governor's office, saying, "The omnibus bill was negotiated over an almost three-month period; there were three times when I've sincerely believed we had a meeting of the minds . . . [but] on each of those occasions, the governor's office came back with what they described as technical changes. And in each of those cases, the quote 'technical changes' included at least three substantive changes."[80]

Another 1999 development originating in the governor's office had a less liberal outcome. The federal TANF regulations released in April 1999 required the governor's office to specify the details of the state's waivers that varied from federal law in order to continue with them. In the fall of 1999, after the close of the legislative session, the Bush administration submitted its outline of the ACT waiver but left out any exemption from the federal cumulative five-year lifetime limit. This meant that recipients (parents and children) who had been operating under the assumption that the federal five-year "clock" would not start for them until after 2002—when the state would adapt its waiver to the federal system—suddenly discovered that they had already used up as much as three years of their five-year lifetime allotment of cash aid. The state's 1995 welfare law had been silent on whether the state was adopting the federal time limit. Most advocates and legislators who were active in welfare policy had understood, however, that the state exempted recipients from the federal limit until 2002, instead employing the five-year "freeze-out." Eric Bost, the DHS commissioner under Bush, also argued that "as a matter of fairness, a reasonable notice to clients at the beginning of the maximum lifetime federal time limit should be provided."[81]

The key issues awaiting the 2001 session included making incremental changes necessary to bring the ACT waiver system into compliance with federal requirements in 2002 (the time limit already having been taken care of) and several relatively liberal proposals coming out of the interim report of the House committee chaired by Naishtat and Maxey.[82] A bigger debate, however, was over money. The state's TANF surplus of a few years earlier was turning into a shortfall. Advocates were concerned that the now-heavy reliance on TANF funds for services that previously were paid for by general revenues would mean that welfare-to-work and other vital services for families leaving welfare would be sharply cut if the TANF block grant were reauthorized at a lower amount or if demand for these other services increased. The state's enthusiasm for using TANF money for other purposes—in particular, to fund child protective services—appeared to have caught up with it.[83]

CONCLUSION

A significant range of organizations participated in Texas welfare reform—as neo-Madison theory would suggest for the second largest state in the union (see Table 5-3). These organizations varied from relatively liberal groups to conservative traditional values organizations. However, the number of groups that participated was limited compared to the numbers in Washington and even in Maryland (a markedly smaller state). Moreover, fewer groups representing low-income people, as well as civil rights organizations representing blacks and Latinos, took part in welfare reform.

As Table 5-3 indicates, a total of 58 outside actors participated in public hearings about Texas welfare reform in 1995 and 1997. This figure compares with 310 groups in Washington and 95 in Maryland. Thirty-two of these groups in Texas were advocacy organizations, nonprofits, unions, and researchers, compared with 142 such organizations in the national debate. Advocates were extremely busy in Texas, however—providing more than 60 percent of all public hearings activity, lobbying legislators and other officials in more informal ways, and working closely with media and with other interest groups. A small handful offered the lion's share of testimony (see Table 5-4). Organized labor played no apparent role in 1995, but it mobilized at the threat of job displacement in 1997. Individuals made up the next largest group, and a smattering of other outside actors participated on different issues related to welfare; none were particularly active or influential, however.

Several categories of actors were almost entirely absent from the debate. Only one state university researcher participated in hearings, and no think tanks or independent researchers were in evidence. Intergovernmental groups participated in 1995, but by 1997 they made no appearance, even though jobs and child care programs were being decentralized across the state. For-profit contractors were even less in evidence in Texas public hearings than they were in Washington, though the largest corporations were active behind the scenes and seemed to have had little reason to appear at legislative hearings. Although policymakers cited the public's concern about welfare reform, there was little evidence that many people were interested in the topic in other than the broadest, most symbolic way. The field was left to a fairly narrow community of groups dominated by a few advocacy organizations.

In some ways, Texas's waiver plan was more lenient toward welfare families than the federal law passed during the 104th Congress. Many participants suggested that some of the more generous (or at least more cautious) provisions were the result of active lobbying by advocacy groups—in particular the CPPP, whose staff often submitted draft legislative language as bills were being written, worked individual legislators, and testified constantly. Policymakers in the mid-1990s were largely unwilling to spend additional state revenues on poor people, however, even with almost $400 million in TANF windfall funds. This attitude drove the policy debate to a

Table 5-3
Texas- and Washington-Based Organizations Involved in Welfare-Related Hearings, by Category

	No. of Organizations/Actors	
Category	**Texas**	**Washington**
Advocates: child advocacy, nonprofit and charitable providers, civil rights[a]	31	112
Individuals	12	38
Intergovernmental	3	64
"Traditional values"	3	14
For-profit companies, business groups	3	19
Miscellaneous	3	7
Professional associations	2	14
Researchers	1[b]	30
Think tanks	0	12
TOTAL	**58**	**310**

Sources: Information from audiotapes and minutes of twenty House and Senate public hearings and Texas Legislature Online website. Author's calculations.

[a]As with national groups, the lines between advocacy and nonprofit service or charitable organizations often are blurry. Some advocacy groups also provided services, and some charitable groups also were committed to advocacy.

[b]This University of Texas researcher technically is a government employee and therefore "inside" government; much like the GAO, however, the University of Texas provided generally well-regarded and objective research.

significant extent. Some of the "generous" clauses, such as a relatively liberal system of exemptions, were motivated at least in part by the fact that the state's scanty benefits made it cheaper in these cases to be generous than tough.

In other ways, the Texas program was notably harsher than the federal law required it to be. The state's cash benefits remained extremely low, and there was little serious interest in raising them substantially until 1999—and then only modestly. The one- to three-year tiered time limits, even with exemptions and the freeze-out policy, were unusually short, although they did not cut off children. The state's 1997 decision to cut funding for the

Table 5-4
Texas Frequent Testifiers

Organization/Actor	No. of Times Testifying
Center for Public Policy Priorities (CPPP)	29
Houston Welfare Rights Organization/Texas Legal Services	12
C. Flynn[a]	9
NASW, Texas Chapter	8
J. Heffernon[a]	8
American Association of Retired Persons (AARP)	7
Texas AFL-CIO	5
Gray Panthers	5
Texas Appleseed Advocacy Fund/Texas Rural Legal Aid	4
Texas Fathers' Alliance	4
Consumers Union	3
R. Arsenault[a]	3
Advocacy, Inc.	3
Texas State Employees' Union	3

Note: These acts of testimony include oral testimony before legislative committees and written testimony or positions registered with no oral testimony given.

[a]Individuals who testified for themselves only.

JOBS/CHOICES programs that were intended to help recipients find and keep suitable employment raised doubts about policymakers' commitment to shifting them into good jobs rather than simply off the rolls. Some Texas policymakers seemed almost proud of its identity as a low-benefit state, and any proposal that cost money—whether it involved a conservative mandate or a liberal benefit— generally was off the table. When the opportunity came to divert money from the TANF windfall into other purposes and free up state general revenues, lawmakers grabbed it, even though Texas jobs and child care programs were underfunded. Although Texas did not rush to cut its programs across the board, one could argue that it had less incentive to embark on a race to the bottom because, at least in terms of benefit levels, it already was pretty close to it.

In Texas, David Ellwood's budget cutters won the day in the mid-1990s, with assistance from social policy critics. Work-oriented reformers faced an uphill battle trying to gain support for additional spending to help people move from welfare to jobs that paid more than the poverty level, even with the TANF surplus.

Despite the intensity of the small community of groups working to represent welfare recipients and the ability of at least one organization to affect the major welfare bill around its essential margins, the narrow range of advocacy perspectives limited their effectiveness. Having only one major voice representing poor families in Texas was a problem. The CPPP's lobbyist himself noted that it would have helped the organization negotiate with lawmakers if a more liberal group—a "grassroots, vocal, rowdy group"—also had been part of the debate, marking a further leftward edge against which his proposals could seem relatively moderate. Instead, as the most active voice of poor Texans (occasionally paired with the Houston Welfare Rights Organization), he and the CPPP by default set the outside boundary for the range of alternatives that received serious consideration. The variety of views that got a hearing undoubtedly was narrower than it would have been with a bigger, more vibrant, and active advocacy community.

It also is worth noting that three of the most effective Texas advocates were either aided by Washington-based organizations (the CPPP received help from the CBPP and CLASP) or were affiliated with organizations funded by the federal government (the Houston organization and the Appleseed Advocacy Fund were affiliated with legal services agencies). Without these groups, the welfare debate in Texas would have been even more constrained.

Certainly, as in Washington and Maryland, other critical factors—not simply the presence and activity of interest groups—contributed to the shape of Texas welfare policy after 1997. Political ideology and culture, party control, the dominant motives of reformers, the characteristics of the state's political institutions, and the relative heterogeneity of the Texas populace, among other considerations, also crucially affected the environment in which these interest groups worked and the policy alternatives that were considered feasible.

The state's conservative "traditionalist" political culture set broad parameters, in terms of the kind of groups that existed and gained support in Texas and with regard to the nature of the state's political institutions and the approaches they took to welfare reform. Rates of public participation and public interest in government were low. The government exhibited a bias toward market approaches to social problems as well as toward the concerns of private interests. Although the state's business powers have diversified, they often dominated politics, as the privatization episode and the orientation of the TWC illustrated. In local politics, the primacy of business concerns also tended to hold, especially in rural areas where a handful of local business and political leaders might control most of a community's resources. Several cities (e.g., Austin, Houston, and San Antonio) had more diversified political environments, but by and large a culture privileging the market, individualism, and self-sufficiency predominated.

Although this culture of self-reliance tended to paint poor people as largely responsible for their situations, few lawmakers resorted to the stereotype of the recipient who produced endless children in pursuit of higher benefits that was prevalent in the Washington debate. Certainly the "who" of welfare reform played a role in limiting the range of policy alternatives: Texas welfare mothers were largely Hispanic and black—groups that historically had been shut out of the political system. The money was just too meager, however, to support the most negative stereotypes.

In 1995 and 1997, the ideological divide between the newly emergent Republicans and generally conservative Democrats also was too narrow to offer a strong incentive to use welfare policy for partisan purposes. Although the ascendancy of the Republican Party in Washington accelerated the pace of welfare reform, the extreme mistrust that marked the federal debate generally was missing in Texas. Even after the Texas Senate went Republican in 1996, the parties' positions on welfare policy remained more similar than different, and the political shifts were more incremental than "revolutionary." The liberal wing of the Democratic Party, though significant in cities such as Houston and Austin, generally was too weak across the state to shift the terms of the new approach in the mid-1990s. This situation changed somewhat when Naishtat gained the chair of the House Human Services Committee in 1999, although policy options still were relatively narrow. The bipartisanship that has marked Texas politics in recent years also helped advocates and others develop relationships with conservative legislators whose party and ideology were not their own. Although most legislators were fairly new to welfare issues in the early 1990s, the generally cooperative relationships helped to ensure that the welfare policy domain, such as it existed in Texas, remained fairly intact.

The state's political institutions have changed markedly since the U.S. Supreme Court's decisions outlawing white primaries, racial segregation, and the malapportionment of state legislatures, as well as the federal Civil Rights and Voting Rights statutes. The structures of Texas government remained remarkably fragmented and nonprofessional, however, particularly considering the size of the state and its $90 billion biennial budget. High turnover within the House and Senate and their committees, the biennial session, meager pay, and an entirely private system of campaign financing meant that crucial policy decisions often were made quickly by citizen lawmakers dominated by the leadership and beholden to well-funded interest groups for information and money. Again, the effort to privatize eligibility determination by granting huge contracts to major corporations—initiated between legislative sessions by the governor, his appointees, and a committee that included the Senate and House leadership—provided ample illustration of these dangers.

The good news from the perspective of low-income Texans, then, was that several advocates in fact played a significant role in the state's welfare reform efforts and were considered effective in representing their concerns, even if they were not always successful in changing policy decisions. The bad news, however, was that the number of groups that were active in welfare politics—especially those representing poor people—was modest. The activity and effectiveness of advocates for low-income families were concentrated largely in a handful of groups. Many interests, including black civil rights and Hispanic organizations, were almost totally absent from their ranks. Although blacks and Hispanics were gaining influence in the state, through greater representation within government and in local political arenas, the state's political elites were still largely white, Protestant, and male. The generally conservative perspective permeating state politics received little serious challenge during the first wave of welfare reform.

NOTES

1. Richard H. Kraemer, Charldean Newell, and David F. Prindle, *Texas Politics*, 6th ed. (St. Paul, Minn.: West Publishing Company, 1996), 24–26. As an example, the authors describe George W. Bush's success when he was operating manager of the Texas Rangers in getting $135 million in public funding to build a stadium for the team. The stadium was sold back to the Rangers on extremely favorable terms. One corporate survey found the state second in the nation in "favorable business climate." For a less academic version of the relationship between Texas politics and business during the Bush era, see Molly Ivins and Lou Dubose, *Shrub: The Short but Happy Political Life of George W. Bush* (New York: Random House, 2000).

2. Recent discussions of partisan politics in Texas include Nicholas Lemann, "All Together Now?" *The New Yorker*, 4 December 2000, 49–53.

3. V. O. Key, Jr., *Southern Politics in State and Nation*, new edition (1949; reprint, Knoxville: University of Tennessee Press, 1984); Kraemer, Newell and Prindle, *Texas Politics*, chapter 1; Kim Quaile Hill and Kenneth R. Mladenka, *Texas Government: Politics and Economics*, 4th ed. (Belmont, Calif.: Wadsworth Publishing Co., 1996). Other groups, including poor whites and Mexican-Americans, also were subject to some of these restrictions.

4. Hill and Mladenka, *Texas Government*, 2–7; Kathryn Larin and Elizabeth C. McNichol, *Pulling Apart: A State-by-State Analysis of Income Trends* (Washington, D.C.: Center on Budget and Policy Priorities, 1997), 8.

5. Hispanics can be of any race.

6. Bureau of the Census, *Statistical Abstract of the United States 1996*, 33, 465, 474, 465, with ethnicity estimates for 1995 from www.census.gov/population/estimates/state/srh/srh95.txt; Nancy Pindus et al., "Assessing the New Federalism: Income Support and Social Service for Low-Income People in Texas," 11, newfederalism.urban.org/html/Txincome.html (accessed March 1998); Center on Public Policy Priorities, "Devolution: Welfare Reform," (Austin: CPPP, 1 September 1997), 1; *State Yellow Book, Fall 1997* (New York: Leadership Directories, Inc., 1997), 1038; *Chronicle of Higher Education, 1997–1998 Almanac Issue*, vol. 44, no. 1, 29 August 1997, 5, 100.

7. *1996 Green Book*, 439–40.

8. Testimony from DHS Commissioner Burton Raiford, 22 March 1995, before Senate Committee on Health and Human Services; *1998 Green Book*, 431; Center for Public Policy Priorities (CPPP), "A Brief Background on Welfare Reform and Welfare-to-Work Policy Changes," (Austin, Tex.: CPPP, 1998) 19; Center for Public Policy Priorities, "Devolution: Welfare Reform," 1.

9. *1996 Green Book*, 452.

10. Lea Isgur, Texas Department of Human Services, memo dated 29 February 1998; U.S. Department of Health and Human Services, Administration for Children and Families, "Change in TANF Caseloads," 14 December 2000, available at www.acf.dhhs.gov/news/stats/caseload.htm.

11. Texas Department of Human Services (DHS), *Demographic Profile of TANF Caretakers, September 1997, Office of Programs Administration and Management Services.* (Austin, Tex.: DHS, 20 February 1998), 12; DHS, *Demographic Profile of AFDC Caretakers*, August 1994, 10.

12. DeAnne Friedholm served as interim commissioner during the first part of the 1995 session. During the 1995 welfare debate, legislators discussed either beefing up the commission's powers or abolishing it; in 1999 they voted to revise the commission's operations and significantly increase its powers. Senate Committee on Health and Human Services, public hearing on multiple bills, 22 March 1995; House Committee on Human Services, public hearing on HB1863, 8 March 1995. See also HB 2641 from 1999 session, enrolled version, available at www.capitol.state.tx.us/tlo/76r/billtext/hb02641f.htm.

13. Interviews.

14. In Texas it is not uncommon for committee chairs to come from both parties, regardless of which has the majority in the chamber.

15. Interviews; Kathryn Brewer Spurgin, "From Rhetoric to Reform: Enacting Welfare Reform in Texas, 1995," Master of Public Affairs professional report, University of Texas at Austin, December 1995, chapter 2; Patrick Joseph Bresette, "The Evolution of Time-Limited AFDC Benefits in Texas: Rhetoric, Reform and Reality," Master of Public Affairs professional report, University of Texas at Austin, May 1996, 21.

16. "A Report to the House of Representatives, 74th Texas Legislature," Committee on Human Services, Texas House of Representatives Interim Report 1994, Harvey Hilderbran, Chairman, 14 October 1994.

17. Texas Conservative Coalition, *Task Force on Welfare Reform, Interim Report 73rd Legislature*, fall 1994.

18. John Sharp, *A Partnership for Independence: Public Assistance Reform Options* (Austin: Texas Comptroller of Public Accounts, 1995).

19. Texas House of Representatives, *House Journal, 74th Legislature, Regular Session*, 7 February 1995, 325; interviews.

20. Sharp, *Partnership for Independence*, 1.

21. Bresette, "Time-Limited AFDC Benefits in Texas," 31.

22. House Committee on Human Services, public hearing on HB 844, 13 February 1995.

23. Spurgin, "From Rhetoric to Reform," 135–36.

24. Interviews; audiotapes of Senate Committee on Health and Human Services hearings on SB 22.

25. Interviews; Texas House of Representatives, *House Journal, 74th Legislature, Regular Session*, 6 April 1995, 1123–27.

26. Pindus et al., "Assessing the New Federalism"; Policy Research Project on Workforce Reform in Texas, *Building a Workforce Development System for Texas*, Lyndon B. Johnson School of Public Affairs, Policy Research Project Report, No. 126 (Austin: University of Texas, 1997), chapter 3.

27. Spurgin, "From Rhetoric to Reform"; Policy Research Project on Workforce Reform in Texas, *Building a Workforce Development System for Texas*; interviews.

28. From Texas State Legislature Web site, "Bill Information, 74th Session, HB 1863, full history"; available at www.capitol.state.tx.us.

29. CPPP, "Welfare Reform"; Texas State Senate, *Senate Journal, Regular Session*, Vol. II, 25 April 1995, 1275; Spurgin, "From Rhetoric to Reform," 81–86, 93–97, 102–04; *1996 Green Book*, 865.

30. Deanna T. Schexnayder et al., "Lone Star Image System Evaluation, Final Report," Center for the Study of Human Resources, University of Texas at Austin, August 1997; interviews. ACT was expanded statewide in 1997, despite a University of Texas study finding that its costs were greater than its benefits.

31. Interviews.

32. Interview; CPPP, "Devolution: Welfare-to-Work Programs," (Austin, Tex.: CPPP, 1997), 1.

33. House Committee on Human Services, public hearing on HB 1863, 8 March 1995, audiotapes.

34. Interviews.

35. Interviews.

36. Keith E. Hamm and Charles W. Wiggins, "The Transformation from Personal to Informational Lobbying," in *Interest Group Politics in the Southern States*,

ed. Ronald J. Hrebenar and Clive S. Thomas (Tuscaloosa: University of Alabama Press, 1992), 174.

37. Interviews.

38. Richard H. Kraemer and Charldean Newell, *Essentials of Texas Politics*, 3d ed. (St. Paul, Minn.: West Publishing Co., 1986), 58.

39. These hearings were on HB 844, HB 1863 (and its committee substitutes), SB 22, SB 62, and SB 554. Texas did not make transcripts of hearings publicly available, nor did it provide readily available witness lists for 1995 (they must be special ordered, at some cost, as part of the minutes or audiotapes from each legislative support services office). In 1997, however, the state began to make witness lists available on the legislature's impressive website. My research indicates that although these lists generally are accurate, sometimes the site indicated that there were no witnesses when the corresponding minutes and audiotapes indicated that testimony in fact was taken. I attempted to be as thorough as possible in piecing together complete witness lists from a variety of legislative sources.

40. The groups involved in welfare policy often are small and underfunded, and one person sometimes does double duty, representing more than one group. Unless I knew that one group was a subsidiary of another (which would have led to double-counting), I counted these groups as separate political entities. As in the national debate, occasionally a representative of one group also would testify for a coalition, in which case I treated the coalition as a separate entity. However, if several representatives testified in the name of one organization, I counted only the single organization. My methodology may skew the count to suggest a somewhat greater number of actors than in fact is the case.

41. House Human Services Committee, public hearing on HB 844, 13 February 1995.

42. Organizations participating in the working group with the Center included the Texas Rural Legal Aid/Texas Appleseed Advocacy Fund, the Texas Legal Services/Houston Welfare Rights Organization, the Consumers' Union, the Texas Alliance for Human Needs, the Industrial Areas Foundation, the Texas Catholic Conference, Texans Care for Children, the National Association of Social Workers—Texas Chapter, the Texas AFL-CIO, the Texas Association of Community Action, Texas IMPACT, ACORN, and the National Association for the Advancement of Colored People (NAACP) Austin chapter. State government actors included the office of Senator Rodney Ellis (D-Houston), the LBJ School of Public Affairs of the University of Texas, the Texas Health and Human Services Commission, DHS, the Texas Council on Workforce and Economic Competitiveness, the governor's office, and the office of Democratic Representative Elliott Naishtat (vice chair of the House human services committee and, as of 1999, chair).

43. For an account of the organization's earlier work in Texas, see Robert H. Wilson, *Public Policy and Community: Activism and Governance in Texas* (Austin: University of Texas Press, 1997), chapter 5.

44. This is not to say that CPPP staffers agreed with the general orientation or hesitated to criticize it. The CPPP was able and willing, however, to work with lawmakers within the existing political framework.

45. Interviews.

46. Policy Research Project on Workforce Reform in Texas, *Building a Workforce Development System for Texas*, 3–19, 23; Pindus et al., "Assessing the New Federalism," 22; interviews.

47. CPPP, "Devolution: Welfare Reform," 6; CPPP, "The Policy Page: The TANF Block Grant and the State Budget, No. 50" (Austin, Tex.: CPPP, 1 August 1997) 2; interviews.

48. CPPP, "Devolution: Welfare Reform," executive summary, 2.

49. The program served only 17 percent of eligible recipients in FY 1994, and the legislature cut JOBS funding further in 1995. In FY 1992–1994, the state left unclaimed almost $42 million in federal JOBS funds. Bresette, "Time-Limited AFDC Benefits in Texas," 165, 190.

50. CPPP, "The Policy Page, No. 50," 2; interviews.

51. CPPP, "The Policy Page, No. 50," 3; interviews; Legislative Budget Board website, available at www.lbb.state.tx.us (accessed 15 February 1999).

52. CPPP, "The Policy Page, No. 50," 3; interviews.

53. CPPP, "The Policy Page, No. 50," 3; interviews.

54. Relations between the House Appropriations Committee and the CPPP later cooled after Center staffers expressed concern about committee decisions publicly.

55. As I note in chapter 2, the new federal law allowed 30 percent of TANF block grant funds to be transferred into state services funded by the federal Title XX social services block grant.

56. CPPP, "The Policy Page, No. 50," 3–7; CPPP, "Welfare Reform Watch," 11–12.

57. CPPP, "The Policy Page, No. 50"; CPPP, "Devolution: Welfare-to-Work Programs," and "Devolution: Child Care," (Austin, Tex.: CPPP, September 1997).

58. Interviews; Texas State Legislature website, "Bill Information, 75th Session," available at www.capitol.state.tx.us.

59. Interviews; CPPP, "The Policy Page: Privatization of Health and Human Services Eligibility Determination, No. 56" (Austin, Tex.: CPPP, 1 September 1997), 2.

60. The Council is composed of the governor, the lieutenant governor, the comptroller, the speaker of the House, the head of the General Services Commission, and the labor commissioner of the TWC.

61. CPPP, "The Policy Page, No. 56," 2; interviews.

62. CPPP, "The Policy Page, No. 56," 2; interviews; Policy Research Project on Workforce Reform in Texas, *Building a Workforce Development System for Texas*, chapter 3.

63. CPPP, "The Policy Page, No. 56."

64. See William D. Hartung and Jennifer Washburn, "Lockheed Martin: From Warfare to Welfare," *The Nation*, 2 March 1998, 11–18; see also Martha M. Hamilton, "Texas

Poor Constitute Rich Prize," *Washington Post*, 26 November 1996, C1; George Rodrigue, "Problems Reported in Privatizing Welfare," *Dallas Morning News*, 17 March 1997.

65. Hartung and Washburn, "From Warfare to Welfare"; CPPP, "The Policy Page, No. 56," 7; interviews.

66. Hartung and Washburn, "From Warfare to Welfare," 14; CPPP, "The Policy Page, No. 56," 3–6.

67. CPPP, "The Policy Page, No. 56," 4; Kevin Thurm, Deputy Secretary of HHS, letter to Michael D. McKinney, M.D., Commissioner of the Texas Health and Human Services Commission, dated 13 May 1997.

68. Hartung and Washburn, "From Warfare to Welfare," 14; CPPP, "The Policy Page, No. 56," 5.

69. Hartung and Washburn, "From Warfare to Welfare," 14; Policy Research Project on Workforce Reform in Texas, *Building a Workforce Development System for Texas*, 26.

70. CPPP, "The Policy Page, No. 56," 5; "Bill Information, 75th Session," available at www.capitol.state.tx.us.

71. Mark Greenberg and Steve Savner, *The Final TANF Regulations: A Preliminary Analysis* (Washington, D.C.: Center for Law and Social Policy, 1999), 30.

72. Quoted in Polly Ross Hughes, "Audit Criticizes State's Oversight of Welfare Reform," *Houston Chronicle*, 2 September 1999, A27.

73. U.S. Department of Health and Human Services, Administration for Children and Families, "Change in TANF Caseloads: Total TANF Recipients by State," as of December 1999; available at www.acf.dhhs.gov/news/state/caseload.htm.

74. Texas Department of Human Services, "Texas Families in Transition, The Impacts of Welfare Reform Changes in Texas: Early Findings," December 1998. See also Polly Ross Hughes, "Welfare Reform in Texas Shows Some Progress," *Houston Chronicle*, 10 December 1998, A1.

75. See Ivins and Dubose, *Shrub*, 90–94, on Bush's use of tough welfare reform for political purposes.

76. Clay Robison, "Campaign 98: Bush Proposes Tougher Welfare Reform," *Houston Chronicle*, 30 September 1998, A21.

77. Polly Ross Hughes, "Bush Announces Grants to Help Churches Keep Poor Off Welfare," *Houston Chronicle*, 12 October 1999, A13.

78. The new vice chair was Glen Maxey, also a liberal-leaning Democrat from Austin. Interviews; Scott S. Greenberger, "Austin Lawmakers Gain Clout in House," *Austin American-Statesman*, 29 January 1999, A1.

79. Center on Public Policy Priorities, "The Policy Page No. 87," 20 May 1999, available at www.cppp.org/products/policypages/71-90/71-90html/pp87.html. Polly Ross Hughes, "76th Texas Legislature: On Welfare, Legislature Goes for Carrot, Not Stick," *Houston Chronicle*, 30 May 1999, 1.

80. Quoted in Hughes, "Welfare Reform in Texas Shows Some Progress."

81. The 1995 House version of welfare reform had required the state to abide by the five-year limit beginning immediately, whereas the Senate bill exempted

recipients until after the state's ACT waiver expired in 2002. During conference, specific mention of the time limit was dropped, although legislative aides have listened to tapes of conference committee proceedings and argue that it was the intent of the conference to forego the federal limit until 2002 and instead implement the five-year "freeze-out." Bost quote from Polly Ross Hughes, "Gov. Bush Is Seeking to Step Up Welfare Cuts," *Houston Chronicle*, 1 October 1999, A1.

82. House Committee on Human Services, Texas House of Representatives, Interim Report 2000, "A Report to the House of Representatives, 77th Texas Legislature," Elliott Naishtat, Chairman, Austin, 5 December 2000.

83. Center on Public Policy Priorities, "The Policy Page: Crouching Budget, Hidden TANF, No. 127," 20 April 2001," available at www.cppp.org/products/policy pages; interview.

6

North Dakota: Welfare Reform on the Northern Plains

Neo-Madisonian concerns about the limits of localism and the effects of a small sphere on diversity in politics found a basis in North Dakota. The state is small; the range and number of actors involved in politics, at least in welfare policymaking, was limited; and the community of organizations representing North Dakota's low-income people was modest and beleaguered. Despite their efforts, they had limited impact on the state's initial foray into welfare policymaking under devolution. In particular, North Dakota's Indians, who made up more than half the caseload, had virtually no role in developing the state's comprehensive program in the mid-1990s. North Dakota's policymakers were dedicated to public service, sincere and hard working, but the state's political institutions were constrained by their informality, the inconsistency with which they operated, and the limited resources on which they had to draw.

North Dakota politics were strongly affected by the state's isolation, small population, and harsh climate, as well as fears of population loss, especially in rural areas. The vast majority of early white settlers were farmers, and agricultural issues have long dominated the state's politics.[1] A strong populist movement blossomed toward the end of the nineteenth century and into the early twentieth century in response to the power of railroads and out-of-state businesses, leading to the rise of the Nonpartisan League (NPL), a farmers' movement with roots in the Socialist Party. Although the NPL held power only briefly, during that time it established major state-owned institutions, including the Bank of North Dakota and a state grain elevator and mill, which remained under control of the state Industrial Commission in the 1990s.[2]

By the 1990s, this populist strain still ran through North Dakota politics, although the state seemed to be dominated by more individualistic, conservative attitudes. In recent years, the state has eagerly sought to bring in outside businesses to diversify the economy and provide jobs, and the percentage of the population occupied in agriculture has plummeted. The "rural Diaspora" has been a real concern—the death rate outpaced births and in-migration in several rural counties—and the state had the lowest growth rate in the nation. In counties dominated by Native Americans, however, the opposite trend has occurred: Returning tribal members and high birthrates have spurred population growth even though unemployment remained extremely high.

These pressures constricted policy options, particularly in social policy. In the mid-1990s, state welfare benefits actually were higher than the national average—apparently a vestige of the state's populist leanings and a time when the majority of recipients were "worthy" white widows. A prevalent and strong ethic of frugality, self-help, and personal responsibility helped to frame welfare reform options, however, and shaped the major decisions about behavioral mandates.

This chapter explores the context of North Dakota's recent welfare overhaul; examines the formation in 1995 of "Training, Employment, Education and Management" (TEEM), the state's waiver pilot program; and looks at the adaptation of TEEM in 1997 to the requirements of PRWORA. As with Maryland and Texas, I consider political pressures inside and outside state government, including the role of the low-income advocacy community and the state's Indian tribes. Finally, I appraise the long-term political implications of devolution for the future of welfare policy in North Dakota.

CONTEXT OF WELFARE REFORM

North Dakota ranked forty-seventh in population among the states in 1995, followed only by Alaska, Vermont, and Wyoming. Its population was 641,000, or substantially less than the welfare caseload in Texas during the same year.[3] The 1994 poverty rate was 10.4 percent—well below the national level—although the median household income ($28,278) also was below the national median of $32,264, reflecting the equitable distribution of income within the state.[4] The state was overwhelmingly white: In 1995, 94 percent of North Dakotans were white, 4.4 percent were Native American, 0.6 percent were black, and 0.8 percent were Asian. The state's four federally recognized Indian reservations were Turtle Mountain (Chippewa), close to the Canadian border; Standing Rock (Lakota and Yanktonai Sioux) in the south, extending into South Dakota; Fort Berthold (Three Affiliated Tribes: Arikara, Hidatsa, and Mandan) surrounding Lake Sakakawea in the west; and Fort Totten (Devils Lake Sioux) toward the east.[5]

North Dakota is very rural; in the 1990s it had no cities with more than 80,000 in population and only four with more than 20,000.[6] The workforce was well educated, but North Dakota's distance from major markets has made attracting outside capital difficult.[7] Statewide, unemployment in the mid-1990s was below the national rate, but it varied widely by region. The three counties with the highest concentrations of Native Americans had official rates that were much higher than average—state data put them at about 50 percent—and Bureau of Indian Affairs data, which count discouraged workers, indicated a 76 percent unemployment rate at Standing Rock Reservation.[8]

Daniel Elazar described North Dakota's political culture as a hybrid of moralist and individualist. The individualism and ethic of self-sufficiency that were typical of western states were tempered by a more stereotypically midwestern sense of social responsibility, particularly in the eastern side of the state—carried in during the 1800s by Scandinavian immigrants and reinforced by the common hardship of people living in such a harsh environment.[9] North Dakotans participated politically at higher rates than citizens in most other states and seemed to hold their elected officials in fairly high regard.[10]

NORTH DAKOTA WELFARE POLICY

The maximum AFDC benefit in January 1996 was $431 per month for a family of three, or $5,172 per year. Over the preceding 26 years, however, the state grant had lost 49 percent of its real value.[11] In FY 1994, the North Dakota caseload was 56 percent white, 1 percent black, about 2 percent Hispanic, 2 percent Asian, and 39 percent Native American. By the end of 1997, Native Americans made up 53 percent of recipients. Total average monthly caseloads dropped from a high in 1993 of 5,982 families to 3,896 by the end of calendar year 1997—a decline of 35 percent.[12] Although welfare use dropped radically in majority white urban areas, caseloads on the state's reservations continued to grow because of in-migration, high unemployment, and severely limited economic opportunities, as well as population growth, shifting the distribution of recipients from majority white to majority Indian.[13]

These changing demographics reflect complicated and volatile social, political, and economic issues that were linked to Indian/non-Indian relations, the tribes' relationship with the federal government, the nature of land set aside for reservations, patterns of economic investment and growth in North Dakota, and controversies regarding the nature and extent of tribal self-government. The politics of welfare reform in North Dakota in the mid-1990s, which were dominated by non-Indian politicians and their constituents, initially seemed surprisingly inattentive to the rapidly changing patterns of the caseload. PRWORA allowed for tribal administration of TANF programs with federal approval, but as of late 2000 no tribe in the state had taken over its own program. Most did not yet have the money, expertise, or administrative capacity to fund and manage one independent of the state. During the 1995 and 1997 legislative sessions in North Dakota, these complex problems received little in-depth discussion. Soon afterward, however, welfare began to force some of them onto the agenda.[14]

The North Dakota Department of Human Services (DHS), which administered AFDC/TANF and other social service programs, was the largest executive agency in the state; it accounted for about one-third of North Dakota's $4 billion biennial budget.[15] During 1995 and into 1997, Henry "Bud" Wessman was DHS director, but his relationship with the legislature soured over mismanagement of the department's new computerized management information system (MIS) for welfare and other programs, forcing his resignation. Carol Olson, the governor's chief-of-staff, later replaced him.

Services were delivered through eight regional centers and locally by decentralized county departments that received part of their funding from the state and federal governments and part through property taxes and other local sources. One social welfare advocate described the state's fragmented approach to structuring human services as "like a roller coaster," with efforts at decentralization quickly followed by attempts to gain greater control by centralizing again. AFDC/TANF was county administered, although JOBS training programs were administered through state and tribal centers. The regional centers and counties differed significantly in their approach to delivering social services, depending on the orientation and "value system" of the county clerks and social services directors, although the counties did have a core group of services that all departments attempted to provide.

Like most other states, North Dakota jumped on the welfare reform bandwagon in response to the Clinton administration's loosened waiver policy. Although the state generally had been slow to innovate, policymakers moved to set up a pilot program in the mid-1990s in response to the general and widely held sense that the system was "broken" as well as growing resentment toward the welfare poor. One legislator who was active in welfare reform said that residents in his very rural district generally knew who was on welfare or collecting food stamps. "Everyone knows each other," he observed. "They talk, [and] it's highly visible if you're accepting public assistance. There's a real work ethic, which leads to a sense of resentment about paying for someone else . . . and I'm seeing them in bars, or they have three kids and they're not married, or kids by different fathers." He and other legislators said that there was a widespread perception that welfare was not "fair."

STATE LEGISLATURE

The North Dakota Legislative Assembly met in Bismarck every two years for a constitutional maximum of 80 days, although legislative committees meet periodically during the interim periods. The legislature was predominately Republican: The Senate had 49 members, of whom 30 were Republicans and 19 were Democrats in the fall of 1997; the House of Representatives had 98 members, of whom 71 were Republicans and 27 were Democrats. The partisan balance was similar in 1995, although in 1993 Democrats led the Senate. Both houses were overwhelmingly white; there was one Native American member.[16] Legislators earned about $12,000 per year while in session and did not receive budgets to maintain their own offices—North Dakota was serious about its citizen legislators.

Legislative Council staff provided modest assistance to committees during the session and the interim periods. On the off-year, legislative staff shrank dramatically.[17] Although some legislators were content with this arrangement, citing the dangers of a too-powerful staff, others noted the difficulty in conducting research on important issues with a legislature that was composed entirely of part-time legislators, most of whom have full-time jobs and little assistance. Not surprisingly, turnover was high: About 27 percent of legislators were new each session. The chair of the House Human Services Committee who took over in 1997 noted that six of her twelve members were freshmen, and several others were new to the committee's issues. She also noted that her committee had been headed by different chairs during each of the two previous sessions.[18]

Legislative rules required that each bill be reported out of committee and either sent to the floor or referred to another committee (which in turn would send it to the floor). All legislation, including amendments, was voted on by the entire chamber.[19] Legislation had to be through committee and voted on by the chamber in which it was introduced by the third week of February—known as crossover—to reach the other chamber in time for deliberation and a vote.[20] Obviously, this time schedule was extremely tight. Legislators noted that with the volume of legislation they had to review—more than 1,000 bills were introduced in 1995, more than half of which became law—they often could not read the various permutations of the legislation on which they voted.[21] Instead, they relied on their colleagues because they had little staff assistance. "Sometimes it's scary," said one legislator. "At first I'd study every bill, but then overnight it would all change."

1995: ESTABLISHING THE TEEM WAIVER PROGRAM

Welfare reform in 1995 began with two 1993 legislative resolutions that directed the Legislative Council to study the design and administration of economic and medical assistance and explore ways to remove work disincentives and increase the self-sufficiency of single mothers.[22] This directive led a statewide welfare reform task force, the state DHS, and the joint Interim Budget Committee on Human Services to develop the TEEM demonstration program. The task force included a range of participants, including advocates and even some welfare recipients. DHS was said to have been reluctant at first to include them in the process—compelled by the then-Democratic Senate—but after the TEEM proposal was well received, the department used their participation as a political selling point.[23] One Native American official noted his frustration at the lack of tribal input, given the importance of Indians to the state's welfare system. TEEM was to combine AFDC, food stamps, and the Low-Income Home Energy Assistance Program (LIHEAP) into a single integrated program, tested in eleven pilot counties. DHS, with unusually broad support, submitted its waiver requests to the federal departments of HHS and Agriculture in fall 1994. They were still being reviewed when the 54th session began in January 1995.[24]

The 1995 session started with SB 2035, the "Welfare Reform Demonstration Project," which in essence gave the legitimacy of legislative approval to what had already happened through the executive agency during the interim. Although the federal government could grant a waiver to a project that had never received legislative approval, the program could not operate without an appropriation of money.[25] Negotiations on the bill were not controversial. Participants noted that it didn't receive much attention in part because it was only a pilot program, not statewide reform. Moreover, before the session DHS, the interim legislative committee, and the welfare task force had successfully developed consensus during the planning process for TEEM. The pilot itself was fairly moderate, with provisions such as higher asset limits and none of the contentious elements that would bedevil the legislature in 1997. The governor's office took no major role in welfare policy in 1995. Governor Edward T. Schafer, a conservative Republican who took office in 1992, had other priorities and left reform efforts to his human resources agency and the legislature.

Senator Russell Thane, a Republican from the Richland area and chair of the Human Services Committee, sponsored the TEEM bill in the Senate. The Senate Human Services Committee held one public hearing in January (see Appendix F for hearings and witnesses).[26] Four government employees testified: one staffer from the Legislative Council, Wessman of DHS, and two DHS staffers. The latter three would become the core group of administration officials shaping welfare over the following two years. The committee voted out the bill with several minor amendments, and it crossed over to the House on January 25. The House Appropriations Committee's subcommittee on human services held one public hearing, on March 8, and the full committee approved the bill unanimously two days later.[27] The final votes in the full House and Senate also were unanimous: 88 to 0 and 48 to 0, respectively.[28] Governor Schafer signed the demonstration legislation on April 12, 1995.

During the 54th legislative session, no one pushed for a family cap, full-family sanctions, shorter time limits, or limits on what recipients could purchase with food stamps or their cash grants. In fact, the proposal called for combining all benefits, even food stamp vouchers, into a single cash lump sum available through an "electronic benefit card." The 1995 TEEM pilot, however, did include provisions designed to shape recipient behavior in other ways and move them into jobs.[29] In addition to the benefit consolidation, TEEM:

- increased asset limits to $8,000 for a family and increased by about 25 percent the amount people could keep from work, with a graduated offset intended to mitigate the work disincentive of welfare;
- exempted one vehicle of any value from the limits altogether;
- exempted savings accounts for purposes such as education and home ownership;
- continued to cover pregnant women for the duration of their pregnancy (a practice in the state since 1991), with the first two trimesters covered by state funds;
- deducted from income determination $175–200 per month per child for child care and reimbursed some child care expenses for people in transition from welfare into work;
- required recipients to sign a "social contract" mandating that they cooperate with paternity establishment, meet training and work requirements, participate in a child health program, and pursue other individualized goals, with grant reduction for noncompliance; and
- placed a heavy emphasis on initial case assessment and subsequent case management.

TEEM built on the JOBS programs established by the federal FSA in 1988 and run by Job Service North Dakota, the state employment agency. The state also contracted with Curtis and Associates, a private for-profit firm, for job preparation and placement. For the first time, recipients were required to participate in training or work activities, including nonpaid work if necessary, unless they were specifically exempted. Families leaving welfare for work were eligible for transitional child care and medical assistance. Finally, TEEM included a detailed evaluation, as required for waivers by federal law. The demonstration initially was expected to affect about 1,250 households a month, or a quarter of the caseload. The state received permission from HHS in September 1995 to start implementing TEEM.[30]

Tribal Participants

Native Americans from the state's four reservations were almost entirely missing from the debate about TEEM.[31] Tribes in North Dakota, like tribes elsewhere, were in an idiosyncratic legal position. They were not under the jurisdiction of the state; several lawmakers commented somewhat bitterly that "they're a sovereign nation" in explaining the relative indifference of many legislators to Indian issues. They did vote for state lawmakers, however, and they were eligible to receive state services, though in some cases additional or alternative programs were provided directly to the tribes by the federal Bureau of Indian Affairs. It was an awkward position—semi-sovereign but wielding little real power—that originated in the federal and state governments' troubled history of relations with the United States' indigeneous people.[32] One official of a heavily Indian county observed, "'Sovereignty' doesn't sit well with many white legislators. It's like a red flag—they see it as something the tribes hide behind." Some state officials seemed to feel that tribal sovereignty precluded state citizenship. Indian and non-Indian relations in North Dakota certainly were strained, though several white North Dakotans hastened to say that they were not as bad as those in South Dakota. Native Americans, however, felt that prejudice—even if unconscious—still ran strong among non-Indians.

Poverty, unemployment, out-of-wedlock births, substance abuse, and other social problems in the state tended to occur in much higher rates among Indians. They generally lived on the state's reservations, however, isolated from the vast majority of white residents. "The issue of the tribes hardly came up at all; welfare reform is not seen as a Native American issue," said one advocate, despite the fact that Indians made up between a third and more than half of the welfare rolls. "You might see them in the shopping malls at Christmas time, but otherwise they're on the reservations, and the interstate doesn't even go through," he commented. White North Dakotans, including many lawmakers, seemed to adopt a policy of neglect, driven by the relative invisibility of most Indians' problems from whites and resentment about their unique sovereignty.

The politics of casinos aggravated this resentment. Lawmakers complained that they didn't know what the tribes did with their casino earnings but that the state was then expected to contribute funds for welfare and other social programs. The state's attorney general gained oversight over casino revenues in the early 1990s, but the resulting reports were not released to the public. One ex-government official described a common attitude: "We've given them casinos, and unemployment is around 2 percent, so who should be out of work?" Several Indians, however, as well as the federal HHS official who oversaw tribal welfare programs, suggested that there was a lot less money flowing from the casinos than many whites thought, in part because the tribes paid a portion of revenues to the management company that actually operated them. Casinos did provide jobs—accompanied by some significant social problems—but fell far short of bringing riches to the reservations of North Dakota.[33]

Indian/non-Indian relations also were aggravated by frequent turnover in tribal governments, which made it harder to attract private economic development into reservation boundaries because contracts honored by one tribal government might not be honored by the next. Government hierarchies were said to be very family-oriented, with employees often related to elected tribal leaders. Although the strong family orientation was a source of pride and strength for many Native Americans in the state, this government instability tended to wreak havoc on the tribes' ability to draw non-Indian investors and economic development.[34] A frequent attitude of whites in the state—similar to that of some whites toward black Americans in urban areas—seemed to be that Indians had contributed to their own problems and were beyond the scope of the state to assist. For many North Dakotans, Indians were identified as "a problem" for the federal government to deal with.

Several participants suggested that Indian representation in state politics came from individual tribal members or, on occasion, from tribal officials but that there were few intermediary groups representing them. One advocate commented on the awkwardness for non-Indian groups in trying to represent Indian concerns. An Indian official who was particularly politically active in state politics suggested, however, that outside groups might carry weight with the legislature where native people often did not. He also noted that the tribes in North Dakota were not a monolithic group and that although they shared many concerns, they also faced different issues.[35]

Nongovernmental Participants

A study of North Dakota interest groups by political scientist Theodore Pedeliski suggested that lobbyists generally were regarded more favorably in the state than is typically the case. The moralistic political culture inhibited influence peddling, but the expertise-strapped legislature relied heavily on interest groups for information. Committee hearings were seen as providing an important opportunity to educate members. Groups with particularly good research capabilities were highly regarded by legislators, as were interest groups that explicitly linked their interests with those of a legislator's constituents. The fact that all bills went to the floor for a vote gave individual legislators a great deal of independence and increased the incentive for interest groups to lobby them.[36] Another 1986 study of interest group influence on state legislatures ranked North Dakota first, noting the part-time citizen legislature, its need for expertise, and the requirement that the full chamber vote on every measure.[37] Nonetheless, the state's cultural norms were said to keep legislators fairly independent of interest group representatives when it came to deciding their votes.

Business interests have long been influential in the state, including the Greater North Dakota Association (GNDA)—the state's leading "peak" business association, which is affiliated with the Chamber of Commerce. Correspondingly, organized labor has been weak; only 14 percent of the state's nonagricultural workers were unionized as of 1993. A greater variety of groups participated in the state's politics than in the past, including some environmental organizations and advocates for disabled citizens and children, reflecting the national growth of such groups since the 1960s. They were fairly weak, however.

North Dakota politics tended to be especially personal because the community was so small. Although the state lacked the sense of an economic and political elite like that in Texas and many other states, the portfolio of active groups in North Dakota politics was skewed toward the middle-class white majority, as well as representatives of the businesses that public officials were so eager to keep within North Dakota borders. Groups representing low-income and minority residents were almost entirely absent. As Pedeliski argued, the most powerful link was between legislators and their constituents, especially those who were influential in numbers or economic resources. This dynamic often left out the concerns of the state's economic and ethnic minorities, however.[38] The absence of groups representing Native Americans was particularly striking. Their interests could be represented through tribal officials, individuals who participated politically, or members of the state Indian Affairs Commission. Often, however, North Dakota government has acted almost entirely without input from the state's Native American citizens.[39]

Interest group strategies have become more sophisticated in North Dakota, as elsewhere, but the top three tactics in a 1988 survey, in order of importance, were contact with committee chairs, contact with rank-and-file members, and participation in committee hearings. Reflecting the uncontroversial nature of the TEEM proposal and the small community of organizations involved, only four interest groups testified at the Senate Human Services Committee hearing on the welfare pilot in January 1995:[40] the director of a county social services department representing the county directors' association; the director of the North Dakota Catholic Conference (NDCC); a representative of the Welfare Advisory Board (who testified at other hearings for North Dakota Legal Assistance); and the director of the People Escaping Poverty Project (PEPP), a Fargo-Moorhead (Minnesota) advocacy group for low-income people that was active in Minnesota and North Dakota. In the House, ten outside actors testified at the Appropriations subcommittee on human services at its sole public hearing. Again, they represented a small core group: the director of the NDCC appeared once more, as did the director of PEPP and the representative of North Dakota Legal Assistance. Another PEPP member testified, as did her three children. Two other people testified: one an ex-recipient and the other her child.

All told, eleven outside actors or organizations participated in the two public hearings during the 1995 legislative debate about welfare reform, offering testimony fourteen times (see Table 6-1). The four advocacy groups testified seven times, providing half of all testimony. Six individuals testified, and one intergovernmental actor participated. No independent researchers,

Table 6-1
Activity of North Dakota Interest Groups in Welfare-Related Hearings, by Category, 54th Session (1995)

Category	No. of Organizations Organizations/Actors	No. of Times Testifying
Advocates: child advocacy, nonprofit and charitable providers, unions[a]	4	7
Individuals[b]	6	6
Intergovernmental	1	1
Researchers	0	0
Think tanks	0	0
"Traditional values" groups	0	0
For-profit companies, business groups	0	0
Professional associations	0	0
Miscellaneous	0	0
TOTAL	**11**	**14**

Sources: Information from minutes of two House and Senate public hearings and testimony (see Appendix F for complete list of hearings and participants). Author's calculations.

[a]As with national groups, the lines between advocacy and nonprofit service or charitable organizations often are blurry. Some advocacy groups also provided services, and some charitable groups also were committed to advocacy.

[b]Four of these individuals were children of the other two.

traditional values groups, professional associations, for-profits, business or trade organizations, unions, or think tanks participated in the public hearings process. All witnesses testified in favor of the pilot program. Going into 1995, there was little disagreement with the direction that the original TEEM program took.

Obviously the active advocacy community in North Dakota was tiny. The NDCC and PEPP were consistently active in testifying about the TEEM pilot; otherwise, however, few people participated in the legislative process. Only PEPP brought welfare recipients to the table. Several groups, including PEPP and the NDCC, also participated in the welfare reform task force during 1994. The number and range of groups participating in legislative hearings were extremely narrow, however. Ultimately, several key advocates would say they felt "used" by state policymakers who listened to their input during the development of TEEM in 1994 and 1995 but went in a significantly stricter direction after the federal bill passed in 1996.

Most advocacy groups were centered in Bismarck. Although they overlapped on some issues, the community tended to be fragmented because so few people were trying to work on so many different social problems. "Working in such a conservative environment, with a diverse group of issues, it's hard for us to be unified," one advocate commented. If one group was known to be active on an issue, the others often turned their attention to other matters because time and staff were in extremely short supply. One retired state official called advocacy in the state "extraordinarily difficult. . . . There must be some geometric progression in population necessary [for group formation]." Another advocate noted, "In other states, there's a network, [even though] it may be small and fairly insignificant. But it doesn't even exist here." Yet another echoed the concerns of the neo-Madisonians when he described the challenges of representing low-income people: "Politics here are very informal, and we don't have well-organized [advocacy groups]," he said, adding, "states like Maryland have more groups, and they have organizations like the Annie Casey Foundation to support them."[41]

Unless people were personally affected by social issues, they tended to ignore them. Those most affected, however, often were least likely to vote or participate in other ways, so they missed out on the legislature's particular attentiveness to constituents. According to one long-time participant in social policymaking, the advocacy community itself was regarded as a special interest rather than as representing a broad range of North Dakotans. There also was a sense that many advocates were "outsiders." Other participants stressed difficulties in getting funding for low-income people in a small state that was so eager to bring in business and jobs and keep them there; there were few foundations or other philanthropic sources of funds.

No groups from outside the state came in to lobby. "We don't usually see that here," noted one legislator. "Some big groups have local lawyers here to lobby, but on the welfare issue not really. [Also,] you don't just pass through North Dakota." Many participants—lawmakers and nongovernmental actors—commented on how little general interest welfare reform stirred in 1995. If there were groups or people who took issue with TEEM, they were not heard from.

1997: CATCHING UP WITH THE FEDERAL BILL

One advocate described a trip he took to Washington in late 1996 on the same plane with a key committee chairperson heading to the National Conference of State Legislatures (NCSL) 1997 winter meeting. On the way to Washington, he said, the chairperson "was talking about all the things they were going to do in the coming session, and welfare wasn't one of them, but on the plane back, that's what [the chair] was talking about: all the changes they would make." The 1996 federal welfare bill took many North Dakota lawmakers by surprise; they were brought up short by the nature and extent of the changes they would be required to make over the eighty-day session in 1997, particularly in the area of child support enforcement. Once it got started, the 1997 legislative debate was more contentious and partisan than it had been in 1995. Although again welfare policy didn't generate widespread public interest—there was said to be a perception that "we did that already"—several new provisions that altered TEEM drew intense disagreement.

Like Maryland, North Dakota opted to give up its waivers and adapt its system to comply with federal TANF requirements. The amended version of TEEM was similar in some ways to the pilot, though it was expanded from eleven counties to all fifty-three. Issues such as child support enforcement, a family cap, and the definition of work generated sharp controversy, however. These alterations were spurred by changes in the federal bill, though only a few, such as provisions for child support enforcement, actually were required by it. Others, such as the family cap and definition of work activities, were state options.

Governmental Participants

The House Human Services Committee took the lead on welfare reform in 1997. HB 1226, the state's comprehensive welfare bill, which DHS formulated, was introduced in mid-January.[42] Rep. Clara Sue Price, Republican from the Minot area, was the new chair of the Human Services Committee, and she made clear that the committee would alter the department's plan significantly by the time it was done. By 1997, relations between DHS and the legislature were strained, reflecting tension over the department's budget practices, charges of secrecy tied to agency efforts to update its computerized welfare tracking system, and other management issues.

The Human Service Committee began hearings in late January with testimony from DHS director Bud Wessman and other department officials, as well as several nongovernmental groups (see Appendix F). Department officials pushed for sufficient funding for the automated "RESPOND" tracking system on which TEEM case management was based and advocated the end of state-funded cash benefits to pregnant women in their first and second trimesters. The bill also proposed to "swap" financing responsibilities between the state and the counties, which were the direct providers of welfare services; the state would take over TANF program costs, and the counties would pay for administration (previously these costs were shared). In its original form, HB 1226 explicitly rejected the family cap. Throughout their testimony, officials in DHS and the legislature expressed concern about the state's ability to meet the new federal work participation rates.[43] The committee invited a welfare expert from the NCSL in Washington to speak to its members in February about the federal bill and its requirements for the state, and debate continued with two more public hearings.[44] The governor's office again was largely uninvolved, and Governor Schafer made little of welfare reform during his 1997 state-of-the-state address.[45]

On February 17, Rep. Robin Weisz, a Republican from the rural Hurdsfield area, introduced an amendment to implement a family cap. According to Weisz, he did this in response to his constituents' concern about "what message the system should reinforce—one of responsibility and adult decisions . . . or 'rewarding' people for irresponsibility?"[46] Rep. Pat Galvin, a Republican from Hazen (just south of the Fort Berthold Indian reservation), supported the cap and was quoted as saying, "I'd be the last person to limit the amount of children [a person can have]. But the government shouldn't pay for it any longer. . . . This loose view of marriage and family has to come to an end soon, and I hope it comes to an end in North Dakota right now."[47] The proposal met with strong disagreement from others, however—as elsewhere, from liberal members who felt that it harmed children and from pro-life conservatives who feared that it would lead to more abortions.[48] Weisz was pro-life, as were most other Republican lawmakers, but he said he did not believe that the family or cash cap (as its proponents preferred to call it) was especially likely to induce abortions. Nor did he believe that the additional monthly payment—between $37 and $90, depending on family size—was likely to induce additional births. "Abortion didn't even occur to me," he commented. Nonetheless, the provision quickly became entangled in the heated combination of antiabortion and "liberal" politics. The final vote on the cap amendment was nine in favor and five against.[49]

The stringent child support enforcement provisions required by the federal bill also sparked sharp disagreement in North Dakota. Legislators resented what they regarded as national government intrusion embedded in a bill that was supposed to give states more flexibility and autonomy. North Dakota had done reasonably well on child support enforcement—in 1994 it ranked nineteenth in per capita collections—and greater federal mandates such as denials of licenses, liens on the property of "deadbeat" parents, and a central "new hire registry" met with strong resistance. Child support provisions made up forty pages of the final sixty-page bill.[50] Several legislators also expressed concern about whether the Indian tribes would elect to run their own welfare programs and what the effect of their decisions would be on the state's ability to meet its work participation rates. Other issues included the appropriate lifetime limit to cash assistance, work participation requirements, how education would be defined for purposes of meeting work requirements, the effects of the financial "swap" with the counties, and the proposal to cut back cash aid to low-income pregnant women.[51]

Ten of the fourteen members of the House Human Services Committee voted in favor of HB 1226 as amended, with opponents largely objecting to the family cap.[52] The full House considered the bill in mid-February, and the cap led to a floor fight. Legislators in the House divided much as committee members had.[53] The House passed the bill 67 to 24, just making the deadline for crossover to the Senate. Democrats tended to oppose the bill, and Republicans supported it, although again abortion politics made unlikely bedfellows.

No one in the House seemed to be very happy with the legislation. Lawmakers who voted against HB 1226 called it "anti-child," and even Weisz was quoted as saying, "This is a terrible bill, but we don't have any choice."[54] House Majority Leader John Dorso, a major proponent of welfare reform, put a more cheerful face on the situation, however, commenting, "The Republican majority has certainly put a heck of a package together as far as welfare reform. I have to take my hat off to them for their diligence and stick-to-itiveness."[55]

Relations between DHS and the legislature further deteriorated when the federal HHS threatened to cut off a $5.5 million welfare automation grant because the North Dakota DHS failed to submit information in the correct form or on time. Republican and Democratic legislators criticized Wessman and the department for the "computer flap," which now threw the DHS budget into disarray. Shortly afterward, the House trimmed the department's budget by more than $22 million from the governor's $1.2 billion request, including cutting funding for the RESPOND system.[56] Several participants also suggested that the controversy inhibited the department's ability to negotiate effectively with the legislature, given its damaged credibility.[57] On March 4, Wessman resigned, and Wayne Anderson, his deputy, took over for the duration of the session until Olson was appointed. Legislators welcomed the change in leadership as an opportunity to reexamine the organization of the massive agency.[58]

The Senate Human Services Committee began its hearings on HB 1226 in early March, with a massive blizzard closing in. Again, child support enforcement and the family cap were the most controversial issues. The same three DHS officials testified at length, as did a representative of the county court clerks, who had jurisdiction over support enforcement; representatives of two business groups that were concerned about the new child support provisions; other county officials; advocates; and several individuals. For the first time, a representative of one of the tribes also participated.[59]

The issue of child care gained new attention. DHS staff testified about the anticipated increase in demand as more recipients went to work, especially given that HB 1226 proposed to exempt only women with children under four months of age. The state had a cap on its child care budget and faced a severe shortage of licensed care workers, particularly in the rural counties—one of which had no licensed child care providers at all.[60] Although the legislature seemed to be unprepared to address the growing need for care, it passed a resolution to order a study of the implementation of welfare reform, including child care, during the coming interim session.[61]

A proposal also was made to delete the family cap. One legislator argued for the deletion, saying, "We would only hurt the child, or all children. Maybe children should be taken from [their] mother for better care." Supporters of the cap remained steadfast, however. The Senate Committee on Human Services finally approved its bill on March 31 by a vote of 4 to 2, with opponents again citing the family cap.[62] The debate in the full Senate also was marked by disagreement over the family cap, although a floor amendment to get rid of the provision failed by one vote. In early April, the Senate approved HB 1226 by a vote of 39 to 8, and it went to conference the next day. The Senate also amended the DHS biennial budget, restoring $4 million and funding for the computer system that the House had cut.[63]

In conference, the cap and child support, predictably, again were the most rancorous issues. Legislators largely recognized, however, that the child support provisions were required by federal law, however much they may have resented it. The family cap was the subject of the angriest debate. Democratic Representative James Kerzman said, "This family cap is a hard area for me; this is only hurting the child. Our goal here is to get these people off assistance." Republican Senator Judy Lee countered, "I don't know of one employer that pays more when you have another family member. This is a cash cap, not a benefit cap, and certainly not a family cap. I have no problem with this."[64] Ultimately, only two Democrats—one senator and one representative—voted to remove it.

Another difference to be resolved was whether to allow more than one year of education to count as a work activity. Senate committee Chair Thane and others advocated more education to help recipients become more self-sufficient. House Chair Price and others successfully opposed this provision, on the grounds that it might endanger the state's ability to meet its federal work requirements and lead to financial penalties. The conference committee approved the bill on April 10, by a vote of 4 to 2.[65]

The next day, the Senate approved HB 1226 by a vote of 30 to 17, and the House endorsed it by a vote of 75 to 17.[66] Although issues crossed party lines, support and opposition correlated to some extent with party identification; Democrats opposed the bill in greater numbers. The divide on welfare reform stood in marked contrast to the almost universal support for the original TEEM pilot program in 1995. Governor Schafer signed HB 1226 on April 17, and it went into effect on July 1, 1997, with the 53-county phase-in to be completed by July 1998. Under TANF, North Dakota would receive $26.4 million annually from the federal government.[67]

Final TEEM System

The final law made several major changes, in addition to instituting the family cap.[68] Specifically, it:

- repealed the entitlement to assistance;
- went with the federal lifetime limit of five years;
- established a computerized intake, assessment, and referral system for all recipients;
- required a behavioral "contract" between the recipient and the state;
- mandated that nonworking parents be limited to two years of cash aid;
- required mothers of children four months or older to work;
- attempted to bundle TANF, food stamps, and low-income energy assistance into one program and move ahead with the EBT system;
- maintained state asset limits at $5,000 for a single-person family and $8,000 for a family of two or more, exempted one car of any value from asset calculations, and established a progressive earnings disregard for one year after recipients began to work;
- instituted progressive sanctions, leading up to full-family benefit termination, if parents did not cooperate with program requirements;
- denied benefits to people who were convicted of drug felonies after the TANF implementation date;
- provided TANF assistance to pregnant women only for their last trimester;
- abolished the cash assistance program for two-parent families, which served about fifty families;
- continued TANF benefits to legal immigrant refugees; and
- adhered to the federal work definitions, limiting recipients to one year of vocational or higher education. The only exemptions from work, other than for mothers with very young children, would be for physical or mental incapacity or disability.

Administration of the program was to be uniform among the counties, though still county-run, even though the federal bill allowed for local variation. Clients who appealed state or county decisions were to receive full hearings. There was no serious discussion of wide-scale privatization or contracting-out of eligibility determination. Several participants suggested that the populist streak ran too deep to allow for large-scale privatization with Lockheed-like corporations.

Unlike Texas, in 1997 North Dakota did not plan to transfer large amounts of TANF money to the Title XX social services block grant or to the child care and development block grant, although it was allowed to transfer as much as 30 percent to these grants. Neither, however, did the state set aside savings from declining caseloads for other welfare-related purposes, as Maryland did. It is worth noting, however, that no North Dakota group conducted the level of financial analysis that the CPPP did in Texas, and it is unclear exactly how the "new" TANF money resulting from dropping caseloads was being apportioned in the state. There is little evidence, however, that the state planned to siphon off "extra" TANF funds to free up general revenues; several participants mentioned the high costs associated with implementing the new TEEM system.

Numerous issues were left unresolved, including the need for greater workforce development and employment assistance; the inadequate child care supply; and the complexities of high tribal unemployment and growing welfare caseloads. The 55th Legislature passed several study resolutions requiring that interim committees and the Legislative Council further explore the relationship between the counties and DHS in social service delivery, implementation of welfare reform, tribal issues, child support, and DHS reorganization and report to the 56th Legislature in 1999.[69] During the 1997 session, the legislature also approved a separate bill outlining the "swap" to reapportion financial responsibility for social services between the state and the counties.[70]

Tribal Participants

The 1996 federal bill authorized tribes to run their own TANF programs, separate from those of the states, negotiating their own work participation rates with the federal government. This provision opened a new set of complicated issues. Several North Dakota legislators were keen on the possibility that the tribes might take over their own programs, thereby spinning them off and not threatening the rest of the state's work participation rates.[71] It was not clear if this proposal would be good for the tribes, however, and they had indicated that they did not feel prepared to run their own programs. A move in this direction would have required significant financial and technical assistance from the state. The mismatch between job growth in the cities and population growth in the reservations raised serious questions about the wisdom of isolating Native Americans still further, unless the state or federal governments were ready to offer a large-scale tribal jobs programs.[72]

The lone representative from the Three Affiliated Tribes who testified at the Senate Human Services Committee's public hearing in 1997 urged the legislature to remember the growing proportion of the caseload that was Indian, include Indians in the policymaking process, and begin to address some of their particular needs. He also stated that his tribe was not in a position to run its own program. Among tribal members, there was a widespread feeling that the TEEM system as it had been revised in 1997 would be harmful to Indians, on the whole. In particular, the decision to limit education to one year came under fire as foolishly hampering recipients' ability to become independent.[73]

Several legislators acknowledged the tension between the state's Indians and non-Indians and the importance of tribal issues for successful welfare reform. One even went so far as to place some of the responsibility for the strained relationship on the legislature, saying, "Maybe it's the legislature's fault. . . . We don't have great relationships with the tribes; we never see them. They give the tribal address at the same time as the governor's address, [but] the legislature has ignored them, and they feel ignored." The chair of the House Human Services Committee suggested that differences in style aggravated the tension. She also stated, however, that in her view it was not indifference but legislators' recognition of their limited understanding of Indian issues that led them in 1997 to steer clear of addressing these issues in the bill and instead to mandate the interim study. On the whole, non-Indians outside and inside the government seemed to be largely unaware of the details of tribal concerns. The director of social services in one Indian county suggested that relations were marked by "seething hostility" just under the surface, for which state officials and their unwillingness to share state funds had been significantly responsible.

Nongovernmental Participants

Twenty-four outside organizations and participants testified or submitted testimony in the 1997 hearings—considerably more than the eleven of the previous session (see Table 6-2). Of these twenty-four, however, only three were advocates for recipients and disadvantaged people: the NDCC, the North Dakota Council on Abused Women's Services (CAWS), and PEPP—slightly fewer than in the prior session. A greater number of intergovernmental actors were involved; the North Dakota Association of Counties, which was understandably concerned with the details of the financial swap, was most active. The representative of the NCSL participated at the request of lawmakers. Ten individuals submitted testimony, six of whom were involved with PEPP. Illustrating the challenges of political participation in a large rural state that is so vulnerable to the vagaries of a harsh climate, the PEPP group's plan to travel from Fargo to Bismarck for the Senate Human Services Committee's hearing in March was thwarted by the spring blizzards of 1997. Instead, they faxed their testimony to the committee chairman.

Table 6-2
Activity of North Dakota Interest Groups in Welfare-Related Hearings, by Category, 55th Session (1997)

Category	No. of Organizations/Actors	No. of Times Testifying
Advocates: child advocacy, nonprofit and charitable providers, unions[a]	3	6
Individuals[b]	10	10
Intergovernmental	6	11
Tribal actors	1	1
"Traditional values" groups	2	7
For-profit companies and business groups	2	2
Researchers	0	0
Think tanks	0	0
Professional associations	0	0
Miscellaneous	0	0
TOTAL	**24**	**37**

Sources: Information from minutes of seven House and Senate public hearings and testimony (see Appendix F for complete list of hearings and participants). Author's calculations.

[a]As with national groups, the lines between advocacy and nonprofit service or charitable organizations often are blurry. Some advocacy groups also provided services, and some charitable groups also were committed to advocacy.

[b]Six of these individuals were PEPP members, but they testified about their own situations rather than for the organization.

A couple of traditional values groups participated this time around. The first, the North Dakota Right-to-Life Association, was most concerned with the family cap. The second, R-Kids, annoyed some lawmakers with its constant presence and focus on broader custody issues that were not addressed in the welfare bill. Business groups testified about child support enforcement provisions. Again, no researchers, independent think tanks, professional associations, contractors, or unions participated. As in 1995, the NDCC was the most active advocate. Representatives of other groups noted that if they knew the organization's executive director was going to testify, they felt less need to do so. Said one, "We know that the Catholic Conference is doing welfare reform well, so other advocates relied on [its executive director]. So it seems like he's doing it alone." The NDCC was the leading opponent of the family cap. In contacts with legislators, the NDCC's director cited extensive research indicating that family caps and benefit levels had little or no influence on the birth rates of women on welfare—apparently, however, to little effect, in part because the session was so short. "Decisions are made in such a short time; they are very complex, and there is not enough time to educate people," he said. "If we had time, we could get rid of the family cap, I believe that." The organization also opposed the end to coverage for pregnant women and cuts in coverage of immigrants and supported exemptions for domestic violence victims.[74]

CAWS also opposed the family cap and loss of cash aid to pregnant women and supported screening and exemptions for victims of family violence.[75] PEPP supported the generous asset limits (as did the other advocates) and the graduated income disregard. It also lobbied for greater child care funding and urged that more than twelve months of educational activities count as work. The group was much less involved in the politics of welfare reform in 1997, however. The director of PEPP noted that after grudgingly accepting and then happily publicizing the influence of advocates on the 1995 TEEM plan, DHS largely shut the doors on them after the federal bill passed. Some participants criticized PEPP for alienating more conservative policymakers and advocates. It was the only group composed at least in part of welfare recipients, however. Almost all of the individual recipients who testified were affiliated with PEPP, and they provided more than a quarter of total testimony. They did not appear to have much influence, however.

No researchers, either from North Dakota universities or from independent organizations, testified about welfare issues. Other than guidance provided by the NCSL, the only source of substantive expertise was from within government: DHS, the Legislative Council, and other state and county agencies. Following welfare reform, the Progressive Coalition, a group whose membership ranged from the North Dakota Farmers Union to social service organizations, started the Putting the Pieces Together (PPT) project. PPT, which was funded initially by the Minnesota-based Northwest Area Foundation, sought to provide information about economic and social policies that affected state residents, as well as leadership development to involve more North Dakotans in the policy process. Although PPT focused largely on health care issues, such as trying to get reluctant state officials to adopt the Children's Health Insurance Program (CHIP), it attended somewhat to welfare. It did not make legislative welfare reform a priority, however, and it continued to face the challenges of fundraising, a small staff, and the larger difficulty of engaging North Dakota residents in the problems facing low-income families.[76]

The general lack of interest in welfare reform was noteworthy. The media, particularly the Bismarck Tribune, covered welfare reform sporadically, and at least one advocate gave the media low marks. Virtually no members of the general public participated. The 1995 chair of the House Human Services Committee commented, "Very honestly, I think a lot of people were disinterested. . . . We didn't get a lot of response, on the whole."[77] For all of the conflict within the legislature over the cap and child support, as well as concern among a handful of interest groups and individuals, the average North Dakotan seemed to be singularly unconcerned, apparently distracted by a winter and spring of blizzards and flooding.[78]

AFTER REFORM

The ability to get recipients into decent jobs probably was the biggest challenge that North Dakota faced. Like other states, it would be aided in meeting national work requirements by the federal caseload reduction credit contained in the HHS regulations released in April 1999. In the long run, however—with the five-year clock ticking—the need to help recipients get into jobs that could support their families remained. This challenge was inextricably linked to the fate of the residents of the state's Indian reservations, where welfare receipt and unemployment were high and economic opportunities extremely limited. Several of North Dakota's distinctive characteristics made finding and keeping good jobs more difficult than in other states. The long distances and harsh climate made transportation particularly problematic, and rural depopulation further exacerbated the problems of providing services such as job placement and child care in sparsely populated communities where poverty was prevalent, if not always highly visible. Moreover, these difficulties were not going to go away: census data for 2000 indicated that during the 1990s, North Dakota had the lowest population growth in the nation—0.5 percent.[79]

Although the statewide unemployment rate had been low in recent years, job growth was concentrated in service industries that were based in the cities, not in rural areas or on the reservations. Removing the value of a car from asset calculations was one attempt to address the transportation problem, but recipients still needed money for a reliable car and expenses such as insurance and maintenance. Child care also was a growing problem. In 16 of the 53 counties, licensed day care was available for fewer than 10 percent of the county's children in 1997.[80] This shortage would only grow deeper as more single parents were pushed into the labor market. It would be particularly difficult for parents in rural areas and those working irregular shifts. Finally, another essential issue was the well-being of families who left welfare for low-wage jobs. North Dakota's work-first orientation—which it shared with most states—would be effective only if there were adequate jobs within commuting distance that paid enough to support a family.

The final evaluation of the TEEM program by Berkeley Planning Associates in March 2000 highlighted a range of the key problems still confronting the state's poor families after implementation of welfare reform.[81] First, the evaluation report described difficulties with TEEM's case management approach. Because of the system's heavy work-first emphasis, recipients often were much more involved with staff at the employment agency than with their TEEM case managers, who were nominally responsible for coordinating all of the services they would receive and providing intensive guidance in the transition to work. Lack of training, inflexibility, fragmentation in the computerized assessment and tracking systems, and sporadic case management "marked by intense periods of communication and long stretches during which there was little contact with clients" made it more difficult for case managers to identify and meet recipients' needs. In addition, the benefits covered by TEEM—TANF, food stamps, and heating assistance—had not yet been fully bundled and continued to operate distinctly, making it more difficult for case managers to provide integrated services.[82]

The report noted that although the welfare caseload had dropped sharply—more than 50 percent—between 1993 and 1998, during 1999 it remained roughly constant, suggesting that people who still were on public assistance would need even greater help to get into jobs. In addition, a larger proportion of adult recipients (62 percent) participated in work activities than in the past; of those who had left welfare in mid-1999, however, only 19 percent had their cases closed because of employment. Sixty-six percent of the cases were closed because of "state policy," such as failure to submit required reports, sign their contract, or other administrative reasons. The proportion recorded as leaving for work had actually declined by 13 percent over the prior year and a half.[83] In September 1999, about 6 percent of closures resulted from sanctions. Lack of transportation and child care were identified as the most serious barriers to work, and when adults did leave welfare for work, 22–30 percent of those who left during the study period returned to cash assistance. The report cited the state for minimal job development efforts and for failing to offer retention services to help recipients keep the jobs they got.

Finally, despite the sharp controversy in the legislature regarding the family cap, the policy seemed to have little impact on caseworkers or welfare parents. Case managers suggested that they did not typically stress the cap with clients, though those interviewed generally were aware of it. Other sources noted that the application of the family cap had been less strict than the legislation suggested. About 160 children were affected by the cap provision; their families lost an average of $90 per month because of it.[84] The evaluation report concluded:

> Although most staff supported the philosophy behind the policy, they were concerned about the well-being of children in families with reduced benefit levels. Regardless of their support for the policy, both clients and staff doubted the efficacy of the benefit cap in affecting family childbearing decisions.[85]

As a preliminary answer to the question of how the new TEEM system actually would be implemented in caseworkers' offices, the evaluation report was disturbing. The federal and state laws laid down new and stringent mandates. Yet caseworkers—the "street-level bureaucrats" of welfare—also had a significant amount of discretion, and the training and support they received were critical in determining what shape welfare reform would take. County social services directors also set the tone and determined which messages filtered down to recipients. The capacity of county and state management and information systems would determine what welfare reform looked like in concrete fact, not just in legislation, over the long haul.[86] North Dakota's TEEM system appeared to be off to a bumpy start.

Tribal issues also loomed large after the 1997 session. The threat of time limits was alleviated somewhat by the technical changes Congress made to PRWORA in 1997 that exempted from time limits residents of Indian reservations with unemployment rates of more than 50 percent. Only the Turtle Mountain reservation consistently faced rates that high, however, according to Job Service North Dakota statistics, meaning that the clock kept ticking for most Indians in North Dakota.[87] Nonetheless, the fact that welfare reform increasingly was a tribal issue started to sink in with legislators, and Indians began to participate politically in greater numbers and with more frequency. Real communication problems still existed, however, and it was still unclear how much influence they would have.

Little major action on welfare reform took place during the 1999 session. There was a failed attempt to allow welfare mothers more time with their children after they were born. North Dakota required mothers to go to work when their children were four months old; the failed proposal would have raised that age to eight months. The legislature agreed to provide limited state financial assistance to tribes that undertook their own TANF programs and to continue the interim studies.[88]

During the 2001 session, an effort to rescind the family cap was unsuccessful. The legislature approved a proposal to codify in state law exemptions from time limits and work requirements for victims of domestic violence. It also loosened the definition of allowable work activities, in part to allow a greater range of options for "hard-to-serve" recipients. (The federal credit for caseload reductions assured policymakers that it would meet federal work requirements.) The other changes the legislature considered were minor.[89]

During the 1997–1998 and 1999–2000 interim sessions, the joint legislative committee continued to meet periodically.[90] The mix of participants who were active in the interim committee proceedings was notably more representative of recipients than that during either the 1995 or 1997 sessions, when the welfare policies were formulated. Tribal officials and other Native Americans were more involved in testifying, including the employment official from Three Affiliated Tribes who was the only Indian to participate in the 1995 and 1997 sessions, as well as the director of the Division of Tribal

Services of the federal HHS (who traveled to Bismarck during both interims). The fact that in the wake of PRWORA the federal government was giving more potential leeway to tribes to run their own employment and cash assistance programs seemed to mobilize North Dakota Indians to engage the legislature and make their desires known. Other advocates—including PEPP, the NDCC, and CAWS—also participated in interim deliberations.

Many legislators and tribal members were eager to explore the possibility that the tribes might run their own TANF programs. It became clear, however, that they did not have the resources to do so without considerable state help. Three Affiliated Tribes indicated the greatest interest in administering a program, and in 2000 it filed a letter of intent with HHS. Its representatives expressed concern, however, that the amount of state funding for tribal TANF programs outlined in North Dakota law was insufficient. The state proposed to provide a sum equivalent to its per recipient spending in 1994 (under AFDC, when the caseload was high and per person spending was relatively modest) multiplied by the number of tribal recipients in 1999. Later that year, however, Three Affiliated Tribes indicated that it was moving ahead with a proposal to HHS to provide case management to tribal recipients while leaving cash assistance grants to the state. It was unclear if HHS would approve the plan.

The idea of tribal TANF programs continued to draw support because of tribes' interest in self-government and the state's desire to avoid penalties for failing to meet federal work requirements. The tribes' lack of infrastructure and experience in running such complex programs presented real hurdles, however, and they indicated that they would need more time for planning and more money from the state to pay for start-up costs.[91] Even with more time and money, the lack of private-sector development on reservations and high unemployment would make moving recipients there from welfare to permanent jobs extremely difficult. The political instability of tribal governments seemed to be unlikely to change in the near future and could make outside business harder to draw into reservation boundaries. One proposed solution was for the state to lure business to areas just outside the reservation, commutable for Indian workers but not subject to contracts with the tribal governments. Another was to encourage reservation residents themselves to start "microenterprises" and other small businesses.[92] Still, a fairly large proportion of Indians faced serious barriers to employment.[93] As one tribal official pointed out, even if Indians had access to programs, they needed to really take advantage of them. The tribes themselves, he said, needed to "maximize all their resources" in anticipation of the major changes that federal welfare reform was rapidly bringing.

In addition to allowing tribes to run their own TANF programs, the tribal TANF regulations also implemented the Native Employment Works (NEW) program to replace tribal JOBS employment programs. NEW gave tribes greater flexibility to define work activities more broadly, including counting higher education beyond the single year prescribed by state law. In North Dakota, most tribal NEW programs would emphasize higher education, allowing recipients who already had high school degrees to attend college as their required work activity. This strategy would help them gain greater skills but would not produce more jobs. The high unemployment rate raised the tough question of whether Indians should be encouraged to move off the reservations to the majority-white cities, where jobs were growing. The history of the government removing Indian children and adults from reservations to boarding schools for "Christianization" and other acculturation programs has given a somewhat sinister cast to any policy designed to encourage economic or cultural assimilation. During 1999 interim committee meetings, however, members discussed again providing incentives to Indians who would be willing to leave reservations for jobs outside.[94]

Welfare reform also raised the larger question of what exactly Indian sovereignty meant in the United States and how it could be reconciled with political pressures from the white majority and other ethnic minorities. Native Americans only gained a degree of real self-determination with the Indian Self-Determination and Education Assistance Act in 1975.[95] Whites had treated them dishonorably for centuries and, many people would argue, had a moral obligation to remediate at least some of these wrongs. What all this meant, however, for a long-term vision of Native American sovereignty was extremely uncertain. Although these questions were much broader than the specific details of the federal and state welfare bills, welfare reform in North Dakota inevitably came back to them.

CONCLUSION

The narrowness of the group of actors that formulated the state's new welfare policy suggests that fears about the effects of narrowing the political sphere were well-founded in North Dakota. The range of types of actors involved in the debate, as indicated by hearings testimony and interviews with key participants, was narrow. The state's welfare recipients, particularly those living on reservations, had little voice in the process of shaping North Dakota's comprehensive response to the national "personal responsibility" act.

The number of groups involved in the debate also was very limited. Only 33 organizations of any type participated in the two legislative sessions over the three years that led up to and followed passage of the federal bill (the period of greatest policy change). This figure compares with 310 in Washington, 95 in Maryland, and 58 in Texas (see Table 6-3). Moreover, the community of actors representing the state's low-income people was extremely small. All told, only five organizations representing poor families participated in legislative policymaking about welfare over the two biennial sessions. No additional nonprofit service providers testified, nor did researchers, unions, think tanks, or professional associations.

Table 6-3
North Dakota- and Washington-Based Organizations Involved in Welfare-Related Hearings, by Category

	No. of Organizations/Actors	
Category	**North Dakota**	**Washington**
Advocates: child advocacy, nonprofit and charitable providers, unions[a]	5	112
Individuals	16	38
Intergovernmental	7	64
Tribal Actors	1	0
"Traditional values" groups	2	14
For-profit companies, business groups	2	19
Researchers	0	30
Think tanks	0	12
Professional associations	0	14
Miscellaneous	0	7
TOTAL	**33**	**310**

Sources: Information from minutes of nine House and Senate public hearings and testimony (see Appendix F for complete list of hearings and participants). Author's calculations.

[a]As with national groups, the lines between advocacy and nonprofit service or charitable organizations often are blurry. Some advocacy groups also provided services, and some charitable groups also were committed to advocacy.

Despite the fact that Indians made up more than half of the welfare caseload over the previous several years, they had virtually no role in shaping the comprehensive welfare system. Native Americans had a greater role later on in discussions about possible state support for tribal TANF programs that was spurred in part by the new options for greater tribal control coming out of HHS in Washington. Until and unless they applied to HHS and received approval to run such a program, however, the state's tribes would live under the North Dakota TANF program that they had so little influence in shaping. They also had little representation in the state legislature. The impact of devolving welfare policy had particular importance for Indians. They have gained power in Washington in the past thirty years, but historically they have had little in the states. Many state governments still have rancorous relationships with the tribes. As one non-Indian advocate noted, "The tribes are at a much greater disadvantage working with local and state than federal government." Devolution shifts policymaking to the governmental level where Indians typically have been politically weakest.[96]

A couple of advocates for low-income people were closely involved in the debate, testifying frequently and trying to reach lawmakers through personal contact and other means. (See Table 6-4 for the most frequent hearings participants.) They made up a tiny group, however, and scored few major victories after the federal bill passed in 1996. In 1999, in fact, one advocate said he stopped going to the legislature during the 1999 session and felt there was little point because it was so unreceptive. Moreover, only a few of these organizations truly could be called "home grown." The NDCC—the most active advocate—represented the two Catholic Bishops in the state. PEPP, the grassroots organization of recipients with a small professional staff, got most of its funding from sources outside North Dakota and divided its efforts between two states, with greater emphasis on Minnesota. The PPT project, which did not participate legislatively but provided information and monitored welfare reform, initially was supported by the Minnesota-based Northwest Area Foundation but lost funding when the foundation shifted focus. Otherwise the advocacy community was small, fragmented among many social issues, and received minimal support from within the state, where some viewed it as its own kind of "special interest." As one tribal official commented, to get an effective advocacy community, "You need population numbers—you need a critical mass." This critical mass obviously did not exist in North Dakota.

Finally, for all the talk about welfare reform as a response to public opinion and devolution as "closer to the people," very few North Dakotans paid much attention to the debate in Bismarck. When I asked one key advocate if there had been any notable increase in the number of organizations or individuals who were interested in welfare policy since the state took over responsibility, he responded, "Definitely not. There were no new groups. There just didn't seem to be people who took an active interest in the process."[97] The media reported on the issue only sporadically, and few North Dakotans participated in any facet of policymaking.

Welfare recipients in North Dakota gained programmatically in some respects. Lawmakers increased asset limits more than in most states, increased the earnings disregard, and attempted to improve case management, even if not entirely successfully. By several other important measures, however, the welfare program became stricter after passage of the federal law. Although some changes were consistent with the federal bill—such as the five-year hard time limit—others were options that state lawmakers and DHS elected to embrace. North Dakota enacted family caps, and mothers with children older than four months in age were required to work. Education counted as

Table 6-4
North Dakota Frequent Testifiers

Organization/Actor	No. of Times Testifying
North Dakota Catholic Conference (NDCC)	6
R-Kids	6
North Dakota Association of Counties	5
People Escaping Poverty Project (PEPP)	3

Note: These acts of testimony include oral testimony before legislative committees and written testimony or positions registered with no oral testimony given. See Appendix F for a complete list of hearings and participants.

a work activity for only one year, except for Indians under the NEW program. Employment programs and child care were limited despite the mandate to work, as were job retention supports. Convicted felons were ineligible for any cash assistance. Full-family sanctions were said to be applied more frequently than in the past. Of the sixty-page 1997 welfare law, only about four pages really dealt with AFDC/TANF, though the law made sweeping changes.[98]

In Maryland, lawmakers largely protected federal and state funds for use by welfare recipients even when this decision did not decrease state costs, in part because of the influence of advocates for poor families; the work-oriented reformers won out. In Texas, the shape of welfare reform in the mid-1990s was driven significantly by budget cutters, with some input by social policy critics, despite intense lobbying by the small number of fairly effective groups.

In North Dakota, however, the design of welfare policy was driven more by lawmakers' fears about the government subsidizing recipients' "irresponsibility," not meeting the federal work requirements, and losing TANF funds. The couple of truly active advocacy groups were unable to dissuade legislators from policies such as the family cap and full-family sanctions. These lawmakers, who could best be described as relative social policy critics, did not go so far as to promote an end to welfare programs, but neither did they want to invest new money in work programs. The state was fiscally conservative—with some reason, given its lack of growth. Its caution may have been excessive, however, considering the urgent need to help recipients get jobs before their five-year time limit hit and the almost $11 million TANF surplus that North Dakota carried at the end of 2000.[99]

The larger political environment, as well as "critical mass," influences the presence and effectiveness of NGOs, particularly advocacy groups for poor people. The political environment also affects the range of policy options that are politically viable. In North Dakota, the political culture stressed self-reliance more than investing in moving poor families to work. There was little history of strong advocacy for low-income families, at least outside the agrarian movement of the past. Although one might expect bias against Indians to explain some of the approach to welfare policy, most lawmakers did not consider welfare an "Indian issue," at least initially. By 1995, the Republican party controlled the House and the Senate, as well as the governor's office; as in Washington, D.C., the key players were part of an increasingly conservative element of the party. The strength of the party also limited the range of policy alternatives because the minority lacked the numbers to negotiate effectively.

North Dakota's political institutions faced important structural limitations, to a great degree as a result of the state's small population and isolation, as well as its political culture, which supported the idea of citizen-politicians rather than professional legislators and staff. Term limits have failed to gain support—with legislative turnover of more than 25 percent each session they probably seemed unnecessary—but change and inexperience among committee members and leadership sharply limited expertise in the mid-1990s. This is not to impugn the seriousness of individual legislators; those with whom I spoke certainly seemed to be dedicated and hard-working. The part-time, biennial legislative schedule severely limited how much knowledge members of the Legislative Assembly realistically could develop, however. The House Human Services Committee had three different chairs during the 1993, 1995, and 1997 sessions.[100] Individual chairs and members might be concerned about and committed to policy issues such as welfare, but unless one takes the position that it is better to know less rather than more about the substance over which one is legislating, the part-time citizen legislature was a real problem for policymaking. This was especially true for issues such as welfare: The interest community, which otherwise might have filled the expertise gap, was small and struggled.

The use of interim committees helped to mitigate the shortcomings of the short biennial legislative session, but even these groups convened only periodically and functioned largely as advisory bodies. The Legislative Council's staff also was small and had limited specialized expertise. The lack of time for deliberation once the session began also made it even more difficult for advocates and others, given their meager numbers, to educate lawmakers on matters that were new to them. Laws were made within eighty days, and large numbers of bills had to be considered and go to the full chamber for a vote. The fact that all legislation went to the floor also made lobbying more difficult for resource-strapped organizations, who had to spread themselves thin rather than focus on a few key legislators or committees. Issues could be complicated, and hearings frequently were scheduled on short notice, making it hard for advocates and others—especially people outside Bismarck—to get to the capitol in time to participate. Even legislators acknowledged the pressures on them to vote on bills about which they were not well informed. The only nonlegislative sources of information during the 54th and 55th sessions were the small DHS staff, a few advocates, and the NCSL staffer from Washington. Time and again, the same three people from the state human services agency testified at meetings of the standing committees during deliberations on TEEM. Although these individuals may have been true experts, having such a small cadre of bureaucrats shaping state welfare policy was troubling.[101]

Finally, the race to the bottom had not taken off in North Dakota as of early 2001. If Congress changed the state maintenance-of-effort requirement or cut block grant levels or if North Dakota faced tighter economic times, however, all bets were off. The state's eagerness to bring new business within its borders suggested that lawmakers would attend first to the interests of these much-desired firms and would be unwilling to spend state money on programs they often perceived as handouts to a nonproductive poor population. Such reluctance could mix with anti-Indian bias, once it was more widely known how large a percentage of the caseload consisted of Native American residents.

Welfare reform in this particular state was largely the activity of a narrow group of legislators and bureaucrats, with limited participation by an even smaller core of advocates. The highly personal quality of politics in North Dakota and the dynamics of welfare policymaking were consistent with this situation. Groups that lacked constituent or personal relationships with lawmakers—Native Americans and welfare recipients—played little role in developing the state's comprehensive welfare program under devolution.

NOTES

1. Elwyn B. Robinson, *History of North Dakota* (Lincoln: University of Nebraska Press, 1966; Institute for Regional Studies, North Dakota State University, undated edition), 202, 146; Larry Remele, "Power to the People: The Non Partisan League," in *The North Dakota Political Tradition*, ed. Thomas W. Howard (Ames: Iowa State University, 1981), 67.

2. Remele, "Power to the People," 66–93; see also Robinson, "The Great Socialist Experiment," in *History of North Dakota*, chapter 15.

3. Bureau of the Census, *Statistical Abstract of the United States 1996*, 33.

4. Ibid., 474, 465; Larin and McNichol, *Pulling Apart*, 8. The state employs a diversified tax system, although it is weighted more heavily toward sales taxes than the national median, and sales taxes tend to be more regressive than income taxes. Bureau of the Census, *Statistical Abstract of the United States 1997*, calculated from table 493, 311.

5. Mary Jane Schneider, *North Dakota Indians: An Introduction* (Dubuque, Iowa: Kendall/Hunt Publishing Co., 1994), chapter 1.

6. Theodore B. Pedeliski, "North Dakota: Constituency Coupling in a Moralistic Political Culture," in *Interest Group Politics in the Midwestern States*, ed. Ronald J. Hrebrenar and Clive S. Thomas (Ames: Iowa State University Press, 1993), 216; *State Yellow Book*, 1029.

7. Randal C. Coon et al., *The State of North Dakota: Economic, Demographic, Public Service, and Fiscal Conditions* (Fargo: North Dakota State University, 1995), 16–23, 65

8. Coon et al., *The State of North Dakota*, 11–12; *State Yellow Book*, 1029; minutes of North Dakota Legislative Assembly Welfare Reform Interim Committee, 28–29 October 1997, and minutes of 1999–2000 House Budget Committee on Human Services; available at www:state.nd.us/lr/minutes.html.

9. Elazar, *American Federalism*, 131–36. See also Robinson, *History of North* Dakota, 554–59, on the cultural values of North Dakotans.

10. Pedeliski, "North Dakota," 217–18. On average, voter turnout in the past has been about 10 percentage points higher than the national mean.

11. *1996 Green Book*, 439, 446, 460–61.

12. This was significantly greater than the national decline of 19 percent during that time. Ibid., 484; 1997 data from North Dakota Department of Human Services, "Temporary Assistance for Needy Families (TANF): Policy Issues" (Bismarck, N.D.: Department of Human Services, 1997).

13. Interviews with DHS officials; see also Rebecca London, Courtney Smith, Kristin Porter, and Kendra Lodewick, "Evaluation of North Dakota's Training, Education, Employment, and Management (TEEM) Program, Final Report," 30 March 2000; available at www.acf.dhhs.gov/programs/opre/ndfr.htm.

14. "Responsible Welfare Reform," *Tribal College Journal* 9, no. 3 (winter 1997–98). Also minutes of Senate Government and Veterans' Affairs Committee on Senate Concurrent Resolution 4030, 1997; testimony by Leo Cummings, Rose LeBeau, and other tribal officials during Interim Welfare Committee hearings on 4 September, 28 October, and 2 December 1997; 10 March and 4 May 1998; available at www.state.nd.us/lr/minutes.html.

15. Kortny Rolston, "Senate Approves Human Services' Budget," *Bismarck Tribune*, 2 April 1997; Don Davis, Janell Cole, and Kortny Rolston, "A Look at the 1997 Agenda," *Bismarck Tribune*, 6 January 1997 (all *Bismarck Tribune* articles available at www.ndonline.com/TribWebPage/Legislature).

16. E-mail to author from North Dakota Legislative Council, dated 8 July 1998; Senator Les LaFountain, Letter to the Editor, *Turtle Mountain Star*, 26 January 1998, 5.

17. Information from Legislative Council Web site; available at www.state.nd.us/lr/council.htm. Also "About the State Legislatures, Term Limits," on website of National Conference of State Legislatures; available at www.ncsl.org.

18. Legislative Council e-mail, 8 July 1998; interviews.

19. Pedeliski, "North Dakota," 219; "How a Bill Becomes a Law," North Dakota Legislative Council (undated, picked up February 1998).

20. Don Davis, "55th Legislature Convenes," and "Lawmakers Face 80-day Schedule Ending April 20," *Bismarck Tribune*, 5 January 1997.

21. "North Dakota Legislative Assembly: Summary of Bills and Resolutions Introduced and Passed," North Dakota Legislative Council (undated, picked up January 1998).

22. "Senate Concurrent Resolution No. 4010" and "Senate Concurrent Resolution No. 4067," 53rd Legislative Assembly of North Dakota, Legislative Council Library, Bismarck. Also testimony of Kevin Iverson, Welfare Reform Project Coordinator for DHS, before Human Resources Division of House Appropriations Committee, 8 March 1995; bill files for SCR 4010 and 4067, Legislative Council Library, Bismarck.

23. Interviews.

24. Interview. Letter from Wayne Anderson, Deputy Director of DHS, to Sen. Russell Thane, Chairman of the Senate Human Services Committee, dated 17 January 1995. Letters from Henry C. Wessman, Executive Director of North Dakota DHS to Administration for Children and Families, HHS (re: Section 1115 Waiver Request), and Bonny O'Neil, Acting Deputy Administrator, Food Stamps Program, U.S. Department of Agriculture (USDA), both dated 6 September 1994. Also at least 34 letters from Gov. Edward T. Schafer, U.S. Senator Kent Conrad, the GNDA, the North Dakota Superintendent of Schools, county social service boards and directors, various state senators and representatives, the North Dakota Job Service (JOBS) director, the NDCC, an ex-welfare recipient, and others to the federal Administration for Children and Families supporting the waiver request. All in bill file for SB 2035, Legislative Council Library, Bismarck.

25. *North Dakota Century Code*, Chapter 459, Senate Bill No. 2035, 1356-7. Rep. Byerly on "enabling legislation," minutes of House Appropriations Committee meeting, 10 March 1995.

26. Minutes of Senate Human Services Committee and House Appropriations Subcommittee on Human Services for SB 2035.

27. The minutes were inconsistent on the final "do pass" vote in the Senate Committee. The roll call record listed the vote as 7 yes and zero no; the report of the standing committee, dated January 19, said the "do pass" vote was 5 yes and 2 no, without identifying the dissenters or the reasons for dissent. There are no records of any House Human Services Committee hearings, and it is unclear why none would have been held. E-mail dated 7 June 1998 from Legislative Council librarian Marilyn Guttromson. Also House Appropriations Committee on SB 2035, minutes, 10 March 1995.

28. Human Services Conference Committee on SB 2035, minutes, 23 March 1995. Also, E-mail dated 7 June 1998 from Legislative Council librarian Marilyn Guttromson.

29. Detail on TEEM from "TEEM Project Summary," North Dakota Human Services Department; available at www.state.nd.us/hms/Teem_sum.htm (downloaded December 1997). Also, written testimony of Kevin Iverson, Welfare Reform Project Coordinator, DHS, before House Appropriations Committee, Division of Human Resources, 8 March 1995, and NDCC, "Welfare Reform in North Dakota," prepared for National Association of State Catholic Conference Directors, June 1997.

30. Written testimony of Kevin Iverson, Welfare Reform Project Coordinator, DHS, before House Appropriations Committee, Division of Human Resources, 8 March 1995. The TEEM evaluation was conducted by Berkeley Planning Associates, which released its final report in March 2000. See "Evaluation of North Dakota's Training Education, Employment, and Management (TEEM) Program," available at www.acf.dhhs.gov/programs/opre/ndfr.htm.

31. I use Native American and Indian interchangeably. The Indians I spoke with in North Dakota tended to refer to themselves that way rather than as "Native American."

32. Schneider, *North Dakota Indians*, chapter 9, describes the dramatically shrinking size and changing configuration of the reservation lands, as treaties were ignored and Indian lands flooded by state projects such as the Garrison Dam in 1954 and the Oahe Reservoir.

33. Interviews; also, John Bushman, Director, Division of Tribal Services, U.S. Department of Health and Human Services, Administration for Children and Families, teleconferencing with interim Welfare Reform Committee, 28–29 October 1997 meeting; minutes available fatrom www.state.nd.us/lr/minutes.html.

34. Interviews.

35. Interviews.

36. Pedeliski, "North Dakota," 218–19.

37. Glen Abney and Thomas Lauth, "Interest Group Influence in the States: A View of Subsystem Politics," paper presented at American Political Science Association meeting, Washington, D.C., August 1986; cited in Pedeliski, "North Dakota," 219.

38. Pedeliski, "North Dakota," 220–37.

39. Ibid., 230.

40. From minutes of Senate Human Services Committee and House Appropriations Subcommittee on Human Services meetings and hearings on SB 2035, available from Legislative Council Library, Bismarck.

41. Interviews.

42. Janell Cole, Kortny Rolston, and Don Davis, "Welfare Reform Bill Debuts," *Bismarck Tribune*, 14 January 1997.

43. Bud Wessman, testimony on HB 1226 before House Human Services Committee, 21 January 1997; Wayne Anderson, testimony on HB 1226 before House Human Services Committee, 20–21 January 1997; both available from Legislative Council Library, Bismarck.

44. It was not always apparent from committee minutes which were public hearings and which were simply committee meetings where public testimony was not invited. I considered hearings/meetings at which people other than legislators spoke, as indicated by committee minutes.

45. Don Davis, "Surprises Few for New Term," *Bismarck Tribune*, 6 January 1997.

46. House Human Services Committee minutes, 17 February 1997, available from Legislative Council Library, Bismarck; interview.

47. House Human Services Committee minutes, 17 February 1997.

48. Ibid.

49. Interviews; also, House Human Services Committee minutes of meetings on HB 1226 and roll call votes, vote #8; both available from Legislative Council Library, Bismarck.

50. Harold A. and Kendra A. Hovey, *CQ's State Fact Finder 1997* (Washington, D.C.: CQ Press, 1997), 295; *North Dakota Century Code for 1997*, Chapter 404, 1488–1548; interviews.

51. Testimony on HB 1226 before Senate Human Services Committee, 4 March 1997, available from Legislative Council Library, Bismarck. Also, text of HB 1226, also available from Legislative Council Library, Bismarck.

52. Testimony on HB 1226 before Senate Human Services Committee, 4 March 1997, available from Legislative Council Library, Bismarck; "Report of Standing Committee on HB 1226," Human Services Committee, 19 February 1997, available from Legislative Council Library, Bismarck.

53. From Janell Cole, "Welfare Cap Debated: Bill Ignores Children Born When Parents on Welfare," *Bismarck Tribune*, 20 February 1997.

54. Quoted in Janell Cole, "Welfare Reform Passes in Late-Evening Session," *Bismarck Tribune*, 21 February 1997.

55. Quoted in Don Davis, Janell Cole, and Kortny Rolston, "GOP Leadership Says Session on Course to Success," *Bismarck Tribune*, 23 February 1997.

56. Ibid.; also, Kortny Rolston, "Senate Approves Human Services' Budget," *Bismarck Tribune*, 2 April 1997.

57. Janell Cole, "$5.5 Million Grant in Danger," *Bismarck Tribune*, 9 February 1997; interviews.

58. Kortny Rolston and Janell Cole, "Resignation 'a Good Thing,'" *Bismarck Tribune*, 6 March 1997.

59. Senate Human Services Committee, minutes on HB 1226, 4 March 1997, available from Legislative Council Library, Bismarck.

60. Memo dated 6 March 1997 from state Office of Intergovernmental Assistance; statistics from Child Care Resource and Referral; available in bill files for HB 1226 from Legislative Council Library, Bismarck.

61. Senate Human Services Committee, minutes on HB 1226, 11 March 1997, available from Legislative Council Library, Bismarck.

62. Senate Human Services Committee, minutes on HB 1226, 31 March 1997; also, roll call vote #7, available from Legislative Council Library, Bismarck.

63. Senate Human Services Committee, minutes on HB 1226, 31 March 1997; roll call vote #7, available from Legislative Council Library, Bismarck; also, Kortny Rolston, "Welfare Reform Given Approval for Family Caps," *Bismarck Tribune*, 3 April 1997; States News Briefs, North Dakota, 3 April 1997, available from Lexis-Nexis Academic Universe. Kortny Rolston, "Senate Approves Human Services' Budget," *Bismarck Tribune*, 2 April 1997.

64. These quotes are from the minutes for April 8. They may not be verbatim, although I took them exactly as they appear in the minutes.

65. Conference Committee on HB 1226, minutes for 4–10 April 1997; also, Conference Committee roll call vote #1; all available from Legislative Council Library,

Bismarck. These quotes are from the minutes for April 8. They may not be verbatim, although I took them exactly as they appear in the minutes.

66. Kortny Rolston and Don Davis, "Welfare System Changed: Five-Year Limit, Benefits Cap Included in Major Overhaul," *Bismarck Tribune*, 12 April 1997.

67. Wayne Anderson, testimony on HB 1226 before House Human Services Committee, 21 January 1997.

68. Most of the following are from North Dakota DHS, "Temporary Assistance for Needy Families (TANF): Policy Issues," 4 March 1997.

69. House Concurrent Resolutions 3031 (child support), 3032 (DHS and the counties), and 3042 (DHS organization); also, Senate Concurrent Resolution 4030 (tribal relations and issues). Section 92 of HB 1226 and Section 31 of HB 1012 required a Legislative Council study of implementation. All for 55th Session in 1997; available from Legislative Council Library, Bismarck.

70. Wayne Anderson, testimony before Senate Human Services Committee, 19 March 1997. Also, text of HB 1041, available from Legislative Council Library, Bismarck.

71. In 1999, the federal HHS released its TANF regulations, including the caseload reduction credit, which ensured that North Dakota—as well as Texas and other states with significant caseload reductions—would meet their work participation requirements. Until then, however, fear about failure to meet federal requirements affected policy decisions. A summary of the regulations is available from www.acf.dhhs.gov/programs/ofa/exsumcl.htm. Regulations governing tribal TANF programs were released in February 2000 and are available at www.acf.dhhs.gov/programs/dts/execsum.htm.

72. House Human Resources Committee minutes; interviews with state legislators and tribal officials.

73. Interviews. This would be alleviated by the federal regulations covering the Native Employment Works program, which replaced JOBS programs on reservations. NEW allowed tribes to define postsecondary education as an allowable work activity. See summary of tribal TANF regulations, available at www.acf.dhhs.gov/programs/dts/execsum.htm.

74. Christopher Dodson, testimony before House and Senate Human Services committees, 20–21 January and 4 March 1997; interview.

75. Bonnie Palecek and Linda Isakson, testimony before Senate Human Services Committee, 4 March 1997.

76. Interviews with project staff; Putting the Pieces Together home page, available at www.nwafdev.org/ndpieces/; Pam Musland, "Progressive Coalition Seeks to Weave Strong Social Fabric in Rural ND," *Union Farmer*, 28 June 2000, available at www.ndfu.org/Ufarmer/06-28-2000-5.htm.

77. Interviews.

78. Kortny Rolston and Don Davis, "For Some, Legislature Lacked Hot Buttons," *Bismarck Tribune*, 13 April 1997; interviews.

79. U.S. Census Bureau, "Table 5. Resident Population of the 50 States, the District of Columbia, and Puerto Rico: April 1, 2000 (Census 2000) and April 1, 1990 (1990 Census)"; available at www.census.gov/population.cen2000/table05.pdf. Also,

Mark Hanson, "Incomes in N.D. Take a Hit," *Bismarck Tribune*, 28 April 1998, and Pam Belluck, "Climate and Finance Conspire to Stunt the Northern Plains," *New York Times*, 19 July 1998, A1.

80. Memo from Office of Intergovernmental Assistance, Office of Management and Budget dated 6 March 1997; child care availability statistics compiled by Child Care Resource and Referral.

81. See Rebecca London et al., *Evaluation of North Dakota's Training, Education, Employment, and Management (TEEM) Program, Final Report, 30 March 2000*, Berkeley Planning Associates for North Dakota DHS; available at www.acf.dhhs.gov/programs/oprc/ndfr.htm.

82. In 2001, the legislature officially changed the name of TEEM to TANF because little remained of the original TEEM pilot program. Most recipients and staff members referred to it as TANF, and the federal government had not allowed the full bundling of food stamps with other benefits. See testimony of Blaine L. Nordwall, director of economic assistance policy for DHS, on HB 1108 before Senate Human Services Committee, 7 March 2001, available at lnotes.state.nd.us/dhs/dhsweb.nsf/ResourceHome/1?OpenDocument.

83. Ibid., 59–60. Imprecision in case closure codes may have played some role in these numbers.

84. On family cap, John Hougen testimony to the Budget Committee on Human Services of the 1999–2000 interim. Minutes for 8 December 1999 available at www.state.nd.us/lr/99minutes.

85. London et al., *TEEM Program*, 39; interviews. Beginning in September 1999, DHS began a pilot program in Rolette County to provide more intensive case services, including job coaching and mentoring. Minutes from Budget Committee on Human Services meeting, 7 October 1999, 4; available at www.state.nd.us/lr/99minutes/hs100699.html.

86. Marcia K. Meyers, "Gaining Cooperation at the Front Lines of Service Delivery: Issues for the Implementation of Welfare Reform," in *Rockefeller Reports*, No. 7 (Albany, N.Y.: Rockefeller Institute of Government, State University of New York, 1998).

87. *1998 Green Book*, 496; Budget Committee on Human Services minutes for 1999–2000.

88. SB 2114 from the 1999 session outlines the minor changes made to the state's system.

89. Blaine L. Nordwall, testimony on HB 1108 before Senate Human Services Committee, 7 March 2001; text of HB 1108, enrolled version, available at www.state.nd.us/lr/.

90. See Welfare Reform Interim Committee minutes for 1997–1998, available at www.state.nd.us/lr/minutes.html; minutes of Budget Committee on Human Services for 1999–2000, available at www.state.nd.us/lr/99minutes.

91. Budget Committee on Human Services minutes, 1999–2000.

92. Interviews. Also, "Responsible Welfare Reform," *Tribal College Journal* (winter 1997–98).

93. One welfare official's estimate was that about 40 percent of one reservation's inhabitants faced these problems. Also, see London et al., *TEEM Report*, on barriers for recipients on reservations, 47.

94. James Shanley, "Welfare Reform Will Create More Misery," *Tribal College Journal* (winter 1997–98): 19. Also, on the history, Jeffrey Hamley, "An Introduction to the Federal Indian Boarding School Movement" in "The Indian Boarding School Movement," *North Dakota History: Journal of the Northern Plains* (spring 1994): 2. Budget Committee on Human Services minutes, 7 October 1999 and 14 September 2000.

95. Schneider, *North Dakota Indians*, 108.

96. Shanley, "Welfare Reform Will Create More Misery," 19; interviews.

97. This advocate did offer one caveat, noting that his organization had worked hard (and with some success) to increase public involvement in the state's debate about instituting a Children's Health Insurance Program and pushed to make it cover a greater number of low-income children.

98. The rest addressed child support, paternity establishment, and the state-county financial swap.

99. Budget Committee on Human Services minutes for 1999–2000.

100. Rep. Clara Sue Price remained chair from 1997 through the 2001 session.

101. Several DHS staff members were cited as knowledgeable and concerned about low-income families. The issue was their small numbers, not their dedication.

7

Conclusion: Welfare as We're Coming to Know It?

By early 2001, welfare reform nationally and in the states was being widely declared a policy victory, although researchers, journalists, and others had begun to explore in more detail what was happening to the families who had left cash assistance. The continued strong economy and shrinking deficit in the late 1990s contributed to a political environment that had, in fact, allowed restorations of some benefits for legal immigrants, as well as creation of the WtW block grant program and CHIP, largely under the control of the states.[1]

Nationally, caseloads dropped by 59 percent between 1993 and 2000. By June 2000, there were fewer than 6 million people on the rolls, compared with a peak of more than 14 million in 1994. This was the lowest level since the 1960s (see Table 7-1). State caseload declines varied from 94 percent in Wyoming, 93 percent in Idaho, and 91 percent in Oklahoma to 27 percent and 28 percent in New Mexico and Rhode Island, respectively.[2] An estimated 63 to 87 percent of the people who left welfare were working at some point after leaving.[3] There was little systematic information to indicate increased child abuse and neglect or a decrease in child well-being. The country saw a drop in the poverty rate from 15.1 percent to 11.8 percent between 1993 and 1999, which was attributed in part to welfare reform.[4] Employment rates among low-income single mothers also increased, from 35 percent in 1992 to 51 percent in 1998.[5]

Many critics of devolution and PRWORA agreed that reform had started off far more auspiciously than they had expected. Implementation was assisted by big state welfare windfalls, the robust economy, and the requirements that states keep up their own welfare spending. At the same time, several

Table 7-1
Changes in National Welfare Rolls

	1940	1950	1960	1970	1980	1990	1994	1996	2000
Average monthly welfare rolls, (thousands), total recipients	1,222	2,233	3,073	7,429	10,497	11,460	14,226	12,649	5,781
AFDC/TANF enrollment as percentage of total U.S. population	0.9	1.5	1.7	3.7	4.6	4.6	5.5	4.8	2.0[a]
Average recipient family size[b]	3.3	3.4	3.8	3.9	2.9	2.8	2.8	2.8	2.6

Sources: 1998 Green Book, Table 7-2 HHS, Administration for Children and Families, available at www.acf.dhhs.gov/ news/tables.htm.

Note: Enrollment data for 1940–1960 are December numbers for 1970 Social Security Annual Statistical Supplement (Table 136). For later years, data are fiscal year monthly averages from Table 7-5 prepared by HHS but exclude foster care recipients in 1980.

[a]The most recent available figure was 2.1, for 1999. Year 2000 has been calculated by dividing total number of recipients in June 2000 by U.S. population figures from 2000 census.

[b]Family size is calculated by dividing total recipients by number of families. This figure understates actual family size for 1936–1950 because the mother or other caregiver was not included as a recipient until after FY 1950. The decrease after 1996 may reflect the increase in child-only cases.

policymakers, such as Governor Tommy Thompson of Wisconsin, made major political and financial investments in welfare reform, which still provided opportunities for credit-claiming and national attention. There was evidence of a bureaucratic "culture shift" within welfare offices in many locations—from eligibility verification to finding new ways to help poor women get and keep jobs.[6] Recipients themselves suggested that they supported work requirements and even offered some support for time limits and family caps, at least in the abstract.[7]

Researchers and media reports also were finding less positive results, however. A major "leaver study" following people who had exited welfare in a range of states found that of those who were working, most had not left poverty. Many had jobs at low pay, often with irregular hours and few benefits, and almost 30 percent returned to the welfare rolls. More than 38 percent reported significant economic hardship, such as going without food or inability to pay rent or other bills. About a quarter of leavers were not working and had no apparent means of support.[8] A growing number of people, especially immigrants and other working families, were using food pantries and other private sources of emergency aid.[9] Use of food stamps and Medicaid declined, in part because of the administrative decoupling of Medicaid from cash assistance, though this trend began to reverse in 1999.[10]

It also appeared that recipients who left the rolls soonest were not always those who were best-equipped for self-sufficiency. Many had been sanctioned off for failing to meet the requirements of states' new programs and were more likely to be among those who were neither working nor receiving assistance. Some researchers expressed concern that a significant number of families never entered the system, dissuaded by state "diversion" policies.[11] It became increasingly apparent that welfare leavers were a diverse group facing a variety of difficulties after exiting the rolls. Although some—in particular, those with more education, better health, and older children—tended to do better post-welfare, others without these advantages appeared to do markedly worse.[12] The proportion of poor children who were receiving AFDC/TANF cash benefits also dropped sharply, from 61.5 percent in 1995 to 43 percent in 1998—declining 10 percent between 1997 and 1998 alone. This decrease indicated that a significantly smaller percentage of children under the poverty level received cash assistance after welfare reform than before.[13]

Most states were not tracking recipients who left welfare, and large national studies generally focused on states with the biggest populations and caseloads, which helped in assessing overall trends but made it difficult to get a picture of the outcomes of the nation's welfare experiment in smaller states.

Finally, as this study and others suggest, the policy processes and decisions under devolution also were changing. These studies also indicate that the concerns that were first raised by James Madison are still worthy of attention. Policymaking within the states was and continues to be different in important ways from that in Washington—and varies widely among them.

THE POLICYMAKING PROCESS

As this book has discussed at length, a range of interrelated factors influence the ways that states make welfare policy. These factors include states' political cultures or dominant ideologies; political party control and strength; the visibility of welfare as an issue; reformers' central political and policy goals; the diversity of state political actors; the professionalism and capacities of political institutions; and the range and strength of interests that participate in the process, including organizations and actors that represent low-income families. Other elements, such as how much money states have and their geography and physical resources, also matter. Although the emphasis of this study is on interest group involvement, it is worth briefly evaluating other factors, especially institutional policymaking capacity. Table 7-2 summarizes and compares a range of key political factors in each of the three states in this study as well as in the national debate in Washington, D.C.

Table 7-2
Selected Political Factors Influencing Welfare Policymaking Processes in State Legislatures and Congress

	Maryland (1995–1997)	Texas (1995–1997)	North Dakota (1995–1997)	U.S. Congress (1994–1996)
Dominant ideology	Liberal–moderate	Conservative–moderate	Conservative–moderate	Conservative
Party control of executive/legislature	Democratic/Democratic	Republican/split	Republican/Republican	Democratic/Republican
Issue visibility	Moderate	Moderate	Low	High
Dominant reformer motivations[a]	Work-oriented reformers	Budget cutters	Social policy critics	—Devolvers —Budget cutters —Social policy critics
Legislative capacity/professionalism	Moderate–high	Moderate–low	Low	High
Availability of expertise to legislature	High–moderate	Moderate	Low	High
Extent of legislative deliberation	High–moderate	Moderate	Low	High
Advocacy presence/effectiveness	High/high	Moderate/moderate	Low/low	High/moderate

[a]See David T. Ellwood, "When Bad Things Happen to Good Policies: Welfare Reform as I Knew It," *The American Prospect* (May–June 1996), for a discussion of these categories on the national level.

Political Influences on Policymaking

First, regardless of whether one subscribes to Elazar's framework of political culture or the various updates of the concept, the residents of different states appear to have varying political ideologies about using public resources to try to solve social problems. Maryland had a basically liberal approach, although it was constrained somewhat by moderate and even conservative elements from the rural and suburban areas west and south of the Baltimore-Washington corridor. Texas was essentially conservative, but it also was influenced by more centrist, at times even liberal, elements from the major cities and the Rio Grande Valley. North Dakota's individualist conservativism was moderated in some areas by its populist threads. Obviously, states such as Alabama, Wyoming, and Oklahoma differ markedly from states such as Vermont, New Jersey, or Minnesota in terms of their predominant public philosophy and ideas about the appropriate role of government in solving social problems.

Political party control of key institutions, especially the governor's office and legislature, and the extent of party competition also influence policy approaches. Democratic-dominated Maryland and Rhode Island have taken very different approaches to welfare policy than Republican-dominated Idaho and North Dakota. This is not a simple or direct relationship: Not all Republican-controlled states have minimalist approaches, and not all Democratic-controlled states provide expansive support to low-income families. Moreover, elements within the parties can be diverse. There tends to be a rough correlation, however, particularly where party competition is absent.

The issue of welfare reform had varying visibility among the states, though in most cases less visibility than in Washington, D.C. The level of partisanship, the size and energy of the advocacy community (which could activate the press), and the existence of one or more good newspapers covering political news in depth contributed to the level of visibility. Both the Washington Post and the *Baltimore Sun*, as well as the Annapolis paper, covered Maryland welfare reform fairly regularly, although they tended to emphasize periodic conflicts and principal events such as full legislative votes and the governor's actions or the sit-in on Delegate Rosenberg's lawn. The major papers in Texas reported on the basic progress of welfare legislation consistently, though again not in detail. In North Dakota, however, the *Bismarck Tribune* reported on the issue only sporadically and in little depth. Whereas welfare reform was front-page news in the major national newspapers such as the *New York Times*, *Washington Post*, and *Wall Street Journal* for the duration of the debate in Washington and beyond, press attention in the state capitals tended to be much more limited.[14] The relative invisibility of state policymaking, despite the rhetoric of greater citizen participation, and the generally limited coverage of welfare and other political issues in the states' newspapers reflected and probably contributed to a widespread public indifference to the details of state welfare reform.

State policymakers responded to a range of policy and political motivations in their approaches toward welfare reform. Borrowing again from Ellwood's framing, the participants included work-oriented reformers who focused on moving recipients into work, even if it cost more; budget cutters, who saw in TANF block grants an opportunity to save state revenues; and social policy critics, who advocated mandates that were designed to delink welfare policy from undesirable recipient behavior. Devolving welfare further was less of a motivation on the state level than the national level. Different motivations prevailed in different states, with implications for their policy outcomes. In Maryland, work-oriented reformers were strongest, as evidenced by the emphasis on preserving excess TANF funds for programs to help people to work. In Texas, budget cutters predominated, and in North Dakota, social policy critics seemed to prevail; the latter regarded reform as a way to stop the system's structure from subsidizing irresponsible behavior.

The diversity of the states' political actors and their constituents appears to have influenced their welfare policymaking approaches; greater diversity generally led to more expansive approaches. In Maryland, the delegations that represented predominantly black Baltimore City and Prince George's County played a central role through their members' legislative leadership and voting power and through the potent interest groups based in the city. Like Maryland, Texas was socially heterogeneous, but its political institutions still were dominated by a fairly conservative, largely white majority (with some exceptions, such as in Houston, Austin, and San Antonio). Representatives of largely black and Hispanic areas helped to block some of the favored initiatives of social conservatives such as the family cap, although interest groups representing blacks and Latinos were largely missing in the mid-1990s. In North Dakota, the only significant ethnic minority in the state—the Indian tribes—was missing from the legislature and had little or no impact on policy decisions.

Policymaking Capacity

On the whole, the policymaking capacities of the states have improved markedly since the 1950s and 1960s, but many still face real limitations with potentially major impact for welfare policymaking. First, state constitutions often contain balanced budget requirements that curb policymakers' ability to increase social spending during tight fiscal times. Where these requirements do not exist constitutionally, they usually exist in statute. With the block grant structure, this limitation places real constraints on state spending if caseloads increase.

State political institutions and processes also vary widely. Seven state legislatures meet only every other year, including those in Texas and North Dakota. In one recent study, nine state legislatures were considered professional; twenty-five were hybrids of professional and citizen legislatures; and sixteen were real citizen legislatures with low salaries, short sessions, and small staffs. Among the states I studied, Maryland was the most professional, with its annual session, moderately high pay (twelfth highest), and sizable staff. Texas legislators also benefited from significant staff resources; with their biennial session and low pay, however, they are considered less professional. North Dakota's biennial and short session, low pay, and very limited staff classify it as a true citizen legislature, like those of a range of states, including Arkansas, Idaho, Maine, Wyoming, Montana, and Utah.[15] This factor limits who can serve in the legislature and can make it harder for legislators to learn and build on their knowledge of the policy areas in which they legislate. In addition, some states have moved during the 1990s to make their legislatures less rather than more professional.[16]

High turnover is common among state legislatures, in part because 18 states have legislative term limits (though none in this study did). States with short legislator tenure—whether because of term limits as in California, Oklahoma, and Michigan or simply because citizen legislators go home to their permanent jobs, as in North Dakota—generally suffer loss in expertise among individual members and committees, as well as loss of long-term cooperative relationships. Power tends to shift to other institutions such as the executive and legislative staff, where it exists.[17]

This shift presents a particular problem in states with citizen legislatures and in small and rural states, where many legislatures lack much in the way of professional staff to pick up the slack. Given that devolution appears to have increased the political power of the state legislatures relative to the governors, it presents a major issue for welfare policymaking. Under the old AFDC waiver system, governors could request waivers from the federal government without the consent of their state legislatures. Under PRWORA, however, the legislatures must appropriate all TANF funds; therefore, their importance grows.

The policymaking process also tends to take place more quickly in the states, with fewer public hearings and less time for deliberation than in the nation's capital. In Washington, welfare reform was debated for more than eighteen months during the 104th session; the committees involved held twenty-five hearings, which lasted from half a day to six days. Even before the reforms of the mid-1990s, welfare was on the agenda—though somewhat further down—from the 1992 presidential campaign through the 1994 midterm elections.

In Maryland, reform was a top priority for several years leading up to the major proposals of 1995 and 1996, with working groups and task forces addressing policy design, although the final public debate took place in nineteen hearings over the two ninety-day annual sessions. There and in the other states, hearings typically lasted from a couple of hours or less to a day. In Texas and, to an even greater extent, in North Dakota, the states' new welfare systems were only one of many pressing issues to be debated and resolved during a very limited time. The Texas legislature held twenty hearings during the two biennial sessions in 1995 and 1997, often considering a slew of related bills in one sitting, with a handful of witnesses. The depth of the discussion during hearings depended to a great extent on how many and which witnesses showed up. North Dakota's Legislative Assembly held a total of nine public hearings over the two eighty-day sessions; the welfare legislation constituted only a small handful of the 900–1,000 bills the legislature considered in each of those sessions. Although the state policymakers I interviewed for this study were sincere and hard working, they were sharply inhibited by lack of time, support, and expertise.

The Role of Nongovernmental Groups in Policymaking

Finally, an equally important issue in the long term for welfare policy—and the focus of this study—is the range and nature of voices that received a hearing during the political debate about welfare reform in Washington and in the state capitals. A greater number of groups and a wider range of perspectives do not guarantee a certain policy outcome, of course; other political factors also play an essential role, as the 104th Congress illustrates. Nor is there some magic number or range of advocacy or other organizations that is "sufficient." A greater number of active groups does increase the likelihood, however, that the concerns of the people who will be most affected by policies will gain a hearing, that more rigorous debate will ensue, and that policymaking will be informed by more and better information. As McConnell, Schattschneider, and others warned, narrowing the "scope of conflict" by sending policymaking to smaller jurisdictions can exclude essential perspectives, especially those of marginalized groups. This study largely bears out the contention that politics within the states entails even less representation of disadvantaged groups than the wider sphere of the national government.

As Table 7-3 indicates, the welfare debate in Washington included the participation of many more organizations that reasonably could be said to represent the interests of low-income families than in the states.[18] Although many of these groups were effectively precluded from major policy influence by the dramatic partisan and ideological shifts of the 1994 election, they existed in large numbers; over time, the lead groups did influence essential details of the federal welfare bill. They counted their victories largely in terms of the provisions they could block and the issues they were able to shape on the margins, and they certainly were not the only political actors working to alter early Republican proposals. Their effect on the final bill was significant and undeniable, however. Every major element of the federal safety net was up for fundamental overhaul, from food stamps to foster care to the EITC and child nutrition programs. Yet the final version of PRWORA was markedly less radical than the original Republican proposals, to a major extent because of the work of these groups.[19]

The debate in the states, not surprisingly, simply included fewer actors representing poor families than in Washington—though how many fewer, at least in two of the three states, was striking. Maryland's community of groups concerned with welfare most resembled that in Washington, and these organizations and actors were very active and fairly influential. Although only two were Washington-based organizations, the proximity of Washington to Annapolis and the presence of often-liberal and politically active Washington suburbanites in Maryland had something of a "spillover" effect on the state's politics generally and this issue in particular. The short distance to Washington made it easier for state advocates to draw on the expertise of national organizations. A diverse mix of federal workers, minority inhabitants, and often educated and fairly wealthy urban and suburban dwellers in the Baltimore-Washington-Annapolis triangle supported the formation and maintenance of state groups. The fact that many effective advocacy organizations were based in Baltimore—less than an hour from the state capital—also helped to increase their presence and effectiveness in the legislative debate.

In Texas, far fewer such organizations participated, despite the fact that the state's population was almost four times that of Maryland's and the welfare caseload was about three times as large. A small group of advocacy "regulars" played a central role in shaping Texas welfare policy. The debate incorporated the perspectives of conservative traditional values groups as well as a few liberal advocacy organizations—a broader range of types of actors than in Maryland. In Texas, however, most participants in welfare politics remained within the same ideological territory, and it was difficult to get support for views that were to the left of center. The main representative of the most active and influential social welfare organization noted the negotiating disadvantages of operating within the relatively narrow range of perspectives found there.

In North Dakota, only a handful of organizations representing the interests of low-income families participated in the welfare debate over two legislative sessions. All were advocacy groups; no researchers or unions took part. Only one Native American official testified over the three years. The state's new welfare policy was formulated in the mid-1990s with almost no substantive input from those who were most affected by it—particularly the Native Americans who made up more than half of the state's caseload. This lack of participation was compounded by broad public indifference and meager media coverage. As the most active Indian official put it, there was a real "critical mass" problem in North Dakota.

Proponents of devolution suggested during the PRWORA debate that when welfare policymaking shifted to the states, it would result in increased interest and a growth in the numbers and activities of actors and groups that participated in the debate on the state level. In the three states in this study, however, that seems not to be the case so far. The number of active groups and actors does not appear to have increased, according to advocates in the states, although in Texas they are said to have become somewhat more organized since the mid-1990s. In North Dakota, there has been no increase in interest or activity among advocates, and welfare policy continues to be of little interest to most residents.

At least one influential Washington advocacy organization has initiated a project to help state-based groups build their policymaking capacities; others also have focused growing attention on the issue. Most Washington groups are short on funding and staff themselves, however, and already are challenged to exercise influence in the single national capital. Foundations tend to be reluctant to fund advocacy; they generally prefer research or direct service.[20]

Table 7-3
Interest Group Participation in Welfare-Related Legislative Hearings: U.S. Congress, Maryland, Texas, and North Dakota, 1995–1997

Type of Organization/Actor	No. of Groups	No. of Times Testifying
Totals		
Washington, D.C.	310	410
Maryland	95	237
Texas	58	160
North Dakota	33	51
Advocates: child advocacy, nonprofits and charitable providers, unions		
Washington, D.C.	112	148
Maryland	46	122
Texas	31	96
North Dakota	5	13
Intergovernmental		
Washington, D.C.	64	83
Maryland	18	28
Texas	3	3
North Dakota	8	13
Researchers		
Washington, D.C.	30	48
Maryland	0	0

Table 7-3 *(continued)*
Interest Group Participation in Welfare-Related Legislative Hearings: U.S. Congress, Maryland, Texas, and North Dakota, 1995–1997

Type of Organization/Actor	No. of Groups	No. of Times Testifying
Researchers		
Texas	1	1
North Dakota	0	0
Think tanks		
Washington, D.C.	12	29
Maryland	0	0
Texas	0	0
North Dakota	0	0
"Traditional values" organizations		
Washington, D.C.	14	19
Maryland	0	0
Texas	3	8
North Dakota	2	7
For-profit companies and business groups		
Washington, D.C.	19	20
Maryland	23	52
Texas	3	4
North Dakota	2	2

(continued on next page)

Table 7-3 *(continued)*

Type of Organization/Actor	No. of Groups	No. of Times Testifying
Professional associations		
Washington, D.C.	14	17
Maryland	3	19
Texas	2	8
North Dakota	0	0
Individuals		
Washington, D.C.	38	39
Maryland	5	16
Texas	12	31
North Dakota	16	16
Miscellaneous		
Washington, D.C.	7	7
Maryland	0	0
Texas	3	9
North Dakota	0	0

Note: Figures for Washington, D.C., include AFDC-related hearings from January 1995 to August 1996. Figures for states include legislative session preceding the national welfare bill (1995 session in Texas and North Dakota, which have biennial legislatures, and 1996 session in Maryland) and session following the federal bill (1997 in all three states). Testimony includes oral testimony and written testimony submitted into the record.

These groups will be hard-pressed to fund and organize an effective presence in fifty different states. Instead, they have tended to focus on jurisdictions with the biggest caseloads, where they can make the most impact for their limited time and money, rather than the small states and jurisdictions where they may be least welcome—though perhaps most needed.

Among the state actors I studied, the most effective were affiliated with organizations with national scope—the Catholic Church and Legal Aid organizations—or had formal or informal relationships with national advocacy groups such as the CBPP. Gaining a presence is likely to be hardest in small, poor, or rural states such as North Dakota—especially in the South and West, where it appears to be particularly difficult to gain the resources and political support necessary to effectively represent the interests of low-income people. In all states, especially these, they simply have a smaller pool of resources and people from which to draw.

It also is worth noting that the vast majority of influential organizations in the states in this study were "top-down" policy and advocacy organizations rather than grassroots membership organizations made up of low-income families themselves. As Piven and Cloward and others have noted, after the periods of economic and social unrest that in the past have spurred the formation of these types of organizations and government responses to them, they are difficult to maintain. Where organizations that rely at least in part on low-income families for support do exist—BUILD in Baltimore or TIAF in Texas—they did not participate in the legislative process leading to welfare reform; instead, they focused on other political venues and priorities. The one exception was PEPP in North Dakota, which participated in the first year of welfare reform there (although the organization actually was based in Minnesota).

Other Political Differences between the Nation and the States

Welfare politics in the states in this study differed from that in the nation's capital in several other ways as well. Most notably, the state debates were significantly less partisan and ideological than in Washington; the level of mistrust was lower. In many ways, this lack of partisanship provided a welcome change from the heated rhetoric of the 104th Congress. It also was symptomatic, however, of the more limited range of viewpoints that received serious consideration in the states. Most actors were in basic agreement about the fundamental assumptions and outlines of reform. The only consistently controversial issue throughout these case studies was the family cap.

In the states I examined, Republicans and Democrats tended to be fairly close ideologically. In Texas and North Dakota, this consensus position was right of center, with few "real liberals"; in Maryland it was somewhat left of center, with a limited number of "true conservatives." By 1995, however, there was broad consensus in all states across the parties about the degenerative effects of "dependency" on welfare mothers and their children and the virtues of work. Very few actors inside or outside state government made the left-leaning arguments—such as those challenging the preference for paid work for poor women versus raising their children—that could still be heard from a few liberal Democrats and advocacy groups in Washington.[21]

Illustrating this relative bipartisanship in the states, the votes on welfare reform legislation often were close to unanimous—in contrast to the national bills, where votes often were sharply divided along party lines. Even after Clinton announced he would sign PRWORA, thus depriving congressional Democrats of political cover, half of the House Democrats opposed it, as did almost half of Senate Democrats. The "scope of conflict" in the federal debate was markedly wider than in any of the states in this study.

POLICY DECISIONS AMONG THE STATES

A wide range of factors contributes to states' welfare policy decisions, and it is impossible to establish a simple link between political inputs and policy outcomes. The results of welfare reform in the states by early 2001 suggested several lessons, however. Most states did make major changes in their welfare systems during the 1990s, especially in moving low-income parents into jobs, indicating that the "institutionalist" predictions of bureaucratic resistance were largely overstated. As Table 7-4 indicates, states' policy decisions have varied widely, well beyond the benefit and income eligibility levels they have always established. The directions they have taken in many ways reflect their historical approaches to poor support before the creation of AFDC in 1935.

Many states took advantage of their new flexibility and money to eliminate AFDC provisions such as low earnings disregards that were widely regarded as inhibiting recipients from moving to work.[22] Five created a state entitlement to assistance. Two—Michigan and Vermont—elected to have no time limit, using state money to cover nonexempt recipients after their federal five years run out. Most states raised their asset limits, and thirteen increased benefits (although only three—including Maryland—kept pace with inflation during the late 1990s). The states used their TANF funds for a broad range of activities, including tax credits for low-income people, substance abuse treatment, assistance with utility bills, homeless shelters, child protective services, Head Start expansion, and block grants to counties. Some uses allowed the states to free up general revenues.[23] Vermont, Michigan, and Minnesota were among the states with relatively expansive approaches to reform, judging by their spending levels and minimal behavioral mandates or other policies that had the effect of excluding potential recipients.[24]

States also used devolution to institute policies that were more stringent than those required by federal law, many of which had the effect of moving recipients off the rolls and lowering costs. Twenty established shorter time limits than the five years provided under PRWORA. In addition to the twelve-month limit for some parents in Texas, Connecticut set a limit of twenty-one months, and Idaho and Indiana established limits of twenty-four months.[25] Twenty-one states elected to institute a family cap. Nineteen required women with children younger than a year old to go to work in the labor force. Idaho was noteworthy in its strict approach to welfare reform: Among other policies, it established the two-year time limit and a practice of counting SSI disability payments as income for the purposes of calculating a family's eligibility for cash assistance, which contributed to the state's 93 percent caseload decline.[26] The southern states, in general, have maintained very low benefit levels, despite their extra block grant funds.[27]

Finally, the states have been implementing their systems in a variety of ways.[28] Some caseworkers have been using their discretion to find exemptions for recipients who otherwise would be removed from the rolls (this was said to occur in Maryland). In other areas, however, caseworker discretion has had less felicitous results—including practices in localities in Illinois, Florida, and Virginia that appeared to treat whites differently from blacks and Hispanics, in some cases providing whites with greater training, education, and other assistance to leave welfare for good jobs.[29]

As Table 7-4 and the preceding chapters indicate, the three states in this study adopted a range of welfare policies. Among other decisions, Maryland preserved the entitlement status of welfare, whereas North Dakota ended it. Texas adopted the variable time limit, whereas Maryland and North Dakota went with the federal five-year maximum. Maryland gave recipients two years of cash assistance before requiring them to work; Texas and North Dakota required them to work sooner. Maryland required parents with children over one year old to work—the federal standard—whereas North Dakota required that women join the work force when their children reached four months of age. Maryland preserved TANF savings in the "dedicated purpose account," whereas Texas aggressively diverted TANF money. Finally, Maryland commissioned a detailed ongoing study of welfare leavers, and five reports had been issued by the end of 2000—far more comprehensive than the follow-up research of either of the other states.

North Dakota did not cut back its relatively large cash grant and instituted relatively generous asset limits, but in most other policy areas it took a fairly stringent approach. Maryland's lawmakers were not universally liberal—they adopted the quasi family cap, and the income levels at which recipients leave the rolls were fairly low—but in most other areas, the state developed a relatively liberal system. Texas had a mix of conservative and moderate provisions, with low benefit levels and short time limits moderated by exemptions for children and the decision to forego the family cap.

These results suggested the relative influence of the advocacy community in each state. Participants in the Maryland legislature, research community, and elsewhere directly attributed provisions such as the dedicated

Table 7-4
Selected State Welfare Policy Decisions

	Maryland	Texas	North Dakota	50 States plus D.C.
Entitlement to assistance	Preserve	Silent	End	5 Preserve 17 End 28 Silent
Time limit	5 Years	—1, 2, 3 years for parents, w/ 5-year freeze-out —5 years cumulative for family	5 Years	20 < 5 Years 29 = 5 Years 2 = No limit
Require work in less than 2 years	No	Yes, immediate	Yes	28 yes 23 No
Family cap	Quasi (benefit to third-party payee)	No	Yes	21 Yes 27 No 2 Flat grant
Age of youngest child work exemption	1 year	4 years, dropping to 1 year by 2002	4 months	19 < 1 year or no exemption 27 = 1 year 4 > 1 year 1= N/A
Asset limits	—Value of any car excluded —$2,000 per family	—Value of car <$4,650 excluded —$2,000 per family w/o elderly member —$3,000 per family w/ elderly member	—Value of any car excluded —$8,000 per family —$3,000 per single person	41 ≤ $3,000 9 > $3,000 1 = no limit
>12 months transitional Medicaid	No	18 months for CHOICES volunteers; 12 months for others	No	—12 for some leavers —39 for 12 months

(continued on next page)

Table 7-4 *(continued)*

	Maryland	Texas	North Dakota	50 States plus D.C.
>12 months transitional child care	Yes	Yes	Provide to families up to 85% state median income	—13 no guarantee —29 guarantee —9 based on income
TANF grant supplantation Protection	Dedicated purpose Account prohibits supplantation	No	No	Not available

Sources: State Policy Documentation Project (a joint project of the CBPP and CLASP), available at www.spdp.org; National Governors' Association, Center for Best Practices, "Round Two Summary of Selected Elements of State Programs for Temporary Assistance for Needy Families," March 14, 1999, available at www.nga.org. For age of child exemption, Jerome L. Gallagher et al., *One Year After Federal Welfare Reform: A Description of State Temporary Assistance for Needy Families (TANF) Decisions as of October 1997*, Occasional Paper no. 6 (Washington, D.C.: Urban Institute, 1998).

purpose account and linking of the grant to the cost of living through the minimum living level to effective lobbying by advocates for poor families. In Texas, policymakers in the mid-1990s welcomed useful information from advocates but were not willing to consider new provisions such as expanded funding for child care and work supports that failed to cut costs and/or welfare rolls—the two most clearly articulated goals of reform there. The debate in North Dakota, most notably about the family cap, was marked by a lack of substantive expertise, either because it was absent within the legislature or because the few advocates who tried to insert it into the debate were largely ignored.

THE FUTURE OF DEVOLUTION

Devolution of welfare policymaking appears to be here to stay, at least for the foreseeable future. President George W. Bush is an ex-governor who identifies even more strongly with the states than his Democratic predecessor. His appointment of Gov. Tommy Thompson of Wisconsin as secretary of HHS in early 2001 reaffirmed his commitment to state autonomy over social programs and indicated that his administration was likely to push for greater devolution—possibly block granting of Medicaid and compensatory federal funding for education (two things Clinton resisted strongly).[30] Bush's

Texas record also suggests a greater role for private, for-profit, and religious organizations, which was quickly confirmed by his creation of a White House office for faith-based programs.

In most states, there was not a great deal of radical policy change in welfare between 1997 and 2001. It appeared that short of a fiscal crisis or other impetus, the period of greatest welfare innovation was drawing to a close, at least for the time being. The states seemed likely to continue to make incremental revisions, and those with waivers, such as Texas, needed to bring their systems into compliance with federal requirements, but few seemed to be gearing up again for fundamental overhaul. The overall policy emphasis was shifting away from the welfare system to broader supports for low-income working people.

The major welfare policy event would be the reauthorization of TANF in Washington in 2002. Going into the debate, however, the politics of welfare had changed significantly. The demand for radical reform of the mid-1990s had been satisfied, and the issue had lost much of its symbolic and strategic value to both political parties. The general public seemed to be largely uninterested in reauthorization, sharing a broad perception that "the welfare problem" had been solved with PRWORA and the drop in caseloads. The "elite" organizations across the political spectrum within Washington—advocates, research groups, policy organizations, and think tanks—were gearing up early, however.[31]

For the first time in more than forty years, Republicans had control of the White House and the House of Representatives after the 2000 elections, by a fairly narrow but not irrelevant margin. The margin between Democrats and Republicans in the Senate was so narrow that policymakers in either party would have to negotiate effectively with those in the other party, as well as with Republican moderates who played a key role in softening the 1996 bill. Although Congressional Democrats could no longer count on Clinton's veto pen, neither did they have to negotiate with his shifting positions on acceptable reform provisions. The governors were likely to fight cuts in block grant funding levels and any attempts to add federal mandates, liberal or conservative. The presence of an HHS secretary who had been an activist governor on the issue of welfare reform and who was willing to spend money—a work-oriented reformer—suggested that the Bush administration might not advocate cutting the grant sharply or adding extensive new state requirements. The major federal tax cut of 2001, however, raised the possibility that the resulting need for budget reductions would increase pressure to cut the block grant.

The scope of issues up for consideration was narrower than during the 104th Congress, and it seemed unlikely that many of the most radical or contentious issues would be seriously revisited: Reinstatement of the entitlement status of assistance and a cutoff of teen mothers were equally unlikely. The volumes of research on the results of welfare reform produced since 1996 also were beginning to find a place in the reauthorization debate. National advocacy groups had been working together and with research organizations and others to determine how best to bring research findings into the debate. Although the general public was not yet tuning in, organizations on the right and left already were grabbing the opportunity to push their key proposals, including policies intended to encourage marriage, an increased role for noncustodial fathers, longer time limits for the hardest-to-serve recipients, and preservation of the maintenance-of-effort requirement.

Finally, welfare recipients themselves had been significantly detoxified in the public and political imagination, at least for the time being. No one was talking about the welfare queen; the emphasis had shifted away from the "undeserving," nonworking mother of children born out of wedlock and toward at least some support for a more sympathetic image of the struggling, low-income, working parent.

Some of the central reauthorization issues for TANF were expected to be:[32]

- *The purposes of the block grant*—whether TANF should be modified to provide support and assistance for working poor families in general, and a wider range of additional state activities for families.
- *Federal TANF funding and state maintenance-of-effort levels*—whether the TANF grant should remain at 1996 levels or even increase, given the likelihood of an eventual economic downturn, and the possibility of providing more assistance to the working poor. Other proposals were likely to relate to cutting the grant because of caseload declines, as well as adjusting individual states' grant levels for population growth, poverty rates, and other factors.[33] Another issue would be whether states should be required to continue to maintain 75–80 percent of their previous spending or be allowed to spend less.
- *Time limits and exemptions*—whether the five-year time limit should be lengthened for families still on welfare that were facing the greatest barriers, whether parents should have their time limit "clocks" stopped while they worked, and whether the 20 percent exemption should be increased, given the size of the caseload decline.
- *State performance measurements*—whether state performance should be gauged by a wider range of measures than caseload declines and work participation, instead including measures such as rates of child poverty and other child well-being indicators, out-of-wedlock birth rates, or measures of family formation.

- *Greater federal standards and safeguards*—whether the federal government should require states to make more effort toward recipients with the greatest problems before removing them from the rolls, given the use of full-family sanctions and other causes of benefit loss and growing poverty among the poorest ex-recipients.
- *Marriage and family formation*—whether the family formation provisions of TANF can or should be strengthened to increase incentives to states and individuals to increase marriage and decrease out-of-wedlock births, especially among low-income families.

The biggest questions in early 2001 were what would happen to the economy and its ability to draw and keep recipients in the labor market and the effect of the federal five-year time limit when it hit in 2002. After the longest expansion in American history, the economy was showing signs of slowing, and many states were beginning to experience budget shortfalls. Between 8 and 36 percent of the caseload decrease during the 1990s had been attributed to the strong economy, and the effect of a downturn on recipients and other low-income workers—particularly once the federal time limit took effect—was a major concern.[34]

In a number of states, the decline in caseloads had been slowing; in several it even began to reverse. If the economy slowed considerably before the reauthorization debate, the slowdown could be used to justify maintaining relatively high block grant levels to support actual or anticipated caseload increases. If it slowed after new grant levels were set, given the financial incentives embedded in the block grant structure, it could spur states to cut back further on their own funding and become more assertive in using TANF funds to free up state revenues.

Another outstanding question was how the courts would interpret welfare policy over time.[35] The U.S. Supreme Court's decision in *Saenz v. Roe* put an end to state policies that paid newcomers at different benefit levels than those already residing in the state.[36] Lower courts and state courts were issuing additional decisions, although the period of liberal activist courts seemed to be over and they turned to addressing fairly narrow issues rather than defining broad "welfare rights."[37]

The relative lack of a "race to the bottom" was attributed to the strong economy, maintenance-of-effort requirements, and the fact that sharp caseload declines coupled with block grant funding had given states far more federal money per recipient, at least for the time being, than they previously received. State policymakers also were motivated by other political considerations, such as the desire to be seen as policy innovators, not just fear of becoming welfare magnets. One could argue that state welfare policy on the whole had become more stringent, but individual state policymakers lacked strong incentive during the 1990s to race downward in large numbers, and federal requirements limited their ability to do so. Whether they face stronger temptation in the future will depend on states' economic conditions, future block grant amounts, and whether maintenance-of-effort requirements are kept up. It also will depend on the political incentives and demands on state policymakers, including demands made by representatives of low-income families.

CONCLUSION

Interest groups are not the only way for the concerns of low-income families to enter the policy process. They also can be represented by receptive legislators, by policy entrepreneurs in the executive branch, by bureaucrats in the welfare agencies, occasionally by favorable public opinion, and sometimes through their own testimony at hearings or other contact with lawmakers. At times they have acted influentially in direct ways such as protests, riots, or civil unrest.

Advocates and advocacy organizations have played and continue to play an essential role in our system, however. They provide information to expertise-strapped lawmakers individually and in public hearings; submit draft legislation; produce accessible information for the media and the public; form coalitions; launch public campaigns; and otherwise persuade and cajole legislators—often acting as "their conscience," in the words of one Maryland committee chair. This study has examined the critical role of interest group participation in shaping the direction of welfare reform, in Washington and in the states. It suggests that the neo-Madisonians were right, at least in the case of welfare policy, when they warned about the repercussions for representation of shrinking the sphere of policymaking.

Given the disadvantages many states face in terms of their policymaking capacities and the ability of poor families' representatives to participate in the debate, our embrace of devolution raises questions about our commitment to equal opportunity, especially for the poor children who make up the majority of welfare recipients. In accepting devolution of social policy to the states and even localities, we seem to have arrived at a moment when we again accept as appropriate the highly uneven approaches to helping poor families that are developing in the states. This devolution means that low-income children in some jurisdictions are growing up with significantly less support and opportunity than those growing up in others, simply because of the state in which their families live.

Devolution also raises questions about our commitment to the ability of citizens to participate in formulating the policies that most affect them. Certainly the size of the political arena is not the only important factor in policymaking. Extending the "sphere of conflict," however, appears to allow low-income families greater opportunity to participate—through advocacy organizations—in policymaking that most affects them. The bottom line is that under devolution, welfare policy tends to be developed less visibly than in the nation's capital, with less deliberation and less knowledge and expertise. It also tends to be formed with less participation by groups representing the people who are most affected by lawmakers' decisions. This is not the case in every state, but it appears to be the case in many. Where it is, policy decisions appear to be less generous or supportive of low-income families than policies outlined in federal law.

Despite the rhetorical and political appeal of decentralization and localism, by shifting welfare policy from the national capital to the smaller jurisdictions of the states and localities, we have in fact moved it into a set of political arenas where the poor families who are its beneficiaries have even less power than they do in Washington. Without at least the presence of a reasonable number of advocates for low-income people in the states, the danger of further "disappearing" the poor and their concerns from the policymaking process only increases.

NOTES

1. Richard W. Stevenson, "Budget Deal, for Now, Takes Back Seat to the Economy," *New York Times*, 7 August 1997; "New Social Provisions," *Washington Post*, 30 July 1997, A12.

2. U.S. Department of Health and Human Services, Administration for Children and Families, "Change in TANF Caseloads: Total TANF Recipients by State, As of June 2000," 28 December 2000; available at www.acf.dhhs.gov/news/stats/caseload.htm.

3. U.S. General Accounting Office, "Welfare Reform: Information on Former Recipients' Status," GAO/HEHS-99-48, April 1999, 18. This source provided data from studies in seven states.

4. *1998 Green Book*, 1303; U.S. Department of Commerce, "Poverty Rate Lowest in 20 Years, Household Income at Record High, Census Bureau Reports," 26 September 2000.

5. Department of Health and Human Services, *Temporary Assistance for Needy Families (TANF) Program, Second Annual Report to Congress, August 1999*, Table 4.1; available at www.acf.dhhs.gov/programs/opre/tanfreports/tan19995.pdf.

6. Marcia K. Meyers, "Gaining Cooperation at the Front Lines of Service Delivery: Issues for the Implementation of Welfare Reform," in *Rockefeller Reports no.* 7 (Albany, N.Y.: Rockefeller Institute of Government, State University of New York, 1998); see also Richard P. Nathan and Thomas L. Gais, *Overview Report: Implementation of the Personal Responsibility Act of 1996* (Albany, N.Y.: Rockefeller Institute of Government, State University of New York, 1998). The Rockefeller Institute is closely following implementation in twenty-three states. Nathan and Gais note that "street level" bureaucrats in the states are far more ambivalent about implementing the pro-

visions of the national bill that are designed to discourage out-of-wedlock births than those that encourage work.

7. Linda Burton et al., "What Welfare Recipients and the Fathers of Their Children Are Saying about Welfare Reform: A Report on 15 Focus Group Discussions in Baltimore, Boston, and Chicago," June 1998; Andrew Cherlin and Pamela Winston et al., "What Welfare Recipients Know about the New Rules and What They Have to Say about Them," Welfare, Children and Families: A Three City Study, Policy Brief 00-1, 2000; both available at www.jhu.edu/~welfare.

8. The other nonworking leavers were believed to be supported by an employed husband or partner. Pamela Loprest, "How Families That Left Welfare Are Doing: A National Picture," Assessing the New Federalism Project (Washington, D.C.: Urban Institute, 1999).

9. Catholic Charities USA, "More People Receive Emergency Food in Spite of Strong Economy: Nation's Largest Social Service Network Sees Dramatic Increase Across Nation," press release, 19 December 2000. Andrew C. Revkin, "Welfare Policies Alter the Face of Food Lines," *New York Times*, 26 February 1999, A1.

10. Marilyn Ellwood, "The Medicaid Eligibility Maze," Assessing the New Federalism Project, Urban Institute, December 1999, available at newfederalism.urban.org/html/occa30.html. Andrew C. Revkin, "A Plunge in Use of Food Stamps Causes Concern," *New York Times*, 25 February 1999, A1.

11. Nina Bernstein, "Studies Dispute Some Assumptions on Welfare Overhaul," *New York Times*, 12 December 2000, A14.

12. Robert Moffitt and Jennifer Roff, "The Diversity of Welfare Leavers," Welfare, Children and Families: A Three City Study, Policy Brief 00-2, September 2000, available at www.jhu.edu/~welfare. Also Wendall Primus et al., "The Initial Impacts of Welfare Reform on the Incomes of Single Mother Families," Center on Budget and Policy Priorities, 1999, available at www.cbpp.org/8-22-99wel.pdf.

13. U.S. Department of Health and Human Services, Indicators of *Welfare Dependency, Annual Report, March 2000*, Table A-5, available at aspc.hhs.gov/hsp/indicators00/wordver/T_A_5.doc.

14. Research has indicated that newspapers are tending to focus less, not more, on covering state politics, despite devolution. I did not have access to coverage in other media outlets such as television news, but I have no reason to believe it was significantly different.

15. See Keith E. Hamm and Gary F. Moncrief, "Legislative Politics in the States," in Virginia Gray, Russell Hanson, and Herbert Jacobs, *Politics in the American States: A Comparative Analysis*, 7th ed. (Washington, D.C.: CQ Press, 1999), 145.

16. See Rosenthal, *The Decline of Representative Democracy*, especially 72–80.

17. John M. Carey, Richard G. Niemi, and Lynda W. Powell, *Term Limits in the State Legislatures* (Ann Arbor: University of Michigan Press, 2000), 125–26.

18. For this study I used legislative hearings participation as an objective measure of group involvement in the welfare debate; extensive interviews confirmed that hearings testimony in fact was a generally accurate indicator of overall participation.

I include advocacy and civil rights groups, nonprofit and charitable providers, researchers, and unions in the group of actors that can represent low-income people.

19. See Weaver, *Ending Welfare As We Know It*, chapter 14, on the strategic and relational politics of various configurations of the national bill.

20. An exception is the W. K. Kellogg Foundation's Devolution Initiative, which is funding a wide range of organizations, from national research groups to state and local advocacy organizations.

21. This preference, of course, also was a "conservative" idea espoused by groups such as the Family Research Council, although they tended to advocate work for poor parents and child-rearing for middle-class mothers.

22. These data were gathered between 1998 and 2000. For more information, see the website of the State Policy Documentation Project, a joint project of the Center on Budget and Policy Priorities and the Center on Law and Social Policy, at www.spdp.org; see also National Governors' Association Center for Best Practices, "Round Two Summary of Selected Elements of State Programs for Temporary Assistance for Needy Families, March 14, 1999"; available at www.nga.org/cbp (downloaded 5 September 2000). See L. Jerome Gallagher et al., *One Year after Welfare Reform: A Description of State Temporary Assistance for Needy Families (TANF) Decisions as of October 1997*, Occasional Paper no. 6 (Washington, D.C.: Urban Institute, 1998), for additional information such as age-of-child work exemptions, although this information is somewhat dated.

23. A Rockefeller Institute study of changes in state spending, issued in 2000, concludes that among four states—California, Georgia, Missouri, and Wisconsin—spending on programs for low-income people was down whereas that for social services that are not means-tested, such as child welfare and mental health, was up "dramatically." See Deborah A. Ellwood and Donald J. Boyd, "Changes in State Spending on Social Services Since the Implementation of Welfare Reform: A Preliminary Report," Rockefeller Institute of Government, February 2000, available at www.rockinst.org.

24. For a discussion of welfare reform in Michigan and Minnesota, see Carol W. Weissert, ed., *Learning from Leaders: Welfare Reform Politics and Policy in Five Midwestern States* (Albany, N.Y.: Rockefeller Institute Press, 2000).

25. Again, Texas time limits included the five-year freeze-out that kept parents off the rolls for that time period, after which they could reapply for assistance. They could use as much as a cumulative total of five years of assistance. Under the state's waiver, children did not lose assistance during the freeze-out period.

26. Timothy Egan, "As Idaho Booms, Prisons Fill and Spending on Poor Lags," *New York Times*, 16 April 1998.

27. States with maximum monthly benefit levels under $250 for a family of three were Alabama, Arkansas, Louisiana, Mississippi, South Carolina, Tennessee, and Texas.

28. See Nathan and Gais, "Overview Report," for a more detailed assessment of implementation across the states.

29. Studies summarized in Steve Savner, "Welfare Reform and Racial/Ethnic Minorities: The Questions to Ask," Center on Law and Social Policy, 2000, available at www.clasp.org/pubs/tanf.

30. Robert Pear, "Shifting of Power from Washington Is Seen Under Bush," *New York Times*, 7 January 2001, A1.

31. Several major TANF reauthorization events were held in the winter of 2001: the Brookings Institution's "Welfare Reform and Beyond" programs as well as "The New World of Welfare: An Agenda for Reauthorization and Beyond," a two-day Washington conference sponsored by the University of Michigan school of public policy. These events were standing room only, despite the fact that reauthorization itself was eighteen months away.

32. Most of this information is from Mark Greenberg et al., *Welfare Reauthorization: An Early Guide to the Issues* (Washington, D.C.: Center on Law and Social Policy, 2000).

33. Congress had threatened a couple of times to cut the size of the block grant, given the states' unspent TANF balances, but Republican governors and others fought the effort. See Judith Havemann, "Senate's Welfare Plan Infuriates Governors," *Washington Post*, 13 March 1999, A2.

34. The Council on Economic Advisors attributed 26–36 percent of the decline in caseloads to the labor market during the years 1993 to 1996 and 8–10 percent of the decline in caseloads to the labor market during the 1996 to 1998 period. See Council on Economic Advisors, "The Effects of Welfare Policy and the Economic Expansion on Welfare Caseloads: An Update," 3 August 1999, 2.

35. See Weaver, *Ending Welfare As We Know It*, 364, and R. Shep Melnick, *Between the Lines: Interpreting Welfare Rights* (Washington, D.C.: Brookings Institution Press, 1994), on the role of the courts in welfare and related policy areas.

36. 526 U.S. 489; 119 S.Ct. 1518; 143 L. Ed. 2d 689 (1999).

37. For information on litigation in the states and localities, see the Welfare Information Network's website at www.welfareinfo.org/litigation.htm.

Appendix A

Selection Criteria for State Case Studies

Criteria	Texas	Maryland	North Dakota	U.S.
Population/rank, 1995	18.7 million/2	5 million/19	641,000/47	263 million/—
Region	South/Southwest	Mid-Atlantic	Midwest/ Northwest	—
Poverty Rate, 1994 (%)	19.1	10.7	10.4	14.5
Median Household Income, 1994	$30,755	$39,198	$28,278	$32,264
Ethnic Diversity, 1995[a] (%)	85 W; 12 B; 28 H; 2.5 A; 0.5 NA	69 W; 26 B; 3 H, 3.6 A; 0.3 NA	94 W; 0.6 B; 0.9 H; 0.8 A; 4.4 NA	83 W; 13 B; 10 H; 3.6 A; 0.9 NA
AFDC Benefits, 1995[b]	$188	$373	$431	$377
Party Control of Governor's Office/ Legislature, 1997	Republican/split	Democrat/ Democrat	Republican/ Republican	—

Sources: U.S. Department of Commerce, Bureau of the Census, *Statistical Abstract of the United States, 1996*; for ethnicity data, www.census.gov/population/estimates/state/srh/srh95.txt; Committee on Ways and Means, U.S. House of Representatives, *1996 Green Book*.

[a]W = white; B = black; H = Hispanic; A = Asian; NA = Native American. Hispanic may be of any race.

[b]Maximum monthly benefit for a three-person family.

Appendix B

National AFDC-Related Hearings during 104th Congress, by Committee, Topic, and Date

U.S. HOUSE OF REPRESENTATIVES

Committee on Agriculture, Subcommittee on Department Operations, Nutrition, and Foreign Agriculture:

"Reforming the Present System," February 7–9 and 15, 1995

Committee on Economic and Educational Opportunities (full committee):

"Contract With America: Hearing on Welfare Reform," January 18, 1995

Committee on Economic and Educational Opportunities, Subcommittee on Early Childhood, Youth and Families:

"Hearing on Contract With America: Child Welfare and Childcare," January 31, 1995

Committee on Economic and Educational Opportunities, Subcomittee on Postsecondary Education and Life-Long Learning:

"Hearing on Job Opportunities and Basic Skills Act," January 19, 1995

Committee on Ways and Means, Subcommittee on Human Resources:

"Contract With America—Welfare Reform," January 13, 20, 23, 27, and 30, and February 2, 1995

"Child Support Enforcement Provisions Included in Personal Responsibility Act as Part of the Contract With America," February 6, 1995

"Welfare Reform Success Stories," December 6, 1995

"The National Governors' Association Welfare Reform Proposal," February 20, 1996

"Causes of Poverty, with a Focus on Out-of-Wedlock Births," March 12, 1996

"Welfare Reform," May 22 and 23, 1996

Committee on Ways and Means, Subcommitte on Oversight and Investigations:

"Hearing on Block Grant/Consolidation Overview," February 9, 1995

U.S. SENATE

Committee on Finance:

"States' Perspective on Welfare Reform," March 8, 1995

"Broad Policy Goals of Welfare Reform," March 9, 1995

"Administration's Views on Welfare Reform," March 10, 1995

"Teen Parents and Welfare Reform," March 14, 1995

"Welfare to Work," March 20, 1995

"Welfare Reform—Views of Interested Parties," March 29, 1995

"Child Welfare Programs," April 26, 1995

"Welfare Reform Wrap-Up," April 27, 1995

"Governors' Proposal on Welfare and Medicaid," February 22, 28 and 29, 1996

"Welfare and Medicaid Reform," June 13 and 19, 1996

Committee on Governmental Affairs:

"Reinventing Government—Efficiency Issues re: Welfare System Reform Proposals," January 25, February 2, 1995 (excluding witness information pertaining only to Department of Defense)

Committee on Labor and Human Resources:

"Child Care and Development Block Grant: How Is It Working?" February 16, 1995

"Impact of Welfare Reform on Children and Their Families," February 28, March 1, 1995

"Filling the Gap: Can Private Institutions Do It?" March 26, 1996

Note: This list includes hearings that took place between January 1995 and August 1996, when the federal welfare bill (PRWORA) was signed into law.

Appendix C

Actors and Organizations Submitting Oral or Written Testimony in Welfare-Related Hearings, 104th Congress

(By Type of Group, Including Number of Times Testified)

INTERGOVERNMENTAL GROUPS AND ACTORS

States

American Legislative Exchange Council, S. Martin

American Public Welfare Association, G. Stangler (testified twice)

California Department of Health and Human Services, Welfare Division, M. Genest

California Department of Social Services, E. Anderson (testified three times)

Colorado Governor R. Romer

Delaware Governor T. Carper (testified twice)

Delaware Department of Health and Social Services, C. Nazario

Delaware Department of Services for Children, Youth and Families, T. Eichler (testified twice)

Florida Governor L. Chiles (testified twice)

Georgia Department of Human Resources, C. Robinson and M. Thurmond

Indiana State Representative D. Young

Kansas Department of Social and Rehabilitation Services, J. Schalansky

Louisiana State Disability Determinations Service, Shreveport, W. Parker

Massachusetts Department of Health and Human Services, G. Whitburn

Massachusetts Department of Revenue, M. Adams (testified twice)

Massachusetts Department of Transitional Assistance, J. Gallant

Michigan Governor J. Engler (testified three times)

Michigan Department of Social Services, G. Miller (testified three times)

Michigan JOBS Commission, D. Stites

Minnesota Department of Human Services, J. Petraborg

National Conference of State Legislatures, J. Campbell (Ohio House of Representatives)

National Governors' Association, T. Carper (Governor of Delaware)

Nevada Governor B. Miller

New Jersey Department of Human Services, W. Waldman

Ohio Department of Human Services, A. Tompkins

Oregon Department of Human Resources, S. Minnich

Former South Carolina Governor C. Campbell

Texas State Representative H. Hilderbran

University of Tennessee, S. Puett

Vermont Governor H. Dean

Vermont Office of Child Support, J. Cohen

Wisconsin Governor T. Thompson (testified three times)

Wisconsin Department of Health and Social Services, Madison, J. Rogers (testified twice)

Written testimony only:

Electronic Parent Locator Network (EPLN) and Consortium of EPLN States

Indiana State Senator L. Kenley

Maryland Foster Care Review Board (citizen board)

National Governors' Association

New Jersey Human Services Department, Division of Family Development, K. Highsmith

New Mexico Citizen Review Board Project, Albuquerque

South Carolina Division for Review of Foster Care of Children

Counties

Butte County (Calif.) Sheriff, M. Grey

Fairfax County (Va.) Office for Children, J. Rosen

Fond du Lac (Wisc.) County Department of Social Services, E. Schilling (testified twice)

La Rue County (Ky.) Health Center, J. Walsh

Los Angeles County (Calif.) Department of Children and Family Services, P. Digre

National Association of Counties, R. Johnson (testified twice)

Newport County (R.I.) Child and Family Services, P. DiBari

Orange County (Calif.) Social Services Agency, A. Doti

Riverside County (Calif.) Dept. of Public Social Services, L. Townsend (testified three times)

Stanislaus County (Calif.) Department of Social Services, J. Davis

Suffolk County (N.Y.) County Executive R. Gaffney

Written testimony only:

City and County of San Francisco, Office of the District Attorney, P. Strauss

Tulare County (Calif.) Office of the Deputy District Attorney, J. Higgins

Local

Chicago Department of Human Services, D. Alvarez

Dallas Mayor S. Bartlett

Florida League of Cities/National League of Cities, E. Austin (Mayor of Jacksonville, Fla.)

Southside Elementary School, Lake Providence, La., W. Bell

Philadelphia Deputy Managing Director W. Parshall

St. Louis Mayor F. Bosley

U.S. Conference of Mayors, C. Cooper (Mayor of East Orange, N.J.) (testified twice)

Written testimony only:

Philadelphia Department of Human Services

Tribal

Written testimony only:

Navajo Nation

Red Lake Band of Chippewa Indians

ADVOCACY/LEGAL/CIVIL RIGHTS ORGANIZATIONS

Advocates for Better Child Support, Inc., S. Brotchie

The Arc (formerly Association for Retarded Citizens of the United States), J. Gardner

Association for Children for Enforcement of Support, Inc., G. Jensen

Bazelon Center for Mental Health Law, J. Manes

Bread for the World, D. Beckmann

Center on Budget and Policy Priorities, R. Greenstein (testified four times)

Center for Law and Social Policy, M. Greenberg (testified three times)

Center for Women Policy Studies, L. Wolfe (testified twice)

Children's Defense Fund, C. Johnson (testified three times)

Children's Rights Council, C. Ewing

Coalition on Human Needs, J. Vasiloff

Community Legal Services, Inc., Philadelphia, J. Stein

Community Nutrition Institute, R. Leonard

Consortium for Citizens with Disabilities, R. Schulzinger (testified twice)

Corporation for Enterprise Development, R. Friedman and C. Wilson (testified twice)

Farmworkers' Justice Fund, M. Hancock

Feed the Children, L. Jones

Food Research and Action Center, R. Fersh (testified twice)

Independent Sector, S. Melendez

Mon-Valley Unemployed Committee, Homestead, Pa., W. Myers

National Abortion and Reproductive Rights Action League, K. Michelman (testified twice)

National Black Women's Health Project, C. Newbille

National Campaign to Prevent Teen Pregnancy, S. Brown

National Caucus and Center on Black Aged, Inc., S. Simmons

National Center for Family Literacy, S. Darling

National Committee to Prevent Child Abuse, A. Donnelly

National Council of La Raza, S. Perez

National Indian Child Welfare Association

National Senior Citizens Law Center, E. Zelenske

National Union of the Homeless/Poor People's Coalition, L. Smith

National Urban League, A. Rowe (testified twice)

National Welfare Rights and Reform Union, Sacramento, Calif., K. Aslanian

National Women's Law Center, N. Campbell

Pennsylvania Welfare Rights Union, Philadelphia, C. Honkala (testified twice)

Philadelphia Unemployment Project, D. Ripley

Public Voice for Food and Health Policy, M. Epstein (testified twice)

Puerto Ricans in Civic Action, M. Ramirez de Ferrer, M.D.

Save Our Security Coalition, A. Flemming

Written testimony only:

Advocates for Youth, M. Clark (testified twice)

American Civil Liberties Union, D. Lewis (testified three times)

Asian & Pacific Islander American Health Forum, Inc./Asian Law Caucus, San Francisco

Child Exclusion Task Force (coalition of ninety-four advocacy groups) (testified twice)

Chinatown Resource Center and the Chinese Community Council, Inc.

Coalition on Women and Job Training

Coalition to Stop Welfare Cuts, Pittsburgh

Day Care Action Council of Illinois (testified twice)

Disability Law Center, Boston

Family Resource Coalition

Jewish Council on Urban Affairs, Chicago

Legal Assistance Foundation of Chicago

Mandel Legal Aid Clinic, University of Chicago

Michigan League for Human Services

National Asian Pacific American Legal Consortium

National Child Abuse Defense and Resource Center

National Child Support Advocacy Coalition

National Congress of American Indians

National Task Force on Violence Against Women

NOW Legal Defense and Education Fund (testified four times)

Parents for Justice

Public Welfare Coalition

SSI Coalition

Taylor Institute, Chicago

Welfare Rights Organizing Coalition, Seattle

Work, Welfare and Families of Illinois, Chicago

Nonprofit Service Providers and Charities

AIDS Project of the East Bay, Oakland, Calif., J. Goldstein

American Association of Community Colleges, R. Smith

American Commodity Distribution Association, Z. Slagle

Archdiocese of New Orleans Department of Community Services, R. Morin

Archdiocese of Philadelphia Nutritional Development Services, P. Temple-West

Bethel New Life, Inc./Evangelical Lutheran Church in America, M. Nelson

Boysville of Michigan, Clinton, Mich., G. Tester

California Child Care and Resources and Referral Network, P. Siegel (testified twice)

Catholic Charities USA, F. Kammer (testified four times)

Catholic Charities USA, S. Daly

Child Welfare League of America, D. Liederman (testified five times)

Covenant House, M. McGready (testified three times)

Crispus Attucks Association, Inc., R. Hollis

Family Service America, Inc., R. Field

Florida Children's Forum, S. Muenchow

Focus: HOPE, W. Cunningham

Goodwill Industries, Manasota, Fla., M. Cook (testified twice)

Indian and Native American Employment and Training Coalition, C. Archambault (testified twice)

Kansas Food Bank Warehouse, V. White

National Black Child Development Institute, Inc., E. Tollett

National Center for Neighborhood Enterprises, L. Earl

National Network of Food Banks, A. Hamel

New Hope Project, S. Schulz

Paternal Involvement Demonstration Project, D. Pate

Project Match/Erickson Institute, Chicago, T. Herr

Religious Action Center of Reform Judaism, D. Saperstein

Seeds of Love Family Day Care Center, M. Moran

United States Catholic Conference, Department of Social Development and World Peace, J. Carr

United Way of America, H. Acres

Wider Opportunities for Women, D. Pearce

Written testimony only:

Adoption Coalition

Ayuda, Washington, D.C.

Council of Jewish Federations

Council of Women's and Infants' Specialty Hospitals

Family Service Agency of San Francisco, Teenage Pregnancy and Parenting Project

Jewish Federation of Metropolitan Chicago

National Association of Public Hospitals and Health Systems

Oakland Chinese Community Council, Inc.

Planned Parenthood Federation of America

SSI Outreach Project, Baltimore

United Cerebral Palsy Associations

United Way of Chicago

YMCA of the USA, Washington, D.C.

YWCA of the USA, New York City

Research Organizations, Academic Experts

Rebecca Blank, Northwestern University

Charles A. Bowsher, U.S. General Accounting Office

Sheldon Danziger, University of Michigan

David T. Ellwood, Harvard University (testified twice)

Michael Fix, Urban Institute

Lawrence H. Fuchs, Brandeis University

Frank Furstenberg, University of Pennsylvania

Robert C. Granger, Manpower Demonstration Research Corporation

Judith M. Gueron, Manpower Demonstration Research Corporation (testified six times)

Sandra L. Hofferth, University of Michigan Institute for Social Research

Marion Howard, Emory University

Herbert D. Kleber, MD, Columbia University

Robert I. Lerman, American University

Glenn C. Loury, Boston University

Rebecca A. Maynard, University of Pennsylvania

Joe S. McIlhaney, M.D., Medical Institute for Sexual Health

Sara McLanahan, Princeton University

Lawrence M. Mead, Princeton University (testified four times)

Ernestine Moore, Skillman Center for Children, Wayne State University

Kristin A. Moore, Child Trends

Linda Morra, U.S. General Accounting Office

Richard P. Nathan, Rockefeller Institute of Government, State University of New York

Marvin N. Olasky, University of Texas at Austin

LaDonna A. Pavetti, Urban Institute

Deborah A. Phillips, National Research Council

Kevin Phillips, *Los Angeles Times*

Jane L. Ross, U.S. General Accounting Office (testified six times)

Louis Rossiter, Virginia Commonwealth University

Sally L. Satel, MD, Yale University

Sarah Shuptrine, Sarah Shuptrine and Associates

James R. Tallon, Kaiser Commission on the Future of Medicaid

Ruth Ellen Wasem, Congressional Research Service, Library of Congress

James Q. Wilson, University of California at Los Angeles

Nicholas Zill, Director of Child and Family Studies, Westat, Inc.

Think Tanks

American Enterprise Institute, Carolyn Weaver

American Enterprise Institute, Douglas J. Besharov (testified twice)

American Enterprise Institute, Charles A. Murray

American Institute for Full Employment, Charles D. Hobbs (testified twice)

Beacon Hill Institute for Public Policy Research, David G. Tuerch

Brookings Institution, Robert D. Reischauer

Cato Institute, Stephen Moore

Cato Institute, Michael D. Tanner

Employment Policies Institute, Carlos Bonilla

Free Congress Research and Education Foundation, Robert B. Carelson (testified twice)

Heritage Foundation, Robert Rector (testified eight times)

Hudson Institute, Michael Horowitz (testified twice)

Hudson Institute, S. Anna Kondratas

Institute for Women's Policy Research, Roberta Spalter-Roth

National Center for Policy Analysis, Peter J. Ferrara (testified twice)

National Center for Policy Analysis, John C. Goodman (testified twice)

Progressive Policy Institute, William Marshall

"Traditional Values"/Social Conservative Organizations

Acton Institute for the Study of Religion and Liberty, Grand Rapids, Mich., R. Sirico

American Fathers' Coalition/Texas Fathers Alliance, Austin, D. Burgess (testified twice)

Children's Rights Council, M. Pitts

Christian Coalition, H. Stirrup (testified twice)

Concerned Women for America, P. Young (testified twice)

Family Research Council, D. Wagner (testified twice)

Federation for American Immigration Reform, D. Stein

Men's Health Network, R. Henry

Minority Mainstream, G. Daye

National Fatherhood Initiative, W. Horn (testified twice)

Project Reality, K. Sullivan

Traditional Values Coalition, A. Sheldon

Women's Freedom Network, C. Young

Written testimony only:

Family Law Reform News, San Francisco

For-Profit Service Providers

America Works, Orange County, Calif., D. MacAllister

Child Care Institute of America, W. Tobin

Child Support Council, D. Grubbs

Child Support Enforcement, R. Hoffman

Cleveland Works, Inc., D. Roth

EDS Government Services Group, G. Newstrom

Policy Studies, Inc., R. Williams

Tonn & Associates, Austin, Tex., C. Langguth

Written testimony only:

Kids Forever Learning Center, Inc.

Outer Limits School

Tessie's Child Care, Inc.

Business/Trade Associations

Apricot Producers of Calif. and Commodity Distribution Coalition, W. Ferriera

Food Marketing Institute, T. Hammonds

National-American Wholesale Grocers' Association and International Foodservice Distributors Association, J. Block

U.S. Chamber of Commerce, J. Joseph (testified twice)

Written testimony only:

American Rehabilitation Association

Grocery Manufacturers of America

National Grocers Association

United States Telephone Association

Organized Labor

AFL-CIO, G. Shea

American Federation of State, County, and Municipal Employees, N. Meiklejohn (testified three times)

Service Employees International Union, AFL-CIO, D. Baker

Written testimony only:

International Ladies' Garment Workers' Union

International Union, United Automobile, Aerospace and Agricultural Implement Workers of America (UAW)

Professional Associations

American Academy of Pediatrics, J. Shonkoff (testified twice)

American Bar Association, M. Haynes

American Society for Payroll Management, D. Salam (testified twice)

National Child Support Enforcement Association, M. Smith

Written testimony only:

American Academy of Matrimonial Lawyers

American Dental Hygienists' Association

American Psychiatric Association

American Psychological Association (testified twice)

Eastern Regional Interstate Child Support Association

National Association of Disability Examiners

National Association of Social Workers

National Society of Professional Engineers

National Treasury Employees Union

Non-Commissioned Officers Association of the United States of America

Individuals (not obvious organizational representatives)

Pamela Cave, Chantilly, Va. (testified twice)

Cari Clark, Springfield, Va.

Sandra M. Corder, Falls Church,Va.

Tamara Elser, Fair Haven, Vt.

Clarissa Pinkola Estes, Denver, Colo.

Edward Allan Faine, Takoma Park, Md.

Tandi Graff, Eugene, Oreg.

Jasmine Gunthorpe, Baltimore, Md.

Amy Hendricks, Temple Hills, Md.

Karen Higginbotham, Opelousas, La.

Carol Hopkins, San Diego, Calif.

Rebecca Kinnard, York, Penn.

George W. Liebmann, Baltimore, Md.

Karolin Loendorf, Helena, Mont.

Gladys Marisette, Topeka, Kan.

Pam White, District Heights, Md.

Written testimony only:

Cindy Backlund, Santa Fe, N.M.

Kim and Shelah Bell, North Salt Lake, Utah

Olivia Brooks, Alexandria, Va.

Margaret Brown, Buffalo, N.Y.

Breda Courtney, Berkeley, Calif.

Seth Farber, New York, N.Y.

Richard Gardner, M.D., Cresskill, N.J.

Pier Geter, Wilmington, Del.

Debora Haskins, Fond du Lac, Wisc.

Lea Higashi, Kent, Wash.

Lisa Karl, Seattle, Wash.

Joyce Kerley, Cypress, Calif.

Kathleen Mallinger, San Diego, Calif.

Hugh Maloney, Ft. Lauderdale, Fla.

Michael March, Boulder, Colo.

Leo Ng, San Francisco, Colo.

Nancy Peterson, Fremont, Mich.

Kathleen Quinn, Havertown, Penn.

Jan and Francis Silver, Washington, D.C.

"Statement of Concern by 470 Law Professors about Welfare Reform"

Bruce Suderow, Washington, D.C.

Thomas D. Sutton, Langhorne, Penn.

Miscellaneous

Church of Jesus Christ of Latter-Day Saints, M. Batemen

Citizens Advisory Council for Public Welfare, Pittsburgh, D. Garner

Citizens Jury on Welfare Reform, Minneapolis, J. Dooley

Written testimony only:

American Association for the Advancement of Retired Persons

Christian Science Committee on Publication for Maryland, D. Burman

Christian Science Committee on Publication

League of Women Voters of Chicago

Note: This list does not include members and delegates to the U.S. Congress who testified or officials from the Clinton administration. The first name listed is the person who first testified for the organization. Thereafter, repeat oral and written testimony by a group representative is noted, although the spokesperson may be different. There inevitably is some subjectivity in assigning groups to categories. I tried to do so by what seemed to be the actor's or organization's primary emphasis.

Sources: Witness and testimony submission lists from welfare-related congressional hearings between January 1995 and August 1996. See Appendix B for complete list of hearings.

Appendix D

Witness Lists for Maryland Hearings[a]

1996 SESSION

I. Senate

FINANCE COMMITTEE

A. SB 238 ("Aid to Families with Dependent Children—Application for Child Support Services—Eligibility"—died in committee)

February 7, 1996:

1. G. Higginbotham and J. Blanton, Maryland Department of Human Resources (DHR), against
2. L. Beauregard, Christian Services USA (CSUSA), for

B. SB 248 ("Work, Not Welfare, Tax Incentives"—signed into law)

February 23, 1996:

1. P. Tiburzi and M. Gordon, Work Not Welfare Coalition, for
2. J. McDermott and J. Zielinski, APG, Inc., for
3. B. Schlossberg, Murry's, Inc., for
4. M. Rosendorf, Hair Cuttery, for
5. H. Barnett, National Association for the Advancement of Colored People (NAACP) of Maryland, for
6. C. Gallion, Maryland DHR, for
7. G. Burner, Maryland Chamber of Commerce, for
8. T. Saquella, Maryland Retailers Association, for

C. SB 778 (Welfare Innovation Act of 1996—comprehensive overhaul)

March 14, 1996:

1. S. Savner, Center for Law and Social Policy, Washington, D.C., no position
2. A. Boer, Associated Catholic Charities, no position
3. K. Goatley, Maryland Food Committee, against
4. A. Ciekot, Action for Homeless, against
5. K. Appleby, Maryland Catholic Conference, against
6. L. Meade, Welfare Advocates, against
7. Maryland Committee for Children, against
8. S. Morgan and S. Buckingham, Maryland Legislative Council of Social Workers (NASW-Md.), for with changes
9. J. Surr, Maryland Association for Education of Young Children, against
10. B. Seabolt, American Academy of Pediatrics, for with changes
11. W. Curry, Prince George's County Executive
12. B. McCann, Howard County Department of Social Services, for
13. L. Fox, E. Russell et al., Maryland DHR, for
14. D. Trumble, Maryland Interfaith Legislative Committee, against
15. B. Smith, Presbytery of Baltimore, "has concerns" (registered, but no show)
16. M. Sanderson, Maryland Association of Counties, against unless amended
17. L. Beauregard, CSUSA, for
18. L. Kauffman, for
19. R. Goodman, Maryland Department of Housing and Community Development, no position
20. E. Russell, Maryland Association of Social Service Directors (written only)
21. Maryland Chamber of Commerce (written only re: child support requirements)
22. County Council of Howard County (written only)
23. Carroll County Department of Social Services Advisory Board (written only)

II. House of Delegates

Appropriations Committee

A. HB 1061

February 29, 1996:

1. J. Levin-Epstein, Center for Law and Social Policy, Washington, D.C., no position
2. K. Appleby, Maryland Catholic Conference, against
3. A. Ciekot, Action for the Homeless, against
4. K. Goatley, Md. Food Committee, against
5. M. Koplov (affiliation not marked, but on panel of advocates), against
6. M. Vanni, Energy Advocates, against
7. L. Meade, Welfare Advocates and Maryland Catholic Charities, against
8. V. Young and S. Buckingham, NASW-Md., for
9. V. Morris and E. Hagen, Maryland Department of Housing and Community Development, for
10. B. Smith, Presbytery of Baltimore, against
11. R. May, Maryland Department of Health and Mental Health, for
12. Collins, L. Fox, E. Russell, and D. Brackington, Maryland DHR, for
13. J. Surr, Association for the Education of Young Children, against
14. H. Bodgan, A. Palmer, City of Baltimore, against
15. P. Roddy, Baltimore County, against
16. M. Sanderson, Maryland Association of Counties, against
17. M. Cullman, Maryland Interfaith Legislative Committee, against
18. B. Seabolt, American Academy of Pediatrics, against
19. J. Siegel, Community Ministries of Montgomery County, against
20. F. Sossi, Maryland Association of Social Service Boards, for
21. P. Sabonis, Homeless Persons Representation Project, against
22. J. Jackson, Advocates for Children and Youth, against
23. L. Rogovin, Maryland Committee for Children, against
24. A. Jones, for

[This bill had no Senate hearings.]

B. SB 778[b] ("Welfare Innovation Act of 1996"—signed into law)

April 2, 1996:

1. J. Surr, Maryland Association for the Education of Young Children
2. Maryland Chamber of Commerce
3. Maryland Catholic Conference, against
4. Maryland Association of Counties
5. Advocates for Children and Youth
6. Maryland Department of Housing and Community Development
7. Maryland DHR
8. NASW-Md.
9. Baltimore Jewish Council
10. Maryland Interfaith Legislative Committee
11. Maryland Food Committee, against

C. HJ 15 ("Federal Rent and Welfare Asistance Programs"—died in committee)

March 21, 1996:

1. L. Beauregard, Christian Services USA, for

Judiciary Committee

D. HB 49 ("Family Law—Noncustodial Parent—Child Support"—reported unfavorably by committee)

January 24, 1996:

1. C. Layman, Maryland DHR
2. J. Norris, Children's Rights Council
3. Welfare Advocates (written only)

Ways and Means Committee

E. HB 1248 ("Work, Not Welfare, Tax Incentives"—cross-listed with SB 248—reported unfavorably by committee)

March 13, 1996: [no positions listed]

1. P. Tiburzi, Work Not Welfare Coalition
2. J. McDermott and J. Zielinski, APG, Inc.
3. B. Schlossberg, Murray's, Inc.
4. P. Berns, Maryland Nonprofits
5. C. Gallion, Maryland DHR
6. G. Burner, Maryland Chamber of Commerce

F. HB 1310 ("Work, Not Welfare, Tax Incentives—Insurance Premiums Taxes"—Governor vetoed because identical to conference version of SB 248)

March 13, 1996:

1. P. Tiburzi, Work Not Welfare Coalition
2. J. McDermott and J. Zielinski, APG, Inc.
3. B. Schlossberg, Murry's, Inc.
4. P. Berns, Maryland Nonprofits
5. C. Gallion, Maryland DHR
6. G. Burner, Maryland Chamber of Commerce
7. T. Saquella, Maryland Retailers Association

G. HB 248 ("Work, Not Welfare, Tax Incentives"—signed into law)

March 26, 1996:

1. P. Tiburzi, Work Not Welfare Coalition

1997 SESSION

I. Senate

FINANCE COMMITTEE

A. SB 186 ("State Lottery Prizes—Reimbursement for Public Assistance Benefits"—reported unsuccessfully by committee)

January 29, 1997:

1. C. Hynes, Maryland Lottery, against
2. L. Beauregard, against

B. SB 672 ("Family Investment Program—Earned Income Disregard"—died in committee)

February 19, 1997:

1. K. Appleby, Maryland Catholic Conference, for
2. L. Meade, Welfare Advocates, for
3. B. Weigel, Maryland Interfaith Legislative Committee, for
4. L. Fox, Maryland DHR, against
5. S. Buckingham, NASW-Md., for
6. K. Goatley, Maryland Food Committee and Action for the Homeless, for

7. J. Schmidt, Advocates for Children and Youth, for
8. Maryland Committee for Children, for (written only)
9. Maryland Jewish Alliance, for (written only)
10. B. Smith, Presbytery of Baltimore, for (written only)
11. J. Johnson, for (written only)
12. Maryland Alliance for the Poor, for (written only)
13. Francis Gallagher Services, for (written only)

C. SB 673 ("Maryland Individual Development Account Act"—died in committee)

Febuary 19, 1997:

1. L. Fox, Maryland DHR, against
2. S. Buckingham, NASW-Md., for
3. B. Warnke, Enterprise Foundation, for (written only)
4. B. Grossman, Corp. for Enterprise Development, Washington, D.C., for (written only)

D. SB 499 ("Welfare Innovation Act of 1997"—signed into law)

Febuary 19, 1997:

1. M. Rosenthal, Maryland Higher Education Commission, for
2. S. Esty and R. McInerney, American Federation of State, County, and Municipal Employees (AFSCME), Council 92, for with amendments
3. F. Bernstein, AFSCME, Washington, D.C., for with amendments
4. G. Middleton, et al., AFSCME Council 67, for with amendments
5. K. Appleby, Maryland Catholic Conference, for with amendments
6. D. Szabo, American Jewish Committee, for
7. A. Collins and L. Fox, Maryland DHR, for with amendments
8. B. Shiprock, Maryland Department of Health and Mental Health, for with amendments
9. P. McIntyre, Medical and Chirurgical Faculty of Maryland/CHASM, for with amendments
10. J. White and E. Gerity, NASW-Md.
11. Y. Gilchrist, Baltimore City Department of Social Services, for
12. P. Borenstein, Baltimore City Department of Health, for
13. B. Bessor, Action for Homeless/Coalition to End Hunger, for with amendments
14. L. Kallins, Maryland Jewish Alliance, for with amendments
15. L. Meade, Maryland Catholic Charities and Welfare Advocates, for with amendments
16. B. Weigel, Maryland Interfaith Legislative Committee, for with amendments

17. J. Schmidt, Advocates for Children and Youth, for
18. P. Townsend, Maryland Hospitals Association, for with amendments
19. L. Zumbrun, Howard County Department of Social Services, for with amendments
20. F. Nastri, J. Williams, and S. Alpert, DrugEnsic System, against
21. B. Benton, Howard County Board of Social Services, for with amendments
22. J. White, NASW-Md., for with amendments
23. B. Seabolt, American Academy of Pediatrics, for with amendments
24. N. Collins and K. Loughran, Maryland Association of Health Maintenance Organizations, against
25. P. Berns, Maryland Association of Nonprofit Organizations
26. V. McCann, Maryland State Treasurer's Office
27. Maryland Alliance for the Poor (written only)
28. Maryland Independent College and University Association (written only)
29. Greater Washington Americans for Democratic Action (written only)
30. Maryland Association of Community Colleges (written only)
31. University of Maryland (written only)
32. Presbytery of Baltimore (written only)

Budget and Taxation

A. SB 521 ("Work, Not Welfare, Enterprise Zone and New Job Creation Tax Credits—Tax Exempt Organization"—referred to interim study)

Febuary 12, 1997:

1. P. Berns, Maryland Nonprofits, for
2. E. Copus, Melwood Training Center, for
3. P. Marshall, NationsBank, for
4. G. Burner, Maryland Chamber of Commerce, for
5. C. Collins, Maryland Association of Community Action Agencies, for
6. B. Ewing, Maryland Food Bank, for
7. A. Coscia, Greater Baltimore Alliance, for
8. H. Cromwell, Maryland Association of Psychiatric Support Services, for
9. P. Townsend, Maryland Hospitals Association, for
10. J. Schmidt, Advocates for Children and Youth, for
11. G. Kormeny, First National Bank, for
12. R. Hoffman, Maryland Works, Inc., for

B. SB 446 ("Family Investment Program—Qualified Employment Opportunity Employees Newly Created Jobs"—unfavorably reported by committee)

March 5, 1997:

1. S. Esty, AFSCME Council 92 and BUILD, for with amendments
2. F. Bernstein, AFSCME, Washington, D.C., for with amendments
3. G. Middleton and J. Somerville, AFSCME Council 67, for with amendments
4. J. Lange, BUILD, for with amendments
5. P. Tiburzi, N. Gordon, and D. McKinney, Work Not Welfare Coalition, against
6. R. Larson, Maryland DHR, against
7. T. Saquella, Maryland Retailers Association, against
8. J. Katay, Maryland Classified Employees Association, for
9. G. Burner, Maryland Chamber of Commerce, against

C. HB 358 ("Social Services—Family Investment Program—Deductions from Assistance Payments to Pay Public Housing Authority"—signed by governor)

March 26, 1997:

1. L. Beauregard, CSUSA, for

II. House of Delegates

Appropriations Committee

A. HB 42 ("Family Investment Program"—died in committee)

January 23, 1997:

1. K. Appleby, Maryland Catholic Conference, for
2. S. Parrot, Center for Budget and Policy Priorities, Washington, D.C., for
3. L. Meade, Welfare Advocates, for
4. K. Mahon, Maryland DHR, against
5. J. Campbell, Baltimore City Office of Employment Development, for
6. L. Rogovin, Maryland Committee for Children, for
7. S. Buckingham, NASW-Md., for
8. A. Ciekot, Action for the Homeless and Maryland Food Committee, for
9. L. Beauregard, CSUSA, for

B. HJ 10 ("Restoration of Federal Support for Vulnerable Populations"—died in committee)

Febuary 18, 1997:

1. C. Marchand, ARC of Maryland, for
2. L. Kallins, Baltimore Jewish Council, for
3. K. Goatley, Maryland Food Committee, for
4. L. Meade, Welfare Advocates, for
5. K. Appleby, Maryland Catholic Conference, for
6. P. Townsend, Maryland Hospital Association, for
7. S. Buckingham, NASW-Md., for
8. B. Weigel, Maryland Interfaith Legislative Committee, for
9. L. Beauregard, Volunteer Veteran's Affairs, for
10. K. Mahon, Maryland DHR, for (written only)
11. B. Smith, Presbytery of Baltimore, for (written only)
12. Maryland Committee for Children, for (written only)
13. M. Bradyhouse, Catholic Charities (written only)
14. Maryland Department of Health and Mental Health (written only)
15. E. Rutner, Greater Washington Americans for Democratic Action, for (written only)

C. HB 653 ("Welfare Innovation Act of 1997"—cross-filed as SB 499, which passed)

Febuary 18, 1997:

1. A. Collins and L. Fox, Maryland DHR, for with amendments
2. P. Beilenson, Baltimore City, for
3. Y. Gilchrest, Baltimore City Department of Social Services, for
4. D. Miller, Greater Baltimore Committee, for
5. B. Shipnuck and T. Davis, Maryland Department of Health and Mental Health, for with amendments
6. P. Townsend, Maryland Hospital Association, for with amendments
7. S. Buckingham, NASW-Md., for
8. B. Weigel, Maryland Interfaith Legislative Committee, for
9. L. Kallins, Baltimore Jewish Council, for with amendments
10. K. Appleby, Maryland Catholic Conference, for with amendments
11. A. Ciekot, Action for the Homeless, for with amendments
12. L. Meade, Welfare Advocates, for with amendments
13. P. McIntyre, MEDCHI/CHASM
14. B. Seabolt, Maryland Chapter of American Academy of Pediatrics, for with amendments
15. B. Benton, Howard County Board of Social Services, for with amendments
16. V. McCann, State Treasurer's Office

17. P. Berns, Maryland Nonprofits, for
18. M. Rosenthal, Maryland Higher Education Commission, for with amendments
19. H. Gee, University of Maryland system, for with amendments
20. J. Schmidt, Advocates for Children and Youth, for with amendments
21. L. Beauregard, for
22. N. Collins, K. Loughran, E. Gwynn, Maryland Association of HMOs, against

D. HB 996 ("Maryland Individual Development Account Act"—bill withdrawn)

Febuary 18, 1997:

1. B. Hecht, Enterprise Foundation, for
2. B. Grossman, Corporation for Enterprise Development, Washington, D.C., for
3. S. Buckingham, NASW-Md., for
4. L. Fox, Maryland DHR, against
5. L. Beauregard, CSUSA, for

E. HB 1140 ("Family Investment Program" [includes anti–job-displacement measures]—died in committee)

Febuary 18, 1997:

1. P. Tiburzi, Work Not Welfare Coalition, against
2. T. Fields, RSC, against (registered view only)
3. D. McKinney, Pizza Hut, against (registered view only—no show)
4. S. Shanahan, Thrift Stores, Inc., against
5. L. Fox, Maryland DHR, against
6. T. Saquella, Maryland Retailers Association, against
7. J. Lange and B. Young, Maryland Industrial Areas Foundation, for
8. R. McInerney, S. Esty, et al., AFSCME Council 92, for
9. A. Hunt, Maryland Department of Labor, Licensing and Regulation, against (written only)
10. L. Beauregard, Washington Veterans Affairs, for
11. G. Burner, Maryland Chamber of Commerce, for (registered view only—no show)
12. L. Mules, Maryland Works, Inc., against (registered view only—no show)
13. Service Master Company, Downers Grove, Ill., against (written only)
14. Dyn Corp., Reston, Va., against (written only)
15. Lowes' Cos., Inc., North Wilkesboro, N.C., against (written only)
16. Hair Cuttery, Falls Church, Va., against (written only)

F. HB 1264 ("Welfare Reform—Temporary Employment"—bill withdrawn)

Febuary 27, 1997:

1. R. Larson, Maryland DHR, against
2. S. Esty, AFSCME Council 92, for with amendments
3. K. Goeller, Maryland Classified Employees Association
4. J. Irick, Maryland Department of Budget and Management, against

G. HB 1375 ("Welfare Reform—Legal Immigrants"—died in committee)

Febuary 27, 1997:

1. L. Kallins, Maryland Jewish Alliance, for (registered view only—no show)
2. D. Maker, Maryland DHR, for with amendments
3. J. Schmidt, Advocates for Children and Youth, for (no show)
4. L. Beauregard, CSUSA, for
5. B. Smith, Presbytery of Baltimore, for (no show)
6. Action for Homeless/Maryland Food Committee/Coalition to End Hunger, for (written only)
7. M. Kennedy, against (written only)

H. SB 499

March 24, 1997:

1. Maryland Department of Health and Mental Health
2. PrimeHealth Corporation, against
3. Maryland Food Committee, for
4. Maryland Classified Employees Association, for
5. Maryland Hospitals Association
6. L. Beauregard
7. American Academy of Pediatrics
8. City of Baltimore, Mayor's Office
9. Maryland Higher Education Commission
10. Presbytery of Baltimore
11. Maryland Catholic Conference
12. Maryland Association of HMOs
13. Action for the Homeless

Ways and Means Committee

A. HB 721 ("Work, Not Welfare, Enterprise Zone, and New Job Creation Tax Credits—Tax Exempt Organization"—referred to interim study by Senate committee)

Febuary 18, 1997 [no positions listed]:

1. P. Berns, Maryland Nonprofits
2. E. Copus, Melwood Training Center
3. P. Marshall, NationsBank
4. J. Schmidt, Advocates for Children and Youth
5. A. Coscia, Greater Baltimore Alliance
6. D. Hutto, Maryland Association of Community Services
7. A. Gross, Woodbourne Center
8. J. Lee, University of Maryland Medical System
9. C. Raggio, Independence NOW
10. K. Sokoya, Family Crisis Center of Prince George's County
11. L. Doyl, Maryland Association of Psychiatric Support Services, Inc.
12. R. Hoffmann, Maryland Works, Inc.
13. E. Garraway, Maryland Independent College and University Association (written)
14. L. Meade, Maryland Catholic Charities (written only)
15. H. Utz, Carroll County Chamber of Commerce (written only)
16. A. Ingram, Association of Community Services of Howard County (written only)

Note: If anything, this list may understate the activity of groups. In at least one case, hearings were mentioned on the legislature's website (www.mlis.state.md.us/), but no witness list was in the bill files from the Legislative Services Department.

Sources: Bill files from Legislative Services Department library; General Assembly website (www.mlis.state.md.us/), "Bills by Subject: Welfare—1996 Regular Session" and "Bills by Subject: Welfare—1997 Regular Session," for information on bill title and committee action; Department of Legislative Services audiotapes for Senate Finance Committee hearings on SB 754 (1996) and SB 499 (1997).

[a]Where available, witnesses' positions on the legislation are noted.

[b]The witness list contained in the bill file had not been filled out. As a rule, the House did not tape hearings, so I re-created this witness list by using copies of testimony contained in the file.

Appendix E

Witness Lists for Texas Hearings

1995, 74TH SESSION

I. House of Representatives

COMMITTEE ON HUMAN SERVICES

A. HB 844 (original comprehensive welfare bill)

February 13, 1995:

1. J. Machado, Austin, against
2. O. McMahan, Waco, for
3. C. Frye, Zion Child Development Center, San Antonio, for
4. D. Burgess, Father's Hotline, Belton, for
5. S. Wade, Sunshine Inn Day Care Center, Kerrville, for
6. J. Ruder, Austin, against
7. P. Bresette, Center on Public Policy Priorities (CPPP), Austin, against
8. J. Tucker, Texas Fathers for Equal Rights, Arlington, against
9. V. Browning, Travis County (Austin) Department of Human Services, against
10. D. Ruffner, Arlington, against
11. B. Aleshire, Travis County Judge, Austin, neutral
12. P. Edwards, Middle Rio Grande Development Council, Uvalde, neutral
13. B. Raiford, Texas Department of Human Services (DHS) commissioner, neutral resource

14. C. Childress, Office of the Attorney General, Child Support Division, neutral resource
15. B. Brower, Texas Legal Services Center, Austin, neutral
16. M. Morris, United Way of Texas, Austin, neutral
17. R. Washington, Texas Dept. of Health, Austin, neutral resource
18. S. Calzonheit, State Medicaid Office, Health and Human Services Commission (HHSC), neutral resource

February 27, 1995:

1. S. Urban, Plum, for
2. B. Raiford, DHS Commissioner, neutral resource
3. M. Henderson, DHS, neutral resource

B. HB 1863 (revised version, more "moderate")

March 8, 1995:

1. J. Sharp, Comptroller of Accounts, neutral resource
2. D. Friedholm, Interim Commissioner, Texas HHSC, neutral resource
3. R. Herskowitz, Comptroller's office, neutral resource
4. P. Bresette, CPPP, neutral
5. G. Enos, North American Morpho Systems, Inc., Austin, neutral
6. P. Coombes, Comptroller's office, neutral resource
7. J. Denton, DHS, neutral resource
8. O. McMahan, for
9. S. Garnett, The Arc of Texas, Fort Worth, for (supported employment provisions)
10. J. Sokolow, Advocacy Inc., Austin, for (supported employment provisions)
11. J. Cooley, Austin, for
12. G. Gonzales, Jr., against
13. B. Green, self and Texas Fathers Alliance, against
14. D. Schexnayder, University of Texas, neutral resource

March 29, 1995:

No testimony. Committee substitute quickly reported favorably and voted approved and passed to House floor with recommendation to pass.

II. Senate

Health and Human Services Committee

A. SB 62 ("Learnfare" bill, to require recipients to attend school to get benefits—died)

March 22, 1995:

1. B. Raiford, DHS Commissioner, resource witness
2. P. Bresette, CPPP, neutral
3. S. Noble, Texas Women's Political Caucus, Austin, registered against
4. L. Lanham, National Association of Social Workers (NASW), Austin, registered against
5. H. Riddering, Texas National Organization for Women (NOW), registered against
6. M. Harris, American Association of Retired Persons (AARP), registered against

B. SB 554 (to require minor parents to live at home or with other adults)

March 22, 1995:

1. P. Bresette, CPPP, neutral
2. S. Noble, Texas Women's Political Caucus, against
3. J. Cooley, for
4. R. Hunt, Teen Parents of Texas, Austin, neutral
5. E. Rodriguez, Teen Parents of Texas, neutral
6. L. Lanham, NASW, registered against
7. H. Riddering, Texas NOW, registered against
8. B. Raiford, DHS Commissioner, registered resource witness

C. SB 22 (comprehensive welfare bill based on Comptroller's "Partnership" report)

March 22, 1995:

1. J. Sharp, Comptroller, resource witness
2. P. Bresette, CPPP, for
3. L. Brown, Coalition of Texans with Disabilities, Austin, for
4. J. Tucker, Texas Fathers Alliance, for
5. M. Bright, The Arc of Texas, for
6. J. Sokolow, Advocacy, Inc., for
7. R. Hunt, Teen Parents, for
8. E. Rodriguez, Teen Parents, for
9. L. Shefman, NASW, for
10. L. Lanham, NASW-Tex., for

11. P. Coombes, Comptroller's Office, neutral resource
12. C. Alexander, Comptroller's Office, neutral resource
13. D. Myers, Texas Commission for the Deaf and Hearing Impaired, neutral resource
14. B. Bower, Houston Welfare Rights Organization, written testimony on
15. P. Brown, Houston Welfare Rights Organization, registered for
16. M. Harris, AARP, Round Rock, registered against
17. B. Raiford, DHS Commissioner, registered resource witness

March 29, 1995:

1. B. Raiford, DHS Commissioner, neutral resource

D. Committee Substitute HB 1863

April 12, 1995:

1. D. Burgess, Texas Fathers for Legal Rights, Belton, against
2. J. Tucker, Texas Fathers Alliance, Fort Worth, against
3. P. Bresette, CPPP, registered neutral
4. C. Alexander, Comptroller's Office, registered neutral resource
5. P. Coombes, Comptroller's Office, registered neutral resource

1997, 75TH SESSION PUBLIC HEARINGS

I. House of Representatives

Committee on Human Services

A. March 31, 1997, Public Hearing:

1. HB 1439 (to establish a cashless welfare system and restrict what recipients may spend money on, preventing TANF money to be used for "sin" commodities such as cigarettes, lottery tickets, or alcohol—passed)

1. B. Bower, for Mary Lovings (Houston Welfare Rights Organization), testifying against
2. P. Bresette, CPPP, against
3. A. Dieter, Gray Panthers, against
4. A. Lovel, Comptroller, neutral
5. D. Shelton, Texas Fathers Alliance, neutral
6. C. Flynn, registered against
7. J. Heffernon, registered against
8. L. Hernandez, NASW, registered against
9. R. Ambrosino, DHS, neutral resource
10. R. Arsenault, neutral

2. HB 1909 (relating to methods used to extend the period of supported employment for recipients of TANF—passed but no funding)

1. B. Bower, for Mary Lovings (Houston Welfare Rights Organization), for
2. P. Bresette, CPPP, for
3. C. Flynn, registered for
4. J. Heffernon, registered for
5. J. Denton, DHS, neutral resource

3. HB 2125 (to create pilot program to establish recipient individual development accounts—died in committee)

1. B. Bower, for Mary Lovings (Houston Welfare Rights Organization), for
2. P. Bresette, CPPP, for
3. C. Flynn, self, registered for
4. J. Heffernon, self, registered for
5. J. Denton, DHS, neutral resource

4. HB 942 (to institute a family cap—died)

1. B. Bower, for Mary Loving (Houston Welfare Rights Organization), against
2. P. Bresette, CPPP, against
3. R. Daly, Texas Catholic Conference (TCC), against
4. A. Dieter, Gray Panthers, against
5. J. Denton, DHS, neutral resource
6. A. Hardy, AARP, registered for
7. C. Flynn, registered against
8. J. Heffernon, registered against
9. N. Engman, Texans Care for Children, registered against
10. J. Jacobson, American Civil Liberties Union (ACLU), registered against
11. L. McGiffert, Consumers Union, registered against
12. H. Baylor, TWC, registered as neutral resource

5. HB 1784 (to roll back benefits for two-parent families and give bonus for working recipients—died in Senate committee)

1. P. Bresette, CPPP, against
2. A. Dieter, Gray Panthers, against
3. C. Flynn, registered against

4. J. Heffernon, registered against
5. J. Denton, DHS, registered as neutral resource

6. HB 2508 (to conduct pilot project and study on finger-imaging in electronic benefits transfer program—died, but passed as rider to appropriations bill)

1. P. Bresette, CPPP, against
2. B. Bower, Mary Lovings (Houston Welfare Rights Organization), against
3. A. Dieter, Gray Panthers, against
4. C. Alexander, Comptroller, neutral resource
5. R. Ambrosino, DHS, neutral resource
6. D. Schexnayder, University of Texas, neutral resource
7. T. Trimble, Acting Commissioner of DHS, neutral resource
8. M. Winfree, WIC program/Texas Department of Health, neutral resource
9. C. Courtney, Texas Retailers Association, registered for
10. C. Flynn, registered against
11. J. Heffernon, registered against
12. R. Arsenault, registered on
13. A. Lovel, Comptroller, registered as neutral resource

7. HB 202 (criminal history and drug use screening of public assistance applicants—died in House committee)

1. D. Shelton, Texas Fathers Alliance, for
2. Rep. B. Solomons, for
3. B. Bower, Mary Lovings (Houston Welfare Rights Organization), against
4. P. Bresette, CPPP, against
5. A. Dieter, Gray Panthers, against
6. J. Denton, DHS, neutral resource
7. A. Hardy, AARP, registered for
8. S. Vaughn, AARP, registered for
9. C. Flynn, registered against
10. J. Heffernon, registered against
11. J. Jacobsen, ACLU of Texas, registered against
12. J. Reese, TAMI, registered against

8. HB 2678 (to require TANF applicant to provide proof of responsibility for each child receiving assistance—died)

1. P. Bresette, CPPP, neutral
2. J. Denton, DHS, netural rosource

9. HB 3428 (assistance to victims of domestic violence, allowing implementation of "family violence option" in federal welfare legislation—passed, effective September 1, 1997)

1. P. Cole, Texas Council on Family Violence, for
2. P. Bresette, CPPP, registered for
3. C. Flynn, registered for
4. J. Heffernon, registered for
5. L. McGiffert, Texas Council on Family Violence, registered for
6. R. Arsenault, registered neutral

10. HB 3431 (assistance to certain legal immigrants—died in committee)

1. W. Beardall, Texas Appleseed Advocacy Fund, for
2. B. Bower, Mary Lovings (Houston Welfare Rights Organization), for
3. A. Dunkelberg, CPPP, for
4. K. Fleshman, UNIR, for
5. L. Hernandez, NASW-Tex., for
6. J. Moritz, DHS, neutral resource
7. D. Austin, registered for
8. R. Daly, TCC, registered for
9. C. Flynn, registered for
10. A. Hardy, AARP, registered for
11. A. Heiligenstein, Catholic Health Facilities/TCC, registered for
12. B. Kafka, ADAPT of Texas, registered for
13. D. Latimer, Texas HomesService for Aging, registered for
14. M. Magruder, Council for Developmental Disabilities, registered for
15. B. Markland, Advocacy, Inc., registered for
16. L. McGiffert, Consumers Union, registered for
17. D. Mintz, JFA, registered for
18. J. Romero, Mexican American Legal Defense and Education Fund (MALDEF), registered for
19. B. Sperry, Childrens' Hospital Association of Texas, registered for
20. S. Vaughn, AARP, registered for
21. C. Lyons, DHS, registered as neutral witness

11. HB 3528 (education and work of TANF parents under age 21 or with school-aged children—died in committee)

1. P. Bresette, CPPP, neutral
2. J. Denton, DHS, registered as neutral resource
3. J. Moritz, DHS, registered as neutral resource

B. April 14, 1997, Public Hearing:

1. HB 2777 (privatization of eligibility determination and service delivery—passed)

1. C. Stewart, HHSC, neutral resource

Economic Development Committee

A. April 1, 1997, Public Hearing:

1. HB 3116 (to prevent job displacement in wage supplementation program—governor vetoed)

1. W. Beardall, Appleseed Advocacy Fund (also Texas Rural Legal Aid), for
2. T. Donoho, State Employees' Union, for
3. R. Levy, Texas AFL-CIO, for
4. D. Simpson, AFSCME, for

2. HB 1639 ("Texans Work" program; same as SB 781—passed)

1. W. Beardall, Appleseed Advocacy Fund, for
2. P. Bresette, CPPP, for
3. R. Levy, Texas AFL-CIO, for
4. D. Pinkus, Small Business United, for
5. L. Dyson, TWC, neutral resource

B. April 15, 1997, Public Hearing:

1. HB 2928 (self-sufficiency fund for recipients; same as SB 1491—died)

1. P. Bresette, CPPP, for
2. Rep. G. Coleman, for

C. April 22, 1997, Public Hearing:

1. SB 1114 (to establish "wheels for work" pilot program for welfare recipients—passed, effective September 1997)

1. Rep. G. Coleman, for
2. P. Hall, TWC, neutral resource

D. May 13, 1997, Public Hearing:

1. SB 1262 (re: Provision of Employment and Training for Certain Public Assistance Recipients—passed)

1. D. Pinkus, Small Business United, for

2. P. Bresette, CPPP, for
3. Rep. E. Naishtat, for

2. SB 1263 (to provide information on EITC to low-income Texans—passed)

1. Rep. E. Naishtat, for
2. L. Macias, TWC, neutral resource

II. Senate

Committee on Health and Human Services

A. March 26, 1997, Public Hearing:

1. SB 1114 ("wheels for work" pilot—passed)

1. P. Bresette, CPPP, for
2. P. Neuman, TWC, neutral resource

B. April 9, 1997, Public Hearing:

1. SB 1263 (to provide information, assistance to apply for EITC—passed, effective September 1, 1997)

1. P. Bresette, CPPP, for
2. P. Hall, TWC, neutral resource
3. F. Moore, on

2. SB 1262 (employment and training programs—passed, effective September 1, 1997)

1. P. Bresette, CPPP, for
2. P. Hall, TWC, neutral resource
3. C. Rush, Family Health Foundation, registered for

C. April 23, 1997, Public Hearing:

1. SB 775 (eligibility requirements for assistance—died in committee)

1. P. Littles, Texas AFL-CIO, against
2. I. Davila, TWC, neutral resource
3. R. Krzesniak, Texas Department of Health, neutral resource

D. May 14, 1997, Public Hearing:

1. HB 1439 (restricting how TANF recipients may spend benefits—passed)

1. B. Bower, Texas Legal Services, on
2. P. Bresette, CPPP, on

2. HB 2777 (privatization of welfare services—passed)

1. R. Evans, Texas State Employees Union, El Paso, against
2. M. Gross, Texas State Employees Union, Austin, against
3. M. Kinsey, CPPP, against
4. S. Noble, League of Women Voters, against
5. W. Beardall, Texas Appleseed Advocacy Fund, on
6. L. Hernandez, NASW-Tex., on
7. R. Levy, Texas AFL-CIO, on
8. L. McGiffert, Consumers Union, on
9. S. Thonton, Texas Impact, on
10. L. Hudson, Texas Department of Health, neutral resource
11. M. McKinney, HHSC, neutral resource

C. May 16, 1997, Public Hearing:

1. HB 1909 (extending transitional assistance—passed but not funded)

1. P. Bresette, CPPP, for
2. B. Bower, Houston Welfare Rights Organization, for

2. HB 942 (to institute family cap—died)

1. P. Bresette, CPPP, against

FINANCE COMMITTEE

A. March 24, 1997, Public Hearing:

1. SB 781 (to create "Texans Work" program involving wage subsidy from JOBS funds—passed, effective September 1, 1997)

1. P. Bresette, CPPP, for
2. R. Levy, Texas AFL-CIO, for
3. R. Bonilla, Comptroller's Office, neutral resource
4. L. Dyson, TWC, neutral resource
5. C. Alexander, Comptroller's Office, neutral resource
6. J. Shahin, DHS, neutral resource

B. April 7, 1997, Public Hearing:

1. SB 781 (continued)

1. L. Macias, TWC, neutral resource

2. C. Nadig, TWCC, neutral resource
3. S. Kibby, Texas PTA, for
4. C. Alexander, Comptroller's office, neutral resource
5. E. Coleman, Comptroller's office, neutral resource
6. B. Graves, DHS, neutral resource

C. April 17, 1997, Public Hearing:

1. SB 1491 (same as HB 2928)

1. P. Bresette, CPPP, for
2. P. Hall, TWC, neutral resource

Appendix F

Witness Lists for North Dakota Hearings

1995, 54TH SESSION

I. Senate

Human Services Committee

A. SB 2035 (TEEM pilot project and waiver request for service integration)

January 10, 1995:

1. J. Smith, Legislative Council
2. K. Iverson, Department of Human Services (DHS)
3. W. Anderson, DHS
4. B. Wessman, Commissioner of DHS
5. C. Daniels, Stutsman County Director of Social Services, representing Directors' Association
6. C. Jackson, People Escaping Poverty Project (PEPP), for[a]
7. P. Ringuette, North Dakota Catholic Conference, for
8. D. Houdek, Welfare Advisory Board, for

II. House of Representatives

APPROPRIATIONS COMMITTEE
HUMAN RESOURCES SUBCOMMITTEE

A. SB 2035 (TEEM pilot project and waiver request for service integration)

March 8, 1995:

1. K. Iverson, DHS, for
2. B. Wessman, DHS commissioner, for
3. D. Schempp, PEPP, for
4. P. Ringuette, North Dakota Catholic Conference, for
5. S. Jackson, PEPP member and self, for
6. M. Anderson, for
7. J. Neucomb, for
8. S. Seeberg, Legal Assistance of North Dakota, for
9. D. Hanson, Jackson's son, for
10. S. Jackson, Jackson's daughter, for
11. K. Jackson, Jackson's daughter, for
12. E. Anderson, Anderson's daughter, for

FULL APPROPRIATIONS COMMITTEE

March 10, 1995:

No testimony—appeared to be committee meeting rather than hearing.

1997, 55TH SESSION

I. House of Representatives

HUMAN SERVICES COMMITTEE

A. HB 1226 (Adaptation of TEEM to federal bill's requirements)

January 21, 1997:

1. B. Wessman, DHS executive director, for
2. W. Strate, Child Support Enforcement at DHS, for
3. W. Anderson, DHS, for
4. K. Iverson, DHS, for
5. D. Painte, Director of North Dakota Indian Affairs Commission
6. S. Papineau, R-Kids, against
7. P. Papineau, R-Kids, against

8. T. Towne, against
9. S. Beehler, R-Kids, against
10. D. Biesheuvel, R-Kids, against
11. K. Kietel, against
12. C. Dodson, North Dakota Catholic Conference

February 5, 1997 (Joint hearing with Appropriations Committee):

1. Sheri Steisel, National Conference of State Legislatures, at committee invitation

February 12, 1997:

1. W. Anderson, DHS
2. W. Strate, DHS
3. T. Traynor, North Dakota Association of Counties
4. C. Dodson, North Dakota Catholic Conference

February 17, 1997:

1. W. Anderson, DHS
2. T. Traynor, North Dakota Association of Counties
3. C. Dodson, North Dakota Catholic Conference

I. Senate

Human Services Committee

A. HB 1226

March 4, 1997:

1. B. Wessman, DHS executive director
2. W. Anderson, DHS deputy director
3. K. Iverson, DHS TEEM
4. W. Strate, Child Support Enforcement, DHS
5. R. Indvik, North Dakota Clerk of the Court Association
6. B. Carlisle, opposed
7. D. Bieshauvel, R-Kids
8. M. Kottre
9. S. Beehler, R-Kids
10. M. Foss, North Dakota Bankers' Association
11. T. Smith, American Council of Life Insurance
12. B. Palecek and L. Isakson, North Dakota Council on Abused Women's Services
13. C. Dodson, North Dakota Catholic Conference
14. L. Cummings, Three Affiliated Tribes/Fort Berthold Reservation
15. V. Hagen-Pond, Right-to-Life Organization
16. K. Hogan, Cass County Social Services director and Reg. V Welfare Reform Task Force

17. T. Traynor, North Dakota Association of Counties (written only)
18. D. Schempp, PEPP director (written only)
19. S. Jackson (PEPP member—written only)
20. J. Maire (PEPP member—written only)
21. A. Brunelle (PEPP member—written only)
22. T. Menge (PEPP member—written only)
23. C. Smith (PEPP member—written only)
24. T. Christianson (PEPP member—written only)

March 11, 1997:

1. C. Bennett, DHS Child Care
2. J. Hougen, DHS

March 19, 1997:

1. W. Anderson, DHS (written)
2. J. Opp, DHS
3. T. Traynor, North Dakota Association of Counties
4. K. Hogan, Cass County Social Services director, Reg. V Welfare Reform Task Force
5. M. Sach, Williams/McKenzie Counties

March 26, 1997:

1. W. Strate, DHS Child Support Enforcement
2. T. Traynor, North Dakota Association of Counties
3. J. Gange, State Supreme Court (staff)

Note: It is not always apparent from legislative records which hearings were public and which were simply committee meetings at which public testimony was not invited. I include hearings and meetings at which people other than legislators spoke, as indicated by committee minutes. This approach might miss hearings at which no one testified, but it also is likely to include committee meetings where only selected DHS staffers were invited for educational purposes. Also, I do not include testimony by House or Senate members.

[a]If clearly indicated in the minutes, position on the bill is indicated. If not, nothing is noted.

Abbreviations

AARP	American Association of Retired Persons
ACIR	Advisory Commission on Intergovernmental Relations
ACLU	American Civil Liberties Union
ACT	Achieving Change for Texans
ADC	Aid to Dependent Children
AEI	American Enterprise Institute
AFDC	Aid to Families with Dependent Children
AFDC-UP	Aid to Families with Dependent Children Unemployed Parent program
AFL-CIO	American Federation of Labor-Congress of Industrial Organizations
AFSCME	American Federation of State, County, and Municipal Employees
ALEC	American Legislative Exchange Council
APHSA	American Public Human Services Association
APWA	American Public Welfare Association
BUILD	Baltimoreans United in Leadership Development
CAP	Community Action Program
CAWS	Council on Abused Women's Services (N.D.)
CBPP	Center on Budget and Policy Priorities
CDF	Children's Defense Fund
CHIP	Children's Health Insurance Program
CLASP	Center for Law and Social Policy
CPI-U	Consumer Price Index for all Urban Consumers
CPPP	Center on Public Policy Priorities (Tex.)
CSG	Council of State Governments

CWL	Child Welfare League of America
DALP	Disability Assistance and Loan Program (Md.)
DGA	Democratic Governors' Association
DHR	Department of Human Resources (Md.)
DHS	Department of Human Services (Tex., N.D.)
DLC	Democratic Leadership Council
EBT	electronic benefits transfer
EDS	Electronic Data Systems
EITC	earned income tax credit
FAP	Family Assistance Plan
FSA	Family Support Act of 1988
FY	fiscal year
GAO	U.S. General Accounting Office
GNDA	Greater North Dakota Association
HEW	U.S. Department of Health, Education, and Welfare
HHS	U.S. Department of Health and Human Services
HHSC	Health and Human Services Commission (Tex.)
HMO	health maintenance organization
JOBS	Job Opportunity and Basic Skills
JTPA	Job Training Partnership Act
LBB	Legislative Budget Board (Tex.)
LIHEAP	Low-Income Home Energy Assistance Program
MALDEF	Mexican-American Legal Defense Fund
MDRC	Manpower Demonstration Research Corporation
MIAF	Maryland Industrial Areas Foundation
MIS	management information system
MLL	Minimum Living Level (Md.)
NAACP	National Association for the Advancement of Colored People
NACo	National Association of Counties
NASW	National Association of Social Workers
NCSL	National Conference of State Legislatures
NDCC	North Dakota Catholic Conference
NEW	Native Employment Works
NFIB	National Federation of Independent Businesses

NGA	National Governors' Association
NGO	nongovernmental organization
NOW	National Organization for Women
NPL	Nonpartisan League
NWRO	National Welfare Rights Organization
OBRA	Omnibus Budget Reconciliation Act of 1981
PAC	political action committee
PEPP	People Escaping Poverty Project
PPI	Progressive Policy Institute
PPT	Putting the Pieces Together
PRA	personal responsibility agreement
PRWORA	Personal Responsibility and Work Opportunity Reconciliation Act of 1996
RGA	Republican Governors' Association
SSI	Supplemental Security Income
TANF	Temporary Assistance for Needy Families
TCA	temporary cash assistance
TEEM	Training, Employment, Education and Management
TIAF	Texas Industrial Areas Foundation
TIES	Texas Integrated Enrollment Services
TWC	Texas Workforce Commission
UAW	United Auto Workers
USCC	United State Catholic Conference
USDA	U.S. Department of Agriculture
WIA	Workforce Investment Act
WIC	Supplemental Feeding Program for Women, Infants, and Children
WtW	Welfare to Work Grant Program of 1997

Selected Bibliography

Abney, Glen, and Thomas Lauth. "Interest Group Influence in the States: A View of Subsystem Politics." Paper presented at American Political Science Association annual meeting, Washington, D.C., August 1986.

Balz, Dan, and Ronald Brownstein. *Storming the Gates: Protest Politics and the Republican Revival.* Waltham, Mass.: Little, Brown and Co., 1996.

Bane, Mary Jo, and David T. Ellwood. *Welfare Realities*. Cambridge, Mass.: Harvard University Press, 1994.

Beer, Samuel H. "In Search of a New Public Philosophy." In *The New American Political System*, edited by Anthony King. Washington, D.C.: American Enterprise Institute, 1980.

Berry, Jeffrey M. *Feeding Hungry People*. New Brunswick, N.J.: Rutgers University Press, 1984.

———. *The Interest Group Society*. Boston: Little, Brown and Co., 1984.

Berry, Jeffrey M., Kent E. Portney, and Ken Thomson. "The Political Behavior of Poor People." In *The Urban Underclass*, edited by Christopher Jencks and Paul E. Peterson. Washington, D.C.: Brookings Institution Press, 1991.

Blank, Rebecca M. *It Takes a Nation: A New Agenda for Fighting Poverty*. Princeton, N.J.: Princeton University Press, 1997.

Bowlby, John. *Attachment and Loss*, Vols. 1 and 2. London: Hogarth Press and Institute of Psychoanalysis, 1969, 1973.

Bresette, Patrick Joseph. "The Evolution of Time-Limited AFDC Benefits in Texas: Rhetoric, Reform and Reality." Master of Public Affairs professional report, University of Texas at Austin, May 1996.

Burke, Vincent J., and Vee Burke. *Nixon's Good Deed*. New York: Columbia University Press, 1974.

Burton, Linda, Andrew J. Cherlin, Judith Francis, Robin Jarrett, James Quane, Constance Williams, and N. Michelle Stem Cook. "What Welfare Recipients and the Fathers of Their Children Are Saying About Welfare Reform." June 1998. Available at www.jhu.edu/~welfare/welfare.pdf.

Cammisa, Anne Marie. *Governments as Interest Groups*. Westport, Conn.: Prager, 1995.

Carey, John M., Richard G. Niemi, and Lynda W. Powell. *Term Limits in the State Legislatures*. Ann Arbor: University of Michigan Press, 2000.

Center on Budget and Policy Priorities. "The Safety Net Delivers: The Effects of Government Benefit Programs in Reducing Poverty." Washington, D.C.: Center on Budget and Policy Priorities, 15 November 1996.

———. "Poverty Rates Fall, But Remain High for a Period with Such Low Unemployment." Available at www.cbpp.org/9-24-98pov.htm (accessed 8 March 1999).

Center for Community Change. "Church and Neighborhood: BUILD-ing Beyond Congregations," organizing newsletter, no. 12, January 1999.
Center for Public Policy Priorities (CPPP). "Welfare Reform Watch." Austin, Tex.: CPPP, 25 July 1995.
———."The Policy Page: Welfare Reform Legislation in the Last Days of the Session, No. 49." Austin, Tex.: CPPP, 23 May 1997.
———. "The Policy Page: The TANF Block Grant and the State Budget, No. 50." Austin, Tex.: CPPP, 1 August 1997.
———. "The Policy Page: Privatization of Health and Human Services Eligibility Determination, No. 56." Austin, Tex.: CPPP, 1 September 1997.
———. "Devolution: Welfare Reform." Austin, Tex.: CPPP, September 1997.
———. "Devolution: Welfare-to-Work Programs." Austin, Tex.: CPPP, September 1997.
———. "Devolution: Impact on Immigrants." Austin, Tex.: CPPP, September 1997.
———. "Devolution: Child Care." Austin, Tex.: CPPP, 1 September 1997.
———. "A Brief Background on Welfare Reform and Welfare-to-Work Policy Changes: Challenges and Opportunities." Austin, Tex.: CPPP, 19 February 1998.
———. "The Policy Page, No. 87." Austin, Tex.: CPPP, 20 May 1999.
———. "The Policy Page, No. 93." Austin, Tex.: CPPP, 30 September 1999.
———. "The Policy Page: Crouching Budget, Hidden TANF," No. 127. Austin, Tex.: CPPP, 20 April 2001.
Cherlin, Andrew, and Pamela Winston, et al. *What Welfare Recipients Know about the New Rules and What They Have to Say about Them*. Policy Brief 00-1. Baltimore: Johns Hopkins University, Welfare, Children and Families: A Three City Study, 2000.
Ciglar, Allan J., and Burdett A. Loomis. *Interest Group Politics*, 4th ed. Washington, D.C.: CQ Press, 1995.
Congressional Quarterly Almanacs, 1969–1996. Washington, D.C.: Congressional Quarterly, 1970–1997.
Congressional Quarterly's Who's Who in Congress, 1995, 104th Congress. Washington, D.C.: Congressional Quarterly, 1995.
Conlan, Timothy J. *New Federalism: Intergovernmental Reform from Nixon to Reagan*. Washington, D.C.: Brookings Institution Press, 1988.
———. *From New Federalism to Devolution: Twenty-Five Years of Intergovernmental Reform*. Washington, D.C.: Brookings Institution Press, 1998.
Cooke, Jacob E. *The Federalist*. Middletown, Conn.: Wesleyan University Press, 1961.
Coon, Randal C., JoAnn M. Thompson, and F. Larry Leistritz. *The State of North Dakota: Economic, Demographic, Public Service, and Fiscal Conditions*. Fargo: North Dakota State University, 1995.
Council on Economic Advisors. "The Effects of Welfare Policy and the Economic Expansion on Welfare Caseloads: An Update." 3 August 1999. Washington, D.C.: Council on Economic Advisors, 1999.
Dahl, Robert A. *A Preface to Democratic Theory*. Chicago: University of Chicago Press, 1956.
Davidson, Chandler. *Race and Class in Texas Politics*. Princeton, N.J.: Princeton University Press, 1990.
Donovan, John C. *The Politics of Poverty*. New York: Western Publishing Co., 1967.
Edsall, Thomas Byrne. "The Changing Shape of Power: A Realignment in Public Policy." In *The Rise and Fall of the New Deal Order*, edited by Steve Fraser and Gary Gerstle. Princeton, N.J.: Princeton University Press, 1989.
Elazar, Daniel J. *American Federalism: A View from the States*. New York: Thomas Y. Crowell, 1972.

Ellwood, David T. "When Bad Things Happen to Good Policies: Welfare Reform As I Knew It." *The American Prospect* (May–June 1996).

Ellwood, Deborah A., and Donald J. Boyd. *Changes in State Spending on Social Services Since the Implementation of Welfare Reform: A Preliminary Report*. Albany, N.Y.: Rockefeller Institute of Government, 2000. Available at www.rockinst.org.

Ferejohn, John. "A Tale of Two Congresses: Social Policy in the Clinton Years." In *The Social Divide*, edited by Margaret Weir. Washington, D.C.: Brookings Institution Press, 1998.

Friedman, Milton. *Capitalism and Freedom*. Chicago: University of Chicago Press, 1962, 1982.

Fox, Lynda G. "Briefing to the Joint Committee on Welfare Reform: Cash Assistance Caseload Trends," Maryland State General Assembly, 6 October 1998.

Gallagher, L. Jerome, Megan Gallagher, Kevin Perese, Susan Schreiber, and Keith Watson. *One Year After Welfare Reform: A Description of State Temporary Assistance for Needy Families (TANF) Decisions as of October 1997*. Occasional Paper no. 6. Washington, D.C.: Urban Institute, June 1998.

Gilens, Martin. *Why Americans Hate Welfare: Race, Media, and the Politics of Antipoverty Policy*. Chicago: University of Chicago Press, 2000.

Goleman, Daniel. *Emotional Intelligence*. New York: Bantam Books, 1995.

Gray, Virginia, and Herbert Jacobs. *Politics in the American States: A Comparative Analysis*, 6th ed. Washington, D.C.: CQ Press, 1996.

Gray, Virginia, Russell Hanson, and Herbert Jacobs. *Politics in the American States: A Comparative Analysis*, 7th ed. Washington, D.C.: CQ Press, 1999.

Greenberg, Mark, and Steve Savner. *The Final TANF Regulations: A Preliminary Analysis*. Washington, D.C.: Center on Law and Social Policy, May 1999.

Greenberg, Mark, et al. *Welfare Reauthorization: An Early Guide to the Issues*. Washington, D.C.: Center on Law and Social Policy, July 2000.

Grodzins, Morton. *The American System: A New View of Government in the United States*. Chicago: Rand McNally, 1966.

Grodzins, Morton, and Daniel Elazar. "Centralization and Decentralization in the American Federal System." In *A Nation of States: Essays on the American Federal System*, 2d ed., edited by Robert A. Goldwin. Chicago: Rand McNally College Publishing Co., 1974.

Gunther, Gerald. *Constitutional Law*, 12th ed. New York: Foundation Press, 1991.

Haider, Donald H. *When Governments Come to Washington*. New York: Free Press, 1974.

Hamilton, Alexander, James Madison, and John Jay. *The Federalist*. Edited by Jacob E. Cooke. Middletown, Conn.: Wesleyan University Press, 1961.

Hamley, Jeffrey. "An Introduction to the Federal Indian Boarding School Movement." *North Dakota History: Journal of the Northern Plains* 61 (spring 1994): 2–9.

Hamm, Keith E., and Charles W. Wiggins. "Texas: The Transformation from Personal to Informational Lobbying." In *Interest Group Politics in the Southern States*, edited by Ronald J. Hrebenar and Clive S. Thomas. Tuscaloosa: University of Alabama Press, 1992.

Handler, Joel F. *The Poverty of Welfare Reform*. New Haven, Conn.: Yale University Press, 1995.

Hartung, William D., and Jennifer Washburn. "Lockheed Martin: From Warfare to Welfare." *The Nation* (2 March 1998): 11–16.

Haveman, Robert, and Barbara Wolfe. "The Determinants of Children's Attainments: A Review of Method and Findings." *Journal of Economic Literature* (December 1995): 1829–78.

Heclo, Hugh. "Issue Networks and the Executive Establishment." In *The New American Political System*, edited by Anthony S. King. Washington, D.C.: American Enterprise Institute, 1978.

———. "The Political Foundations of Antipoverty Policy." In *Fighting Poverty: What Works and What Doesn't*, edited by Sheldon H. Danziger and Daniel H. Weinberg. Cambridge, Mass.: Harvard University Press, 1986.

Hedge, David M. *Governance and the Changing American States*. Boulder, Colo.: Westview Press, 1998.

Heinz, John P., Edward O. Laumann, Robert L. Nelson, and Robert H. Salisbury. *The Hollow Core*. Cambridge, Mass.: Harvard University Press, 1993.

Hero, Rodney E. *Faces of Inequality: Social Diversity in American Politics*. New York: Oxford University Press, 1998.

Hill, Kim Quaile. *Democracy in the Fifty States*. Lincoln: University of Nebraska Press, 1994.

Hill, Kim Quaile, and Kenneth R. Mladenka. *Texas Government: Politics and Economics*, 4th ed. Belmont, Calif.: Wadsworth Publishing Co., 1996.

Hochschild, Jennifer. *What's Fair?: American Beliefs about Distributive Justice*. Cambridge, Mass.: Harvard University Press, 1981.

———. *Race, Class, and the Soul of the Nation: Facing Up to the American Dream*. Princeton, N.J.: Princeton University Press, 1995.

Hovey, Harold A., and Kendra A. Hovey. *CQ's State Fact Finder 1997: Rankings Across America*. Washington, D.C.: CQ Press, 1997.

Howard, Thomas W. *The North Dakota Political Tradition*. Ames: Iowa State University Press, 1981.

Hrebenar, Ronald J., and Clive S. Thomas. *Interest Group Politics in the Southern States*. Tuscaloosa: University of Alabama Press, 1992.

———. *Interest Group Politics in the Northeastern States*. University Park: Pennsylvania State University, 1993.

———. *Interest Group Politics in the Midwestern States*. Ames: Iowa State University Press, 1993.

Hula, Kevin W. *Lobbying Together: Interest Group Coalitions in Legislative Politics*. Washington, D.C.: Georgetown University Press, 1999.

Imig, Douglas R. *Poverty and Power: The Political Representation of Poor Americans*. Lincoln: University of Nebraska Press, 1996.

Ivins, Molly, and Lou Dubose. *Shrub: The Short But Happy Political Life of George W. Bush*. New York: Random House, 2000.

Jencks, Christopher. *Rethinking Social Policy: Race, Poverty, and the Underclass*. Cambridge, Mass.: Harvard University Press, 1992.

Johnson, Cathy M. "Who Speaks for the Children: Representation in the Policy Process." Paper presented at American Political Science Association annual meeting, Washington, D.C., September 1994.

Kaiser/Harvard Program on the Public and Health/Social Policy. *Survey on Welfare Reform*. Menlo Park, Calif.: Henry J. Kaiser Family Foundation, January 1995.

Katz, Michael B. *The Undeserving Poor*. New York: Pantheon Books, 1989.

———. *The Price of Citizenship: Redefining the American Welfare State*. New York: Metropolitan Books, 2001.

Kellam, Susan. "A Conversation with Maryland's Lynda Fox." *Public Welfare* (spring 1996): 24–30.

Key, V. O., Jr. *Southern Politics in State and Nation, New Edition*. Knoxville: University of Tennessee, 1984.

King, Desmond S. "Citizenship as Obligation in the United States: Title II of the Family Support Act of 1988." In *The Frontiers of Citizenship*, edited by Ursula Vogel and Michael Moran. New York: Macmillan, 1991.

Kingdon, John W. "Ideas, Politics, and Public Policies." Paper presented at American Political Science Association annual meeting, Washington, D.C., September 1988.

———. *Agendas, Alternatives and Public Policies*. New York: HarperCollins, 1984, 1995.

Kraemer, Richard H., and Charldean Newell. *Essentials of Texas Politics*, 3d ed. St. Paul, Minn.: West Publishing Co., 1986.

Kraemer, Richard H., Charldean Newell, and David F. Prindle. *Texas Politics*, 6th ed. St. Paul, Minn.: West Publishing Co., 1996.

Larin, Kathryn, and Elizabeth C. McNichol. *Pulling Apart: A State-by-State Analysis of Income Trends*. Washington, D.C.: Center on Budget and Policy Priorities, 1997.

Layton, Charles, and Mary Walton. "Missing the Story at the Statehouse." *American Journalism Review* (July–August 1998).

Leach, Penelope. *Children First: What Society Must Do—and Is Not Doing—for Children Today*. New York: Vintage Books, 1995.

Leadership Directories, Inc. *State Yellow Book, Fall 1997*. New York: Leadership Directories, Inc., 1997.

Lemann, Nicholas. *The Promised Land: The Great Black Migration and How It Changed America*. New York: Vintage Books, 1992.

———. "Citizen 501(c)(3)." *Atlantic Monthly* (February 1997): 18–20.

———. "All Together Now?" *New Yorker*, 4 (December 2000): 49–53.

Levine, Phillip B., and David J. Zimmerman. "An Empirical Analysis of the Welfare Magnet Debate Using the NLSY." University of Wisconsin-Madison Institute for Research on Poverty Discussion Papers, DP #1098-96, July 1996.

Lieske, Joel. "Regional Subcultures of the United States." *Journal of Politics* 55 (November 1993): 888–913.

Lippincott, Ronald C., and Larry W. Thomas. "Maryland: The Struggle for Power in the Midst of Change, Complexity, and Institutional Constraints." In *Interest Group Politics in the Northeastern States*, edited by Ronald J. Hrebenar and Clive S. Thomas. University Park: Pennsylvania State University, 1993.

London, Rebecca, Courtney Smith, Kristin Porter, and Kendra Lodewick. *Evaluation of North Dakota's Training, Education, Employment, and Management (TEEM) Program, Final Report, 30 March 2000*. Berkeley Planning Associates for North Dakota Department of Human Services, available at www.acf.dhhs.gov/programs/opre/ndfr.htm.

Maryland Catholic Charities, Division of Community Services. "Welfare Reform: 15 Positive Policies, 15 Welfare Reform Issues Addressed by Advocates in Maryland." Available at www.catholiccharities.md.org/welfare.htm.

Maryland Department of Human Resources. "Report on Legislation Enacted During the 1998 Session." Available at www.dhr.state.md.us/dhr/profile.htm.

———. Written testimony of Lynda G. Fox, Deputy Secretary for Programs and Local Operations. "Briefing to the Joint Committee on Welfare Reform: Cash Assistance Caseload Trends," 6 October 1998.

Maryland Department of Legislative Services. *General Assembly of Maryland: List of Committees and Roster, 1998 Session*. Annapolis: Maryland Department of Legislative Services, 1998.

Maryland General Assembly. "Senate Bill 499, Enrolled Bill." Annapolis, Md.: Department of Legislative Services, 1997.

———. *Joint Committee on Welfare Reform: Report of the 1996 Interim*. Annapolis, Md.: Department of Fiscal Services, 1996.

———. *Maryland Session Laws of 1996*.

———. Bill files for 1995: SB 754. Annapolis, Md.: Legislative Services Reference Library.

———. Bill files for 1996: SB 238, SB 248, SB 778, HB 1061, HJ 15, HB 49, HB 1248, HB 1310, HB 248. Annapolis, Md.: Legislative Services Reference Library.

———. Bill files for 1997: SB 186, SB 672, SB 673, SB 499, SB 521, SB 446, HB 358, HB 42, HJ 10, HB 653, HB 996, HB 1140, HB 1264, HB 137, HB 721. Annapolis, Md.: Legislative Services Reference Library.

Maryland Governor's Commission on Welfare Policy. "For the Good of the Whole. . . : Making Welfare Work." Final Report. June 1994.

Maryland Governor's Press Office. "Maryland at the National Forefront in Welfare Reform Efforts and Initiatives." 30 June 1997.

———. "Comments by Governor Parris N. Glendening, Executive Order Signing: Displacement and Family Investment Program." 30 June 1997.

McConnell, Grant. *Private Power and American Democracy*. New York: Alfred A. Knopf, 1966.

McFarland, Andrew S. "Interest Groups and the Policymaking Process: Sources of Countervailing Power in America." In *The Politics of Interests*, edited by Mark P. Petracca. Boulder, Colo.: Westview Press, 1992.

Mead, Lawrence M. *The New Politics of Poverty*. New York: BasicBooks, 1992.

Melnick, R. Shep. *Between the Lines: Interpreting Welfare Rights*. Washington, D.C.: Brookings Institution Press, 1994.

Meyers, Marcia K. "Gaining Cooperation at the Front Lines of Service Delivery: Issues for the Implementation of Welfare Reform." *Rockefeller Reports*, no. 7. Albany, N.Y.: Rockefeller Institute of Government, State University of New York, June 12, 1998.

Milkis, Sidney M., and Michael Nelson. *The American Presidency: Origins and Development, 1776–1990*. Washington, D.C.: CQ Press, 1990.

Moffitt, Robert A., and Jennifer Roff. *The Diversity of Welfare Leavers*. Policy Brief 00-2. Baltimore: Johns Hopkins University, Welfare, Children and Families: A Three City Study, September 2000.

Moynihan, Daniel Patrick. *Maximum Feasible Misunderstanding*. New York: Free Press, 1969.

———. *The Politics of a Guaranteed Income*. New York: Random House, 1973.

Murray, Charles. *Losing Ground: American Social Policy, 1950–1980, Tenth Anniversary Edition*. New York: BasicBooks, 1994.

Nathan, Richard P. "Federalism—The Great 'Composition.'" In *The New American Political System*, 2d ed., edited by Anthony King. Washington, D.C.: American Enterprise Institute, 1990.

Nathan, Richard P., and Thomas L. Gais. "Overview Report: Implementation of the Personal Responsibility Act of 1996." Federalism Research Group, the Nelson A. Rockefeller Institute of Government. Albany: State University of New York, October 1998.

Newshour with Jim Lehrer. Transcript from "Strictly Business" (14 October 1996).

Nightingale, Demetra Smith, and Robert H. Haveman. *The Work Alternative*. Washington, D.C.: Urban Institute, 1995.

Norris, Donald F., and James X. Bembry. "Primordial Policy Soup, Bureaucratic Politics, and Welfare Policy Making in Maryland." *In The Politics of Welfare Reform*, edited by Donald F. Norris and Lyke Thompson. Thousand Oaks, Calif.: Sage Publications, 1995.

Norris, Donald F., and Lyke Thompson, eds. *The Politics of Welfare Reform*. Thousand Oaks, Calif.: Sage Publications, 1995.

North Dakota Catholic Conference (NDCC). "Welfare Reform in North Dakota." Prepared for National Association of State Catholic Conference Directors. Bismarck, N.D.: NDCC, 1997.

North Dakota Century Code. 1995, 1997.

North Dakota Department of Human Services, Children and Family Services Division. *North Dakota's Children: A Chartbook Perspective 1993*. Bismarck, N.D.: Department of Human Services, August 1993.

———. "Temporary Assistance for Needy Families (TANF): Policy Issues." Bismarck, N.D.: Department of Human Services, 4 March 1997.

———. "TEEM Project Summary." Bismarck, N.D.: Department of Human Services. Available at www. state.nd.us/hms/Teem_sum.htm (accessed December 1997).

North Dakota Legislative Assembly. Senate Concurrent Resolution No. 4010, 53rd Legislative Assembly. Bismarck, N.D.: Legislative Council Library, 1993.

———. Senate Concurrent Resolution No. 4067, 53rd Legislative Assembly. Bismarck, N.D.: Legislative Council Library, 1993.

———. Minutes of Human Resources Division of House Appropriations Committee on SB 2035, 54th Legislative Assembly. Bismarck, N.D.: Legislative Council Library, 1995.

———. Minutes of Senate Human Services Committee on SB 2035, 54th Legislative Assembly. Bismarck, N.D.: Legislative Council Library, 1995.

———. Minutes of Human Services Conference Committee on SB 2035, 54th Legislative Assembly. Bismarck, N.D.: Legislative Council Library, 1995.

———. Proposed House Bill No. 1226, #78211.0100, 55th Legislative Assembly, 1997.

———. Minutes of Senate Human Services Committee on HB 1226, 55th Legislative Assembly. Bismarck, N.D.: Legislative Council Library, 1997.

———. Minutes of House Human Services Committee on HB 1226, 55th Legislative Assembly. Bismarck, N.D.: Legislative Council Library, 1997.

———. Minutes of Human Services Conference Committee on HB 1226, 55th Legislative Assembly. Bismarck, N.D.: Legislative Council Library, 1997.

———. House Bill 1012, 55th Legislative Assembly. Bismarck, N.D.: Legislative Council Library, 1997.

———. House Bill 1041, 55th Legislative Assembly. Bismarck, N.D.: Legislative Council Library, 1997.

———. House Bill 1108, 57th Legislative Assembly, 2001. Available at 222.state.nd.us/lr/.

———. House Concurrent Resolutions 3031, 3032, and 3042, 55th Legislative Assembly. Bismarck, N.D.: Legislative Council Library, 1997.

———. Senate Concurrent Resolution 4030, 55th Legislative Assembly. Bismarck, N.D.: Legislative Council Library, 1997.

———. Minutes of Welfare Reform Interim Committee, 1997–1998. Available at www:state.nd.us/lr/minutes.html.

———. Minutes of Budget Committee on Human Resources, 1999–2000 Interim. Available at www:state.nd.us/lr/minutes.html.

North Dakota Office of Intergovernmental Assistance. Child care memo dated 6 March 1997. Bill files on HB 1226. Bismarck, N.D.: Legislative Council Library, 1997.

Olson, Mancur. *The Logic of Collective Action*. Cambridge, Mass.: Harvard University Press, 1965.

Osborne, David. *Laboratories of Democracy*. Boston: Harvard Business School Press, 1988.

Patterson, James T. *America's Struggle Against Poverty, 1900–1994*. Cambridge, Mass.: Harvard University Press, 1994.

Pedeliski, Theodore B. "North Dakota: Constituency Coupling in a Moralistic Political Culture." In *Interest Group Politics in the Midwestern States*, edited by Ronald J. Hrebrenar and Clive S. Thomas. Ames: Iowa State University Press, 1993.

Peterson, Paul E., and J. David Greenstone. *Race and Authority in Urban Politics: Community Participation and the War on Poverty*. Chicago: University of Chicago Press, 1973, 1976.

———. "Racial Change and Citizen Participation: The Mobilization of Low-Income Communities through Community Action." In *A Decade of Federal AntiPoverty Programs*, edited by Robert H. Haveman. New York: Academic Press, 1977.

———. *The Price of Federalism*. Washington, D.C.: Brookings Institution Press, 1996.

———. *City Limits*. Chicago: University of Chicago Press, 1981.

Peterson, Paul E., and Mark C. Rom. *Welfare Magnets: A New Case for a National Standard*. Washington, D.C.: Brookings Institution Press, 1990.

Petracca, Mark P. *The Politics of Interest: Interests Groups Transformed*. Boulder, Colo.: Westview Press, 1992.

Pindus, Nancy, et al. "Assessing the New Federalism: Income Support and Social Service for Low-Income People in Texas." Washington, D.C.: Urban Institute, 1998. Available at newfederalism.urban.org/html/Txincome.html (accessed March 1998).

Piven, Frances Fox, and Richard A. Cloward. *Regulating the Poor: The Functions of Public Welfare*. New York: Vintage Books, 1971.

———. *Poor People's Movements: Why They Succeed, How They Fail*. New York: Vintage Books, 1979.

Policy Research Project on Workforce Reform in Texas. *Building a Workforce Development System for Texas*. Lyndon B. Johnson School of Public Affairs, Policy Research Project Report, no. 126. Austin: University of Texas, 1997.

Primus, Wendall, Kathryn Porter, Margery Ditto, and Mitchell Kent. *The Safety Net Delivers*. Washington, D.C.: Center on Budget and Policy Priorities, 1996.

Primus, Wendall, Lynette Rawlings, Kathy Lavin, and Kathryn Porter. *The Initial Impacts of Welfare Reform on the Incomes of Single Mother Families*. Washington, D.C.: Center on Budget and Policy Priorities, 1999.

Quadagno, Jill. "Race, Class, and Gender in the U.S. Welfare State: Nixon's Failed Family Assistance Plan." *American Sociological Review* 55 (February 1990): 11–28.

———. *The Color of Welfare: How Racism Undermined the War on Poverty*. New York: Oxford University Press, 1994.

Reed, Adolph L., Jr. "The Underclass Myth." *The Progressive* 55 (1991): 18–20.

Remele, Larry. "Power to the People: The Nonpartisan League." In *The North Dakota Political Tradition*, edited by Thomas W. Howard. Ames: Iowa State University Press, 1981.

Rieder, Jonathan. "The Rise of the Silent Majority." In *The Rise and Fall of the New Deal Order*, edited by Steve Fraser and Gary Gerstle. Princeton, N.J.: Princeton University Press, 1989.

Rivlin, Alice M. *Reviving the American Dream: The Economy, the States and the Federal Government*. Washington, D.C.: Brookings Institution Press, 1992.

Robertson, David B., and Dennis R. Judd. *The Development of American Public Policy: The Structure of Policy Restraint*. Glenview, Ill.: Scott Foresman, 1989.

Robinson, Elwyn B. *History of North Dakota*. Institute for Regional Studies, North Dakota State University [undated]. Original edition, Lincoln: University of Nebraska Press, 1966.

Rodrigue, George. "Problems Reported in Privatizing Welfare." *Dallas Morning News*, 17 March 1997.

Rosenthal, Alan. *The Third House: Lobbyists and Lobbying in the States*. Washington, D.C.: CQ Press, 1993.

———. *The Decline of Representative Democracy: Process, Participation and Power in State Legislatures*. Washington, D.C.: CQ Press, 1998.

Rovner, Julie. "Draft Welfare Regulations Draw Fire from States." *Congressional Quarterly* (20 May 1989): 1191–94.

Salamon, Lester M. "The Stakes in the Rural South." *The New Republic* (February 20, 1971): 17–18.

Sarvasy, Wendy. "Reagan and Low-Income Mothers: A Feminist Recasting of the Debate." In *Remaking the Welfare State*, edited by Michael K. Brown. Philadelphia: Temple University Press, 1988.

Schattschneider, E. E. *The Semi-Sovereign People*. Hinsdale, Ill.: Dryden Press, 1975.

Schexnayder, Deanna T., et al. "Lone Star Image System Evaluation, Final Report." Austin: Center for the Study of Human Resources, University of Texas at Austin, August 1997.

Schick, Allen. *The Federal Budget: Politics, Policy, Process*. Washington, D.C.: Brookings Institution Press, 1995.

Schlozman, Kay Lehman, and John T. Tierney. *Organized Interests and American Democracy*. New York: Harper and Row, 1986.

Schneider, Mary Jane. *North Dakota Indians: An Introduction*. Dubuque, Iowa: Kendall/Hunt Publishing Co., 1994.

Schwarz, John E. *America's Hidden Success: A Reassessment of Public Policy from Kennedy to Reagan*, rev. ed. New York: W. W. Norton and Co., 1988.

Shanley, James. "Welfare Reform Will Create More Misery." *Tribal College Journal* 9 (winter 1997–98): 19–21.

Sharp, John. *A Partnership for Independence: Public Assistance Reform Options*. Austin: Texas Comptroller of Public Accounts, January 1995.

Skocpol, Theda. "The Limits of the New Deal System and the Roots of Contemporary Welfare Dilemmas." In *The Politics of Social Policy in the United States*, edited by Margaret Weir, Ann Shola Orloff, and Theda Skocpol. Princeton, N.J.: Princeton University Press, 1988.

———. *Protecting Soldiers and Mothers: The Political Origins of Social Policy in the United States*. Cambridge, Mass.: Belknap Press of Harvard University Press, 1992.

———. *Boomerang: Clinton's Health Security Effort and the Turn against Government in U.S. Politics*. New York: W. W. Norton and Co., 1996.

Skowroneck, Stephen. *The Politics Presidents Make: Leadership from John Adams to George Bush*. Cambridge, Mass.: Belknap Press of Harvard University Press, 1993.

Spurgin, Kathryn Brewer. "From Rhetoric to Reform: Enacting Welfare Reform in Texas, 1995." Master of Public Affairs professional report, University of Texas at Austin, December 1995.

State Legislative Leaders Foundation. *State Legislative Leaders: Keys to Effective Legislation for Children and Families*. Centerville, Mass.: State Legislative Leaders Foundation, 1995.

States News Service. "States News Briefs, North Dakota." (3 April 1997).

Stone, Deborah. *Policy Paradox: The Art of Political Decision Making*. New York: W. W. Norton and Co., 1997.

Storing, Herbert. *What the Anti-Federalists Were For*. Chicago: University of Chicago Press, 1981.

Super, David, et al. *The New Welfare Law*. Washington, D.C.: Center on Budget and Policy Priorities, 1996.

Teles, Steven M. *Whose Welfare? AFDC and Elite Politics*. Lawrence: University Press of Kansas, 1996.

Texas Conservative Coalition. *Task Force on Welfare Reform, Interim Report 73rd Legislature, Fall 1994*. Austin: Texas State Legislature, 1994.

Texas Department of Human Services. *Demographic Profile of TANF Caretakers, September 1997*. Austin, Tex.: Office of Programs Administration and Management Services, 20 February 1998.

———. *Demographic Profile of AFDC Caretakers, August 1996, August 1995, August 1994*. Austin, Tex.: Office of Programs Administration and Management Services, 1996, 1995, 1994.

———. *Texas Families in Transition, The Impacts of Welfare Reform Changes in Texas: Early Findings*. Austin, Tex.: Executive Office of Planning, Evaluation, and Project Management, 1998.

Texas House of Representatives, Committee on Human Services. "A Report to the House of Representatives, 74th Texas Legislature," Texas House of Representatives Interim Report 1994. 14 October 1994.

———. Minutes of Various Public Hearings. 74th and 75th sessions. House Communications Division.

———. *House Journal, 74th Legislature—Regular Session*. February 7, April 5, 6, 10, 1995.

———. *Senate Journal, 74th Legislature—Regular Session*. April 25, May 3, 24, 1995.

Texas State Senate, Committee on Health and Human Services. Minutes of Various Public Hearings. 74th and 75th sessions. Senate Staff Support Services.

Thomas, Clive S., and Ronald J. Hrebenar. "Interest Groups in the States." In *Politics in the American States: A Comparative Analysis, 6th Edition*, edited by Virginia Gray and Herbert Jacob. Washington, D.C.: CQ Press, 1996.

Tiebout, Charles. "A Pure Theory of Local Expenditures." *Journal of Political Economy* 64 (October 1956): 416–24.

Tindall, George Brown, and David E. Shi. *America: A Narrative History*, 3d ed. New York: W. W. Norton and Co., 1992.

Trattner, Walter. *From Poor Law to Welfare State: The History of Social Welfare in America*, 5th ed. New York: Free Press, 1994.

Tribal College Journal. "Responsible Welfare Reform" issue. Vol. 9 (winter 1997–98).

Truman, David M. *The Governmental Process*. New York: Alfred A. Knopf, 1964.

U.S. Advisory Commission on Intergovernmental Relations (ACIR). *The Federal Role in the Federal System (A-86)*. Washington, D.C.: ACIR, 1981.

———. *RTS 1991: State Revenue Capacity and Effort*. Washington, D.C.: ACIR, 1993.

———. *Changing Public Attitudes on Governments and Taxes, 1993*. Report S-22. Washington, D.C.: ACIR, 1993.

U.S. Department of Commerce. *Statistical Abstract of the United States*, 1996. Washington, D.C.: Bureau of the Census, 1996.

———. *Statistical Abstract of the United States, 1997*. Washington, D.C.: Bureau of the Census, 1997.

U.S. Department of Health and Human Services. Letter from Deputy Secretary Kevin Thurm to Michael D. McKinney, Commissioner of the Texas Health and Human Services Commission, dated 13 May 1997.

———. "Change in Welfare Caseloads: Total AFDC/TANF Families by State, As of June 2000." Washington, D.C.: Administration for Children and Families, 2000.

———. *Indicators of Welfare Dependency, Annual Report, March 2000*, Table A-5. Available at aspe.hhs.gov/hsp/indicators00/wordver/T_A_5.doc.

U.S. General Accounting Office (GAO). *Welfare Reform: States Are Restructuring Programs to Reduce Welfare Dependence*. GAO/HEHS-98-109. Washington, D.C.: GAO, 17 June 1998.

———. *Welfare Reform: Information on Former Recipients' Status*. GAO/HEHS-99-48. Washington, D.C.: GAO, April 1999.

U.S. House of Representatives. Committee on Ways and Means, *Where Your Money Goes: The 1994–95 Green Book*. Washington, D.C.: Brassey's, 1994.

———. Committee on Ways and Means. *1996 Green Book*. Washington, D.C.: Government Printing Office, 1997.

———. *1998 Green Book*. Washington, D.C.: Government Printing Office, 1998.

———. Committee on Agriculture, Subcommittee on Department Operations, Nutrition, and Foreign Agriculture. "Reforming the Present Welfare System," February 7–9 and 15, 1995. Serial No. 104-02. Washington, D.C.: Government Printing Office, 1995.

———. Committee on Economic and Educational Opportunities. "Contract With America: Hearing on Welfare Reform," January 18, 1995. Serial No. 104-10. Washington, D.C.: Government Printing Office, 1995.

———. Committee on Economic and Educational Opportunities, Subcommittee on Early Childhood, Youth and Families. "Hearing on Contract With America: Child Welfare and Childcare," January 31, 1995. Serial No. 104-22. Washington, D.C. U.S. Government Printing Office, 1995.

———. Committee on Economic and Educational Opportunities, Subcomittee on Postsecondary Education and Life-Long Learning. "Hearing on Job Opportunities and Basic Skills Act," January 19, 1995. Serial 104-4. Washington, D.C.: Government Printing Office, 1995.

———. Committee on Ways and Means, Subcommittee on Human Resources. "Contract With America—Welfare Reform," January 13, 20, 23, 27, and 30, and February 2, 1995. Serial No. 104-43 and 104-44. Washington, D.C.: Government Printing Office, 1995.

———. Subcommittee on Human Resources. "Child Support Enforcement Provisions Included in Personal Responsibility Act as Part of the Contract With America," February 6, 1995. Serial No. 104-6. Washington, D.C.: Government Printing Office, 1995.

———. Subcommittee on Human Resources. "Welfare Reform Success Stories," December 6, 1995. Serial No. 104-37. Washington, D.C.: Government Printing Office, 1995.

———. Subcommittee on Human Resources. "The National Governors' Association Welfare Reform Proposal," February 20, 1996. Serial No. 104-48. Washington, D.C.: Government Printing Office, 1996.

———. Subcommittee on Human Resources. "Causes of Poverty, With a Focus on Out-of-Wedlock Births," March 12, 1996. Serial No. 104-52. Washington, D.C.: Government Printing Office, 1996.

———. Subcommittee on Human Resources. "Welfare Reform," May 22 and 23, 1996. Serial No. 104-62. Washington, D.C.: Government Printing Office, 1996.

———. Subcommittee on Oversight and Investigations. "Hearing on Block Grant/Consolidation Overview," February 9, 1995. Serial No. 104-29. Washington, D.C.: Government Printing Office, 1995.

U.S. Senate. Committee on Finance. "States' Perspective on Welfare Reform," March 8, 1995. S. Hrg. 104-339. Washington, D.C.: Government Printing Office, 1995.

———. "Broad Policy Goals of Welfare Reform," March 9, 1995. S. Hrg. 104-278. Washington, D.C.: Government Printing Office, 1995.

———. "Administration's Views on Welfare Reform," March 10, 1995. Washington: U.S. Government Printing Office, 1995.

———. "Teen Parents and Welfare Reform," March 14, 1995. S. Hrg. 104-349. Washington: U.S. Government Printing Office, 1995.

———. "Welfare to Work," March 20, 1995. S. Hrg. 104-140. Washington: U.S. Government Printing Office, 1995.

———. "Welfare Reform—Views of Interested Parties," March 29, 1995. S. Hrg. 104-759. Washington: U.S. Government Printing Office, 1995.

———. "Child Welfare Programs," April 26, 1995. S. Hrg. 104-130. Washington: U.S. Government Printing Office, 1995.

———. "Welfare Reform Wrap-Up," April 27, 1995. S. Hrg. 104-327. Washington: U.S. Government Printing Office, 1995.

———. "Governors' Proposal on Welfare and Medicaid," February 22, 28 and 29, 1996. S. Hrg. 104-791. Washington: U.S. Government Printing Office, 1996.

———. "Welfare and Medicaid Reform," June 13 and 19, 1996. S. Hrg. 104-875. Washington, D.C.: Government Printing Office, 1996.

———. Committee on Governmental Affairs. "Reinventing Government—Welfare Reform," January 25, February 2, 1995. S. Hrg. 104-567. Washington: U.S. Government Printing Office, 1995.

———. Committee on Labor and Human Resources. "Child Care and Development Block Grant: How Is It Working?" February 16, 1995. S. Hrg. 104-17. Washington: U.S. Government Printing Office, 1995.

———. Committee on Labor and Human Resources. "Impact of Welfare Reform on Children and Their Families," February 28, March 1, 1995. S. Hrg. 104-25. Washington: U.S. Government Printing Office, 1995.

———. Committee on Labor and Human Resources. "Filling the Gap: Can Private Institutions Do It?" March 26, 1996. S. Hrg. 104-472. Washington: U.S. Government Printing Office, 1996.

University of Texas Center for the Study of Human Resources. *Lone Star Image System Evaluation, Final Report*. Austin, Tex.: Lyndon B. Johnson School of Public Affairs, August 1997.

Verba, Sidney, Kay Lehman Schlozman, and Henry Brady. "The Big Tilt: Participatory Inequality in America." *The American Prospect* (May–June 1997): 74–80.

Vidich, Arthur J., and Joseph Bensman. *Small Town in Mass Society: Class, Power and Religion in a Rural Community*. Princeton, N.J.: Princeton University Press, 1968.

Walker, David. *The Rebirth of Federalism: Slouching Toward Washington*. Chatham, N.J.: Chatham House Publishers, 2000.

Walker, Jack L. "The Origins and Maintenance of Interest Groups in America." *American Political Science Review* 77 (June 1983): 390–406.

———. *Mobilizing Interest Groups in America: Patrons, Professions, and Social Movements*. Ann Arbor: University of Michigan, 1991.

Weaver, R. Kent. "Ending Welfare as We Know It." In *The Social Divide: Political Parties and the Future of Activist Government*, edited by Margaret Weir. Washington, D.C.: Brookings Institution Press, 1998.

———. *Ending Welfare As We Know It*. Washington, D.C.: Brookings Institution Press, 2000.

Weaver, R. Kent, and William T. Dickens. *Looking Before We Leap: Social Science and Welfare Reform*. Occasional Paper. Washington, D.C.: Brookings Institution Press, 1995.

Weir, Margaret. *Politics and Jobs: The Boundaries of Employment Policy in the United States*. Princeton, N.J.: Princeton University Press, 1992.

——— "Political Parties and Social Policymaking." In *The Social Divide: Political Parties and the Future of Activist Government*. Washington, D.C.: Brookings Institution Press, 1998.

———. *The Social Divide: Political Parties and the Future of Activist Government*. Washington, D.C.: Brookings Institution Press, 1998.

Weir, Margaret, Ann Shola Orloff, and Theda Skocpol. *The Politics of Social Policy in the United States*. Princeton, N.J.: Princeton University Press, 1988.

Weissert, Carol W., ed. *Learning from Leaders: Welfare Reform Politics and Policy in Five Midwestern States*. Albany, N.Y.: Rockefeller Institute Press, 2000.

Welfare and Child Support Research and Training Group, School of Social Work, University of Maryland. *Life After Welfare: Fifth Interim Report*. Baltimore: Family Investment Administration, Maryland Department of Human Resources, March 1998.

"Welfare Bills Suffer from Politics," *Atlanta Constitution*, 12 July 1996, R4.

Williams, Lucy A. "The Abuse of Section 1115 Waivers: Welfare Reform in Search of a Standard." *Yale Law and Policy Review* 12, no. 8 (1994): 8–37.

Wilson, Robert H. *Public Policy and Community: Activism and Governance in Texas*. Austin: University of Texas Press, 1997.

Winnicott, D. W. "The Theory of the Parent-Infant Relationship." In *Essential Papers on Object Relations*, edited by Peter Buckley. New York: New York University Press, 1986.

AUDIOTAPES

Maryland General Assembly. Audiotapes of Senate Finance Committee hearings on SB 778, 14 March 1996. Department of Legislative Services, Annapolis.

———. Audiotapes of Senate Finance Committee hearings on SB 499. 19 February 1997. Department of Legislative Services, Annapolis.

Texas State House of Representatives. Human Services Committee. 74th Session. Public Hearings: February 13, February 27, March 8, March 29, 1995.

———.75th Session. Public Hearings: March 31, 1997.

———. Economic Development Committee. 75th Session. Public Hearing: May 13, 1997.

Texas State Senate. Health and Human Services Committee. 74th Session. Public Hearings: March 22, March 29, April 12, 1995.

———. 75th Session. Public Hearings: April 9, May 4, May 16, 1997.

———. Finance Committee. 75th Session. Public Hearings: March 24, April 7, 1997.

WEBSITES AND DATABASES

American Public Human Services Association (formerly American Public Welfare Association): apwa.org
Baltimore Sun: www.sunspot.net
Bismarck Tribune: www.ndonline.com
Center on Budget and Policy Priorities: www.cbpp.org
Center for Public Policy Priorities: www.cppp.org
Maryland Catholic Charities: www.catholiccharities.md.org/welfare.htm
Maryland Department of Human Resources: www.dhr.state.md.us/
Maryland General Assembly: mlis.state.md.us/
Maryland Governor's Office: www.gov.state.md.us/
National Conference of State Legislatures: www.ncsl.org
National Governors' Association: www. nga.org
North Dakota Catholic Conference: www.ndcatholic.org
North Dakota Department of Human Services: www.state.nd.us/hms/dhs/htm
North Dakota Legislative Assembly committee minutes, including interim Welfare Reform Committee: www.state.nd.us/lr/minutes.html
North Dakota Legislative Council: www.state.nd.us/lr/council.html
Northern Lights Periodicals Database: www. northernlight.com
State Policy Documentation Project (a joint project of the Center on Budget and Policy Priorities and the Center on Law and Social Policy): www.spdp.org
Texas Legislative Budget Board: www.lbb.state.tx.us
Texas Legislature Online: www.capitol.state.tx.us/tlo
Urban Institute: newfederalism.urban.org

Index

Page numbers with a t indicate tables.

J

K

L

U

V

W

Z